Exploring Marx's Capital

Historical Materialism Book Series

The Historical Materialism Book Series is a major publishing initiative of the radical left. The capitalist crisis of the twenty-first century has been met by a resurgence of interest in critical Marxist theory. At the same time, the publishing institutions committed to Marxism have contracted markedly since the high point of the 1970s. The Historical Materialism Book Series is dedicated to addressing this situation by making available important works of Marxist theory. The aim of the series is to publish important theoretical contributions as the basis for vigorous intellectual debate and exchange on the left.

The peer-reviewed series publishes original monographs, translated texts, and reprints of classics across the bounds of academic disciplinary agendas and across the divisions of the left. The series is particularly concerned to encourage the internationalization of Marxist debate and aims to translate significant studies from beyond the English-speaking world.

For a full list of titles in the Historical Materialism Book Series
available in paperback from Haymarket Books, visit:
https://www.haymarketbooks.org/series_collections/1-historical-materialism

Exploring Marx's Capital

Philosophical, Economic,
and Political Dimensions

Jacques Bidet

Translated by
David Fernbach

Preface to the English edition by
Alex Callinicos

Haymarket Books
Chicago, IL

First published in 2005 by Brill Academic Publishers, The Netherlands
© 2006 Koninklijke Brill NV, Leiden, The Netherlands

Published in paperback in 2009 by
Haymarket Books
P.O. Box 180165
Chicago, IL 60618
773-583-7884
www.haymarketbooks.org

ISBN: 978-1-60846-028-1

Distributed to the trade in the US through Consortium Book Sales and
Distribution (www.cbsd.com) and internationally through Ingram
Publisher Services International (www.ingramcontent.com).

This book was published with the generous support of Lannan
Foundation and Wallace Action Fund.

Special discounts are available for bulk purchases by organizations and
institutions. Please call 773-583-7884 or email info@haymarketbooks.org
for more information.

Cover design by Ragina Johnson.

Printed in the United States.

Entered into digital printing June 2021.

Library of Congress Cataloging-in-Publication Data is available.

Contents

Foreword to the English Translation of Jacques Bidet's *Que faire du 'Capital'?*

Alex Callinicos

The appearance in English of Jacques Bidet's outstanding study of Marx's *Capital*, first published in 1985 as *Que faire du 'Capital'?*, is an important intellectual event. It makes available to the English-speaking world the first book by one of continental Europe's most important and influential left-wing political philosophers. Moreover, occurring as it does at a time of renewed intellectual interest in *Capital*, it is likely to help shape Anglophone discussion of the nature and future of the Marxist critique of political economy.

Bidet's book, drawn from an 800–page doctoral thesis entitled 'Economie et dialectique dans *Le Capital'* and submitted at the University of Paris-X Nanterre in 1983, came at the end of one great wave of attention to Marx's masterpiece. This gathered strength in the course of the 1960s – important landmarks are the collective work by Louis Althusser and his collaborators, *Reading 'Capital'* (1965), and Roman Rosdolsky's great commentary on Marx's *Grundrisse*, *The Making of Marx's 'Capital'* (1968). Though serious critical scrutiny of *Capital* and its manuscripts preceded the political radicalisation of the late 1960s and early 1970s (and in some cases, at least, cannot be taken as in any serious sense an anticipation of this development),[1] one dimension of the renaissance of Marxist theory that the events of 1968 and after helped to stimulate was an exploration of the philosophical and political significance of Marx's economic writings. Finding one's away around the conceptual architecture of *Capital* was widely taken to be a precondition of being able to engage in more concrete enquiries: this was, for example, a feature of the 'state-derivation' debate in Germany and Britain during the 1960s and 1970s.[2]

---

[1] For example, Ilienkov 1982
[2] See Holloway and Picciotto 1978 and Clarke 1991.

Indeed one of the most original and influential intellectual enterprises in the recent history of Marxism, David Harvey's development of a 'historical-geographical' materialism, gravitates around a close reading and conceptual opening out of *Capital*.[3]

Exploring Marx's 'Capital', as I have already noted, appeared when this great bubble of politico-philosophical investment in Marx's economic thought had apparently burst. It is in any case a slightly puzzling anomaly that, while many distinguished works of Marxist political economy appeared in France during the 1970s, there was no sustained follow-up there to the exploration of the conceptual structure of *Capital* that Althusser and his students had inaugurated, not simply in his and Etienne Balibar's well-known essays but in the contributions to the original edition of *Reading 'Capital'* by Roger Establet, Pierre Macherey, and Jacques Rancière (which were not included in the 1968 edition on which translations are usually based and are therefore and regrettably much less widely known). The one major exception was Gérard Duménil's *Le Concept de loi économique dans 'Le Capital'*, published in 1978 with a preface by Althusser in the famous 'Théorie' series in which *For Marx* and *Reading 'Capital'* first appeared. (Duménil's remarkable book is discussed briefly and critically by Bidet in Chapter VI below.)

When publishing *Exploring Marx's 'Capital'*, Bidet must have seemed doubly isolated. Not only was he engaging in a form of enquiry practised by few other French Marxists, but the book appeared when Marxism was more or less eclipsed intellectually both by the powerful political reaction orchestrated by the *nouveaux philosophes* in the late 1970s and by the rise of poststructuralism, associated with figures such as Gilles Deleuze, Jacques Derrida, and Michel Foucault and widely interpreted as requiring the abandonment of Marxism.[4] An unfriendly reader might find confirmation that what Bidet was undertaking was essentially outdated in the acknowledgement this book found from the disgraced Althusser, who, in one of the two autobiographical texts in which he sought to make sense of how he had come to murder his wife, cited *Que faire du 'Capital'?* in support of his own interpretation of Marx.[5]

---

[3] Harvey 1982.
[4] For contemporary responses see Anderson 1983 and Callinicos 1982.
[5] Althusser 1994, pp. 236–7.

It would, however, be more accurate to say that Bidet refused to capitulate to a mean and reactionary time. He followed the publication of *Exploring Marx's 'Capital'* by launching, in collaboration with Jacques Texier, the theoretical journal *Actuel Marx*. This established itself astonishingly quickly as the premier journal of Marxist and post-Marxist theory in French, with a significant readership throughout the Latin world. The success of the journal (from whose editorship Bidet retired in 2005) helped to develop the networks necessary to hold what proved to be the first in a series of International Marx Congresses at the University of Paris-X Nanterre in 1995. Now regularly held at the same venue at three-yearly intervals, the Congress has been one of the flagships in the efforts by Marxists to move from defiance in the face of the triumph of liberal capitalism at the end of the Cold War to the pursuit of new lines of intellectual enquiry and militant activity in the very different political context defined by events such as Seattle, Genoa, 9/11, and the invasion of Iraq. Finally, the *Actuel Marx 'Confrontation'* book series referred to above has published a number of intellectually distinguished works, including *Théorie générale*, Bidet's most ambitious attempt so far to pursue the lines of argument first opened in *Exploring Marx's 'Capital'*.

The *Leitmotif* of all Bidet's work can be summed up the title of his most recent book – 'Explication and Reconstruction of *Capital*'. It is fair to say, however, that the balance has shifted increasingly from explication to reconstruction over the past twenty years. The latter preoccupation was already present in *Exploring Marx's 'Capital'*: the subtitle of the book's first edition was 'Materials for a Refoundation'. But the focus here is on a close critical reading of Marx's economic writings. This translation appears when Anglophone philosophers and economists have reinvigorated detailed scrutiny of Marx's economic concepts and theories.[6] What, then, is distinctive to the reading that Bidet offers here?

Exploring Marx's 'Capital' shares the assumption common to the critical scholarship of the past generation in treating *Capital* not as a more or less transparent window on the world, but as a complex, articulated conceptual structure that requires strenuous interpretation. In this spirit Bidet addresses a wealth of different issues – for example, the skilled labour problem, the

---

[6] See, for example, Arthur and Reuten (eds.) 1998, Campbell and Reuten (eds.) 2002, Bellofiore and Taylor (eds.) 2004.

intensity of labour, the nature of value theory itself, productive and unproductive labour, ideology, the value-form, the Sraffian critique of Marx. He treats them all with a combination of rigour and erudition that is always a source of illumination even when his arguments fail to persuade. Amid these extremely rich discussions, two over-arching themes are worth emphasising here.

The first concerns the texts that Bidet discusses. One feature of the explosion of research into *Capital* was the growing recognition that Marx's book was the tip of a vast iceberg of manuscripts composed mainly during the decade 1857–67, and almost all unpublished till after his death. Another distinguished commentator, Enrique Dussel, has distinguished between four drafts of *Capital* – the *Grundrisse*, written in 1857–8, which provided the basis on which Marx drafted and then published in 1859 *A Contribution to the Critique of Political Economy*; the *1861–3 Manuscript*, intended as a continuation of the *Contribution*, but only published in part as *Theories of Surplus-Value* by Kautsky in 1905–10 and in full in the 1970s (it is available in English as Volumes 30–4 of the Marx-Engels *Collected Works*); the *1863–5 Manuscript*, the first recognisable draft of the three volumes of *Capital*, from which Engels edited and published Volumes II and III after Marx's death, and now in the course of publication in the definitive MEGA edition of Marx's and Engels's complete works; and Volume I, which Marx himself managed to publish in 1867, and reworked for the second edition of 1873 and the French translation of 1875.[7]

The *Grundrisse* became a reference point in Marxist discussion of *Capital* from the 1960s onwards, thanks in particular to Rosdolsky's groundbreaking work. But Bidet's is one of the first commentaries to take the full measure of the *1861–3 Manuscript*.[8] His treatment of Marx's texts is distinctive methodologically as well as philologically. One consequence of the discovery of the *Grundrisse* by Marxist theorists in the 1960s and 1970s was that many of them made this text the template on the basis of which to interpret Marx's later drafts, including *Capital* itself. This tendency was especially pronounced by those influenced by the German 'capital-logic' school and by the Italian 'workerist' tradition, represented in the English-speaking world by those

---

[7] Dussel 2001a.

[8] Vygodski 1974 is an important Soviet commentary that stresses the importance of the *1861–3 Manuscript*, though it seems to rely exclusively on the extracts published as *Theories of Surplus-Value*.

identified with 'open Marxism': Toni Negri, for example, argues that in the *Grundrisse* revolutionary subjectivity has not yet been suffocated by the 'objectivism' that prevails in *Capital*.[9]

Bidet sets himself strongly in opposition to this entire approach. As he has put it more recently:

> The *Grundrisse*, which is made too often into the object of an ill-thought-out academic cult, must read for what it is, as a 'sketch': as a rough draft (of genius), with its attempts and errors. One cannot take all the products of this exploratory investigation as constitutive of a theory.[10]

He describes his own approach thus:

> Unlike other commentators, I do not look for the 'truth' of *Capital* in the earlier versions: I hold that Marx worked like an ordinary researcher, only producing a new version in response to its predecessor's insufficiency with respect to the project he is pursuing, and having no reason to explain why he made the changes to which he is led.[11]

In this focus on the process of conceptual recastings that Marx undertakes in successive drafts, Bidet is very close to the approach pursued by Dussel, for example in his own very detailed commentary on the *1861–3 Manuscript*.[12] But this leads us to a second theme, Bidet's distinctive treatment of Marx's Hegelian heritage. The *Grundrisse* is the economic manuscript where Hegel's influence is most evident, notably in Marx's widespread use of Hegelian terms and motifs. Those who treat the *Grundrisse* as the benchmark for Marx's economic thought tend also to stress the conceptual continuities between Marx and Hegel (though this is not universal: Negri is an exception). So does Bidet's demotion of the *Grundrisse*'s interpretive significance imply that he belongs to the anti-Hegelian camp? Althusser's citation of *Exploring Marx's 'Capital'* as support for his own views seems to imply that the answer to this question is 'Yes'. For, of course, Althusser is most famous for the claim that

---

[9] Negri 1984; for open Marxism see, for example, Bonefeld, Gunn and Psychopedis (eds.) 1992.
[10] Bidet 2004, pp. 102–3. Part 1 of this book is largely (though not solely) devoted to summarising the findings of *Exploring Marx's 'Capital'*.
[11] Bidet 2004, p. 10.
[12] Dussel 2001b.

an 'epistemological break' separates the 'ideological', 'humanist' Marx of the early 1840s from the 'scientific' works of Marx's maturity, above all *Capital*.

Bidet's position is more complex. For Althusser, the presence of Hegelian categories in works such as the *Grundrisse* is an ideological 'survival' of Marx's pre-scientific problematic. For Bidet, however, it plays a more ambiguous role: Hegelian thought functions as an 'epistemological support/obstacle' in the construction of Marx's theory. At the start of the *Grundrisse*, Marx famously commits himself to 'the method of rising from the abstract to the concrete'.[13] This method, which clearly reflects the influence of Hegel's *Science of Logic*, informs Marx's attempt in successive drafts to proceed from a set of highly abstract concepts – those through which, in particular, the labour theory of value is stated – by introducing, step by step, more complex determinations. The contrast between the intimidatingly formal exposition of Chapter 1 of *Capital*, Volume I, 'The Commodity', and the profusion of empirical detail in which, for example, Marx treats financial markets in Volume III, Part 5, may serve as illustration of this process. It is intended in part to overcome the major problem that Marx's most important predecessor, David Ricardo, encountered when he sought to make the labour theory consistent with everyday economic phenomena where commodities evidently do not exchange in proportion to their labour values.

But one major problem that Marx encounters concerns what he will call in Part 2 of *Capital*, Volume I, 'The Transformation of Money into Capital'. How, in other words, does a sum of money under capitalist economic relations expand thanks to the generation of a profit? Bidet argues in Chapter VI below that, in the *Grundrisse* and the *Primitive Version* of the 1859 *Contribution*, Marx tries to offer a 'dialectical' solution to this problem. In other words, modelling his procedure on the transitions through Hegel moves from one category to another in the *Science of Logic*, Marx seeks to show how money becomes capital through conceptual analysis of the functions of money and the distinction between use-value and exchange-value. In *Capital*, Volume I, however, Marx abandons this 'dialectical' strategy and introduces a conceptual discontinuity where once he relied on alleged continuities. He shows that money becomes capital once labour-power becomes a commodity that is sold on the market on terms leading to its exploitation and therefore to the production of surplus-value, thanks to which capital is able to valorise itself

---

[13] Marx 1973, p. 101.

and expand.[14] It because of Hegel's influence that Marx was able to construct a model of science through which he could begin to overcome the problems he had inherited from Ricardo, but, in order to bring his project closer to a conclusion, he had to try to liberate himself from this influence: 'The Hegelian legacy is thus decisive. But it also constitutes the principle of a vast field of "epistemological obstacles".'[15]

Like Dussel, Bidet sees the arduous process of conceptual rectification that Marx pursues across successive drafts as marking intellectual progress: thus he criticises commentators for not noticing that the second edition of *Capital*, Volume I, is 'much superior' to the first.[16] But Bidet's is not a triumphalist narrative in which the truth is finally unveiled at the end of *Capital*, and not just because Volume III is, famously, unfinished. Indeed, one of his most important findings – that, as reported in the preceding paragraph, there is a conceptual discontinuity between the labour theory of value outlined in Part 1 of *Capital*, Volume I, and the theory of the capital relation that begins to be developed in Part 2 – becomes, in more recent works, the starting point of an ambitious critique of Marxism. Most systematically in *Théorie générale* Bidet argues that, in Part 1, Marx develops a theory of market production that cannot be reduced to the subsequent account of the capitalist mode of production proper. The market economy thus abstractly conceptualised belongs to a broader 'metastructure' of modernity that comprises as well the factor of 'organisation' at work in state bureaucracy and corporate hierarchies alike. Capitalism and 'collectivism' are both contingent realisations of the abstract 'matrix of possibilities' constituted by the metastructure. Consequently, although Bidet remains critical of 'dialectical' interpretations of *Capital*, he is now open to the idea that a larger dialectic is at work in modernity.[17] His current theory plainly merits critical attention in its own right.[18] Important though this discussion undoubtedly is, one can nevertheless read and gain much from *Exploring Marx's 'Capital'* without knowing anything about, let alone taking a position on its author's later development. It is good to have this fine book in English.

---

[14] For more recent versions of this argument, see Bidet 1990, pp. 67–73, and Bidet 2004, pp. 99–110.

[15] Bidet 2000, p. 277. See, in addition to Chapter VII below, Bidet 2004, pp. 81–2.

[16] Bidet 2004, p. 76.

[17] See Bidet 2005, a critique of Arthur 2002.

[18] See the critical discussion of Bidet 1999 in Callinicos 2006, §1.2.

References

Althusser, Louis 1994 [1992], *L'Avenir dure longtemps, suivi de Les Faits*, Paris: Stock/IMEC.
Althusser, Louis et al. 1973 [1965], *Lire 'le Capital'*, Paris: Maspero (4 vols.)
Althusser, Louis and Etienne Balibar 1970 [1968], *Reading 'Capital'*, London: NLB.
Anderson, Perry 1983, *In the Tracks of Historical Materialism*, London: Verso.
Arthur, Christopher J. 2002, *The New Dialectic and Marx's 'Capital'*, Historical Materialism Book Series, Leiden: Brill Academic Press.
Arthur, Christopher J. and Geert Reuten (eds.) 1998, *The Circulation of Capital*, Basingstoke: Palgrave.
Bellofiore, Ricardo and Nicola Taylor (eds.) 2004, *The Constitution of Capital*, Basingstoke: Palgrave.
Bidet, Jacques 1985, *Que faire du 'Capital'? Materiaux pour une refondation*, Paris: Klinksieck.
Bidet, Jacques 1990, *Théorie de la modernité, suivi de Marx et le marché*, Paris: Presses universitaires de France.
Bidet, Jacques 1999, *Théorie générale: Théorie du droit, de l'économie et de la politique*, Paris: Presses universitaires de France.
Bidet, Jacques 2000, *Que faire du 'Capital'? Philosophie, économie et politique dans 'Le Capital' de Marx*, Paris: Presses universitaires de France.
Bidet, Jacques 2004, *Explication et reconstruction du 'Capital'*, Paris: Presses universitaires de France.
Bidet, Jacques 2005, 'The Dialectician's Interpretation of *Capital'*, *Historical Materialism*, 13, 2: 121–46.
Bonefeld, Werner, Richard Gunn, and Kosmas Psychopedis 1992, (eds.) *Open Marxism*, 2 vols., London: Pluto.
Callinicos, Alex 1982, *Is there a Future for Marxism?*, Basingstoke: Palgrave.
Callinicos, Alex 2006, *The Resources of Critique*, Cambridge: Polity.
Campbell, Martha, and Geert Reuten (eds.) 2002, *The Culmination of Capital*, Basingstoke: Palgrave.
Clarke, Simon (ed.) 1991, *The State Debate*, Basingstoke: Palgrave.
Duménil, Gérard 1978, *Le Concept de loi économique dans 'Le Capital'*, Paris: Maspero.
Dussel, Enrique 2001a, 'The Four Drafts of *Capital'*, *Rethinking Marxism*, 13, 1: 9–26.
Dussel, Enrique 2001b [1988], *Towards an Unknown Marx*, London: Routledge.
Harvey, David 1982, *The Limits to Capital*, Oxford: Blackwell.
Holloway, John, and Sol Picciotto (eds.) 1978, *State and Capital*, London: Edward Arnold.
Ilienkov, E.V. 1982 [1960], *The Dialectics of the Abstract and the Concrete in Marx's 'Capital'*, Moscow: Progress.
Marx, Karl 1973 [1939], *Grundrisse*, Harmondsworth: Penguin.
Negri, Antonio 1984 [1979], *Marx Beyond Marx*, South Hadley: Bergin and Garvey.
Rosdolsky, Roman 1977 [1968], *The Making of Marx's 'Capital'*, London: Pluto.
Vygodski, V.S. 1974 [1965], *The Story of a Great Discovery*, Tunbridge Wells: Abacus.

Author's Preface to the English Edition

It might seem a risky venture for me to update for English readers a book on Marx published twenty years ago, especially when its origins go back to a doctoral thesis now thirty years old. Even reading it afresh is a test. What could I have written in those days?

When it appeared in 1985, at the very time of a massive trend against Marxist writings, this book was neither read nor received as it might have been – at least, not in France. For a decade or more, Marx disappeared from bookshops and study programmes.

At the start of a new century, however, in radically new historical conditions and a globalised scholarly environment, it seemed that it could well provoke fresh interest and questions. A new generation of readers of *Capital* are emerging, along with informed scholars. I therefore re-read this 'youthful' work with a view to a new French edition, which appeared in 2000. This reading was inevitably retrospective, starting from the point I had then reached with my *Théorie générale* – this last being precisely an 'attempt to refound Marxism' and thus the (provisional) end-point of a journey that began with the present book.

Two obvious questions governed my re-reading: had not historical changes and new paradigms made my thesis obsolete? And was the road from *Que faire du 'Capital'* (1985) to *Théorie de la modernité* (1995) and *Théorie générale* (1999) coherent and credible?

I reached the conclusion that this work of 1985 could and should be reproduced today without changes. I continue to subscribe to the positions it puts forward and the interpretation/interrogation it offers, which, indeed, formed the starting-point of my further development.

This book presents several distinctive features in relation to other works of its kind.

At the ideological level, it adopts a resolutely detached position, as indicated on the first page, where I stress that my aim is not any kind of 'Marxist philosophy' but rather 'a philosophical investigation of the Marxist theory of history'.

At the level of philology, it rejects certain biases that are (still) too widespread. First of all, the tendency to present the Marxian corpus as a coherent ensemble, in some sense co-present in the mind of its author, as if 'Marx's thought' existed in such a way that every fragment of this (sacred) text could be illuminated by another. Or, again, to represent the development of his theory as a royal road, a progressive construction following a linear series of discoveries and enrichments. Not to mention the reverse procedure that so tirelessly alleges a deterioration from the *Grundrisse* to *Capital*. What I am specifically interested in is the sequence of successive drafts of *Capital*, understanding Marx as one would any other scientist, who only writes a new version in order to *correct* the previous one. I investigate in each case therefore the reasons for these corrections, in which – as I see it – Marx successively *jettisoned* the preceding versions. I show that his procedure was broadly 'experimental', in the sense that in feeling his way ahead he sought support from all available philosophical categories, the Hegelian ones in particular, and that when he let go of this remarkable débris it was because it finally proved inadequate for his purpose. This is the thesis of the epistemological support/obstacle.

At the theoretical level, this book is entirely oriented to deciphering the juridical, political and ideological dimension that is immanent in the economic relationship itself, the idea that it is here, above all, that Marx was an innovator, the discoverer of a new 'continent'. It anticipates in this way the 'institutionalist' reading of Marxist theory that is today taking shape, providing it with both a theoretical foundation and a philological support. Negative evidence of this is the chapter I devote to the 'neo-Ricardian' studies that were so important in the 1970s. This shows, in fact, the vacuity of a positivist re-interpretation of Marxist theory as pure economics, the 'production of commodities by means of commodities' – in which, by definition, only one institution exists, that of the market. And this one institution means no institution, since institutions exist only in the antinomy of possible alternatives, the antinomic co-implication between the contractual contractuality of the market and the central contractuality of the plan.

At the political level, the book turns on the question of the relationship between market and capital – a decisive question. For, if Marx can rightly be seen as the classic author of the workers' movement, this is not because he wrote any socialist doctrine. It is because he developed a powerful theory of the imbrication of capitalism and market, one of his objectives being to establish that socialism presupposes the abolition of the market. I show in this book, however, that Marx did not only distinguish the concept of market from that of capital, he in a sense *separated* these two determinations of the modern form of society from one another. This led me to an optimistic conclusion that I expressed in the Preface to the Japanese and Serbo-Croat editions (1986): the idea of drawing support from this conceptual separation to think through the actual use that socialism could make of the market. But Marx, for his part, only separated the two the better to unite them. The task I faced thus proved harder than I had anticipated. The entire concept had to be revisited.

This was why I took up the challenge of re-developing *Capital* 'in a rational order', in other words writing a 'general theory' of modern society that would overcome the gaps in Marxism. This took me on several detours, and a few returns back over the ground of classical contractual theory. I would like then to briefly explain the elements of continuity and of rupture that mark the long road that led from *Que faire du 'Capital'* to *Théorie générale*.

Capital dramatises right from the start the relationship between market and capital. Volume One commences with an abstract theory of the market as the social logic of production (Part One). It goes on to show how this is implicated in a logic of a different kind (Part Three). Those without means are forced to sell their labour-power, and at a price that assures its purchaser an accumulation of surplus-value, by virtue of which society is not made up simply of individuals who exchange, but also of antagonistic classes. The proclamation of equality and freedom is turned into its opposite. I show here, however, how Marx failed in his project of a genuinely 'dialectical' development of this reversal. What he produced was, in actual fact, a purely 'analytical' presentation.

I must add that, when I wrote the present book, I found this result quite satisfactory. It was only gradually that the *dialectical necessity* became apparent to me, if by this we mean a conceptual form that makes it possible to conceive, at the same time and without confusion, not just the structure and its movement, the system and its contradiction, but also what is and what must be, necessity and freedom, force and right.

The only revision I would need to make to the text, therefore, bears precisely on the question of the dialectic, which I sometimes treat here in a rather negative fashion. Readers will note however that the thesis of the epistemological support/obstacle underlines the presence of a philosophical basis that is often pertinent. If I have left the text all but unchanged, it is because my criticisms essentially focus, as the reader will be able to see, on certain inadequate uses that Marx made in his preparatory drafts of various categories borrowed from the Hegelian system. An inadequacy that was amply confirmed, in the later versions, by his abandonment of these references, too hastily canonised by scholarly exegesis.

I have, therefore, not revised my thesis that Marx failed in his attempt to present *dialectically*, and thus to think in this way, the relationship between market and capital – and more generally, I would add today, the modern form of society. The dialectical requirement is certainly constantly present in Marx's theorising – which even provides the most powerful illustration of it available –, but it remains freighted here with a questionable historico-teleological perspective, leading from the era of market relations, via the apogee of capitalism, to the supposedly post-market relationships of socialism (or communism). In this interpretation, its development fuelled the great utopia of the twentieth century.

I was thus led to resume my theoretical work by starting from the basis of more complex presuppositions, outside of which no 'dialectic of modernity' would be possible. It is impossible to begin the theory of the modern economy with the figure of the *market* alone, referring only to the freedom-and-equality of exchange. The other rational pole of the productive social co-ordination, antinomic and of the same epistemological rank, that of *organisation*, is immediately bound up with the market, and so, correlatively, the necessity of a central contractual freedom-and-equality, in a relationship of mutual co-implication that defines the social condition of modern man. There is no 'free' market without a 'free' will that establishes it, and that as such can also establish its opposite: some form of organisation. No 'modern freedom' without 'ancient freedom'. No rational market, if it is not limited (determined) by organisation. That is what modernity *proclaims*, at least to the extent that it *claims* to establish the modern juridico-economic order: this is what I call the 'metastructure' of modernity. And that is also, in all its complexity, what always proves to be already 'turned into its opposite' in the 'structures', i.e. the class relations specific to modern society, and in which the question of revolution is permanently raised.

Such was the guiding thread of my subsequent research, sketched out in *Théorie de la modernité* and developed in *Théorie générale*, as an alternative to Habermas's 'reconstruction'. It thus seems to me that I have pursued in these three works, through experiments and breaks, one and the same research project, the object of which is to conceive together capitalism and the alternative to capitalism. It was only very gradually that the dialectical concepts of 'metastructure' (opposed to superstructure) and 'structure' (in which organisation, the homologue of the market, constitutes the other basis of modern class, the other constitutive moment of capital) emerged in their full theoretical and political implications, and correlatively, the concepts of the world-system. This is how the connections with other systemic undertakings are made clear, for example those of Habermas, Rawls and Bourdieu. And it is likewise how other requirements are integrated, such as those raised by linguistic philosophy, and other implications such the ecological, for example. But the essential wellsprings of this undertaking were already at work in the initial investigation presented in this book, which sought in effect to clarify a set of connected questions raised by Marx's *Capital*, and that are more than ever on the agenda today.

The object here was to think through the relationship between the quantitative moment that the analysis we call 'economic' presupposes, and the qualitative moment of the relations between individuals and classes, an imaginary and a practical relationship, that are inherent to politics. And to construct, against 'textbook economics', a *political*-economic conceptuality.

These lines of this research form the foundation for a new work, *Explication et reconstruction du 'Capital'* (2004), which now occupies the key place in a theoretical ensemble aiming at a 'refoundation of Marxism'. This book proposes, on the one hand, an explanation of Volume One of *Capital* in the spirit of the present work, and, on the other hand, a reconstruction along the systematic lines of my *Théorie générale*. It seeks to raise a formidable challenge: to show that *Capital* can only tackle the questions it presents on condition of being reconstructed on an expanded basis, according to the twin 'poles' of the metastructure, market and organisation, and its twin 'aspects', economic and legal-political. My hypothesis here is that Marx was mistaken in placing an exposition of the *market form* at the start of his work, in order to show that this generated, at the end of the concentration of capitals, an *organised form* available for socialist revolution. These two polar 'mediations' actually have the same fundamental epistemological level, and form the two factors of the modern class relationship. It is on this basis that it is possible and necessary to address all the problems of capitalism: value, money, fetishism, alienation, class, class struggle, exploitation, reproduction, hegemony, nation-state, world system, and socialist alternatives. The objective is to write a new version of Marx's theory, on an improved theoretical foundation, and in this way more realistic and responding better to the present requirements of political struggle.

This research is the prelude to another, designed to complete the cycle of this 'refoundation of Marxism'. It will develop, on this conceptual basis, the interpretation of the process of globalisation and the *altermondialiste* perspective. The aim is to produce a *cosmopolitanism from below*, analysing the relationship between the imperialist world-system and the new world-form that is appearing on the horizon of ultimodernity.

April 2006

Editorial note

I have changed nothing in my 1985 text, which originated in a thesis defended at the University of Paris-X in 1983, 'Économie et dialectique dans *Le Capital*', 800 pages, apart from inserting references to my more recent works on the same subjects, and making a very few cuts and precisions. The interpretation of *Capital* I propose here has been continued, as I mentioned above, in two further books: *Théorie générale* (1999), and especially *Explication et reconstruction du 'Capital'* (2004). But it is pursued also in many other publications. I would refer on the one hand to the *Critical Companion to Contemporary Marxism* edited by Jacques Bidet and Stathis Kouvelakis (2007). This particularly contains – besides an introduction suggesting the use that can be made of *Capital* today, and a study of the proposed interpretation of Kôzô Uno – an article titled 'New Interpretations of *Capital*'. The Bibliography attached to the present book also gives various recent articles that extend the present study in different directions. Finally, readers can find on my web site <http://perso.wanadoo.fr/jacques.bidet>, among other pieces, a *'Commentaire du Capital'* that follows Parts One and Two of Volume One paragraph by paragraph.

Introduction

It is generally accepted that Marxism represents a part of contemporary theoretical culture. Problems begin when the question is raised as to the conditions and limits within which its categories are legitimate, make a genuine contribution to the knowledge of the history of societies, and can form the principle for a transformative intervention in our own society.

These are the questions I intend to put to Marx's discourse, applying myself to its essential element, the theory of the capitalist mode of production as presented in *Capital*.

My project has nothing to do with a 'Marxist philosophy'. It is, rather, a philosophical investigation of the Marxist theory of history. It is based on a certain recognition of the crisis that today affects Marxist thought in its various forms.

The dominant Marxist *philosophical* discourse drew its strength from the fact that it took up the humanist tradition and turned it into a critique of capitalist society and a universal social project. It saw in the proletariat the figure of universal Man, who had to liberate himself and establish the age of reason. Strong objections have been raised against this kind of discourse. Is not the specific object of the categories of historical materialism the forms of the various modes of production that are always particular, and the always determinate fields of possibility that they present? Do not these categories simply dissolve when the attempt is made to mobilise them in the teleological schema of a philosophy of history?

A more restrained use of Marxism has also been made, oriented above all towards the analysis of the *economic-social-political* frameworks of capitalist societies. This is, in fact, where its fruitfulness seems to be most clearly displayed: examination of a social formation starting from the question of the ownership of its means of production (and, more generally, from the categories of historical materialism) incontestably yields decisive information. And yet this approach is prey to a double difficulty, even within Marxism itself. This is firstly *on the side of its object*: capitalist societies are taking ever more complex forms (property being diversified, so that the determination of classes on this basis becomes more problematic), and are interpenetrating in a process of globalisation that seems to create between nations cleavages analogous to those existing between classes, at the same time as 'postcapitalist' societies (based on the 'abolition of capitalism') have emerged that raise the question as to what extent analogous categories are applicable to them. The other difficulty is *on the side of the theory* that grasps this object. The theory of the capitalist mode of production indeed gains its coherence and its unity only from the principle on which it is founded: a definite conception of value, the starting category of the system, about which debate has never ceased, without ever reaching a decisive result or even making appreciable progress. It goes without saying that this initial uncertainty resonates through the entire edifice, making the subsequent categories of surplus-value, exploitation, etc. problematic, as well as the very characterisation of socialism as a fundamentally different type of society.

This is the reason, moreover, why a different kind of discourse has made itself more insistently felt in recent years: a discourse on the foundations of the theory of *Capital* and aiming at its 'reconstruction'. This has taken different forms: examination of the articulation of the various aspects of the system and its specific 'logic', elucidation of the starting category of value. It also bears on Marx's relationships to Hegel and Ricardo. But here, too, the results do not seem decisive. If we have come to a clearer understanding of the importance of the question of the specific order of theoretical presentation (even though the prevailing tendency of this has been more a re-integration into the Hegelian matrix), the question of the initial categories remains quite unresolved. Even those who, referring to the work of Sraffa, Ricardo's 'logical' successor, have rightly shown that Marx effected a far deeper break with Ricardo than he himself imagined, his introduction of 'labour-value' being a radical innovation, have not – it seems to me – been able to draw the implications of this. They have rather sought to base the same theory on different principles.

For all these reasons, a return to the foundations of the theory of the capitalist mode of production seems imperative to me today, inseparable from analysis of the organisation of categories and the determination of their object. A reading of commentaries shows how many of the basic questions have not received the analytical treatment that they require from the perspective of the history of science: above all the categories of 'labour-value', 'labour-power' as commodity (along with the value/price couple that characterises it), and 'productive labour' (in the articulation of structure and tendency in which it is inscribed), even the 'value-form', without even speaking of the general categories implicit in the discourse of *Capital*.

The perspective of the history of science brings with it, I believe, several complementary requirements. To examine the final result as the system that it claims to constitute, but also as the fruit of successive corrections and attempts, successful or not – in short, in terms of its genesis, which the recent publication of the last essential manuscripts finally enables us to reconstitute. To confront at each stage of its drafting the philosophical scaffolding (often Hegelian) and the socio-economic matrix (often Ricardian), and to appreciate the work that is effected in this encounter. And to analyse the categories on this basis, according to the place in the presentation that defines them.

More precisely, this perspective prescribes a study based on a problematic of the '*epistemological support/obstacle*'. I mean by this that, from 1857 on, Marx's project of a theory of the capitalist social system sought expression with the aid of the method and figures of discourse of Hegelian philosophy, and that he found here a certain measure of support and a possibility of deployment, but at the same time an obstacle and cause of stagnation and confusions. Confusions that echo in the uncertainties of contemporary Marxist discourse.

I focus therefore on the period stretching from the first complete draft, that of the *Grundrisse*, to the final versions of *Capital*. A period referred to as Marx's 'maturity', but which is still marked by a series of deep breaks, the genetic study of which, from the standpoint that I indicate, does not seem to have been previously conducted.

Yet an analysis of this kind can only be carried out as a function of a certain idea of the result towards which Marx was tending, and that he achieved more or less fully. A certain idea of what this theory could be in its adequate formulation. In short, what it had to be, given what it is, given the logical constraints inherent to the conceptual field opened up.

The thesis I propose presents therefore a double aspect.

One aspect concerns the object of the theory. I see its specificity as deriving from the *political*-economic character of the space that it constitutes: it articulates a set of categories, each of which – starting with value – must be interpreted as at the same time 'economic', 'social' and 'political'. And this is precisely where the main difficulty lies, a difficulty that constantly threatens a fall into economism or sociologism. Yet there is no Marxist theory unless this cleavage is overcome in a conceptualisation in which questions of production, of power and of representation interfere at each level.

The other aspect concerns the genesis of this problematic. Marx found support in Hegel's *Logic*, and yet only constructed his system by distancing himself from this, in particular by progressively (but never totally) overcoming a well determined series of epistemological obstacles resulting from the Hegelian dialectical mode of exposition and the Hegelian conception of science. It is thus by following this path (which means asking each time why Marx changes his text), and not the reverse (seeking the truth of a version in its predecessor), that we can reach the real problems that the constitution of this theoretical discourse raises.

Chapter One
Preliminary Methodological Remarks

1. Pathways: 1857 to 1875

The texts to be examined here are situated in a period that is very precise in its starting date, 1857, when Marx elaborated his overall plan and his first general sketch, but quite vague as to its conclusion. 1875 marks the approximate end of the period relevant here, with the completion of the French edition. Between these two dates, the essential elements of Marx's masterwork, *Capital* or the theory of the capitalist mode of production, were developed in a number of successive and comparable versions.

It is necessary to distinguish first of all (1) *three successive manuscripts*, punctuated by plans that restructure and redefine the problems studied with a view to a projected new version, and (2) *three editions of Capital*.

1.i First economic manuscript (1857–8): the *Grundrisse der Kritik der politischen Ökonomie*. This is the first general sketch of the work, based on the idea of a systematic development from abstract to concrete, and also presenting a quite clear view of the principal steps in this development, particularly its beginning with the concept of value, and the pivotal articulation of value and price of production, through which Marx escaped from the conceptual space of Ricardo. This manuscript realised only a part of the broad programme that Marx had set for himself at this time. But it already covered the space of the future *Capital*, albeit unevenly, the contents of Volumes Two and Three being still only embryonic. It was finished in January 1858.

Marx directly went on to write and publish (1859) *Zur Kritik der politischen Ökonomie*, which would develop into the future Part One of Volume One, devoted to the initial categories of commodity and money.

In 1859, he drafted a *plan* comprising the division into three books that we know today, also defining the sections of Volume One.[1]

1.ii The second economic manuscript (December 1861 to July 1863)[2] comprises:

– a version of Volume One (continuation of *Zur Kritik*);
– a version of Volume Three;
– *Theories of Surplus-Value*, intended as the basis of a fourth book, devoted to the history and critique of previous economic thought.

This manuscript contains a new and very detailed plan of Volumes One and Three, written after *Theories* in January 1863, and reflecting the theoretical clarifications that this had brought, especially on the notion of 'capital in general' which plays an essential role in the organisation of the exposition.

1.iii The third economic manuscript (1863–5) comprises a new draft, still provisional, of the three books.[3] There is also an important text here, designed to go at the end of Volume One but which Marx decided to omit. It is titled 'Chapter 6. Results of the Immediate Process of Production'.[4]

---

[1] K. Marx 1974b, pp. 969–80.

[2] [This manuscript is spread over twenty-three notebooks (*Hefte*), and its first authoritative edition is in the *Marx-Engels-Gesamtausgabe* (MEGA). It forms Band 3 of the Zweite Abteilung of the MEGA that contains all economic writings of Marx and Engels, and this volume is in turn divided into six parts: Teil 1 to Teil 6. All this is now available in English translation as Vols. 30 through 34 of the Marx/Engels *Collected Works*. Volume 30 contains Notebooks I through VII, on the production process of capital, together with the first part of *Theories of Surplus-Value*. Vols. 31 and 32 continue the *Theories*, and after these are concluded in Vol. 33 they are followed in the same volume and Vol. 34 by supplementary material on the subject-matter of the later Volume One of *Capital*, together with material on the problems later dealt with in Volumes Two and Three, especially the transformation of surplus-value into profit. – Translator's notes are placed here in brackets throughout.]

[3] Doubt persists on the subject of Book One, for which no draft corresponding to this second manuscript exists (Galander 1979, p. 1260).

[4] [English translation in *Capital* Volume One, trans. Ben Fowkes, (Marx 1976), pp. 941–1084.]

There are then the three editions of *Capital*, Volume One,[5] which we shall variously refer to here.

2.i The first edition (1867), particularly characterised, in relation to later editions, by a different presentation of Chapter 1 and the existence of an 'Appendix' which is an alternative version of this.[6]

2.ii The second German edition (1873), including a version of Chapter 1 that is broadly based on the 1867 Appendix.

2.iii The French edition (1872–5), in fascicles, translated by J. Roy and revised by Marx, who took the opportunity to refashion his text in many places.[7]

Subsequent editions were the work of Engels. The fourth edition, which became the 'canonical text',[8] follows in essentials the second German edition, with certain additions that Marx wrote for the French version.

---

[5] [The first English edition, translated by Samuel Moore and Edward Aveling under Engels's supervision, appeared in 1886. It was translated from the third German edition prepared by Engels in 1883, the year of Marx's death, which closely follows the French edition of 1872–5 as well as the second German edition of 1873. As Engels explains in his Preface to the English edition (Marx 1976a, p. 110), Marx had noted a few further changes for a projected English translation planned some years earlier, but Engels 'did not consider [him]self at liberty to make use of [these] otherwise then sparingly'. Two points about naming and numbering should also be noted. Firstly, whilst Marx always described *Capital* as made up of different *books*, and the French edition follows the German in titling these as *livres*, Engels presented the English edition as the first *volume*, a usage retained in the 1976 Penguin translation by Ben Fowkes which is cited here. Secondly, for the French edition, Marx changed the numbering of chapters and parts, and this is followed in the English editions. In the German editions Part Two, 'The Transformation of Money into Capital', is a single chapter, but in the French and English editions it is divided into three chapters (4, 5 and 6); the seven sections of Chapter 24 are made into separate chapters (26 through 32); and the eleven chapters of Part Seven are grouped into a Part Seven (Chapters 23 through 25) and a Part Eight (Chapter 26 through 33). Wherever the English edition reads significantly differently from the German or French as cited by the author, this is made clear in a note.]

[6] This 1867 edition was republished in 1980 by Gerstenberg Verlag. P.D. Dognin has provided a French translation of its first chapter and the Appendix under the title *Les 'sentiers escarpés' de K. Marx* (1977).

[7] I shall discuss this text on a number of occasions. Reference should also be made to the important introduction that J.P. Lefebvre provided to his recent new translation of *Le Capital* for Éditions Sociales, bringing new information on J. Roy and the editing of this French translation. See also my article 'Traduire en allemand *Le Capital*' in G. Labica 1986.

[8] This is the edition reproduced in the *Marx-Engels-Werke*, Vol. 23.

2. The history of science perspective

The great interest of this sequence, running from the *Grundrisse* to the French edition, is clearly that it provides us with a series of successive corrections and re-editings, teaching us something quite different about Marx's theory from what can be seen in the final text. It forms the basis for a task which, in my view, has never been carried out completely and which I shall now try to define: to analyse the heuristic instruments used by the author and the epistemological obstacles overcome, and, in this way, to read the final result through the trajectory of its genesis, interpreting everything in it that remains inadequate by the goal that develops in the movement and the logical constraints that progressively assert themselves.

It should be emphasised that the predominant tendency in Marxist philosophical literature (of whatever 'obedience') has been and remains to read this history in reverse: interpreting *Capital* in terms of the *Grundrisse*, and the latter in terms of the *1844 Manuscripts*. In short, the hermeneutic path that leads back to Hegel and situates the discourse of *Capital* in a revolutionary-humanistic metaphysics. That this is the way to a theoretical neutralisation of Marxism seems to me to have been clearly established by the work of Louis Althusser, who showed that the opposite direction is the proper one: the production, starting from categories borrowed from German philosophy and classical economics, of a new discourse articulated on specific categories that do not form a system together with the first ones.[9]

The writings of Althusser and his school thus constitute here an important reference. The present debate, however, will essentially be of a different nature, centred not on the cleavage between the period of youth and the period of maturity, but on a series of breaks that can be noted within the 'mature' period. And this terrain is still insufficiently explored. The work of Rosdolsky, for example, which is exemplary in many ways, and studies the transformations effected in the drafting of *Capital*, tends to underestimate the theoretical effect of the shift in the philosophical instruments that Marx successively uses.

---

[9] I have explained in the Preface above why I was led to qualify this kind of appreciation. My *Théorie générale* reinscribes the project of *Capital* in the context of modern political philosophy. But this in no way contradicts the programme I set myself here, starting from the thesis of the 'epistemological support/obstacle', in which the 'support', moreover, figures positively as the philosophical element – with presuppositions that I have subsequently sought to deploy in the concept of 'metastructure'.

Everything happens as if, despite completing the construction of his system, Marx says fundamentally the same thing from the *Grundrisse* through to *Capital*, just with differences of language. Soviet and East-German works such as those of Vygodsky, concerned above all to show a process of maturation, scarcely leave room for an epistemological view or the philosophical elements that form an obstacle. While there is free examination of technical points, the specifically economic categories, there is a kind of rule of silent respect for the philosophical scaffolding that is deemed unchangeable. And even the most systematic and exhaustive West-German studies, those of the 'Projektgruppe Entwicklung des Marxschen Systems', too often behave as if philosophical figures did not have a different bearing on Marx's work from one text to another.

In short, if this period of maturity has been the subject of several works, in the wake of the classic texts of R. Rosdolsky (1969) and H. Reichelt (1970), its history in terms of the role of the philosophical matrix of the discourse, its mutations and its effects in terms of epistemological supports/obstacles, still remains largely to be written.

3. The perspective of reconstruction of the system

The main difficulty in undertaking this approach is that it is possible only retrospectively, starting from a conception of the point of arrival, or even from a representation of the optimal formulation of the theory. And this, we have to say, is what is lacking most of all in the literature on this question: reflection on the foundations of the theory, the articulation of categories, the context of their applicability.

In point of fact, it is clear that Marx never wrote a new version without having the previous one in mind; he always wrote *something different* from the earlier text, in different words, in a different order; he only wrote *corrections*. But these are still not always easily readable. The difficulty in this respect is not simply that it was not his custom to point out his rectifications or embark on self-criticism (especially in relation to texts that had not been published). It is because these 'corrections' only exist as such in the light of a particular conception of the final work, or of what its theoretical content should be. It is only on this basis that one can conceive of a process of 'maturation'. In short, it is on the basis of a certain representation of the final result, the theory of the capitalist mode of production (pertaining to historical materialism), that it is possible to represent what supports, or obstacles, Marx found in his initial stock of categories, in relation to the new theorisation that was under way.

In this respect, a certain division of labour between economists and philosophers has been highly damaging. For the former have undoubtedly been more concerned with the overall 'system' of *Capital*, the compatibility between its different volumes, the articulation of its parts and aspects. But these problems turned out to be enveloped within the work in a language that belongs to philosophy. And philosophers, for their part, frightened off by so much technicality, have remained on the threshold. By and large, moreover, in recent years, it has often been the economists who have taken the bit between their teeth and started to undertake on *Capital* work of a philosophical character. The recent books by G. Duménil (1978) and H. Denis (1980) provide good examples.

The inadequacy of so many commentaries is no longer a function of ignorance of the texts and their order of succession, but, rather, of the theory presented in *Capital*, which will be the main object of the present investigation. 'Genetic' study is productive only to the extent that the representation of the finished work that inspires it is correct, and likewise the completion or reconstruction that it proposes.

Chapter Two
Value as Quantity

I start here with the most paradoxical aspect of Marx's project. It is the most contested, in that, even among Marxists, the operational character of the mathematical figures of surplus-value has always been in question. But also the most unavoidable, since an explicit intent runs through *Capital* from start to finish, that of constituting a science in the modern sense of the term, constructing a homogeneous space in which magnitudes are considered and calculation is possible.[1]

The radical novelty of Marx's project, however, escaped him, and is manifest today, I believe, in a singular fashion. If contemporary neo-Ricardianism is the logical development of Ricardo's thought – if it must be accepted that Ricardo, no more than Adam Smith, did not base himself on 'labour-value' but essentially saw labour only as a commodity with a price – we are forced to reconsider the idea that Marx had of his continuity with his classical predecessor. And we must ask, at the same time, what are the consequences of the surprising fact that Marx was, unknown to himself, the first to tackle the question of 'labour-value', and what are the difficulties attached to the project of constituting this category designed in principle to homogenise the 'economic' space?

---

[1] Chapters 2 and 3 are summed up in synoptic form on pages 195–217 of my *Théorie de la modernité*. The theory of value, re-interpreted in terms of a 'use-of-labour theory of value', is a central theme of my *Théorie générale*. (See especially sections 211D and 232A.)

Now, this project comes up against old problems of quality that are summed up in terms of the 'complexity' or 'intensity' of labour, problems that the classics, in their perspective, could resolve easily, but which, in *Capital*, despite Marx's strategies which alternately attribute them a (very suspect) simplicity or postpone them to later, experience a significantly different fate.

I propose therefore to start by showing why the category of 'labour-value', far from being the touchstone of a scientistic interpretation of Marx, as claimed for example by A. Negri,[2] constitutes the strong point, albeit the hardest to grasp, from which this theory shows that it transcends a merely quantitative significance (though without losing this reference) and is to be understood as a theory of class struggle.

I shall seek at the same time to analyse why the Marxist literature that deals with these questions is so frequently marked by a great incoherence: not only is *Capital* is nothing more than the final step in an unfinished journey, which must be followed from 1857 to 1872 (or even beyond) in its successive *corrections*, but there is still a long way from the projects announced at the start of Volume One to their realisation in the work as a whole, as a function of the logical possibilities inherent in this 'special object'. And I shall show how these questions, seemingly marginal and particular, concern the status of the category of value and the object of this theory.

1. Constructing a homogeneous economic space: a Marxian project that breaks with political economy

At the start of his discourse in *Capital*, Marx stakes out an explicitly epistemological position on the relationship between the theoretical space he defines and the possibility of introducing measurement into it. This is a very commonplace idea, general to scientific procedure well before Marx: there is only measurement in science in relation to an object to be measured, by the 'simultaneous construction of the object and its measure'.[3]

The project of homogenising economic space was clearly nothing new. It was implied in the physiocratic reproduction schemas, and above all in the reference to labour that is common to the English classics. What was radically

---

[2] Negri 1979, pp. 39 & 55.
[3] Dostaler 1978, Vol. 2, p. 40.

new was the project of homogenising it in terms of 'embodied labour'. And the paradox is that Marx largely failed to notice this novelty. So much so that Marxist tradition frequently assimilates the Marxian theory of value to that of Ricardo. The recent interpretation (cf. C. Benetti and J. Cartelier, in the wake of Sraffa) that asserts a total break in this respect is the one I see as correct. And I want to show how it is verified when we examine how the classics deal with the quantitative treatment of the 'qualities' of labour such as its level of skill or intensity. In this way, the nature of the tasks facing a theory of labour-value will be shown *a contrario*.

Smith, as is well-known, defined the value of a commodity by the quantity of labour that could be 'bought' by it, or that it 'commanded'. But this quantity was weighted by two kinds of 'qualities'.

The first of these is *skill*. 'There may be more labour . . . in an hour's application to a trade which it costs ten years' labour to learn, than in a month's industry at an ordinary and obvious employment.'[4] The labour market, Smith added, broadly sanctions this natural imperative by the difference in wages that the various levels of skill command. The second 'quality' is the *hardship* that belongs to the nature of certain work.[5]

The problem raised by the qualitative differences between types of labour is thus 'resolved' very simply in terms of differences in wages, by the mediation of competition on the labour market. The economic space is thus homogenised not by labour itself, but by the labour that wages purchase, by labour as commodity.

Ricardo, in his *Principles of Political Economy and Taxation* (Chapter 1 'On Value', Section 1) openly criticised Smith, rejected the idea of the 'quantity of labour commanded'[6] and proposed to return to the definition of value in terms of the quantity of labour needed for production, just as Marx was later to do.

The continuation of his text, however (Section 2), shows that, in reality, Ricardo does not depart from Smith's position. He does indeed appear to shift the question to new ground. In substance, he asks how it is possible, given that quantity of labour is what determines value, to calculate the weighting introduced by its qualitative elements, skill and intensity? But the

---

[4] Smith 1974, p. 134.
[5] Smith 1974, pp. 134, 202.
[6] Ricardo 1971, pp. 57–8.

response he provides surreptitiously returns us to the point of departure. Ricardo emphasises that 'the comparative skill and intensity of labour . . . operates *equally*' (my emphasis: J.B.) at successive times, and thus does not modify the 'variations in the relative value' that is the object of his study.[7] He goes on to refer to Smith as the writer who correctly treated this question by reference to the labour market.

Thus Marx, when he tackled the question of the quantitative transformation of the 'qualitative' aspects of labour ('complexity', 'intensity') in the context of his project of homogenisation of an 'economic space', only found in his supposed predecessors a type of solution in contradiction with his theory of labour-value: a solution in terms of labour as commodity. He thus faced a difficult problem, given that, as against the classical bourgeois economists, his concern was to conceive these 'qualities' – which remain *within labour* itself and which cause a problem when the attempt is made to calculate value *in terms of labour* – within the strict field of labour, independently of the question of wages.

2. Paralogisms of Marx the measurer

The orthodox reading, deliberately sanctifying, and the hostile reading, naturally simplifying, have both maintained, for opposite reasons, the idea that Marx's statements on 'labour-value' formed a coherent and stable ensemble. I shall show here the contradictions through which they actually developed, even within the so-called period of maturity, and the background of uncertainty as to the relationship between the substance and its measure against which the assertions of *Capital* are made.

It is *The Poverty of Philosophy* that must serve as the starting-point here, since it was in this text that Marx adopted unequivocally for the first time this theory of value, from Ricardo as he believed. The procedure he followed here would be repeated in future writings: from asserting that the measure of value was labour-time, he immediately went on to consider *skilled* labour as producing more value in the same time.[8] And he presented the solution to this problem as self-evident: it is a function of 'competition'. At the same

---

[7] Ricardo 1971, p. 64.
[8] Marx 1976b, p. 53.

time, Marx introduced 'simple' labour 'which has become the pivot of industry' as the unit of measure. This is labour deprived of skill: 'Quality no longer matters. Quantity alone decides everything; hour for hour, day for day.'[9] We may note the leap from mere 'quantity of labour' to the standard of measurement, labour deprived of 'skill' because uniformly mechanised.

A famous passage in the *Grundrisse* (where some people read a great dialectical feat) effects an analogous slippage in the same terms, but now adding a further category, that of 'abstract labour', which functions on both levels: 'labour as such . . . abstract labour', and 'purely abstract, purely mechanical labour'.[10]

This amalgam is further developed and enriched in *A Contribution to the Critique of Political Economy*. The paralogism once more bears on the 'simplicity' of labour, which undergoes the same uncontrolled doubling of meaning. We are first presented with what in *Capital* is called abstract labour, in the following terms: 'uniform, homogeneous, simple labour', 'simple labour, labour, so to speak, without any qualitative attributes'.[11] Then comes the slippage: 'This abstraction, human labour in general, *exists* in the form of average labour which, in a given society, the average person can perform. . . . It is *simple*[12] labour which any individual can be trained to do. . .'.[13] In short, just like the 'abstraction' in the *Grundrisse*, the *Critique*'s 'simplicity' designates first of all the category of 'abstract labour' that ignores concrete differences, and then the *actual* uniformisation of labour arising from mechanisation and the subjection of the great majority of workers to this. Note that we find the same polysemy again in a further term: 'labour pure and simple [*die Arbeit schlechthin*]', which operates both in the sense of abstract labour[14] and that of simple labour.[15]

The existence of these slippages, which are also found in other texts, is highly surprising, since Marx already distinguishes perfectly well the two couples abstract/concrete and simple/complex, and yet has them interfere with each other at a certain moment in his theorisation, in connection with

---

[9] Marx 1976b, pp. 53–4.
[10] Marx 1973c, pp. 103–4.
[11] Marx 1971, p. 30.
[12] [Marx inserts here the footnote: 'English economists call it "unskilled labour".']
[13] Marx 1971, p. 30.
[14] Marx 1973c, pp. 103–4.
[15] Marx 1973c, p. 323.

the determination of an average. It is all the more important to explain this curious procedure in that it leaves significant traces in the construction of *Capital*.

I put forward here the following hypothesis. This procedure is an attempt to combine the determination of the 'substance' of value and that of its 'measure', with a view to mastering the problem presented for the theory of 'labour-value' by the existence of labours of differing 'quality'. Marx seeks to establish a standard presenting the characteristics of the substance itself, of such kind that, by relating the different kinds of labour to this standard, he relates them to the substance. What he seeks is in some sense a *substantive standard*. This is what we must now examine more closely.

3. *Capital*: the categories of measurement undermine the theorisation of the substance to be measured

Capital broadly clarifies the presentation of the *Critique*. It repeats it in two sections. In the first section of Chapter 1, Marx articulates the *substance* of value, the 'expenditure of human labour-power'.[16] Skilled labour is then postponed to the second section, when the question of measurement has already been settled.

Yet the question of knowing whether skilled labour produces more value in the same time is unavoidably forced on Marx, as a point that is undoubtedly secondary but still indispensable to resolve in principle so that the quantitative space of value is mastered.[17]

But Marx has trouble mastering this aspect of his discourse, decisive as it is. And it is not surprising that the articulation of the three 'reductions' that, in a sense, constitute the start of his presentation, should generally be so poorly understood.

The *first* reduction is the consideration of abstract labour. A negative operation: the particularity of different labours is 'left aside', retaining what is common to them all, the property of being expenditure of labour-power.

---

[16] Marx 1971, p. 128.

[17] It strikes me as significant that critics of Marx perceived from the start that there is a difficulty in seeking to define value in terms of the expenditure of labour whilst simultaneously taking skill into account. For example, Böhm-Bawerk (1926), Bernstein (1899), Pareto (1902–3), etc.

To speak correctly, there is no 'reduction', different qualities are not translated into something common. The particular qualities are left aside, with only their common quality retained. In this way, the *substance* of value is defined as the expenditure of labour-power.

This yields the principle of quantitative comparison of different labours producing different commodities and constituting different branches. In the commodity structure, this comparison between branches is effected spontaneously, by the 'law of value' in its initial aspect as a law of the market: commodities are exchanged for one another as a function of the labour-time they require.

The *second* reduction concerns the transition from 'individual' labour to 'socially necessary' labour. It designates the second aspect of the 'law of value' as a law of the market: within a particular branch, the value of a particular commodity is established as the average level of labour required. In their combination, these two aspects define the commodity structure, with the double relationship that competition presupposes: between branches and within a branch.

This second reduction thus translates 'qualitative' differences into quantitative; if value is determined by the time socially necessary, the individual labour that, thanks to its level of skill, intensity and productivity[18] produces the commodity in question in less time, asserts itself as producing more value in the same time. Otherwise expressed, definition of the conditions of equality of labours establishes at the same time their inequality in three dimensions: skill, intensity and productivity.

The *third* reduction is that of 'complex' labour to 'simple'. We may well suppose (and Marx's assertion that 'experience shows that this reduction is constantly being made'[19] may be interpreted in this sense) that what is again at work here is the rule of competition. In reality, however, while the second reduction *immediately* belongs to the theory, this is not the case with the third. The theory of labour-value maintains a reduction to socially necessary labour-time: in *average* conditions of skill, intensity and productivity. The question of complex labour, here opposed to simple not as to an *average* but to its *unit of measure*,[20] raises right away, on the contrary, a problem for the theory. It

---

[18] Marx 1976a, p. 129.
[19] Marx 1976a, p. 135.
[20] Ibid.

re-introduces in effect, tangentially, the very question of the 'kind' of labour that had been explicitly excluded by the initial founding assertion, that which defined value by abstract labour, expenditure of labour-time. Far from being an extension of the second reduction, the third seems to bring with it a kind of return that risks a re-appearance of concrete labour, after this was excluded so as to open the quantitative space of value.

That Marx has trouble mastering this 'third reduction' appears most strikingly, to my mind, in the well-known passage at the start of *Capital* where he makes a strange equation between *abstract* and *simple* (or even *average*) labour:

> But the value of a commodity represents human labour pure and simple, the expenditure of human labour in general. And just as, in civil society, a general or a banker plays a great part but man as such [*der Mensch schlechthin*] plays a very mean part, so, here too, the same is true of human labour. It is the expenditure of simple labour-power, i.e. of the labour-power possessed in his bodily organism by every ordinary man, **on the average**, without being developed in any special way. *Simple average labour*, it is true, varies in character in different countries and at different cultural epochs, but in a particular country it is given. More complex labour counts only as *intensified*, or rather *multiplied* simple labour, so that a smaller quantity of complex labour is considered equal to a larger quantity of simple labour. **Experience** shows that this reduction is constantly being made.[21]

It is striking to find once more here the same slippage as in the earlier texts: from *abstract* labour, labour in general, *die Arbeit schlechthin*, to its privileged support, the ordinary man, *der Mensch schlechthin*, who accomplishes *simple* labour. The formulation is less clear than in the *Critique*, where we read: 'This abstraction, human labour in general, exists in the form of average labour. . . . It is *simple* labour'.[22] But the essential is the same: 'the same is true of human labour. It is the expenditure of simple labour-power'.[23] In short, labour in general exists in the ordinary man in an immediate fashion, in the light of which those kinds of labour of a higher degree can be grasped only indirectly by way of this substantive standard.

---

[21] Ibid. [Italics for Marx's emphases, bold for J.B.'s.]
[22] Marx 1971, p. 31.
[23] Marx 1976a, p. 135.

The anthropological connotation of the text is plain: ordinary man is promoted to the rank of man in general.

It seems to me, however, that this humanist thematisation is not an end in itself, but there is also a philosophical *recourse* here that responds to an extra-philosophical intention: that of resolving problems arising from the specific theoretical matrix set up at the start of *Capital*. More precisely, Marx seeks to escape from the trap I have described above: he tries to successively take into account the different 'kinds' of labour without cancelling the initial operation that made abstraction from the kind of labour. The procedure consists of situating the various more skilled kinds of labour on a scale that relates them to the unit of a 'substantive standard'. For the question of a standard is no longer here simply that of choosing a certain *quantity* of duration. It concerns *quality*: the unit adopted has to have the character of a substance, to be pure metal, as opposed to the 'enriched alloys' of complex labour. Simple labour can only play the role of unit here because abstract labour takes on the features of simple labour: 'it is simple labour'; 'it is the expenditure of simple labour-power'. Simple labour becomes a substance because it is supposed to be the simple 'expenditure of labour-power'. The first, quantitative, principle of the measure of substance, labour-*time*, is thus supplemented by a second, which bears on the *quality* of the labour standard. Its quality will in a sense be not to have a quality, so that it can be just a pure element of substance. And the substantive character of this labour standard is communicated to the skilled labour of different kinds, since these are measured by the multiplication of this element by a number: they are 'multiplied simple labour'. In this way, their qualities are transformed into quantities. But at the price of a serious confusion: the assimilation of abstract labour to simple labour.

We thus see how this question of simple labour leads well beyond the familiar classical question of the 'reduction of complex labour', even beyond quantitative analysis. It involves an interference between the determination of the measure of value and that of its substance. The theory of measurement forms the critical test for the theory of substance and its determination.

Hence the necessity to examine in what manner *Capital* actually carries through the project, announced in its opening pages, of a translation of qualitative differences (of productivity, skill and intensity) into quantity. Does Marx manage to effectively master a quantitative space that would be that of an 'economy'? Do its founding categories enable us to conceive such a problematic? Or do they not put in place, surreptitiously, a quite different one?

4. In what sense does more productive labour produce more value? The articulation of structure and dynamic

The interference of the 'quality' of labour on the quantity of value produced is expressed first of all in the category of productivity: more productive labour, Marx explains, constitutes an 'intensified' labour, producing more value in the same time. In this sense, this is a very clear and simple point in his theory, a moment at which the 'transformation of quality into quantity' seems to have been mastered in an explicit and adequate rational schema. It is important however to understand why this 'transformation' does not reach a calculable conclusion.

It actually has two facets, which designate in their relationship the structure of the capitalist market as based on labour-value.

Between one period and another, the global variation of *average* (or social) productivity does not modify the amount of value produced: 'an increase in the productivity of labour will also supply more products in a given day . . . a given value is spread over a greater mass of products'.[24] This proposition only makes explicit the thesis of the determination of value by socially necessary labour-time. The global elevation of the productive power of labour thanks to the introduction of machinery, the application of science or the improvement of natural conditions, does not modify the quantity of value produced.

Within the same period, the *particular* productivity of each competing enterprise is translated by differences in the amount of value produced. This is how the use of a more efficient machine, as long as it is not yet generalised, 'convert[s] the labour employed by the owner of that machinery into labour of a higher degree [*potenzierte*], by raising the social value of the article produced above its individual value'.[25] 'The exceptionally productive labour acts as intensified labour; it creates in equal periods of time greater values than average social

---

[24] Marx 1976a, p. 661.
[25] Marx 1976a, p. 530.

labour of the same kind'.[26] Curiously, Marx applies here to this labour-creating extra surplus-value the term 'potenzierte' labour ('complexe' in the French, 'intensified' in the English) that he generally reserves for skilled labour, which alone is mentioned in the general presentations where he explains the simple/complex couple.[27] But he does so in a quite particular sense. 'Complex' labour here means labour that, because it possesses a higher productivity, creates a commodity of less 'individual value' but which is sold nonetheless at the same price as the commodity of its competitors, or at a price slightly below. This work creates a greater quantity of social value in the same time. In this particular sense, the definition of 'complex' labour is inherent in the notion of value, in the 'law of value'. It denotes the way in which the market structure presents a principle of historical dynamism, a form that promotes the increase in productivity.

It is understandable that the question of the 'reduction' of complex to simple labour is not reduced here to that of a calculable transformation, and it would be vain, moreover, to try and present its 'general rule' (since the gain obtained depends on the more or less productive character of the technical innovation, and does not follow any definite principle). Marx elaborates here the concept of a dynamic object, the process of capitalist accumulation. He defines a historically determined structure, that of a mode of production possessing an inherent tendency. We can thus understand how the definition of value as a quantity, because it is situated within the definition of the social relation and its dynamic (where the contradiction already comes to a head), fails to contain it in the positivity of measurement.

5. Skilled labour as a zone of paralogism

Against current interpretations, I propose to show that, in the theory of the capitalist mode of production, skilled labour can only be tackled in the context of 'more productive' labour, that is, according to the model analysed above: the theory does not authorise any specific consideration concerning the increase in value that this more skilled labour might produce *as such*.

---

[26] Marx 1976a, p. 435.
[27] Marx 1976a, pp. 137 & 661.

The paradox is that Marx totally failed to recognise, at least in his explicit discourse, this theoretical constraint. And I will therefore start by showing the enormous resistance he opposes to it throughout *Capital*, in the form of a series of paralogisms based on pseudo-categories. We shall go on to see what path, followed by Marx but not recognised, the logic of his system imposes. And why this marks a break with any economistic perspective, and the instauration of the perspective of historical materialism.

5.i *The paralogism of evidence*

The text in the first chapter of *Capital* that presents Marx's explicit thesis on complex labour appears very strange if confronted with the methodological principles that the author himself proclaims:

> More complex labour counts only as intensified, or rather multiplied simple labour, so that a smaller quantity of complex labour is considered equal to a larger quantity of simple labour. **Experience shows that this reduction is constantly being made.** A commodity may be the outcome of the most complicated labour, but through its *value* it is posited as equal to the product of simple labour, hence it represents only a specific quantity of simple labour. The various proportions in which different kinds of labour are reduced to simple labour as their unit of measurement is established by a social process that goes on **behind the backs of the producers**; these proportions therefore appear to the producers to have been handed down by tradition.[28]

We are quite right to be surprised by this appeal to experience, and wonder what it actually is here that this might offer. *Capital*, in fact, does not claim to start from experience, but to lead us to experience, to the 'phenomena', to appearance as it is given to us, in other words to explain this by the means of concepts that do not belong to experience but must first of all be produced.

In capitalist society, the 'experience' according to which exchange between commodities is regulated in the last resort by necessary labour-time *precisely does not exist*. Already in Chapter 1, the category of fetishism is introduced, its object being to account for the fact that 'experience' does not attest to value

---

[28] Marx 1976a, p. 135; [Italics for Marx's emphases, bold for J.B.'s.] Cf. Marx 1971, pp. 31–2.

as quantity of embodied labour. We may deduce from this that experience also does not enable us to say that skilled labour yields more value.

The fragility of Marx's position can be read in the internal contradiction of his text: between the assertion that this reduction is a 'fact of experience' and the idea that it is produced 'behind the backs of the producers [*hinter den Rücken der Produzenten*]'. And we may well believe that it is a sense of dissatisfaction that led Marx to revisit this question in a further text, which gives the question a quite different sense.

There is a further passage in *Capital*, inserted in the French edition, that takes up the problem and adds a supplementary argument, though an equally specious one:

> The values of the most varied commodities are everywhere expressed *indistinctly* in money, i.e. in a certain amount of gold or silver. In just this way, the different kinds of labour, represented by these values, have been reduced in different productions to sums determined by one and the same kind of ordinary labour, labour that produces gold or silver.[29]

The procedure here is inadmissible, taking up a passage from the *Grundrisse* the content of which can also be summed up in the same way:[30] all labours are represented 'indistinctly' in the general equivalent, thus in just one kind of labour; complex labour is thereby reduced to simple labour. The reduction to abstract labour, promoted to the rank of experience and made visible in the money commodity, is taken as evidence and guarantor of the reduction of complex labour to simple, thus of the legitimacy of these categories. The exchange of the products of different labours for money (product of a labour called simple) proves that they are exchanged according to the supposed degree of complexity of these labours.

5.ii *The jeweller's paradigm*

It is in the same perspective that Marx develops certain notions that can have no legitimate place in his system. I shall show that these represent different attempts to backtrack on a break that rightly follows from the very nature of the first principles of *Capital*.

---

[29] Marx 1983, fasc. I, p. 198; my emphasis: J.B. [This passage does not appear in the English edition.]
[30] Marx 1973c, p. 846.

These are articulated first of all in the singular figure of the jeweller, in an account that is so theoretically improper that it merits being studied and deciphered. This can be seen in the three variants of the same theme: in the *1861 Manuscripts*, the German edition of *Capital*, and the French edition.

The German text, in the canonical fourth edition, occupies a middle position. The passage in question here reads:

> All labour of a higher, or more complicated character than average labour is expenditure of labour-power of a more costly kind, labour-power that has cost more time and labour than unskilled or simple labour-power, and which therefore [*daher*] has a higher value. This power being of a higher value, it [therefore] [*daher*] expresses itself in labour of a higher sort, and therefore [*daher*] becomes objectified, during an equal amount of time, in proportionally higher values.[31]

The thesis appears to be simplicity itself. It consists in a connection between three terms that is taken as self-evident. There are two relationships that I shall call XY and YZ. The line of argument is as follows:

from X = higher costs of training,
to Y = a higher value of labour-power, and hence
to Z = a higher labour creating more value.

A certain embarrassment surrounding this question, however, is already signalled in the history of the German editions. The first three of these contain, instead of the last *daher* ('therefore') the word *aber* ('but'), which gives the following proposition: 'This power being of a higher value, it [therefore] [*daher*] expresses itself in labour of a higher sort, but [*aber*] becomes objectified, during an equal amount of time, in proportionally higher values.'[32] It was Engels, in the fourth German edition, who changed *aber* to *daher*, thus making the text more coherent.

The *1861 draft* already contained the same thesis and the same formulae. But it gave a curious argument for point Y, concerning the 'higher value of skilled labour-power': 'When reference is made to labour as a measure of value, it necessarily implies *labour of one particular kind* [. . .] **the proportion**

---

[31] Marx 1973a, pp. 211–2; Marx 1976a, p. 305; cf. also Marx 1972, p. 231.
[32] Cf. Marx 1980, 163–4.

which the other kinds bear to it being easily ascertained by the respective remuneration given to each.'[33] I emphasise the surprising conclusion that Marx suppressed in *Capital*, where the same passage appears, but dishonestly cut off in mid-sentence after 'easily ascertained'.[34] It is clear, in fact, that the ending brings us back to precisely to what the theory is designed to exclude: the determination of the amount of value produced by that of wages paid.

The French edition (1872) differs clearly enough from the German to see here a deliberate intervention by Marx, which can only be interpreted as a correction:

> Let us admit . . . that, compared with the labour of the cotton-spinner, that of the jeweller is labour of a higher power, that the one is simple labour and the other complex labour expressing a skill harder to train and rendering more value in the same time.[35]

This text invites us to conclude from labour-power being *'harder to train'* that it has the capacity to produce more value in a determinate time. It would appear, therefore, that the central reference to the value of labour-power (Y) has disappeared. Only one ratio is proposed here: XZ, that of the 'harder' training (X) to the greater value created (Z), whereas the German text distinguished two successive relationships, XY and YZ.

In reality, the apparent superiority of the French text resides in its vagueness, the hesitation it has in saying that the value of skilled labour-power affects the value of its product. Its interest consists in the relative censorship it imposes on the propositions advanced in the German version. A censorship, however, that only makes the problems it bears more evident.

Each of the two propositions in the German text, both XY and YZ, is unacceptable in terms of the requirements of the theory presented in *Capital*.

XY is a paralogism of the effect of training on the value of labour-power. Can one really say that the costs (X) of training increase the value (Y) of labour-power? I shall show below (Chapter 4) that this proposition has only

---

[33] Marx and Engels 1988a, p. 91. [Italics for Marx's emphases, bold for J.B.'s.]

[34] Marx 1976a, p. 306, n. 20. [This footnote, as attributed, is in fact a quotation from J. Cazenove, *Outlines of Political Economy*, published in 1832, which Marx presumably endorses.]

[35] Marx 1983, fasc. I, p. 197.

a generic legitimacy, and cannot be applied to particular wage-earners without paralogical effect.

YZ is a paralogism of the skilled worker as machine. Can one really say that a higher value (Y) of labour-power translates into a greater value (Z) of product? Clearly not. It is the very object of the theory of surplus-value that there is no necessary relationship between the amount of value that labour produces and the value of labour-power itself; an increase in the latter only reduces surplus-value. Training costs, which come under the category of 'necessary subsistence' (in the broader sense) cannot have, *qua* costs, an effect on the value of the product. Those explanations that, basing themselves on this text of Marx, seek in the higher value of skilled labour-power the principle of the production of a greater value in the same time, stray into a machine analogy, such as Adam Smith uses in *The Wealth of Nations*.[36]

The analogy is deceptive. If the machine does indeed transmit its own value to the product, this is not the case with human labour-power. Variable capital (*v*) does not represent a magnitude transmitted to the product, but a determinate quantity of value that disappears in the worker's consumption, her labour creating in the same time a magnitude equal to $v + s$, which is in no way determined by the value of the 'subsistences' consumed. The costs of education, which come under this category of 'subsistence', can thus have no effect, *qua* costs, on the value of the product.

It is remarkable and perfectly logical that the deceptive metaphor of the machine indifferently serves two distinct usages: to depict XY, the idea that training, by the cost it incurs, raises the value of the labour-power of the individual receiving it, and equally YZ, the idea that labour-power with a higher value creates more value.

What it actually relates to is the idea of a *transfer* of value from an original labour (X), first to the productive power (Y) that it forms and then to the product of this (Z). But this transitivity is precisely what characterises constant capital such as machinery, and not living labour, the value of which is not the object of a transfer but simultaneously of a consumption (*v*) and a production ($v + s$). The paralogism comes from treating variable capital as constant capital.

---

[36] Smith 1974, pp. 203–4.

YZ is also a paralogism of the category of 'uniform rate of profit'. We should finally note that this correlation between the value of labour-power and that of its product, which the 'machine' analogy grasps at a static level, may also be analysed in terms of the dynamic (in a sense) moment of the theory, that of the market. And this is what Marx does in the text that opens Part Two of Volume Three, where he puts forward the idea that the equalisation of rates of surplus-value is a real tendency of the system. This means that, if simple labour is paid 1 unit when it produces 2, it should be assumed that complex labour paid 2 units will produce 4. Thus, Marx explains, differences in skill create differences in wages but not in exploitation, since they correlatively create differences of value in the product: 'If the work of a goldsmith is paid at a higher rate than that of a day-labourer, for example, the former's surplus labour also produces a correspondingly greater surplus-value than does that of the latter.'[37]

This tendency, Marx adds, is accomplished through 'the advance of capitalist production and the progressive subordination of all economic relations to this mode of production'. Despite being always braked in reality by various obstacles, a general theoretical study, which supposes that 'actual conditions correspond to their concept',[38] can treat it as accomplished.

But the whole problem lies precisely in determining the nature of this mysterious law which tendentially assures the 'equal rates of surplus-value'. Neither this question, nor even the category of an equal rate of surplus-value itself, seem to me to have been properly studied. Marx, in fact, did not produce a theory of it, deferring it indefinitely to his future book on wages. It seems to me that he actually came up against a difficulty of principle. A law of this kind should not be confused with that ensuring the equalisation of the rate of profit, which involves the *redistribution* of surplus-value, therefore of the value produced. It can only be a law logically prior to this – which indeed is why Marx treats it as a preliminary ('we now assume . . .'),[39] a law concerning the production of this surplus-value. But, at the very heart of this 'law', there appears a proposition logically prior to the question of surplus-value itself, and concerning simply the level of *value* (that is, of commodity production

---

[37] Marx 1981, p. 241.
[38] Marx 1981, p. 242.
[39] Marx 1981, p. 241.

in general): the assertion that skilled labour produces more value in the same time.

The conclusion is already implicit (or should be, but it escapes such excellent commentators as Rubin):[40] either such a proposition can be founded at the theoretical level of Chapter 1 of Volume One, that of commodity production as such (as *abstract* form, not historical stage), or else it cannot be founded at all, in which case the subsequent category of a 'general rate of surplus-value' has to be considered inoperative.

If, however, we look for what basis Marx has for the sense of evidence that he (literally) displays, we have to investigate the nature of the paradigm chosen: the jeweller, an ancient creature already invoked by Adam Smith and Ricardo.[41] This is a precapitalist type of profession on which capital finds it hard to impose its 'real subsumption'. It is suited to the imaginary experience of a labour whose fruits might seem to have a higher value. It is only with the development of capitalism and its specific tendencies that this play of false categories becomes impossible, precisely because the field of value is now fully asserted, in all its coherence and with the constraints that constitute it – a field in which 'skilled labour' occupies a very determinate place, which cannot be that of a 'superior labour' in general, nor that of a superior 'kind'.

This is what we must now examine more closely.

5.iii   *Rectification: the collective labourer*

There is a passage in the 'Results'[42] that provides the correct treatment of this question as it arises from the theory of extra surplus-value. Marx explains that, at the level of the workshop or firm, thus of 'individual capital', given the unity of the production process and the process of valorisation, the 'collective worker [*Gesamtarbeiter*]',[43] as producer of the product, is also the producer of the commodity and the indivisible former of the value that it

---

[40] Rubin 1978, p. 222.

[41] Smith 1974, p. 207; Ricardo 1971, p. 12.

[42] Marx 1976a, pp. 1021–4, 1052–5.

[43] This term denotes here the totality of workers in the enterprise. In other theoretical contexts *Gesamtarbeit* can refer to the total labour of the commodity-producing society (Marx 1973a, p. 87: cf. Marx 1976a, p. 165), or again to combined labour in general (Marx 1973a, p. 346; cf. Marx 1976a, pp. 445–6). The present case is one of a very specific concept.

contains. The commodity offered on the market, whose value is determined by socially necessary labour-time, is the product of the workshop as a whole, and only acquires at this level the characteristics of concrete and abstract labour by which it produces a certain commodity in a certain time, the various qualities of labour-power existing only in their agency.[44]

It is significant, moreover, that Part Five of Volume One, which deals systematically with the factors determining the amount of surplus-value (and thus value) produced, introduces in place of the former triptych productivity/intensity/skill (factors that weight the average social *duration* that defines value), a new problematic of duration/productivity/intensity, marked by the absence of any category such as skill or specialisation. This absence flows logically from the development of Part Four, which shows that the commodity, in terms of both exchange-value and use-value, is the fruit of collective labour.

Nothing authorises us to assign specialised labour a greater share in the value produced. The debate actually leads back to that of 'socially necessary labour-time', which is developed on two levels. On the one hand there is *intensity*, which we still have to study; on the other hand there is *productivity*. And it is within the latter that specialisation makes its appearance, its (unequal) development going hand in hand with that of the modernisation of machinery and the organisation of labour. The incidence of specialised labour on the increase in value can neither be individualised nor applied to a particular category of workers. It is set in the context of extra surplus-value, which Marx defines as an effect of the overall productivity of the workshop, in other words the rise in the productive power of the collective labourer.

Formally, 'specialisation' is thus given the place that 'skill', in the sense of dexterity occupied in the first definition of socially necessary labour-time in *Capital*, in the group skill/intensity/productivity.[45] It is just, as we shall come on to see, that it is integrated into the last of these, reducing the triptych to two terms: intensity/productivity. This topic, which defines a relationship to an *average*, ends up finally absorbing the other topic, complex/simple labour, which refers to simple labour as its *unit*, its substantive standard.

The problematic of the different 'levels of skill' of labour and their specific products or values, inherited from the classical economists, with its solutions

---

[44] Cf. Marx 1972, p. 399 in the same sense.
[45] Marx 1976a, p. 129.

in terms of production costs or remuneration of the worker, is thus revoked in the 'Results', and in Parts Four and Five of Volume One. Marx thus arrives at a standpoint conforming to his theoretical premise of labour-value: strict disconnection between value of labour-power and value produced, between labour and its 'price'. The break with political economy is complete.

6. Intensity: closure and fracture of the quantitative space

The question of intensity seems to be the one where the mastery of quantity is most readily and completely effected. Yet this mastery, being only metaphorical, only closes one quantitative space to define another, one that cannot yet be named.

In Volume One of *Capital*, Marx introduces the question of intensity of labour as early as Part One, when he defines value as 'labour-time socially necessary', necessary that is given the average degree of *skill, intensity* and *productivity*.[46] But the most important developments arise in Part Four, where he shows how in manufacture and modern industry the intensity of labour tends to increase, as a function of both the fragmentation and the regularisation of labour, as well as the shortening of the working day; then, in Part Five, which systematically examines the respective effects of variations in *duration*, *intensity* and *productivity* on the amount of value produced and its division between surplus-value and wages; and, finally, in Part Six, where intensity is related to the form of wages (particularly piecework) and to the level of wages in different countries.

As I see it, Marx analyses 'more intense' labour in terms of three main problematics. First of all, in the context of the production of a definite commodity: he indicates here a disparity in relation to the intensity needed to produce this commodity in average time, and defines 'something like' the extra surplus-value that attaches to labour of higher productivity in relation to its competitors. In the second place, the tendency to intensification is analysed as a global characteristic of capitalist society; it is then defined in terms that refer to absolute surplus-value. And, thirdly, Marx envisages it as characteristic of a particular branch taken as a whole and opposed to other

---

[46] Marx 1976a, pp. 130–1 & 660.

branches: what is again pertinent here, as in the first case, is a disparity, but one of a different kind, this time in relation to the average intensity of labour in the society considered as a whole.

I shall show that the first problematic is bound up with a differential schema of value, the second with a dimensional schema, while the third leads to a point of equivalence that also expresses the need to supersede these.

6.i *Intensity: a 'differential' problematic of value (as extra surplus-value)*

The definition of value as *'social value'*, the time necessary on average for the production of a particular commodity, implies that this social value can be counterposed to *'individual values'* that differ from the average precisely in that the labours that form them vary in their level of skill, intensity or productivity. We have already seen how, in relation to productivity, Marx developed the couple 'social value'/'individual values', and the idea that 'intensified labour . . . creates in equal periods of time greater values than average social labour of the same kind'.[47] Intensity readily lends itself to the same analysis: labour of average intensity is counterposed to labour of greater or lesser intensity, creating a correspondingly greater or lesser amount of value.

The framework of analysis here is still that of the branch, identified with a particular type of commodity. Marx raises the question of intensity in relation to piecework[48] and the world market.[49] It is clear that those capitalists whose workers perform a more intense labour in relation to those of their competitors benefit from an increase in surplus-value, analogous to that derived from a higher productivity, and that this can only be analysed as arising from a difference, due to this higher degree of intensity, in relation to the time socially necessary for the production of *this* commodity, thus in terms analogous to those of extra surplus-value.

But only analogous, since the factors tending to re-absorb the extra surplus-value by a generalisation of the technical process that is temporarily more productive are very clear, just as those tending to maintain different levels of

---

[47] Marx 1976a, p. 435.
[48] Marx 1976a, p. 694.
[49] Marx 1976a, pp. 701–2.

intensity between one enterprise and another. Something 'extra-technical' thus lies at the heart of the determination of the economic magnitude.

6.ii *Intensification: a 'dimensional' problematic of value (as absolute surplus-value)*

While the texts that we have just examined tackle 'intensity' in the same way as productivity is tackled in Chapter 14 in the context of analysis of the *structure*, preliminary and principle of a historical dynamic, 'intensification' intervenes within this structure as its *tendency*, bound up with the stages of capitalist development: manufacture and modern industry bring greater uniformity and density of labour, and hence its intensification.[50]

In this new perspective, no longer synchronic but diachronic, the quantitative reference is of a quite different order. For intensity no longer characterises individual labours in their difference from the average, but rather this *'average labour'* itself. This is no longer grasped as a differential element, but as a second constitutive dimension of value in general. In short, the *differential* conception is replaced (or supplemented) by a *dimensional* conception: the quantity of labour is now defined by the relationship of its two dimensions: the extensive amount or duration, and the intensive amount or intensity.[51]

As I see it, this analytical development is freighted with a rich ambiguity. While appearing to confirm the quantitative path, it brings us towards its breaking point.

On the one hand, we can read here the triumph of quantitativism, again with a reference to productivity but this time in opposition to it. The general rise in intensity is distinguished from the rise in productivity in that the former produces an addition of value in society.[52] But the two are equivalent inasmuch as they each constitute quantitative figures, qualities translated into quantities.

On the other hand, however, the fact is already signalled here that labour is only 'condensable', analysable in terms of its intensive 'dimension', because it is an expenditure of *human* labour-power, irreducible to clock time, to a simple natural quantity.

---

[50] Marx 1976a, pp. 455–6, 458, 534–5.
[51] Marx 1976a, pp. 534–5, 683–4.
[52] Marx 1976a, pp. 660–1.

6.iii *The paradox of the quantitative indifference of general intensification. The myth of the nation becoming uniformly more hard-working*

Marx finally introduces intensity as a characteristic specific to various branches. What is pertinent here is once more a discrepancy, as in the first case, but a discrepancy of another kind, in relation to the average intensity of labour in the society under consideration as a whole. This introduction however is highly elliptical, being contained in a further assumption. Suppose, Marx says, that all the branches of industry align themselves with the branch where labour is most intense. This is a kind of thought experiment aiming to push to their final conclusion the consequences of the initial defining propositions on the relationship of intensity to quantity of value:

> If the intensity of labour were to increase simultaneously and equally in
> every branch of industry, then the new and higher degree of intensity would
> become the normal social degree of intensity, and would therefore cease to
> count as an extensive magnitude.[53]

This is what I call the 'paradox of the nation becoming uniformly more hard-working'. It expends more labour-power, since all branches of industry are aligned with the most intense ones, yet at the moment of this alignment the extra thus constituted 'ceases to count as an extensive magnitude' because it establishes a new ordinary degree of intensity, and from this fact the nation *produces less value!*

This is certainly a myth, a discourse to which no empirical experience can correspond. But it is a logical myth: the pursuit of the intrinsic logic of the categories beyond the terrain on which they can be properly applied, a pursuit that enables us to grasp their outer limits as well as the significance of these.

In reality, the analyst may genuinely hesitate between two solutions. On the one hand, the axiom that defines labour as the substance of value, and the couple duration/intensity as the two dimensions determining its magnitude, should lead us to maintain to its logical conclusion the idea that, when intensity grows, so does the amount of value produced. On the other hand, however, and conversely, the treatment of value as a quantity defined as a function of

---

[53] Marx 1976a, pp. 661–2. [In the French edition, the final phrase 'as an extensive magnitude' is omitted.]

average conditions at a given time leads us to maintain that, once the extra intensity is generalised, it ceases to be a principle of increase in the magnitude of value.

In this sense, the dilemma is only apparent, and the paradox finds its solution in the field of quantitative space. The movement of general intensification, in so far as it expresses the finality of capitalism, tends not to an increase in value produced, but to the accumulation of *surplus-value*. This involves a specific 'movement', but one that can be equivalently represented either by the dimensional schema that sees every intensification as a disguised extension of labour-time or alternatively by the differential schema that assimilates it to a gain in productivity. What is at work here is simple a convergence of the two figures, expressing equivalently in the quantitative space the effect of the qualitative alteration represented by the general intensification: the increased accumulation of surplus-value.

In reality, however, a residue remains. For the very origin of the paradox is doubly inadequate. The *geometric* metaphor that underlies the dimensional schema is inadequate, for there are not two 'real' dimensions. We do have an available unit for duration, that of natural clock time, but intensity can only be 'taken into account' as a function of an average expenditure of human energy. The *technical* metaphor that underlies the differential schema is equally inadequate; for more intense labour is in no way more productive labour, bringing additional use-value only in relation to the extra expenditure.

The *naturalist* metaphor bound up with the dimensional schema, and the *technical* metaphor bound up with the differential schema, both only appear to ensure a mastery of the quantitative space, by translating into quantity the quality of greater or lesser intensity. But because they are simply metaphors, they can do this only by disguising something essential, which is expressed only through its metaphoric displacement: the *social* concept of intensity, and through it the concept of value, that has still not been produced.

This then indicates the path that our investigation must now take: to determine in what way the figures are metaphorical, and to take as our object the concealed point that they denote.

Conclusion

The space of 'labour-value' is anything but the platitude that is so often imagined. On condition, to be sure, that we understand how it was, before Marx's discourse, a *terra incognita*, and that the classics, as soon as they perceived it, set sail for a different continent, that of *economics* ('political economy' being political only in a weak sense). The minimal difference that inaugurated the discourse of 'historical materialism' was *to examine labour for itself*, outside of the question of wages. With this aim, Marx found himself facing a new task: to produce a homogenisation of the field, a translation of persisting 'qualities' of labour into quantities, *without passing by the external detour of wages*. And this forced him to provide an analysis of labour that the classics had not produced.

Marx's effort to construct this homogeneous space is expressed in the difficult development that stretches from *The Poverty of Philosophy* to the various editions of *Capital*. Though he determined early on, well before his terminology was established, the principal categories (abstract/concrete labour, socially necessary labour), invalid interferences continue to resurge in his discourse. They particularly mark the tendency to impress on abstract labour the determination of 'simple', 'undifferentiated' or 'average'.

Even *Capital* is marked by this disturbing reaction of the categories of measurement on the theorisation of the substance to be measured. Three distinct aspects are raised in Chapter 1. First of all, the cleavage of concrete/ abstract labour. Then the reduction of labour to 'socially necessary labour'. And, finally, a further reduction, though still only projected, of complex labour to simple labour. This project is that of the 'substantive' standard, the simple element of the substantive matter. It is understandable then that Marx's entire analysis concerning this reduction of complex to simple must necessarily spur an elaboration of the 'substance' itself.

The category of *productivity*, of 'more productive' labour, provides an initial reference, and so full of promise that we may well ask whether it does not constitute the universal operator of this translation from complex to simple. It must be noted, however, that it only does this by instituting a framework of structure and tendency (which, as we shall show, distinguishes this discourse from a different discourse on labour, that of Ricardo).

We shall see, though, how Marx stubbornly seeks other ways of showing how *skilled* labour produces more value in the same time. He appeals first of all to evidence, which is scarcely suited to establish a primary abstract category, the very object of which is to lead us finally on to experience. Then he gets into a series of paralogisms around the figure of the 'jeweller', i.e. propositions of which none is compatible with the starting principles. It is only in Part Four that he implicitly arrives at the only solution possible, when he abandons this precapitalist paradigm and asserts that the 'collective worker' (of the capitalist enterprise) forms the product of his value globally, according to the unity of the process of production and valorisation, in such a way that individual assignment of the production of value is superseded, though within the limits of this framework.

Intensity, the last of the quantitative particularities that remain after abstract labour has been established, ensures both the closure and the fracture of the quantitative space. Marx broaches it rhapsodically at a number of levels, but develops two schemata above all: the *differential* one that grasps it in terms of the technical metaphor of productivity (and extra surplus-value), and the *dimensional* one supported by a geometric, naturalist metaphor of a second 'dimension' (and of absolute surplus-value). These metaphors deal well enough with the object that they tackle, but their inadequacy leaves a residue that is precisely the question still left beyond the 'greater or lesser' intensity: that of *expenditure* itself as determination of the substance of labour in so far as this is not exhausted in its quantitativity, in other words the social field, or the *political*-economic field in the strongest sense.

Chapter Three
Value as Sociopolitical Concept

Our examination of the notion of *'labour-value'*, so strongly contested, has brought to light a further notion that is still more controversial, that of the *'expenditure of labour-power'*. It is precisely at the pivot between these two that I see the conversion effected that gives these categories their sociopolitical sense.

Marx certainly had a good deal of trouble in defining these initial terms. He came up against obstacles that tradition has obscured by attributing an uncertain and purely metaphorical meaning to other notions that go together with this expenditure: 'labour-power' and its 'consumption' in the wage relationship.

To designate the latter as a political-economic relationship, however, is trivial unless the equally political-economic nature of the value categories it presupposes is properly defined. Without this, the interpretation would break down into an economic discourse on quantity and a sociological discourse on social relations. And if promotion of labour-value has often served economistic tendencies, its rejection with the purpose of reconstructing the theory around the wage relationship ends up making it a concept that can be used any which way, leading only to confusion between different modes of production.

The articulation labour-value/money/capital is thus the place where the key question of the capitalist mode of production is defined, that of *socialisation*.

It is in this element of abstraction, and in its specific logic, that labour is performed, as the production of social wealth. But according to what rationality and what contradictions? What is the link between the expenditure of human energy and the consumption of labour-power? Between domination and acquiescence? Between the economic and the political relationship? All these questions bear above all on the current debate on the theory of the state and the articulation between state and capital.

1. Value as expenditure

Intensity would seem the element most readily recoverable for the conception of value as quantity. Yet our analysis has demonstrated the limit of this reduction. It is this limit that we now have to explore. A limit at which will emerge, precisely from the contrast between *time* as 'measure' and *labour* as 'substance', the sociopolitical determination inherent to the unity of the concept of 'labour-time'.

1.i *From the negative sense of value to its positive sense*

With the question of intensity, we find ourselves at the very articulation of the double determination of value as 'magnitude' and as 'substance', for the problematic of *average* intensity implies the notion of *intensity as such*, contained in the definition of abstract labour as expenditure, which is nothing other than the definition of value: 'all labour is . . . expenditure of human labour-power, *in the physiological sense*, and it is in this quality of being equal, or abstract, human labour that it forms the value of commodities'.[1]

This proposition certainly possesses a negative sense: negation of everything pertaining to the division of labour that presents a particular character. This negation permits the homogenisation of its object and thus its apprehension in quantitative terms. It makes value into a magnitude which can be measured, and is measured by the duration of labour.

But this operation is far from being purely negative, since it also defines what remains when we abstract these particularities: a *'physiological expenditure'*. And the question precisely arises as to why what remains after abstraction of the particular and constitutes the object of the concept of value has to be

---

[1] Marx 1973a, p. 61; Marx 1976a, p. 137; my emphasis: J.B.

designated as something 'physiological' in nature, and as forming an expenditure. The initial response here is that abstract labour is not just a mere 'amount of time': it is the duration of *labour*, the exercise of a *force*.

This is indeed a constitutive dimension of what Marx presents (p. 132) as his *'discovery'*. At first sight, the 'concrete/abstract labour' distinction of Chapter 1, Section 2 seems to bring nothing new in addition to that of 'use-value/value' in Section 1. It looks as if everything had been said already in this first section. Has not Marx already defined the *substance* and measure of value? As he concludes here: 'Now we know the *substance* of value, it is *labour*. We know the *measure of its magnitude*. It is *labour-time*.'[2] But, in actual fact, Section 2 does introduce something new: duration is specified more precisely as duration of labour, of an expenditure that is not adequately measured by duration, precisely because it is expenditure of labour-power. When we move on from the commodity (Section 1) to labour (Section 2), the abstraction, which bears not on the product but on the act of producing, makes manifest the particular relationship of measurement and substance. Measurement is necessarily contrasted with substance and subordinated to it. What is required here is a *theory of the substance*, to explain how the quantity of expenditure is regulated in definite social relations.

We first need to elucidate the political-economic significance of the 'physiological' reference.

1.ii   *The difficult birth of 'expenditure' in Marx's discourse*

In the *Grundrisse*, in a long and well-known passage, Marx formulates a double critique of Adam Smith, who defines value by the quantity of labour understood as 'a sacrifice of the same quantitative magnitude'.[3] 'Philosophically', labour is not a divine curse. Economically, sacrifice is 'a purely *negative* characterisation', yet: 'Something that is merely negative creates nothing. . . . Labour *alone* produces; it is the only *substance* of products as *values*.'[4] Labour as substance of value is a *'positive, creative activity'*.[5]

---

[2] Marx 1976a; Marx's emphases. [The passage in which this occurs, though present in the French edition, was apparently deleted by Marx in the second German edition, but restored by Engels for the English edition.]

[3] Marx 1976a, p. 610.

[4] Marx 1976a, p. 612; Marx's emphases.

[5] Marx 1976a, p. 614; Marx's emphases.

Marx remains prisoner here of a philosophical play of oppositions that we can anticipate by denoting it as an *epistemological obstacle*. Let us compare the two problematics:

Grundrisse opposes	SACRIFICE	to positive creative activity = SUBSTANCE of value
Capital opposes	EXPENDITURE *abstract* labour = SUBSTANCE of value	to *concrete* labour

We should note, more broadly, that the notion of 'expenditure' is still almost non-existent in the *Grundrisse*. It is certainly mentioned,[6] but in a usage that is not retained in *Capital* (a point I shall return to in Chapter 10). And the prevailing terms denoting the relationship of labour to its product are those of '*objectivity*' or '*materialised*', '*realised*'. In the *Critique*, 'expenditure' appears from the start to define what *Capital* will name 'value',[7] though the notion is neither thematised nor taken up. And the manuscripts of 1861–3 go much further into *objectification* (which we must equally consider an epistemological obstacle inasmuch as it is located outside the cleavage pertinent here, between concrete and abstract labour, being applicable to either).

In parallel to this, and as counterpart to this anthropological theme of 'objectification', the category of labour 'time' is developed in the *Grundrisse* in a *naturalistic* sense: 'as effect . . . it is measured only by the measure of this force itself. The measure of labour is time.'[8] I shall come back to the abyss of difference that there is between measurement in terms of 'force' and of 'expenditure'. 'Just as motion is measured by time, so is labour by *labour-time.*'[9] In this sense, in *Zur Kritik*, the abstraction of the content is entirely oriented to the problematic of quantification, and the problem of sacrifice versus expenditure is avoided.

On the other hand, the question returns with a vengeance in *Capital*, where 'expenditure' abounds, figuring as key term in the three passages that define

---

[6] Marx 1973c, p. 294; cf. Marx and Engels 1988a, pp. 59, 60.
[7] Marx 1971, p. 29.
[8] Marx 1973c, p. 613.
[9] Marx 1971, p. 30. Marx's emphasis.

value.[10] Marx takes up again the confrontation with Smith,[11] but in a very different sense. He shifts the former distinction (sacrifice that creates nothing/labour that produces), for it is now expenditure that is attributed the 'formation of value', while 'it is in this quality of being concrete useful labour that it produces use-values'. The critique he makes of Smith is now far more nuanced: Smith was not totally wrong as far as the capitalist wage-labourer is concerned; he simply forgot that this expenditure is 'also man's normal life-activity'.[12]

The schema of expenditure, which Marx constitutes here as one of opposition between 'sacrifice' and 'normal activity', is highly charged, yet very enigmatic at this moment in the analysis. We shall see in what sense his theory implies it in this very duality. But it is already clear that the *Grundrisse*'s opposition between 'sacrifice' and 'labour' set up an obstacle to the establishment of an adequate categorial ensemble. To oppose 'labour' to 'sacrifice' was certainly justified to the extent that the point was to criticise Smith for giving a 'psychological' foundation.[13] But the polemic led Marx to expel the 'sacrifice' from labour altogether, to empty this of a certain content, and clearly already a social one. This is what the introduction of the theme of expenditure is designed to correct.

Capital is particularly insistent that the expenditure of human labour-power constitutes the positivity of 'value', which cannot be taken as a simple 'abstraction'. And this text sounds like a denial of the equivalent passage in the *Grundrisse*:

> [T]he labour objectified in the value of commodities is not just presented *negatively*, as labour in which abstraction is made from all the concrete forms and useful properties of actual work. Its own *positive* nature is brought out, namely the fact that it is the reduction of all kinds of actual labour to their common character of being human labour in general, of being the *expenditure* of human labour-power.[14]

---

[10] Marx 1976a, pp. 130, 135, 137.
[11] Marx 1976a, p. 137.
[12] Marx 1976a, p. 138, n. 16.
[13] Marx 1973c, p. 613.
[14] Marx 1976a, pp. 159–60; my emphases: J.B.

1.iii 'Expenditure' in the classical economists: introduced and dismissed

Adam Smith, in Chapter 5 of *The Wealth of Nations*, introduces a related idea, that of 'hardship'. But he makes this a characteristic of certain 'sorts of work'. This amounts to locating it on the side of the division of labour, of *concrete labour*, and thus also the side of the nature of things, in this way naturalising the wage relationship in respect to the *performance* of labour. (Even though remuneration, for Smith, is partly linked to a relation of forces.) Moreover, this relative hardship of different kinds of labour, unlike Marx's 'intensity', is translated into a homogeneity of the economic field only by the external route of the labour market, i.e. a differential remuneration, on the basis of which it can be maintained for instance that if labour is harder, more value is produced. In sum, the economism of the market solves the problem of the 'natural' diversity of jobs.

Ricardo, when he seeks to define an invariable measure of value in his 1823 manuscript 'Absolute Value and Exchangeable Value', puts forward a hypothesis that is highly significant of his entire approach. Any commodity, he explains, can certainly serve as measure at a particular moment, but not through time, since its relative value varies. There is said to exist, however, an invariable 'natural standard':

> [L]abour is that standard. The average strength of 1000 or 10,000 men it is said is nearly the same at all times. A commodity produced in a given time by the labour of 100 men is double the value of a commodity produced by the labour of 50 men in the same time.[15]

Ricardo tends here to represent labour as an objective and positive magnitude, and seeks an invariant. Hence the myth that human power does not vary through time, or that it varies very little, enabling an 'approximate' solution. But is this power something that man possesses and *can* expend? Or does he *actually* expend it? Ricardo's proposition abolishes the possibility of this difference, thus naturalising the notion of labour-power.

Marx speaks of 'average power' in his project of homogenisation – though what he needs, if seemingly analogous to this, is in fact completely different. For he does not assume it is stable, but, on the contrary, that it 'varies in

---

[15] Ricardo 1951, p. 381.

character in different countries and at different cultural epochs'.[16] This forbids comparison between one period and another. And, above all, it no longer refers to the power that men on average *possess*, but to the *expenditure* of this power.

In short, where Ricardo moves from expenditure of labour to average equality of powers conceived as a constant standard, Marx, developing the concept of the *substance* of value at the same time as that of its *measure*, sticks with the exercise of expenditure: 'If we leave aside the determinate quality of productive activity, and therefore the useful character of this labour, what remains is its quality of being an expenditure of human labour-power.'[17] Despite the tendencies to the contrary that I have indicated, Marx globally *de*naturalises.

1.iv   The Marxian reversal: intensity denaturalises duration

The slippage is scarcely perceptible, but it is considerable none the less: from Ricardo referring to the power that people *possess*, to Marx referring to the power that they *expend*. The nuance is decisive. For, in this way, the exercise of labour-power ceases to be natural and becomes social. Intensity seems at first to be the qualitative character most recoverable for quantity: with respect both to its physical expenditure and as element of abstract labour, it seems to provide the very paradigm of what Marx calls 'potenzierte' labour. And he grasps it precisely as the second (intensive) dimension that combines with the extensive dimension (duration) to define the quantity of labour.[18] But the spatial metaphor meets a limit: intensity reacts on duration and transforms it. Duration being given, intensity appears as the historical element making clear that duration is not given after all, and that the time 'socially necessary' to produce things is determined by class struggle. Value and abstract labour do not yet define any determinate class relationship, but the question of intensity already denaturalises duration and labour, 'Socially necessary' time can only be that of a 'socially regulated' expenditure. And that returns us to the principle of social regulation of expenditure specific to any society, in

---

[16] Marx 1976a, p. 135.

[17] Marx 1976a, p. 134.

[18] Marx 1976a, pp. 508 ff.

other words to class relations. For the question of expenditure immediately evokes that of the social compulsion to expenditure.[19]

We can thus grasp the critique that Marx made of Ricardo: he did not define abstract labour as such. Connected to this, I believe, is the fact that Ricardo ignored intensity (the problem of expenditure): 'He recognizes no change either in the length of the working day or in the intensity of labour.'[20] His world was a different one, that of variation in relative values, not of the absolute principle of value.

The question of expenditure must, in this respect, be analysed starting from the relationship it has with the category of 'labour-*power*', such as this functions in the frequent references Marx makes to 'human labour-power'. We have to understand that, in the theoretical framework established in Chapter 1 of *Capital,* the pertinent determination, that which defines value, is *expenditure* [*Verausgabe, Ausgabe*] and not the *exercise* of a power, in the sense that the value produced by labour does not derive from the overall functioning of this power (which could be conceived as the ensemble of food + expenditure), but simply from expenditure. Just as money does not smell, so value does not bear an immediate reference to the reconstitution of labour-power, the 'input' needed to balance the expenditure. The concept of expenditure of labour-power tells us nothing initially as to its reproduction, in the sense of the reproduction of the workers in the system under consideration. The rationality of the commodity system as presented in Section 1 implies only an equilibrium between 'exchanging producers', an abstract category that does not correspond to that of the individual worker. This worker appears here in terms of her 'expenditure' of labour, not her reconstitution. This is not a simple problem of the order of presentation, but concerns the 'double articulation' that characterises this theory as a theory of class struggle and that is heralded in the presentation even before the class relationship is introduced. It is something that cannot be grasped by the vulgar historicising

---

[19] This compulsion, moreover, always ultimately concerns individuals. Which is why we cannot accept Dostaler's orientation according to which 'it is not the labour of the individual that becomes abstract' (Dostaler 1978b, p. 74). This formulation goes together with the globalising interpretation that he gives to the theory of value, which allegedly concerns social relations and 'not the objects exchanged' (p. 83). This analysis is a response to that which attributes to Marxian 'labour-value' a naturalist foundation (for instance Lippi 1976).

[20] Marx 1976a, p. 660.

interpretation that sees Section 1 as presenting the precapitalist commodity relationship: workers appearing here only in the perspective of their expenditure of labour-power.

The novelty that the notion of labour-'power' brings with it must be recognised in its full amplitude; it may however be hidden, as it is in the value of 'labour-*power*'. As we know, the classical economists wrote of the 'value of labour', and by introducing the category 'value of labour-power' Marx provides the means to distinguish between the value of this power and the value it produces, and thus to formulate the theory of surplus-value. But the effect of the pseudo-concept 'value of labour' is not just to obscure the question of surplus-value. By censoring at the same time the notion of labour-'power', it hides the question of the *substance* of value, which we begin to understand involves labour, but in its relationship with the class structure.

Nothing in all this gets rid of quantity. On the contrary: more intense labour produces more value. It is simply that the definition of value by abstract labour opens up both the homogeneous space of the economy in which quantitative analysis is deployed, and also the space of class struggle. Value, as quantity, is also, by being the quantity of an expenditure of socially regulated labour-power, a social relationship in a specific sense that includes the political dimension.

2. 'Transformation of expenditure into consumption of labour-power'

The apostrophes round this heading do not mean it is a quote. In fact, this is a formulation that does not figure anywhere in Marx's discourse, though I believe it should do so: the transformation of money into capital is precisely in one of its aspects a 'transformation of expenditure into consumption of labour-power'. And this follows from the logic of the concepts of a theory of the 'mode of production' in which expenditure is inscribed in a space defined here by the articulation of compulsion and politics. The metaphor of 'consumption of labour-power', frequently present in the texts[21] but neglected by the tradition, does have a theoretical meaning, connecting the political

---

[21] Marx and Engels 1988a, pp. 54 & 57; Marx 1976a, p. 995 ('Results') & p. 270.

theme of 'domination' with the economic determination of labour as expenditure and as quantity. It depicts the political-economic articulation.

2.i *The Ricardian system has no place for compulsion*

If Ricardo overlooked this expenditure, it was because he could not see the compulsion to expenditure. In other words, the *wage relationship* as a relation of forces in the context of production does not constitute an element in his system.

This is indeed the import of Marx's criticism of Ricardo: all is not said when the distinction is made between two *magnitudes* of value, that of the subsistence necessary for labour and that which labour produces. It is not sufficient to establish the *possibility* presented by the difference between the worker's consumption and his productivity, what has to be explained is why this possibility exists as a *necessity* in the capitalist mode of production. In other words, Ricardo ignores 'the cause of the existence of surplus-value', keeping simply to 'the cause that determines the magnitude of that value'.[22] In this way, he tends to confuse the presentation of the technical conditions of productivity with an explanation of its origin [*Ursprung*].

The same criticism is also expressed in different terms. Ricardo understands relative surplus-value but not absolute surplus-value: 'He recognizes no change either in the length of the working day or in the intensity of labour, so that with him the productivity of labour becomes the only variable factor.'[23]

This criticism bears on the wage relationship as 'compulsion [*Zwang*]', in the sense that this denotes the 'cause' of surplus labour, the reason why surplus labour is performed. This compulsion should be understood in the broadest sense: it bears clearly on the *whole* labour, which must be such as to produce a surplus, and thus include a surplus labour. It is here that the theoretical distance between Marx and Ricardo is apparent, in that only Marx bases himself on 'labour-value': Ricardo sees an antagonism involving *distribution*, but for Marx this originates in the realm of *production*, defined as a relation of compulsion.[24]

---

[22] Marx 1976a, p. 651.
[23] Marx 1976a, p. 660.
[24] Marx 1969, p. 405.

A specific space is constituted here, that of historical materialism, the relation of forces (contradictory relationships) at the interference of economics and politics. For Ricardo, the economy is, in a sense, neutralised, considered outside of social antagonisms, with the element of compulsion being hidden in the form of contract. Attentive as he was to confrontation over the level of wages, he did not attribute the wage relationship itself a specific place within his system of categories. The wage relation remains unconsidered, inasmuch as, being perceived as eternal nature (finally realised), it is not recognised in its historical *fragility* – the particular forms that maintain and reproduce it, but also contain the possibility of its collapse. Marx uses the term 'economy' in a neological sense (which commentators do not seem to have noted) when he uses it, from the *Grundrisse* to *Capital*[25] to denote the social content of the specific relationships of a mode of production. This means denoting the wage relation itself, in an unprecedented sense, as belonging to the object of this new discourse, or again it means creating this new discourse, that of historical materialism, which integrates the sociopolitical into its primary concepts.

2.ii *Hegel at the halfway point*

Hegel, by incorporating into the unity of his philosophy the formerly disconnected fields of economics, ethics and politics, certainly showed Marx the way. But it is especially important to understand the limits of his intervention, and to do so perhaps more clearly than Marx did himself.

Paragraph 67 of the *Philosophy of Right* emphasises, echoing the critique made by Rousseau of the 'contract of enslavement', that the alienation of one's entire working time means the extinction of freedom. This inversely defines the wage relation as a site of freedom. It may be surprising, then, to find Marx invoking this text of Hegel so unambiguously.[26] For, in actual fact, *Capital* effects a genuine reversal of Hegel's problematic.

Hegel's analysis of the wage relationship is set within the paradigm of power and manifestation, or substance and accident. A power is the totality of its manifestations. To alienate this totality is then to alienate completely

---

[25] Marx 1973c, pp. 304 ff.; Marx 1971, p. 51; Marx 1976a, p. 764; Marx 1978, p. 303.
[26] Marx 1976a, p. 272, n. 3.

the power that is my personality. This is *slavery*. But, if I alienate these manifestations only in part, or for a definite time, the substance is unaffected: I remain free.

If we look closely at Marx's statements on this point, he takes the opposite position to the texts he appeals to. For him, in fact, the worker alienates *his* (labour-)*power*, as indicated by the very title of the chapter: 'The Sale and Purchase of Labour-Power'. Hegel, following Rousseau, produced at the same time a philosophical critique of slavery and a speculative justification of wage-labour as a relationship of freedom. Marx presents here a critique of wage-labour, which he reveals as a situation of force in which the labour-*power* itself is committed, and not just one or other of its manifestations. And this is shown by the paradoxical fragmentation in the text of the category of property. On the one hand the worker is 'the free proprietor of his own labour-capacity, hence of his person'; he has it 'at his *disposal* [*über sie verfügen*]'.[27] But his power is only that of being able to put it at the temporary disposal [*zur Verfügung*] of the capitalist; who purchases the (labour-)power and thus becomes, we have to say, its new proprietor.

Hegel, as we see, lies halfway between the classical economics and Marx. He goes beyond the notion of the 'sale of labour', but does not go as far as the 'sale of labour-power'. He analyses the wage relationship in this passage as the sale of particular *manifestations* of this power, an act that has only an external connection with the power itself.

Marx, on the contrary, defines wage-labour as alienation of 'labour-power' or 'labour-capacity', previously identified with one's own person. While Hegel's worker remains the owner of his labour-power, Marx's worker, by selling his labour-power, loses his ownership of it. But, at this point, a division appears in Marx's discourse, and thus also a transformation in the concept of property: despite 'alienating' his labour-power, the worker does not 'renounc[e] his rights of ownership to it'.[28] He is thus both proprietor in so far as he 'disposes' of it, and non-proprietor since he has sold it and someone else has bought it. This division of property is not adequately expressed by the category of 'hire' that Marx introduces ('just like a horse he had hired for the day'[29]), which simply denotes a division of property between two owners

---

[27] Marx 1976a, p. 271; my emphasis: J.B.
[28] Marx 1976a, p. 271.
[29] Marx 1976a, p. 292.

who share its disposition. In other words, the category of labour-power as commodity and the category of property applied here do not exhaust the wage relationship but have only a metaphorical value. For a 'disposition' of this limited kind cannot be understood as instrumental, but only as domination, i.e. as a political relationship. The division of 'disposition' effects a genuine transformation of the concept, which we must now examine.

2.iii   *Wage-labour as a 'political' category in 'economic' theory*

There thus exists, at the junction between Parts Two and Three of *Capital*, Volume One, a necessary moment at which Marx breaks with the succession of 'quantitative' categories to introduce the juridico-political determinations inherent to the wage system (just as the juridical presuppositions of the category of value are presented in Chapter 2 of Part One). This requisite transition, that of the 'formal subordination of labour to capital', an expression that designates this inaugural moment of capitalist relations of production at the point when they have not yet modified the productive process, is found in the various successive versions: of 1857–8, of 1861–3, of 1863–5, and finally of 1867. The set of categories it introduces, which Marx returns to later in connection with the 'real' subordination, is absent from the discourse of classical economics, and signifies a change of terrain in relation to it: inscription of the analysis of capitalism in the problematic of the mode of production, the contradictory unity of economics and politics.

The political category makes an appearance in classical economics with the notion of 'labour commanded', but this is a false entry, or rather an actual exit. We know how, in Adam Smith's exchange perspective, every purchase of a commodity is conceived as a 'purchase of labour' (which is how, moreover, Smith avoids commodity fetishism) or 'command' over it; and how the value of a commodity is measured by the labour that it thus 'purchases' or 'commands'. But the very use that is made here of the political category of 'command' to designate the value relationship in general as an exchange relationship is paid for by a de-politicisation of the wage relation. On the one hand, the 'command' is attributed to the *commodity* that 'purchases' (in the sense that it 'commands'), while, on the other hand, this command is applied both to the *product* of labour as well as to the living labour 'purchased'. The term 'command' here does not comprise any of the determinations that it finds in *Capital*, where the 'command' is exercised by the capitalist and bears on the performance of work by the wage-labourer. Adam Smith's terminology, in reality, makes the exchange relationship, metaphorically enhanced into a 'command', the model of the wage relationship, and thus de-politicises it.

Marx explicitly rejects this conception.[30] For him, it is the appropriation of the very particular commodity that is labour-power which determines recourse to the register of political categories.

In the function of capitalist direction Marx distinguishes two aspects, one concerning the connection necessary for any process of collective work, the other concerning exploitation. It is the latter, deriving from the antagonism between capital and labour, to which he links the necessity of supervision, *Oberaufsicht*.[31] But a mode of production exists only in the contradictory unity of these two functions, which relates to the unity of the processes of production and valorisation. And it is in this double (yet single) respect that the capitalist 'consumes' labour-power. This, for him, is a use-value presented for his consumption as a functionary of capital, a use-value by which the productive power of capital is realised.[32] The category of 'consumption of labour-power', in so far as it refers to the theory of the mode of production, must be understood in terms of the interaction of technique and politics, in their specific contradictory unity.

In this logic, it seems necessary to go further and relate this double aspect of capitalist management identified by Marx to the dualities of use-value and value, concrete and abstract labour, which Marx placed at the head of his theory. On the one hand, there is the necessary connection of the different parts of *concrete* labour carried out by different agents. 'All directly social or communal labour on a large scale requires, to a greater or lesser degree, a directing authority, in order to secure the harmonious cooperation of the activities of individuals.' On the other hand, because the 'determining purpose' of capitalist production is 'the greatest possible production of surplus-value', the wage relationship develops a 'resistance to the domination of capital' and 'the pressure put on by capital to overcome this resistance'.[33] If this is the

---

[30] Marx 1973c, p. 471; Marx 1988, p. 92; Marx 1972, pp. 138–9 (on the so-called 'power of purchasing').
[31] Marx 1976a, pp. 448–9.
[32] Marx 1973c, p. 307.
[33] Marx 1976a, p. 448.

case, then the category of abstract labour undergoes here what should rightly be called a 'transformation', which is actually no more than an aspect of the transformation [*Verwandlung*] of money into capital that forms the subject and title of Part Two. The 'expenditure in the physiological sense' becomes, in the capitalist relationship, a *compulsory* expenditure.

The 'political' character of this compulsion derives from the divided disposal, which does not just mean that the capitalist has labour-power at his disposal only for a time, and that this limitation reduces his power. Far more broadly, and in relation to this structural feature (the ability to change employer), the divided disposal of the capitalist over labour-power clearly pertains to the reasons that the workers find to work, and that make them work sufficiently, in other words the capacity of the capitalist class to assert itself as the 'directing' class in the Gramscian sense, to rally the workers to general perspectives of social life and the social purpose of labour. A relationship is thus established that goes beyond the relations between individuals: a 'class' relationship, since the relationship of 'dominant to dominated' comes to be mediated by the relationship of individuals to their class and of these classes to each other. The political instance is thus located at the point of this articulation of expenditure and compulsion. It is implied in the very category of labour-value.

The novelty of the categorical configuration introduced by Marx, in my view, is something quite different from the trivial idea that labour relations are *also* power relations. It effects a coupling of economic and political categories at the most fundamental level, in such a way that these two orders cannot then be completely dissociated: the economic category of labour-value is only a semi-concept, lacking operational value, outside of this concept of 'consumption', i.e. a definite type of social compulsion to produce.

To sum up, if the substance of value is abstract labour, *expenditure*, it is coupled in the mode of production with its correlative, the social *compulsion* for this expenditure (a market compulsion exercised over the workers by the capitalist class), with which it forms, in the unity of the concept, a social and class relationship. And the question thus arises as to the usefulness of the category of 'labour-value' in general, for every society, and particularly for 'socialist' society in a programmatic and normative use. But, before confronting this question, we must first consider its articulation with another essential determination of value, that of money.

3. Money and labour-value constitute one and the same point of rupture between Marx and Ricardo

The question of money takes us back to a point preceding the wage relationship presented in the previous section: we return now to the first abstract moment of labour-value, to which belongs a certain theory of money. Marx constructed this theory in opposition to Ricardo, thematising it as the site of his break with him. I propose to show how this is profoundly justified, and that the delimitation which Marx effects between his predecessor and himself anticipates very pertinently the recent reading of Ricardo in the wake of Sraffa. The parting between two theoretical orders, which is manifested at the level of money, is of the same nature as that which has been sketched out in our analysis of labour-value: it concerns money as a political-economic category.

3.i Marx's critique of Ricardo on money

After claiming to have been the first to extract the notion of 'abstract labour' and base a theory of commodity production on it, Marx makes the same claim about 'value'. While starting from the Ricardian conception, he puts forward a set of criticisms centring on the relationship between value and money, by which he defines the specificity of the new theoretical field he is establishing.

These criticisms, sometimes extended to 'political economy' in general, figure in some elliptical notes to Chapter 1 of Volume One.[34] Their brevity should not lead to underestimating their importance, which is explained only in terms of the great project of 'Volume Four', the substance of this making up *Theories of Surplus-Value*, the critique of previous doctrines. If *Capital* is explicitly inscribed in a history of theoretical production, as a re-elaboration of earlier findings, these scattered formulations are decisive keys for its interpretation. We shall therefore pay the closest attention to the various texts in which Marx developed the themes that these notes in the first chapter refer to.

These texts figure above all in the *Grundrisse*,[35] *Critique*,[36] and particularly *Theories of Surplus-Value*, which provides the most comprehensive presentation of the question.[37]

---

[34] Marx 1976a, p. 173, n. 33; p. 174, n. 34; p. 177, n. 38.
[35] Marx 1973c, pp. 140–74.
[36] Marx 1971, pp. 60–3.
[37] Marx 1969, pp. 164–72; Marx 1972, pp. 54 & 131–7, esp. pp. 136–9.

Let us examine Marx's critique point by point.

(i) Ricardo is essentially interested in the *'magnitude of value [Wertgrösse]'*. This idea is repeated in most of the texts cited: Ricardo, at the very moment when he superseded his predecessors by formulating the project of a theory entirely in terms of a notion of value based on quantity of labour, remained a prisoner of the 'quantitative' aspect. He neglected in fact the *'value-form'*. In this context, what this 'form' denotes above all is abstract labour as such, labour which represents itself 'as abstract general labour', which is the 'specific form in which labour is an element of value'.[38]

(ii) If Ricardo neglects this form, it is because he sticks with *relative value*, something that in turn tends to lead back to a value 'in use-values', the opposite of its formal determination. Marx insists at several points on the ambiguity of relative value, which on the one hand designates the quantitative determination, *'magnitude of value* in contradistinction to the quality of having *value* at all', and on the other hand, 'the values of a commodity expressed in use-value'.[39] Marx's critique evidently bears first of all on those anti-Ricardians such as Bailey who rejected the notion of absolute value (and, against them, Marx shows how objects are comparable and measurable only because they belong to the same space, defined here by abstract labour as *'substance'* of value). But it also touches Ricardo, who does not take absolute value as his object of study, but rather the variation in relative values, in such a way that the measure of value is not found in the 'labour-substance' but in other commodities.

(iii) This insufficiency is expressed in the Ricardian theory of *money*, which does not immediate link money to the concept of value. 'Hence he does not grasp the connection [*Zusammenhang*] of *this labour* with *money* or that it must assume the form of money.'[40] 'Therefore he has not understood that the development of money is connected with the nature of value [*den Zusammenhang der Geldbildung mit dem Wesen des Werts*].'[41]

Altogether, then, this is one and the same criticism in three different facets. Keeping just to the measure or magnitude of value, Ricardo fails on:

the *form*, which is that of abstract labour in its particular historical (commodity) determination;

---

[38] Marx 1972, p. 137; cf. p. 131.
[39] Marx 1972, p. 132; Marx's emphases.
[40] Marx 1969, p. 164; Marx's emphases.
[41] Marx 1972, p. 137. Cf. also Marx 1971, p. 62, etc.

the *substance*, which is labour itself, and not the relationship to other commodities;

money, which pertains to the nature of value, because it is the form adequate to its substance.

3.ii   *The meaning of Marx's statement that 'money is connected with the nature of value'*

Ricardo opens the first chapter of his *Principles* with a section devoted, via a critique of Adam Smith, to the question of the *foundation* of value, the principle that governs exchange. He finds this in the quantity of necessary labour. But, from Section 2 on, he leaves 'absolute value' thus defined for what will constitute his real object: the variation in relative values. The question of the foundation is now overlaid by that of *measurement*. More broadly, Ricardo investigates the principles of the wealth of nations, i.e. accumulation. He considers that this is greater according to how large the share of profit is in the distribution between wages, profit and rent. Hence the question of magnitude at the beginning, and thus of its *measure*.

However, as he starts to establish in Section 4, the existence of fixed capital introduces a disturbing factor, which modifies the rule of measurement by necessary labour. Organic composition varies between different capitals, yet they have to be remunerated according to their magnitude. Thus, when the rate of profit falls, the products of sectors rich in fixed capital are depreciated in relation to others. Hence the need to establish an 'invariable measure' of value that remains unaffected by variations in the rate of profit, and thanks to which it is possible to determine, when two commodities vary relative to one another, the real nature of their relative variation, as distinct from the 'curious effect' that accompanies any modification in the rate of profit. Here is the second and *true* basis of the Ricardian edifice, disconnected from labour-value. It is in this theoretical context that Ricardo is led, in Section 6 of his Chapter 1 on value, to turn to metallic money, the production of which is deemed to rest on a type of capital with an average proportion of fixed capital, and which from this fact (if we abstract from the variability of its conditions of production) will play the role of instrument of 'invariable measure'. It is clear that money is introduced here, at the start of the *Principles*, for a quite different purpose than it is at the start of *Capital*: it does not indicate the essence of value, but simply its measurement. This money, moreover, must be considered as the true paradigm of an invariable standard of value (which his successors set out to construct). For this role is conferred on it by virtue of the supposed organic composition of the capitals that produce it, and not of its specific function in exchange. In the Ricardian definition of value (even relative value), money does not appear *as money*.

When Ricardo studies the question of coinage for itself, in Chapter 27 of the *Principles*, it emerges that money in its metallic form is indeed a commodity. But not the other way round: the commodity is not originally money, abstract labour. In sum, passing from absolute to relative value (from the first to the second section of Chapter 1 of his *Principles*), Ricardo turns away from the relationship between the commodity and the worker to sketch a world of commodities to which labour itself belongs. He thus neutralises the question of labour into that of the comparative productivity of production techniques. This slippage from absolute to relative value is also, to this extent, a slippage back to use-value, as Marx emphasises, obscuring value as founded on abstract labour.

The absence of money from the essence of value in Ricardo is the absence of abstract labour. This is the basis of Marx's claim to have initiated the problematic of abstract labour. For although the classics, when they talk about 'labour' in general, seem to take this into account, they do not provide a concept of it, as they do not consider its relationship to money as the adequate expression or form of value, the expression of abstract labour.

We have therefore to read the celebrated Section 3 of Chapter 1 of *Capital* as essentially directed against Ricardo. 'Now, however, we have to perform a task never even attempted by bourgeois economics. That is, we have to show the origin of this money-form.'[42] A project of this kind is anything but incidental. To derive money from value is to reverse the Ricardian problematic. This origin does not just conclude that money is a commodity, but that the commodity, in so far as it is value, is money. As Marx puts it, 'The difficulty lies not in comprehending that money is a commodity, but in discovering how, why and by what means a commodity becomes money.'[43] In effect, money is not deduced just as the practical instrument that brings a solution to the problems of would-be exchangers, who would otherwise be condemned

---

[42] Marx 1976a, p. 139.
[43] Marx 1973a, p. 107; Marx 1972, p. 186.

to barter. As a commodity whose use-value is rejected and whose value (its reference to abstract labour) thus constitutes its sole definition, it denotes the social nature of the commodity, which is to be produced by a certain expenditure of labour, as the fruit of a determinate system of compulsion. The absence of money in Ricardo's discussion of value is thus the absence of politics. It is the index of a quite different theoretical universe, that of a general economics that overlooks the particular determinations – the sociopolitical determinations – of the mode of production.

Marx's discourse in Part One of *Capital*, though it does not yet include the class determinations required for a mode of production, is nonetheless open to these from the start. For, just as *expenditure* is only a semi-concept, requiring *consumption* for its completion, so too *money*, which depicts expenditure because it is the presence of labour 'as such' in the principle of the commodity relationship, raises the question of *power*, in actual fact of capital as a power relation.

This is what escapes Ricardo. And the Marxian critique of his conception of capital will confirm this.

4. Value and capital as semi-concepts

A problem appears, in fact, when we consider the close analogy that exists between the two criticisms that Marx formulates against Ricardo, concerning *money* on the one hand and *capital* on the other. In the *Grundrisse*, for example, the critique of Ricardo is explicitly developed not in the 'chapter on money' but rather in the 'chapter on capital', yet it is in the same register: Ricardo tends to stick with quantity, with the materiality of wealth, with use-values and distribution; he neglects the economic form.[44] This double critique can, in one sense, be understood quite simply: we can say that Ricardo's economism is expressed at both levels, value and capital, which moreover are for him one and the same. This might be sufficient, if Marx's critique did not also constitute the reverse side of his theses on money and capital, and on their connection as determinate historical forms. For the question that is now raised – and I will leave Ricardo at this point to examine the specific problems of Marx's theory – is that of knowing to what order this celebrated blind

---

[44] Cf. Marx 1973c, pp. 316, 348–53.

point of Ricardo's belongs: the sociopolitical dimension that escapes Ricardo and that I have analysed as the relationship between expenditure and consumption of labour-power, between work and compulsion. In what different senses is this determined in Marx's theory at the level of money (the commodity relation) and at the level of capital? At what level of analysis is the principle of the contradiction of the capitalist mode of production conceived? And, especially, how should we understand the category of *'latent' contradiction* that frequently expresses this articulation between the level of money and that of capital?

I propose here to pursue in Marx's texts the origin of this question, a quite surprising one, and to show how a certain clarification of the problematic is progressively effected, though its ultimate conclusions do not seem to have been actually drawn.

There is present in Marx's work, in effect, a symptomatic *displacement* of the 'political' theme, first of all inserted at the level of the commodity relation, then divided between this and the capitalist relation, and finally reserved to the latter, without the implication of this shift being really made explicit by the author, even though it determines the status of his categories. I shall follow these three moments, which correspond to three particular texts: the 'Comments on James Mill', the *Grundrisse*, and *Capital*.

4.i   The 'Comments on James Mill': a premature politicisation

There exists in Marx's Paris notebooks of 1844, alongside the famous *Economic and Philosophical Manuscripts*, a lesser-known text commenting on James Mill's *Elements of Political Economy*, which presents, still in philosophical style but very explicitly, the entire thematic constellation that I have analysed (money, abstraction, compulsion, poverty), and locates this at the level of the exchange and commodity relationship as such. This text, moreover, dates from a time when Marx had not yet taken up the Ricardian legacy, and had yet to adopt the definition of value as 'quantity of necessary labour'. The paradox is that, in this period of his 'youth', when the theory of value was as yet scarcely conceived, let alone becoming the cornerstone of Marx's theory of the capitalist mode of production, it appears in Marx's work as most highly charged with an essential dimension that, in the culminating text, Part One of *Capital*, is scarcely more than implicit and, as it were, buried under censorship: the *sociopolitical* dimension.

Money, as mediator of exchange, effects an 'abstraction' denoted as alienation:

> [T]he *mediating activity* or movement, the *human*, social act by which man's products mutually complement one another, is *estranged* from man and becomes the attribute of money, a *material thing* outside man.[45]
>
> This *mediator* now becomes a *real God*.
>
> The mediating process between men engaged in exchange is not a social or human process, not *human relationship*; it is the *abstract relationship* to private property, and the expression of this *abstract* relationship is *value*, whose actual existence as value constitutes *money*.[46]

What merits particular attention in this text is the fact that the theme of alienation or estrangement, which in the *Economic and Philosophical Manuscripts* illustrates the category of *wage*-labour, is defined here on the contrary at the level of *commodity* production in general. This is, indeed, already bourgeois society, but it is grasped at the level which Marx will later qualify as the most abstract (in the order of presentation), that of the commodity relationship as such. Between the 'Comments on James Mill' and the ensuing *Manuscripts* the category of alienation thus descends a level in the order of presentation: from money to capital.

Marx also develops, moreover, in these 'Comments', a category of labour that fits the same system as that of exchange-estrangement: *Erwerbsarbeit*, 'labour to earn a living'. 'The relationship of exchange being presupposed, *labour* becomes *directly labour to earn a living*. . . . The product is produced as *value*, as *exchange-value*, as an *equivalent*.'[47] This labour, which Marx defines as abstract because it ceases to correspond to individual 'need' but is subjected to 'external' or 'social needs', is performed under 'compulsion [*Zwang*]'.[48]

In sum, it is the commodity division of labour that 'turns man . . . into an abstract being, a machine tool'[49] and constitutes a relationship of mutual power and violence.[50]

Capital, as we know, will essentially transpose these themes to the level of the capitalist relationship (and the 'Comments on James Mill' already prefigure

---

[45] Marx 1975, p. 212; Marx's emphases.
[46] Marx 1975; Marx's emphases.
[47] Marx 1975, pp. 219–20; Marx's emphases.
[48] Marx 1975, p. 220.
[49] Ibid.
[50] Marx 1975, p. 226.

this). Everything happens as if the problematic of historical materialism, in the course of its development, led to these sociopolitical categories being reserved in their primary sense for relations between classes.

We may ask however whether this theoretical purification was effected without a residue, if it did not have as its counterpart an overly radical 'de-politicisation' of commodity categories. Or rather if Marx fully faced up to the greatest difficulty of a theory of the capitalist mode of production, which I have named its 'double articulation':

> the commodity articulation, which taken in itself can only be considered as functional;
> the capitalist articulation, though the contradictions of this, as well as its sociopolitical dimensions in the broad sense, can only be considered on the basis of the categories specific to the commodity articulation.

4.ii   *The* Grundrisse *as experimental text*

In the *Grundrisse*, the commodity relationship is integrated into a recapitulation of world history in three stages: (i) that of the 'relations of personal dependence' within primitive communities; (ii) that of 'personal independence founded on *objective* dependence' (the commodity epoch); (iii) finally, 'free individuality, based on the universal development of individuals and on their subordination of their communal, social productivity as their social wealth'.[51]

In this context, the category of 'abstraction' is not that of Part One of *Capital*, that of the 'concrete labour/abstract labour' couple, but still that of the 'Comments on James Mill'. For this abstraction immediately rises up to the concrete, it belongs to the order of purposes. It denotes, in fact, the general commodity separation between the individual, his work and his product as a *disturbance* in the order of utility and purpose. In this sense, Marx defines it as reification, *Versachlichung*, submission to social relations, *Unterordnung*, the negation of the individual and his purposes.[52] Commodity society is like this because in it money becomes the 'purpose' of economic activity.[53]

---

[51] Marx 1975, p. 158.
[52] Marx 1973c, p. 157.
[53] Marx 1973c, p. 151.

But, having reached this point, Marx's text stops short. The discourse on money as the disturbing and defining purpose of commodity society appears as an impossible discourse. When, in the *Grundrisse*, such contradictions are introduced, they are illustrated by specifically capitalist relations, as in the case of the 'mercantile estate' whose activity is governed by the quest for money.[54] In short, the hypothesis is not applied to the commodity relationship in general. Why is this? The reply is unambiguous: the distinction between use-value and value (or money) only involves a contradiction to the extent that it offers the possibility of a production whose purpose is value and no longer simply use-value. Now, this possibility does not exist in the commodity relationship as such, except in the limiting case of hoarding, which, far from expressing the essence of commodity production, denotes rather its point of extinction. Only the capitalist mode of production, *capital as such*, is defined by the logic of abstract wealth.

It is significant that the designation (at the level of commodity relations) of 'use-value' and 'value' as 'opposed' [*entgegengesetzt*] disappears between the first and second editions of *Capital*.[55] This actually brings a (relative) rectification, which we must now proceed to analyse.

4.iii Capital: *what is a 'latent' contradiction?*

In Chapter 6, I shall study the progression, from one version to another, of the Marxian conception of the transition from money to capital. For the moment, I limit myself to one point only: the 'political' categorisation that the *Grundrisse* develops in the 'chapter on money' is assigned in *Capital* to the specifically capitalist relationship, with the effect that the commodity relationship as such (Part One) becomes the object of a strictly 'technical' exposition. I shall now consider the advance and the limits that this development represents.

In Part Two of *Capital*, Marx seems, as it were, to arrange problems in a rank order. He distinguishes two types of relationship, one of which, money (C–M–C), has use-value as its purpose, the partner's commodity, while the other, capital (M–C–M), has value as its purpose, or more precisely, the

---

[54] Marx 1973c, p. 148.
[55] Marx 1980, p. 13; Marx 1973a, p. 61; cf. Marx 1973c, p. 137.

indefinite increase in value.[56] This latter implies the particular commodity that is labour-power, and its value and use-value – inscribed in the same space – are contrasted: the difference between labour-time and the time needed for the production of labour-power comes to constitute the principle of a *contradictory* relation of production, in the sense that the purpose of this is no longer use-value, the natural purpose of work, but rather surplus-value, and is characterised by this fact as a contradiction between worker and capitalist. The latent contradiction becomes a real one.

Capital thus unpicks the explosive charge that is attached to the commodity relationship in the *Grundrisse*, and translated there into the anthropological discourse of alienation and reification. In my view, as I shall go on to show, the discourse of *'fetishism'* that is substituted here for that of *'reification'* is something quite different: no longer a discourse on man, but rather a discourse on ideology, on the ideological form specific to commodity relations. It is not a discourse on human *nature*, but rather on the *representations* of exchangers.

What *Capital* expresses better, thanks to the strict division of its elements of exposition (something that is lacking in the *Grundrisse*) is the simple *latency* of the contradiction at the level of the commodity relationship as such, which is presented in its functional reality, certainly including a principle of contradiction (for it implies a tension between the private and the social), but not a principle of the development of this contradiction. Here, in fact, the problems that seem at first to form a 'vicious circle' are 'resolved'.[57] The contradiction only appears as a principle of development with the introduction of the particular commodity that is labour-power: between the concrete purpose that pertains to labour and the abstract objective, surplus-value, that pertains to the structure of capital. It is the 'mode of production' that defines the contradiction's principle of development. The abstract matrix of commodity production is not a mode of production.

If this is the case, then, just like expenditure and consumption, value and capital are also defined as semi-concepts. In the same manner as the wage relationship as a relationship of domination and consumption only provides the concept of expenditure of labour-power, of abstract labour forming value,

---

[56] Marx 1973c, pp. 230–1.
[57] Marx 1971, pp. 61 & 88.

because it represents the system of social regulation of expenditure, so it is only by becoming capital that value comes to express the contradictory significance of the couple by which it is defined. Two aspects of the same problem: the compulsion to produce is established to the extent that the abstract purpose is asserted.

We can understand, therefore, the convergent set of criticisms addressed to Ricardo, formulated in the same terms whether they pertain to value or capital, which he grasps as a *quantity*, but not as a *qualitatively* determined relationship, not with reference to the abstract, the non-use-value, and thus also to compulsion and domination.

We can also appreciate the theoretical import of the category of this contradiction's 'latency', which indicates both the functionality of the system that the initial moment defines and the explosive charge that it already bears, yet completely contains because it is not yet a class relationship. We thus glimpse the necessity of an adequate conception of each.

We can finally divine also the crucial problem that such a theoretical matrix – essentially uniting value to abstract labour and thus to money, and uniting expenditure to consumption of labour, in short the value relationship to the capital relationship – will pose to the Marxian project of a socialist society, to this other normative discourse on labour.

5. Value and socialisation of labour: Marx's inconsistent socialism

There is a key moment at which Marx appears to forget everything he has told us about value: when he turns to consider socialism. So conscious elsewhere of the difficulties and contradictions inherent to the construction of socialism, he does not seem to perceive that these are inscribed in the very matrix of the concept of value that he has himself developed. And this forgetfulness is undoubtedly heavy with consequences.

5.i *The theory of value in the critique of utopia*

The Ricardian socialist John Gray had proposed the suppression of capital as a private institution and its replacement by a national capital with the double function of storehouse and bank. The 'commodity' relationship would persist between this capital and the individual producer-exchangers, on the basis of labour-value: they would obtain 'certified' time-chits corresponding to the labour-time included in their respective commodities. Utopia, Marx says. For a system of this kind would have no means of making individual labour into a *'social labour'*. In other words, nothing indicates the motivations or compulsions by which the individuals would work coherently together.[58]

The capitalist mode of production contains an immanent principle of socialisation of labour. Marx offers a theory of this, characterised by a double articulation.

On the one hand, there is the abstract level of commodity production as such. It is only on the market that 'individual' labour acquires the character of social labour, and verification is made whether this labour: a) responds to the norms of average intensity, skill and productivity, in the absence of which it represents a lesser *'individual value'* and will exchange for a correspondingly lesser counterpart; b) responds to a demand proportionate to supply, in the absence of which the market price will differ from the value. Commodity *socialisation* is thus something quite other than an accounting certificate or *verification* – it refers to a structural *incentive*: a) for a definite expenditure of labour-power in a given time; b) for an appropriate choice of the object produced and the manner of producing it.

In specifically capitalist production, the second level of articulation, the same is true, with the important difference that the market incentive for expenditure of labour-power and choice of product no longer bears directly on the worker, but is exercised via the pressure of the capitalist who has to make him work. *Socialisation is thus asserted as a class relationship,* a political relationship, a relation of domination. Socialisation by the mediation of value is realised by a process that mobilises power. The abstraction (the 'detour by abstract labour') does not just signify a negation of the determinations of concrete labour, but a specific 'movement' that involves the expenditure and thus the consumption of labour-power (since this is here a commodity), and finds its conceptual expression only in a definite system of domination.

It is from this analysis of the actual functioning of a society that Marx develops his critique of 'the labour money utopia'. This utopia implicitly

---

[58] Cf. Marx 1971, pp. 83 ff.

assumes that it is sufficient to 'measure',[59] to 'establish in an authentic manner',[60] the labour-time spent, and to exchange as a function as this, in order for supply to match demand and for the fluctuations of commodity production to cease. A mistake, Marx says. Value is not 'measured', but *established* in the confrontation of the market, which, if it is left in place, will drag the 'time-chits' into its mechanism.

5.ii 'Gotha': the utopia returns

It is surprising then to find these famous time-chits reappear in the *Critique of the Gotha Programme*, this time in Marx's own doctrine. We should bear in mind that this is the most systematically argued presentation that he left us on the question of socialism:[61]

> [T]he individual producer gets back from society – after the deductions – exactly what he has given it. What he has given it is his individual *quantum* of labour. For instance, the social working day consists of the sum of the individual hours of work. The individual labour time of the individual producer thus constitutes his contribution to the social working day, his share of it. *Society gives him a certificate stating* that he has done such and such an amount of work . . . and with this certificate he can withdraw from the social supply of means of consumption as much as costs an equivalent amount of labour. The same amount of labour he has given to society in one form, he receives back in another.
>
> Clearly, the same principle is at work here as that which regulates the exchange of commodities as far as this is an exchange of equal values.[62]

We should note that Marx proceeds with caution and restricts his assertions to the question of the 'distribution of means of consumption'.[63] Also that he has explained in Volume Two of *Capital* how 'these chits are not money. They

---

[59] Marx 1973c, p. 138.

[60] Marx 1973c, p. 155.

[61] Lenin gave this problematic of verification a striking emphasis. In *The State and Revolution*, he explains that 'the immense majority of functions' under capitalism, both economic and political, are functions of 'book-keeping'. In my *Théorie générale* (Section 834), I propose a new interpretation of the *Critique of the Gotha Programme*.

[62] Marx 1974c, p. 346; my emphases: J.B.

[63] Marx 1974c, pp. 346 & 348.

do not circulate.'[64] It is clear, however, that a project of this kind only makes sense to the extent that the question of labour-time rules the whole of economic life and is translated into the prices fetched by various products. In effect, the very idea of time-chits supposes that the labour-time provided by the worker can be compared with the time embodied in the commodities withdrawn.

The question of comparing individual labour with social labour, however, can only be resolved by the transformation of one into the other, by socialisation, as Marx has himself demonstrated. And we stumble here on an enormous paradox: having developed a new concept of value, Marx is unable to apply it to socialism. What does the text cited above actually say? On the input side, society 'measures' individual labour. On the output side, it supplies a product in terms of social labour-time. This is to present the problem of socialisation, of the relationship between individual and society – precisely that which Marx aims to deal with here – as resolved in advance. It adapts the concept of value in such a way as to empty it of its substance and its object.

'[N]ow, in contrast to capitalist society,' Marx explains, 'individual pieces of labour are no longer merely indirectly, but directly, a component part of the total labour.'[65] This reference to immediacy does indeed seem to present two facets, one negative and critical, envisaging the project of a socialisation that would do without market mediation, and the other positive, indicating a perspective of the extinction of that which makes the mediation necessary, in other words the contradiction within society.

It is, in fact, in this ideal sense that the *Critique of the Gotha Programme* (despite formulating so well the inherent 'defects' of socialism as it emerges from capitalism) mobilises the category of value. '[P]rinciple and practice are no longer at loggerheads', which means that 'the exchange of equivalents' now exists 'in the individual case' and not merely 'on average'.[66] But how is the miracle of transubstantiation performed, of individual labour into social labour? This 'direct' socialisation? That is something Marx is unable to explain.

Or, rather, he indicates at several points the principle involved: the fact that production is performed according to a collectively drawn-up plan. But

---

[64] Marx 1978, p. 434.
[65] Marx 1974c, p. 345.
[66] Marx 1974c, p. 346.

this reply clearly gives rise to many other questions. How are these decisions made and applied? How will *labour* itself appear with its adequate content and 'normal' intensity? How is a general interest combining individual interests determined? How are general objectives translated into norms for individuals? What are the motivations?

Marx does not need to justify his lack of response to these questions; they were not the object of his theory. *Capital* only seeks to provide a concept of the *capitalist* socialisation of labour. But, in the *Critique of the Gotha Programme*, Marx puts forward an aberrant principle, a real diversion of the theory of value, when he writes that, under socialism, there will be (given the impossibility of exploitation) 'the same principle . . . which regulates the exchange of commodities',[67] and proposes the notion of time-chits as following from his theory in *Capital*.

It is not the 'same principle' at all. And there is an ambiguity here, in my view, that is nowhere removed in Marx's work and finds expression in diverging assertions. On the one hand, there are texts like *The Poverty of Philosophy*, in which Marx maintains, against Proudhon and basing himself on Ricardo, that value is not the category of the 'new social world' but, rather, of the present society.[68] On the other hand, in the *Critique of the Gotha Programme* and also in *Capital*, we see Marx apply this concept of value to the socialist future. With differences, to be sure, since, on the one hand, the 'fetishism' that attributes value to the products themselves is overcome, the social relations having become (miraculously!) *transparent*, while, on the other hand, the category of value will now function outside of the 'law of value' in the sense of law of the market. But the kernel persists: consideration of the labour-time socially necessary will be the principle of planning, and, as we see here, also of distribution.[69]

But this turn from the present to the future does not involve simply a change of epoch, of the concept's field of application. The very concept of value has been changed. What is now involved is a category of 'legislation': 'the regulation of labour-time and the distribution of social labour among various production groups becomes more essential than ever, as well as the

---

[67] Ibid.
[68] Marx 1976b, p. 123.
[69] Cf. Marx 1973c, p. 172.

keeping of accounts on this'.[70] A discourse of this kind cannot apply the concept of value elaborated in *Capital* and the *Theories of Surplus-Value*, this being a concept of contradiction. The discourse here is a directive one, which proposes to install the rational in the real.

This conceptual shift, effected in the Marxian discourse about socialism, evacuates the political from the relations of production and leads to considering it in a *separate* fashion in the form of a theory of the state, of which it is now possible to announce the coming end and its dissolution into 'the administration of things'.[71]

At the same time, this new recourse to the category of value opens the way to an *economics without politics*, as witness the development of an economic discourse based on value as legislative category. This discourse is undoubtedly necessary, but it should recognise its limitations, which are not only external (in the sense that there would 'also' be social and political contingencies) but also internal.

In short, Marx presents two discourses on value. That of *Capital*, a scientific discourse, which explains the motive forces and contradictions of a society. And that of the *Critique of the Gotha Programme*, which prescribes an organisational principle that is both technical and ethical. Marx does not clearly establish the relationship between these two discourses. I shall return to this point in the last chapter, to show the ways in which this ambiguity heralded certain interpretations that persist in contemporary debate. But it was necessary to tackle this question already here, to the extent that it expresses *a contrario* the specificity of the discourse on value in *Capital*, as a discourse of contradiction.

We can now understand how Marx's failure to perceive the duality of his discourses on value contributed to preventing the question of labour-value being linked to the order of politics and the state in an adequate fashion.

6. Labour-value and the state

The analysis of value as a political category, as proposed above, makes it possible to consider the 'state form' in its 'internal' relationship to the relations

---

[70] Marx 1981, p. 991.
[71] Marx and Engels 1987, p. 268 (*Anti-Dühring*).

of production, as against everything in the Marxist tradition that tends to consider it as a superstructure outside of the economic base.

As C. Luporini (1979) has shown, *Capital* is characterised by the fact that Marx considers civil society here in abstraction from the state. J.-P. Cotten[72] qualifies this analysis: Marx stresses state intervention in the historical origin of capitalism, but still conceives this as something external and instrumental. We may add that Marx also raises the question in a less external sense in relation to factory legislation.[73] But here, too, he does not offer a theoretical elaboration.

A. Tosel[74] insists correctly on the 'tenuous' character of the link between Marx's critique of the political and his theory of value. There is something missing in the discourse of *Capital*, the absence of an articulation between bourgeoisie and state, considered in the perspective of the place of the bourgeois class in the relations of production. I propose here to tackle this in connection with another absence, that of the development of the property/organisation relationship defined as the double facet of the capitalist function.[75] This is clearly a large problem, and one broadly debated today, that of the 'derivation of the state' – a problem with two facets. On the one hand, the state as organisational site of the capitalist class, a theme developed from very different orientations, which stress either the reconciliation of particular interests, or the national realisation of this unity, or the domination of the monopolist fraction, or the series of ever new responses at each stage in order to deal with new crises, contradictions and problems. On the other hand, there is the state as site of the relation between classes: domination, but also reconciliation (the compromises needed to win the agreement of the workers), and as site of emergence of decisive contradictions. These two aspects are evidently bound together. I shall confine myself here to the second, which more directly connects with my own problematic.

In reaction to certain orientations that insist on the first aspect, tackling the state on the basis of the category of 'capital' and privileging its regulatory intervention in reproduction and accumulation, there is now a tendency that aims at a less external and less functional conception, seeking to show how

---

[72] Cotten 1979, p. 330.
[73] Marx 1973c, p. 624.
[74] Tosel 1979, p. 49.
[75] Cf. Marx 1973c, p. 651.

the state expresses the relation of wage-labour as itself a relation of domination. L. Cartelier, for example, explains that the wage relationship is itself 'the minimal form of state'. It is by way of the state that the socialisation and submission of the wage-earners is ensured, and it is defined by the relation of production itself. The mutual externality of economics and politics is thereby overcome.

This project is amply justified in principle. But it is totally compromised, in my view, by the means chosen to conduct it. The author proposes in effect to abandon the terrain on which Marx tackles this question, that of 'labour-value'. For her, commodity relations socialise the owners of means of production, not the workers, who are only socialised in the wage relationship, termed a 'state' relationship: 'we call this type of submission contained in the wage relationship a state function'.[76]

My own view is quite the contrary. It is on the terrain of the commodity and its interpretation as labour-value that Marx lays the basic foundation of a theory of the state as specific moment of a relation of domination. The category of labour that opens his presentation (the couple of concrete and abstract labour, the latter expressing the 'expenditure' of labour in general) already implies in itself the social principle of the performance of this expenditure, a principle realised by the wage relation, in which the 'consumption' of labour-power forms the reverse side of expenditure. The Marxist theory of the state exists as such only through the *homogenisation of terrain* between value and wage-labour, which derives from this relationship of expenditure and consumption. There is thus not, on the one hand, an exchange that socialises the capitalists, and, on the other hand, wage-labour 'set to work'[77] that socialises the workers through the monetary relationship, but, rather as I have shown, a double articulation in which the compulsion exercised by the capitalists on the workers is first of all that which the market exercises on them, the ensemble forming a 'mode of production', a mode of 'useful expenditure' of labour, which is a definite mode of domination.

And this terrain is indeed that of the state, that is, of a certain exteriority to the wage relationship. Not simply because the state represents the common interest of the capitalist class (at the same time as its site of organisation and

---

[76] Cartelier 1980, p. 77.
[77] Cartelier 1980, pp. 78–9.

of internal confrontation), but because this 'domination through wage-labour' has its mediation here. As we have seen, the celebrated 'disposition [*Verfügung*]' has nothing instrumental about it (misdeeds of the 'reification' metaphor!); the effective performance of labour implies acquiescence in definite social and cultural conditions. And these are determined not at the level of the individual wage relationship but in the society as a whole, in a confrontation sanctioned by instances of the state. The expenditure of labour-power assumes its 'consumption', in other words, class domination, but because there is class struggle, this can only be ensured by the *acquiescence* of the working class, in terms of compromise. The state is not the site of reconciliation of interests of different classes, but, on the contrary, the site of compromise: class struggle is not total war, but a moving compromise that embodies the momentary state of the balance of forces, persisting by definition until the moment that the system is abolished. The dominant class must therefore pay the price, by showing its ability to ensure the existence of 'general services'. And, as far as the immediate wage relation is concerned, it must accept the assertion of 'norms' that preside over social life, in particular over the conditions in which labour is performed.

The Marxist tradition has broadly thematised contradiction and theoretically devalorised the categories that make it possible to consider the *continuity* of the system. And yet, if these are not recognised, there is a strong risk of revolutionary reason being disarmed. As long as the wage-earners have not constituted a new and credible universal, prefiguring a different model of production, this relative universal around which the dominant class gathers, and in the name of which it obtains the useful expenditure of labour, will continue to impose itself.

Conclusion

Starting from the Marxian project of a homogenisation of 'economic' space to make quantitative analysis possible, we have seen how the founding category, that of labour-value, reveals its other face, a socio-political one. For the *'expenditure'* of labour-power, far from enclosing the proposal in physiology, asserts itself as the *social* substance of value. Labour-time is not the time of physics: intensity denaturalises duration. The time socially necessary, as prescribed by the market, establishes itself in the social antagonism in which expenditure is compulsion. Thus the definition of value by abstract labour opens up both the homogeneous space of an economy, susceptible to quantitative analysis, and the space of class struggle.

This is what the classical economists 'did not see' when, homogenising in terms of remuneration, they failed to confront labour itself as a bipolar process, in which what is expenditure for the worker is, for the capitalist, the 'consumption of labour-power'. They did not consider this expenditure because they did not consider compulsion. Marx thus inaugurated a theory in which the wage *relationship*, as a relation of domination, is a constitutive moment, which was not the case for 'political economy'. Beyond the impulse that Hegel provided with his philosophical analysis of the relationship of work and domination and the wage-relation in particular, Marx thus constituted, in the space of historical materialism, the *'economic basis'* of the capitalist mode of production, in which economics is always immediately political. Not just in the sense that labour-value constitutes only a semi-concept with no operative value outside of a definite concept of domination, a definite type of social compulsion to produce. But also because this domination, far from being instrumental, presupposes an acquiescence with its reasons, its 'hegemonic' universal.

The thesis of the inherence of money to value is connected to this theory of labour-value. This thesis is directed against Ricardo, and important precisely because it is here that Marx defines his break with him, and thus the distinction of two fields (which we find today in the opposition between Marxism and neo-Ricardianism). It is explicitly formulated in *Theories of Surplus-Value*, but its presence in *Capital* can also be shown. Ricardo sees only the quantity of value, he does not see its 'form'; he does not see that money belongs to the very nature of value. But this is above all because he does not see the *substance* of value (abstract labour, expenditure), of which money is the form only because its abstraction is adequate to this. The absence of money from value in Ricardo is thus the absence of the political, of what in Marx is the presupposition of the political in value.

But nothing is more difficult to think through than this articulation between the political or social antagonism and the economic matrix. I denote this problem as that of the 'double articulation' of the socialisation of labour under capitalism: at the most abstract level, the compulsion is that of the market, while 'concretely' the capitalist class exercises it over the wage-earning class.

The relationship of one level to the other is expressed in particular by the notion of a contradiction 'latent' in the first, which becomes effective in the second. A 'latency' that should be understood in the context of the progress of the exposition of the structure – but a structure that is unique. From this fact, value and capital are defined as *semi-concepts*, just like expenditure and consumption. It is one and the same problem: the compulsion to produce is established as a function of the abstract character of the goal.

This essential liaison between labour-value and the particular mode of social compulsion becomes manifest when we realise Marx's astonishing blunder in the utopian turn he gives the theory of value in his discourse on socialism. When he deploys the category of labour-value in a strictly legislative or normative fashion, outside any problematic of contradiction, he believes he is holding to 'the same principle'. He then comes up with the very formulations he had so rightly displayed as utopian: forgetting that in this social division of labour and wealth it is impossible to determine the quantities that each person gives and receives outside of a concept of the socialisation of labour – such as capitalism provides with its 'double articulation'. This utopian formulation disconnects the categorical unity specific to historical materialism. It opens the way to an economy without politics, a denial of social contradiction, an underhand diversion of the discourse, which, while operating with seemingly identical categories, ceases to be that of historical materialism and risks, on the contrary, becoming a discourse of concealment and domination.

With value, however, Marx presented us in *Capital* with the category that is most explosive because most anti-utopian: referring to the *expenditure* of labour-power, it is only a semi-concept that appeals to its other half, that concerning the definite relations of social domination and *compulsion* implied by a particular mode of production. The concept of value that belongs to the field opened up by the theory of the mode of production denotes how the political is inherent to the economic, how contradiction, class struggle, the political and the state are *irrepressible*.

Applied to the present debate on the Marxist theory of the state, this analysis thus leads to precise conclusions. It shows – as against those who try and consider the relationship between state and capital starting from the wage or monetary relationship alone, and propose in this way to reconstruct Marxist theory around the relationship of exploitation but outside of the theory of labour-value – that the wage compulsion, in which the state intervenes at the level of domination as well as the level of hegemony: (i) on the one hand has its foundation prior to the state organisation, in the most basic and most pregnant structure, that of the market, and is, in this respect, a market compulsion, but a compulsion exercised by a class with the mediating intervention of the state; and (ii) on the other hand, is conceived as the compulsion to produce, to expend labour-power. In a word, it shows the impossibility of basing a discourse of capitalist wage domination outside of the social form that structures it, and outside the object – labour – on which it bears; in short, outside the law of value. It also makes it possible to understand how, if at this abstract level of the wage relation in general, no 'theory of the bourgeois state', its particular forms or attributes, is yet possible, it is certainly in the relationship of this moment to the original moment of labour-value that the articulation of the *political* to the economic must be posed.

The question of the state itself must be conceived, just like the whole system of categories, in relation to the progress of an exposition that proceeds from the abstract to the concrete. And this is why it will be developed in the new category that is introduced along with the wage relationship, the category of labour-power, which we shall now go on to tackle.

Chapter Four
Value and Price of Labour-Power

The two previous chapters have shown the double
aspect of value, quantitative and sociopolitical, and
the category of labour-power will manifest a similar
ambivalence, characteristic of the theoretical space
opened by Marx's exposition. The paradox here is
that the value/price couple will form the principle
for 'de-economising' the discourse.

This may be surprising. For this couple, inasmuch
as it applies to labour-power just as to any other
commodity, initially appears to express a specifically
economistic moment of the theory. Does not the
category of price refer to market mechanisms? And
does not even that of value, reduced to the category
of means of subsistence, give labour-power a similar
status to that of the ingredients of its production?
As far as the presentation of absolute surplus-value
is concerned, it might be thought that the only
arbitrary aspect was the magnitude of the unpaid
part (s), with the paid part (v) being more or less
naturalised. Relative surplus-value would thus be
defined as a modification of absolute surplus-value
that does not affect is 'real' content (and, on this
point, Marx's Ricardian presentation acquires a certain
verisimilitude). All this runs in the direction of a
functionalist and economistic reading, in which
reproduction of labour-power 'at its value' appears
as a requirement of the system.

Marx, moreover, only discloses his specific approach rather belatedly (and very imperfectly at that). Which is why, before going on examine his statements in *Capital*, it is necessary first of all to introduce a few considerations on the origins of this element of his thinking. All the more so, in that the essential texts of 1863 were published in English translation only in 1982, and have not yet appeared in French.

We have to remember first of all that, until the period 1863–5, Marx tended to define the normal wage as a *minimum*. The correction that Engels made in a note to *The Poverty of Philosophy*[1] is well known, but often taken for a mere 'change of judgement', the transition to a less pessimistic 'opinion' of capitalism. In my view, however, it is something quite different: a theoretical shift that shatters the rather economistic context in which the question of wages was previously raised. In the texts before 1857, this was defined as corresponding to the minimum necessary for the reproduction of labour-power.[2] The *Grundrisse* provided a philosophical transposition with the theme of pauperism as supposed product of capital: 'abstract, objectless poverty'.[3] This 'miserabilist' variant of the theme of alienation stretches over several pages. The *1861–3 Manuscripts*, however, break quite clearly with this conception: the problematic of pauperism is reduced here to that of the capitalist wage relationship: '*absolute poverty* . . . obliged to offer his labour capacity as such for sale as a commodity'.[4] But this is as far as it goes. And the question is hardly broached in *Theories of Surplus-Value*. In short, the whole doctrine, or at least its dominant note, is that of a *minimum* economic normality constituted by value, around which the market price fluctuates. And the anthropological figure of poverty/alienation (based on a historical teleology: emancipation leads from this poverty to true wealth) provides philosophical backing for a kind of functionalism of the system conceived as a system of domination.

As I see it, this shift of 1863–5 (in which we see Marx decisively abandon the notion of wages as a minimum) must be linked to another shift, more theoretical in nature, and which can hardly be taken as a mere change of opinion: the modification of his plan. Until this point, Marx intended to study

---

[1] Marx 1976b, p. 125.
[2] Marx 1977a, p. 209; Marx 1973c, p. 892.
[3] Marx 1973c, pp. 452–4.
[4] Marx and Engels 1988a, p. 40; Marx's emphasis.

wage-labour in a separate book. And it is interesting to note in what terms he then characterised respectively the two discourses on wages: the one that he gave at that time in the context of his study of 'capital in general', and the other that he intended to give, later on, in the 'book on wage-labour'.[5] The first discourse continued to assume that labour-power was sold at its value.[6] It was thus not simply a question of conceiving wages as a minimum (letters to Engels of 20 May 1865 and 24 June 1865), but the fact that the only topic here was the *value* of labour-power, while the question of its *price* would be postponed to a later treatise devoted to the 'real movement' of wages. Now, Marx eventually abandoned this plan, and integrated these questions, partially at least, into *Capital*. Rosdolsky explains how the initial project was to present the capitalist relationship in its 'pure' form, but that, in reality, 'the strict separation of the categories of capital and wage-labour . . . could only be taken up to a certain point'.[7] In my view, it is necessary to go further: the first plan, inspired by the Hegelian articulation of essence and phenomena, led Marx to dissociate the value and price of labour-power, and this fuelled a certain economism. It tended, in fact, towards the constitution of a discourse organised around the 'economic normality' of value, with the theme of the vital 'minimum' bringing a supplement of revolutionary spirit. And this is why I propose to show how the best combined treatment of these two questions, as we find it in *Capital*, introduces a shift at this level which leads to these categories being presented in a more adequate fashion as elements of a theory of class struggle (and not simply of class domination).

These questions are far from clear in Marx's exposition, and the fluctuations in his terminology are already evidence of this. (Thus, from one edition to the next, the fall in wages is referred to first as a 'fall in value', then as a fall in wages 'below their value'.[8]) Nevertheless, the couple of value and price of labour emerges as a constraining matrix that gradually permeates the presentation and gives it a logic that is in no way economistic.

---

[5] Cf. Marx 1973c, p. 419; Marx and Engels 1988a, pp. 43, 184–5.
[6] Marx and Engels 1988a, pp. 173, 184.
[7] Rosdolsky 1980, pp. 61–2.
[8] Marx 1973a, p. 547, n. 1. [This footnote does not appear in either the French or English editions.]

1. A non-normative problematic of the norm

The problematic of the value of labour-power was only established belatedly in Marx's exposition, since the 'canonical' statements that supersede the conception of a minimal wage date from 1865; furthermore, the system of categories that it implies are nowhere subjected to a systematic analysis comparable to that of Part One on value, even though this would have been equally necessary. A set of notions are presented however around the central core of value and price: normal/minimal, reproduction, movement, contract/theft, tradition, and so on. These are not there by chance, but introduced by certain constraints of the problematic, which Marx is far from fully recognising yet which orient the development of his discourse. My intention is thus to explore the logic of this moment of the system at which labour-power is defined as a commodity, and to make explicit the presuppositions of the categories deployed.

I want to show, as I have done with the category of value, how Marx bases his presentation of a political-economic space on these economic categories themselves, here price and market, driving them to a kind of limit from which they acquire on the rebound an 'original' modification. In other words, the dialectical development of the system is not to be sought in a Hegelian spirit being tacked on as supplement, but rather in the specific development itself.

1.i   *The dual reference of value*

We can start from the formulations in *Wages, Price and Profit*, which are substantially repeated in both the *Grundrisse* and *Capital*. Although these propositions are very well-known, it seems that they have not yet received the analytical study they deserve.

'The value of the labouring power is formed by two elements – the one merely physical, the other historical and social.' In every society a 'traditional standard of life' is established, which satisfies 'certain wants springing from the social conditions in which people are placed and reared up'.[9] This historical element forms part of the value of labour-power, but can be driven down to

---

[9] Marx 1973d, pp. 71–2; cf. Marx 1976a, pp. 274–6. [This text was delivered as a speech to the General Council of the International Working Men's Association, and composed for this purpose in an English not always fully colloquial.]

an 'ultimate limit' corresponding to the means of subsistence 'indispensable' to the physical reproduction of the working class. Finally, wages may sink even below this 'mere physical minimum', but this goes beyond the framework of the simple wage relationship, as the 'physical perpetuation of the race' can then be ensured only by public assistance.

I shall term the model indicated here by Marx the 'MN model'. It effectively proposes two theoretical reference points:

On the one hand, the *minimum* value of labour-power, or M;
On the other hand, its *normal* value, or N.

The level of wages can thus be depicted on a straight line punctuated by two points (. . . M . . . N . . .) and develops in the three zones thus determined.

The *normal value* (N) represents the 'necessaries absolutely indispensable' for the working class 'to maintain and reproduce itself'. Marx takes up here the approach of the classical economists, adding that the normal state of life includes the satisfaction of a set of 'natural' needs, but 'the number and extent of his so-called necessary requirements, as also the manner in which they are satisfied, are themselves products of history'.[10] This idea is, in a sense, a simple commonplace, but, for Marx, it conceals here a relatively new ambition: to lay down the principles, thanks to the theory of the capitalist mode of production, that will make it possible to understand how such 'products of history' are formed. We should also note that he associates with this the idea, which we shall return to, of 'tradition': 'traditional standard of life',[11] resting on a set of 'customary means of subsistence'.[12]

The second reference is the *minimum value* (M). This corresponds to a quantity of means of subsistence below which labour-power can no longer be supplied 'at normal quality'. This limit forms a 'vital minimum [*das physische Minimum*]' which can be located 'below the normal value of labour-power'.[13] Below this vital minimum, labour-power is not placed adequately on the labour market, and so the question of the reproduction of the relations of production experiences various complications, with corresponding solutions. This minimal limit is linked with a further limit, in this case a maximum,

---

[10] Marx 1976a, p. 275.
[11] Marx 1973d, p. 71.
[12] Marx 1981, p. 177.
[13] Marx 1981, p. 874.

that of the daily quantity of labour provided. Two conditions are actually required for the reproduction of labour-power in its normal quality: a minimum of subsistence and a maximum of labour, with a certain trade-off existing between the two.

It should also be noted – not that this point is specifically addressed by Marx, but it does tacitly articulate his discourse – that the idea of a norm is applied here in turn to two different objects:

> The *'normal state'* of life: 'His means of subsistence must therefore be sufficient to maintain him in his normal state as a working individual.'[14] This notion refers to the 'normal value' of labour-power. This is point N.
>
> The 'normal quality' of labour-power: 'the value of every commodity is determined by the labour-time required to provide it in its normal quality'.[15] This implies the existence of a minimum subsistence. The 'norm' here thus relates to the idea of a 'minimum limit' of the value of labour-power, and not that of normal value. This is point M.

This clarification of concepts, still entirely formal, introduces us to the very particular manner in which the question of wages is posed in the theory of the capitalist mode of production.

The *normal* level (N) relates, in my view, to a historical determination of needs, in which – even if these are analysed as effects of production – they cannot be adequately defined as a condition of it in the precise sense of a condition of reproduction of labour-power as such. It exceeds the level M that would suffice to ensure the supply of labour-power 'in its normal quality', implied by the nature of the tasks to be performed. A 'relative autonomy' is thus introduced that prevents the capitalist mode of production being conceived as a mere 'system of production' reproducing its own conditions (even on an expanded scale).

It is important to understand that the notion of a *norm*, which characterises this relative autonomy, denotes not nature but culture, and moreover the antagonistic moment in this; more precisely, the result of the history of this antagonistic relationship, inscribed in duration. This is illustrated by a passage, rarely discussed as it exceeds the limits of the positivist *koinè*, in Chapter 10

---

[14] Marx 1976a, p. 275.
[15] Marx 1976a, p. 277.

on the working-day, in which 'the voice of the worker' is raised to 'demand a normal working day'.[16] This voice denounces the 'robbery' involved in prolonging labour beyond the terms of the 'contract'. Let us not be deceived: what is defined as 'robbery' here is in no way exploitation. It is not the extortion of surplus-value, but simply its 'abnormal' extension. A theme taken up again in Chapter 12: 'The surplus labour would in this case be prolonged only by transgressing its normal limits . . . by a *usurpation* of part of the domain of necessary labour-time.'[17] The norm thus designates the articulation of the balance of rights to the balance of forces. The latter is not a suppression of any right: both the 'exchanging' parties keep their rights. But: 'Between equal rights, force decides.'[18] In short, the norm designates, at a definite level of material development, the moment of class struggle, in so far as it establishes certain results and is constantly established by these.

The *minimum* level (M) is that corresponding to the conditions indispensable for the reproduction of labour-power as a use-value for capitalist production. It is often tempting to interpret this as a functional requirement of the system that the capitalist mode of production forms, or even a premise of any political economy: does not labour-power *have* to be reproduced? In actual fact, it can be shown that one of the particularities of this system is its 'openness' to external labour-power, which enables it to avoid such systemic requirements. And it is then apparent how this concept of 'minimum value' cannot be ultimately inscribed in a schema of reproduction, in the form of a minimum functional prerequisite, but that it is rather determined – and this is also how the status of the concept of value in general is determined in the capitalist mode of production – in the contradictory movement that it designates. In short, the reproduction of capital should not be understood as reproduction of a society. No more at this level than the previous one does the Marxian matrix lend itself to functionalism. But a study of these movements in the value of labour-power cannot be undertaken before the notion of the *price* of labour-power is also established.

---

[16] Marx 1976a, pp. 342–3.
[17] Marx 1976a, p. 431; my emphasis: J.B.
[18] Marx 1976a, p. 344.

1.ii   *The price of labour-power, or wages*

Let us assume that the couple 'value/price of labour-power' corresponds in a preliminary sense – though not adequately, as we shall go on to show – to the general distinction between value and market price, applied here to the commodity labour-power: value is 'the centre of gravity' of market prices,[19] the axis round which these fluctuate as a function of variations in supply and demand. Marx takes up here a notion familiar to the classical economists, who – beyond the 'market price of labour', its 'current' or 'accidental' price – investigated its 'value' or 'natural price'.[20] He simply corrected this couple to refer to the price and value of labour-*power*.

But when he applied himself more precisely to the movement of wages, Marx showed how far this first approach which aligns labour-power with the condition of any commodity in general – so that it 'fluctuates around its value' – remains formal and inadequate.

Let us refer to the passages on trade unionism appended to the 'Results', where Marx does express himself initially in terms of such fluctuations. He describes the trade-union struggle as a struggle to maintain wages at the level of their value:

> [T]he *value of labour-power* constitutes the conscious and explicit foundation
> of the *trade unions*. . . . The *trade unions* aim at nothing less than to prevent
> the *reduction of wages* below the level that is traditionally maintained in the
> various branches of industry. That is to say, they wish to prevent the *price*
> of labour-power from falling below its *value*.[21]

What the trade unions confront is, in effect, the fluctuating movement of supply and demand, the 'law of the market'. But the continuation of this passage shows that the notions of market and price here possess a quite singular character, which we shall seek to elucidate. '[W]hen the capitalist negotiates with each man *singly*', he can exploit the need of individual workers **'which exists independently of the general relations of supply and demand'**. We are here on quite different ground from that of the market. 'The workers combine in order to achieve *equality* of a sort with the capitalist in their *contract*

---

[19] Marx 1981, p. 279.
[20] Marx 1981, pp. 677–8.
[21] Marx 1976a, p. 1069; Marx's emphases.

concerning the sale of their labour. This is the *rationale* (the logical basis) of the *trade unions*.'[22]

It is necessary here to gather up the various theoretical elements, inevitably scattered throughout *Capital*, concerning the question of prices, and show that both the category of *market* and the cleavage between value and price cannot have the same meaning for the particular commodity that is labour-power as they do for commodities in general. And this question, decisive for defining the very object of the theory of the capitalist mode of production, is only illuminated if we manage to overcome the epistemological obstacle that derives from the notion of price as representing an initially *negative* content, that of a discrepancy or modification in relation to value, of such a kind that we initially find condensed under this term, and in the couple that it forms with value, questions pertaining to different moments of the theory, and all the more so in that the diverse nature of these differences has not been clarified.

The relationship that the two classes maintain with exchange and the market is not of the same kind as in the case of ordinary commodities, and problems of a different order lie concealed beneath the single term 'price'. For commodities in general, the value/price difference always has the immediate sense of a shift in the division of surplus-value among capitalists. This is the case with the theory of the transformation of value into *price of production*, which ensures the equalisation of the rate of profit between branches. The same goes for *market price*, which fluctuates around the former. These two concepts, introduced in Volume Three after Volume One has dealt entirely with the theory of surplus-value as a global social relationship, the division of the value produced between workers and capitalists, only bear (immediately) on the redivision of surplus-value among the latter. The same also applies to the particular category of price bound up with the theory of *extra surplus-value* developed in Volume One (Part Four, Chapter 12). This derives in particular from the fact that certain capitalists, producing in conditions of optimal productivity, obtain a relatively higher surplus-value even if they reduce their prices below the 'social value', the effect being an unequal division of surplus-value among capitalists in this branch. In these three cases, the category of price (even if it is quite evident that this relates at least indirectly,

---

[22] Marx 1976a, pp. 1069–70; Marx's emphasis signalled by italics, my own by bold: J.B.

in a mediated fashion, to the question of the value of labour-power, given that the theory of the capitalist mode of production forms a coherent system) immediately designates simply the problem of the redivision of surplus-value among capitalists.

What characterises, on the contrary, the category *price of labour-power* (in the couple 'value/price of labour-power') is that its immediate object involves the division of the value produced between workers and capitalists, not a redivision of surplus-value among the latter. This is, accordingly, a category that, as distinct from that of market price – to which it is at first tempting to assimilate it – pertains to the field of Volume One of *Capital*, i.e. pertains *immediately* to the theory of surplus-value. And this follows from the fact that, on the 'labour market', proletarians appear both as commodities, subject as such to the considerations of Volume Three and thus being ascribed a market price that tends to vary with supply and demand, and as exchangers who 'exchange' not among themselves but with the other class in a relationship of exploitation, where what is at issue, in the question of price, is the division of the value produced between the two classes.

We can thus understand the limitations of the analogy between the market in the ordinary sense of the term and the 'labour market', as well as of this single term being used for both 'competition' among capitalists and 'competition' among workers. Paradoxically, the movement of variation in the price of labour-power around its value derives, as Marx emphasises in his passage on trade unions, from the ability or otherwise of the 'sellers of labour-power' to overcome their mutual competition – a situation that is normally the general one of sellers in a market – and constitute themselves as a relatively unified social force.

The very fact of the market, where labour-power appears as subject to fluctuations in supply and demand, endows this with a 'market price'. But the question of price (as opposed to value) cannot end here, because of the nature of the relationship it has to the category of 'market', where it appears not only as object (commodity subject to fluctuation) but also as actor. And because the tendency of this action is to constitute a unified social force facing up to another social force, the 'labour market' presents itself as a class relationship, a market 'of two classes', i.e. where the competitive relationship does not find its logical outcome – in the sense of one in conformity with class interests – within the class itself, by the elimination of a portion of its members at the end of an economic strategy (innovation, mechanisation, etc.), but in the fact that a political force emerges that is capable of prejudicing the interests and power of the other class. Without anticipating our analysis of the category of social class, which we shall come on to later, it is already possible to maintain that the 'value/price of labour-power' couple forms the touchstone of a non-economistic interpretation of *Capital*.

For any modification in the conditions of payment for labour-power, the theory thus raises the question of whether this is a movement in the price of labour-power or in its value. This is why we must now examine the specificity and various relationships of the respective movements of the value of labour-power and of wages (the price of labour-power). This is a necessary condition for establishing the object of these concepts.

2. Movements of value and movements of price

Both the value of labour-power and its price possess modes of variation or 'movements [*Bewegungen*]' that are connected yet distinct, and define at this level the articulation between the structure and its tendency. Marx did not explicitly acknowledge this theme, but he moved towards it spontaneously, as a function of the principles guiding his procedure. I want to show how, as against any positivistic structuralism, it is this that governs the concept of class struggle.

I shall analyse, in turn, what I propose to call the 'formal' and the 'real' devalorisation of labour-power, the first denoting simply a fall in the *value* of the means of subsistence, the second the reduction of their amount in terms of *use-value*, a reduction in the standard of living.

2.i   *The distinction of these movements in the formal devalorisation of labour-power*

As we already know, Marx presents in Part Four of Volume One the theory of relative surplus-value, which is also a theory of a fall in the *value* of labour-power; the value of wage goods in effect declines with the rise in productivity.[23] But, in Part Five, he also analyses – and this is the point we shall focus on

---

[23] Marx 1976a, pp. 429–30; cf. Marx 1981, p. 210.

here – a movement in the *price* of labour-power, in relation to that of its value and dominated by this, but distinct from it all the same.

The increase in productivity, Marx explains, tends to determine a movement of decline in value [*Wertbewegung*] of labour-power. For example, it might previously have taken 8 hours out of a 12-hour day to reproduce a variable capital with a value of 4 shillings. If productivity increases by a third, this variable capital will only have a value of 3 shillings,[24] which means it is realisable in 6 hours. 'Nevertheless,' Marx continues:

> even when circumstances allow the law to operate, subsidiary movements may occur. For example, if, as a result of an increase in the productivity of labour, the value of labour-power falls from 4 shillings to 3, or the necessary labour-time from 8 hours to 6, the price of labour-power might well fall only to 3s. 8d., 3s. 6d. or 3s. 2d. . . . . The amount of this fall, the lowest limit of which is 3 shillings (the new value of labour-power), depends on the relative weight thrown into the scale by the pressure of capital on the one side, and the resistance of the worker on the other.[25]

Two distinct movements are defined here.

On the one hand, a movement in the *value* of labour-power arising from the historical tendency of the capitalist mode of production to increase productivity: this, by its effect on the production of wage goods, lowers their value and thus that of labour-power. This 'law of motion' is nothing but the law of value applied to a particular commodity, labour-power, under capitalist conditions. More precisely, it denotes the tautological moment of the definition of the value of labour-power by that of the means of subsistence. And the whole interest of this passage in *Capital* is to show that a movement of this kind has under capitalism only a purely virtual reality: that of a 'limit'. The new value of the means of subsistence (here 3 shillings) only forms the 'minimum limit given by the new value.'[26] This implies that the tautological definition does not say all that there is to be said: there is something about the wage relationship that means that the definition forms only a limit, and thus, in a sense, a mere virtuality.

---

[24] [The new English translation of *Capital*, published in 1976, still adheres to Marx's use of the old money. The pound was divided into 20 shillings (s.), and these in turn into 12 pence (d.).]

[25] Marx 1976a, pp. 658–9; cf. Marx 1973a, pp. 545–6; Marx 1978, p. 210.

[26] Marx 1973a, p. 546.

And it is in this sense that Marx indicates, on the other hand, a movement in the *price* of labour-power. He explains in fact that the law of value encounters subsidiary movements [*Zwischenbewegunen*], 'obstacles' that can be analysed in terms of 'movement'. This price movement resists the decreasing movement of value. Thus, the movement in the value of labour-power as defined by the general rise in productivity is one thing, while the movement in its price brought about by this movement in value is something else.

When we analyse the relationship between these two movements, it appears that a value/price couple is defined here that is quite different in kind from that applying to commodities in general. It is specified by the nature of the wage relationship itself: wages are not provided in the form of wage goods, but in the money form, that of a universal equivalent which its holder, the wage-earner, goes on to exchange against the commodities he needs. This particularity defines the possibility of a specific dissociation between value and price: in actual fact, between the movement of the value of subsistence goods and the variation in 'wages'.

Let us examine the particular nature of the labour-power 'commodity'. The theory offers a double determination of it: in relation to the value of means of subsistence, and in relation to the monetary character of the wage relationship. And the second of these appears here as the principle of an 'obstacle-creating movement [*Zwischenbewegung*]' to the first. An obstacle in the sense of something able to oppose the formal devalorising and transform it into an actual valorising. The capitalist can only make this virtual movement in the value of labour-power effective by obtaining a change in the wage contract, a reduction in the nominal level of wages, thus an alteration in the established rules and norms. The configuration of capitalist social relations as relations of power is thus characterised here by the contradiction between the *relatively stable* character of the wage (fixed in money) as a traditional element, since every wage situation once acquired establishes, from the very fact of its existence, a 'tradition', and thus also a point of support, a 'position'; and on the other hand the *relatively variable* character, tending to fall, of the value of subsistence goods, arising from the fact of the general and continuous development of productivity in capitalist society. (This model ignores inflation, but it can be transposed to contemporary situations, where the workforce stick to the inverse yardstick of the 'traditional' division of the fruits of growth and a correlative increase in purchasing power.)

Here, the 'movement in value' of labour-power and the movement of its 'price' are analysed in terms of class struggle, in two different registers.

The first of these, which simply reflects the developmental trend in the value of wage goods, is analysed as the result of competition *between capitalists*. The second expresses a specific moment of the economic struggle between *capitalists and wage-earners*. The struggle around the price of labour-power, as distinct from what happens to its value, is conducted at different levels: branches of industry, individual firms, etc. The movement in the value of labour-power linked to relative surplus-value is relatively unified. That of its price, on the other hand, is relatively dispersed, depending on the balance of forces established at each of these levels.

This specificity of the value/price relationship applied to labour-power translates into the following 'curious effect': the price movement, in the sense denoted by *Zwischenbewegung*, rebounds on that of value. In effect, the brake that the workers' resistance brings to the mechanical alignment of the price of labour-power to its decreasing value can be analysed as an element that modifies the value and its movement itself, by favouring a growth in the mass of working-class means of subsistence. It stamps on a *value* that productivity tends to decrease a principle of growth, at least in so far as this resistance determines lasting effects; a new 'standard of living'. And this rebound on the magnitude of value is also a rebound for its concept.

We should understand that Marx's analysis of the configuration of capitalist relations of production and the conclusions that may be drawn concerning its effects on the conditions of a modification in 'standard of living' have an abstract character. Historical study of the development of labour-power bears on the whole conditions of its existence and its employment, which the rise in productive forces is constantly changing, creating new objective needs and implying their partial satisfaction. And it goes without saying that the satisfaction of new needs, in other words a rising level of material consumption, can go together with a deterioration in the material conditions of existence. But we can understand also the importance of the division that Marx makes here between the value of labour-power and its price: it expresses the *determinate* presence, in his theory, of the category of 'relation of forces' that prevents the analysis of the historical effects of the development of the productive forces from being transformed into a functionalist deduction of the value of labour-power. The relations of production are analysed, even at the most abstract level as here, as a system of 'positions' in the military sense. The same will also be found, in a negative fashion, in the other aspect of the question.

2.ii *The distinction of these movements in the actual devalorising of labour-power*

In the texts of *Capital* that deal not with relative surplus-value taken abstractly but with the historical development of the tendencies of the capitalist mode of production that are linked to this, the distinction between the movement in the value of labour-power and that of wages is less simple: Marx seems sometimes to use the two categories indifferently in his presentation of the same laws of development. This is particularly the case in those passages in Volume One that deal with the tendencies to a fall in wages: Chapters 14, 15 and 25 devoted respectively to manufacture, large-scale industry, and the general law of capitalist accumulation.

In reality, as I see it, Marx analyses these tendencies on the basis of a double determination that defines a problematic analogous to that of formal devalorisation. Firstly, there is the development of the capitalist division of labour, marked by mechanisation, simplification and fragmentation, which has the result that the labour-power required by the capitalist no longer needs to present the same characteristics of robust adult strength and skill: it can thus be produced in a shorter time. There follows from this – and this is the second aspect – a modification in the *labour market*: the generalised employment of women, children and foreigners, adding to the competition that machinery already exerts on the worker, and leading to a significant over-supply of workers in relation to the jobs on offer (it is the category of the labour market that has to be analysed here).

Marx's different presentations of this subject actually mingle the categories of *value*, governed by the first aspect, and *price*, determined by the second.

With *manufacture*, there appears a group of workers who have no need of training, and the value of labour-power accordingly falls.[27]

With *large-scale industry*, it appears increasingly clear that this actual devalorisation affects not only skill, but also the mass of means of subsistence needed for its production and reproduction. Also that it is realised via the

---

[27] Marx 1976a, pp. 460–1.

mediation of a market on which men, women and children compete with each other. Devalorisation means here that labour-power is produced 'in its normal quality' in a shorter time, the costs inherent to the subsistence of women and children now constituting the *norm* of the value of labour-power.[28]

The same approach is applied to the 'commercial employee' and to supervisors.[29]

In what way is the problematic defined here of the same nature as the previous one? The content is different: formal devalorisation affects both N and M, the normal and the minimum value, but does not affect the quantity of use-values corresponding to these; actual devalorisation, on the contrary, expresses an impoverishment, a reduction of N to M. But there is a common matrix, the assertion of an 'economic law': purely virtual or at least not mechanical in character, because it is 'counteracted' by certain tendential properties of capitalist relations of production, in such a way that the real movement of the price of labour-power is distinguished from the abstract movement of value. This is why, even if in Marx's texts the notions of value and price of labour-power appear to be closely linked or even indissociably interchangeable, their distinction – or, more precisely, their necessary coupling – assumes none the less a major theoretical importance.

The mechanism here is reversed: the 'devalorisation of means of subsistence' was, for the wage-earner, a resource to be grasped, whereas the 'simplification of the labourer needed' is, on the contrary, a counter-resource. But what these have in common is precisely this polarised field of support/obstacle: the labour market as a (non-closed) field of class struggle. A quite specific market in the sense of a 'two-class' market, in which the market relationship is a class relationship: the possibility of overcoming the competitive situation of the workers depends on their ability to unite against the capitalist class and thus escape the situation of atomisation defined by the development of a market – to constitute themselves into a relatively unified social force, i.e. a class.

The devalorisation of labour-power thus takes place via the mediation of a market and, consequently, a price movement. But the intervention of the

---

[28] Marx 1976a, pp. 489, 527.
[29] Marx 1981, pp. 402, 414–15.

price category, which one might have believed would take us into a field of 'purely economic' mechanisms, since the fluctuation of prices in general derives from a pure law of supply and demand, expresses, on the contrary, the fact that the study of wage movements can only be adequately conducted in terms of value if the connection between the internal relations of the working class – its tendency and capacity to unite – and its relationship to the capitalist class is taken into account. The specific character of the 'value/price of labour-power' couple is thus decisively due to the fact that it defines a structure of class struggle: the question of value is never settled simply by the effect of a change in the conditions required for the reproduction of a system of production and its agents, but by the mediation of a 'market' on which the question of the constitution of class unity is played out.

The relations between the concepts of value and price cease then to appear simply as relations of exteriority, a relationship of essence to appearance, a transition from the more abstract to the more concrete. The concept of price 'modifies' the concept of value, giving it an *original* modification. Value is established in a struggle defined here by the question of price, which expresses the concept of value as a concept of class struggle. The concept that the presentation necessarily goes on to introduce, that of the price of labour-power, has a rebound effect on the first concept, that of its value, and, in this way, determines the status that this has in the theory of the capitalist mode of production, a status which is not purely economic.

What I mean by an *original* modification is that it does not pertain to a more 'concrete' moment of the presentation, a moment that would be located further on in an order leading us progressively towards the empirical, or towards the expression of an essence. This is not something that could have been the object of a 'later volume', such as Marx had originally conceived. The category of price, in the sense developed here, determines the presentation at a level just as essential as that of value. For, in the same way that we saw how intensity denaturalised duration, so here price denaturalises or 'de-economises' value, thus defining the very status of the theory right from the start.

We should note that here again the conception of the presentation, which tends to postpone the moment of competition and market to Volume Three, basing itself on a certain problematic of 'dialectical' development from essence (figured by value) to phenomenon (figured by price), far from being a guarantee against economism, on the contrary provides the theoretical conditions for it.

3. The non-functionalist character of the system: its 'openness'

This articulation of value and price will serve us as a guide in exploring the confines of the system, the zone in which these categories cancel each other out only by producing particular and various effects, but effects that complete their definition.

3.i The 'reduction of the price of labour-power below its value'

The *upward movement* of wages expresses a relative unity between the value and price of labour-power, every advance in price becoming the basis of 'tradition' simply by its very existence.

The *downward movement*, on the contrary, is characterised by a specific disjunction between the price and the value of labour-power, which Marx refers to as the 'reduction of wages below the value of labour-power'. The fall in wages does not actually have the effect of rigorously restricting and suppressing needs that were historically felt and asserted, thus defining the value of labour-power. This latter displays on the contrary a *relative* persistence, such that the fall in wages must be characterised initially as the infraction of a certain 'normality'. This is what the texts that tackle this question indicate. The following passage is typical:

> In the chapters on the production of surplus-value we constantly assumed that [normal] wages were at least equal to the value of labour-power. But the forcible reduction of the wage of labour beneath its [correct] value plays too important a role in the practical movement of affairs for us not to stay with this phenomenon for a moment. In fact, it transforms the worker's necessary fund for consumption, within certain limits, into a fund for the accumulation of capital.[30]

---

[30] Marx 1976a, pp. 747–8.

The French version, which adds the words 'normal' and 'correct' as indicated, together with the notion of 'reduction', completes the sense of this 'forcible reduction' below the value of labour-power.

Two distinct ideas are thus often associated: the tendency to reduce wages below the normal value of labour-power (thus to go from N to M), and the tendency of wages to sink below the minimum M.

There is an apparent contradiction in the fact that the same processes are both described by Marx as a *devalorisation* or fall in wages below the value of labour-power. A divergence can be marked here between two versions[31] or successive editions.[32] But this contradiction is only apparent: for the very idea that the value of labour-power 'corresponds to historical needs' implies the possibility of a degradation of 'traditional standards'. The fall in price below value denotes the first phase of the process, at which it appears as theft, an infraction of traditional norms. Devalorisation then denotes the normalisation of the situation, the establishment of a new tradition at a lower level of consumption.[33]

As a whole, then, the *relative unity* of the upward movement, in the sense that a prolonged rise in the price of labour-power tends to raise recognised needs and thus the actual value of labour-power, should be opposed to the *relative disunity* of the downward movement, in the sense that crossing the axis of value leads only with greater difficulty to a downward shift in the axis itself, i.e. the devalorisation of labour-power, after being initially characterised as an apparent fall in wages below value. The value axis thus forms a line of resistance: the traditional standard, internalised as a norm, is an element in the relation of forces. According to Marx, it is around this that economic struggle, trade-union defence, is organised.[34] The latter is defensive not by necessity, but because it is based on the 'position' provided by the acquired situation. This, Marx says, is the 'conscious and explicit foundation' of trade-union action.[35] But no position is ever guaranteed, no tradition assured, and the value of labour-power can also regress.

---

[31] Marx 1976a, p. 276; Marx 1973a, p. 187.
[32] Marx 1973a, p. 547, n. 1.
[33] Cf. Marx and Engels 1988a, p. 184, which explicitly develops this point.
[34] 'Results'; Marx 1976a, p. 1069.
[35] Ibid.

Here, again, the couple of value and price of labour-time escapes an economistic fate. And it is now the category of value itself (and not only that of price, as we previously saw), that breaks open the space of the market, or again displays it as a 'two-class market'. The market here is a class relationship, and the class relationship takes the form of a market. There is both a connection between members of a class (the working class), the constitution of its unity, and, at the same time, its relationship to another class.

3.ii   *The Marxian concept of pauperism*

The second difference between the upward and downward movements of wages is that the latter encounters the other theoretical reference, that of the minimum value of labour-power: point M. Evidently, here the 'fall in wages below the value of labour-power' acquires a new meaning, since the situation is reached at which labour-power no longer finds in wages the means of reconstituting itself as such, in other words of reproducing its ability to perform its role in the production process.

The interest of the analysis that Marx finally reaches in *Capital* (after feeling his way as we have seen) is that it rises above a descriptive approach and constructs a specific concept of pauperism as a social relationship specific to capitalism.

Marx puts forward a capitalist 'law of population',[36] characterised by the alternation between technical innovations generating unemployment and extensive developments requiring new labour. He relates this phenomenon to that of the industrial cycle. He sees a functional connection here, but one from which the dominant class draws such secondary benefits that it comes quite naturally to constitute an objective ('production of a relative surplus population').[37]

What should hold our attention here is the nature of the social relationship that is defined at the margin but within capitalism (and through it, the general relationship between capitalism and its 'outside'). The *pauper* is, in effect, the intermittent agent of the cyclical system, an agent who, as a result of this intermittent status, is not fully reproduced by the wage relationship, but either

---

[36] Marx 1976a, pp. 781–802.
[37] Marx 1976a, p. 789.

by a subsistence that he finds outside capitalist production, or thanks to allocations deducted from overall surplus-value. In the latter case, his relationship to the capitalist class is no longer that of an exchange (the purchase and sale of labour-power) based in law and giving certain rights, but that of a free allocation. Stripped of the juridical features attaching to the commodity category of labour-power, this relationship thus loses its connection with the 'norms' (in the sense indicated above) attaching to it. Hence the precariousness that may, in due course, ensure a better 'disposal' over labour-power.

This category of pauperism bears an important lesson as to what the 'structure' and its 'reproduction' means under capitalism. The reproduction of a capitalist 'system' does not mean the reproduction of a 'society', it does not imply that its 'members' or agents are reproduced. Even if mass consumption becomes a condition of its development (and if, to this extent, it can be an objective of the ruling class), even if capital finds itself faced with a class that necessarily demands its reproduction, this is not a requirement of the system, which does not imply the reproduction of its agents at even their minimal value. This can be called the essential *openness* of the system.

4. A hierarchy of values of labour-power?

What is the meaning of the notion of the value of labour-power, and how pertinent can it be, when applied to various categories of wage-earners or particular individuals? I want to show here the theoretical conditions that make it possible to overcome the economism that almost invariably obscures this question.

4.i Did Marx fall into economism?

The well-known texts in which Marx lists the constitutive elements of labour-power mention three kinds of costs: (i) the worker's subsistence costs; (ii) the costs of maintaining his family; (iii) costs involved in occupational training.

This list naturally leads Marx to the question of the differences in value between labour-powers. Now, it often seems as if he only tackles this question with respect to the last of these three elements, that of *training*. This is actually the only principle of differentiation that he indicates in Part Two, in the pages where he defines labour-power as a commodity: skilled labour presupposes training, thus an additional production time, which increases the value of the labour-power under consideration.[38] And this is also the only point that leads him to consider, starting in Part Four, the historical tendencies of the capitalist mode of production in this regard. He explains here how a new disparity sets in at the stage of manufacture.[39] And this representation of unequal values of labour-powers based on unequal training costs is also found in several other texts.[40]

Marx even puts forward the idea of an objective foundation for the hierarchy of wages which cannot conceivably be questioned as long as capitalism lasts:

> Upon the basis of the wages system the value of labouring power is settled like that of every other commodity; and as different kinds of labouring power have different values, or require different quantities of labour for their production, they *must* fetch different prices in the labour market. To clamour for *equal or even equitable retribution* (sic.) on the basis of the wages system is the same as to clamour for *freedom* on the basis of the slavery system.[41]

We are led therefore to the 'accounting' interpretation: 'it is necessary to count' in the value of complex labour-power the costs inherent to its professional training. An economistic interpretation, in the sense that the concept of value no longer intervenes directly in explaining a contradictory development, but only after the event, by way of a means of measurement (which it certainly is) of what has been produced.

The idea is conveyed elsewhere that a confrontation over the magnitude of value of labour-power does not include any 'purely technical' element that could be isolated as such. If it is true that, at a generic level, the distribution of value produced cannot be determined *a priori* but is effected by the clash of classes, in conditions constantly being renewed by the development of the productive forces and the progressive constitution of the working class as organised force, this problematic is applied also to the different fractions of

---

[38] Marx 1976a, p. 305.

[39] Cf. Marx 1976a, pp. 460–1.

[40] Examples are Marx 1973c, pp. 323–4; Marx 1988, pp. 44 & 64; Marx 1972, p. 148; Marx 1973d, p. 56; Marx 1981, pp. 394, 402, 511–12.

[41] Marx 1973d, pp. 56–7; Marx's emphases.

the totality of wage-earners, who, confronting capital in different historical conditions, are in a better or worse position to obtain satisfaction. And this is indeed the way in which Marx analyses the conditions of the 'devalorisation' of the labour-power of commercial employees and the fall in the wages of supervisors. He shows, in particular, how the general spread of education brings these wage-earners into direct competition with others 'accustomed to a lower standard of living' or with a more numerous 'class'.[42] Just as in the general presentation of the effects of mechanisation and fragmentation of labour, he brings out the fact that, because the qualities required of labour-power are now shared among a broader group or even in abundance, a shift is effected in the balance of forces, obliging members of these strata to reduce their 'standard of living'. We see in these examples how the 'devalorisation' of these categories of labour-power affects in the same fashion the costs of education, this becoming socially less costly to the extent that it is generalised,[43] likewise the total costs of 'subsistence' and 'maintaining a family', since a 'lower standard of living' must now be accepted.

In sum, we find in Marx an approach to this question that goes beyond an accounting treatment of the specific costs involved in the production of 'complex' labour-power, a reference to the levels of requirement specific to various social categories, and to their capacity, according to historical circumstances, to obtain satisfaction. But nowhere does he offer a satisfactory theoretical formulation.

4.ii *Paralogisms of prevalent interpretations*

The value of labour-power includes the costs inherent to maintaining a family, and to the education and professional training of children. This proposition is evident enough once we take for granted that labour-power is a commodity and, more generally, that the capitalist relations of production are also relations of reproduction. But the question arises as to in what way this *abstract* proposition, abstract in that it concerns initially the *general* principles of the distribution of value produced between the two classes, can be applied to *particular* fractions of the wage-earning class or to *individuals*.

---

[42] Marx 1981, pp. 511–12.
[43] Marx 1981, pp. 415.

In this perspective, there are only two solutions. Each has been proposed several times over, and yet it is easy to demonstrate that they are based on serious theoretical confusions.

The first solution considers the increase in wages as the *retroactive payment* of additional costs involved in professional training. The confusion at work here is between the concept of the production of labour-power and the concept of the production of means of production. For the latter, the process involved is *prior* to their existence as a commodity, which crystallises in them a certain labour-time. Their production is their *origin*. For labour-power, on the other hand, its production consists in its individual and collective *reconstitution*. If we consider that an additional value is fixed in specially trained labour-power, either by virtue of the 'training work' performed by the individual in question, or of the 'educational work' carried out on him or her, or again of the total social costs involved in this training, we remain clearly in the same irrational explanation based on a machine metaphor.

As against this retrospective path, but in the same inter-individual problematic, others have sought a *prospective solution*, implicitly assuming that each stratum of 'complex labour-power' more or less reproduces 'its own race'. The 'calculation' of the value of the labour-power of a particular stratum then includes the training cost of its 'natural' successors, the children of these workers.[44] This procedure, besides the fact that it shares the same confusion between labour-power and machine, reproduction and origin, also involves an additional misconception. It proceeds as if the individual value of complex labour-power included by its nature – by the very fact of its characteristic operation – the costs of a *specific and analogous* training of its children. Or as if the system tended to settle categorically the problem of the reproduction of the particular strata of labour-power that it required.

4.iii   *Proposed theorisation: the articulation of the general and the individual*

Should establishing this double impasse lead us to question the existence of a relationship between the character of complex labour-power and a determinate level of value?

Certainly not. But, as the preceding analysis shows, if there does indeed exist on the market, summoned by the growth in the productive forces, a

---

[44] Cf. Baudelot et al. 1974, p. 219.

better trained set of labour-powers whose 'production' time has been longer, any procedure that would attribute to such a skilled labour-power *individually* a higher value by virtue of the training it has received or that it procures for its progeny is complete nonsense.

First of all, we have to restore the concept of the 'value of labour-power' to the level of abstraction that is specific to it. And this apparent 'relegation', far from withdrawing its operational character, makes it possible, on the contrary, to assign it its true status. Let us consider its position in the presentation of *Capital*. In analysing the *tendencies* of capitalism, Marx displays the contradictory demands of the productive forces, which require at least certain fractions of wage-earners to be skilled, and the capitalist relations of production, the logic of which is to reduce the 'value of labour-power', i.e. to compress training costs. This consideration intervenes in the analysis of the historical development of the capitalist mode of production. Here, it is perfectly operational, in the sense that it makes it possible to investigate the *strategies* of the different classes – that of the capitalist class that restricts training or distributes it with a strict perspective of profit, and that of the proletariat which struggles to obtain it – and to account for certain aspects of capitalist *accumulation* as the accumulation of surplus-value.

Secondly, the concept also shows its pertinence at the most concrete level, but at the price of an (apparent) movement of *redirection*, so that paradoxically the costs of training, far from being the cause of a higher value for certain labour-powers, are actually its consequence. If, in a certain social stratum, in effect, the worker is able to obtain for his children a longer training, this is *because* the value of labour-power, the 'traditional standard of living', is higher there. An *apparent* inversion of the relation of cause and effect, but in reality simply a necessary correction of the schema of production of labour-power based on the machine analogy.

Moreover, once the question of the value of labour-power is posed in these terms, it becomes clear that the opposition between the costs of *training* (certain of which are specific to skilled workers) and the costs of *subsistence* (common to all workers) ceases to be relevant. The various categories of wage-earners possess different 'standards of living', which are ultimately explained by the particular circumstances of their confrontation with capital. (And we also find here the same 'political' categorisation as that which presided over the consumption of labour-power, i.e. its 'expenditure' in terms of the theory of labour-value: there is no difference of principle between what, in the wage situation of a particular hierarchical category, derives from its struggle, and what derives from what capital offers in order to obtain the necessary consensus.) Within this 'standard', training does not occupy a theoretically privileged position. The same set of historical circumstances is responsible for the fact that certain categories of workers are able to 'wrest' from capital both better conditions of existence and training for their children.

The distinction between labour-powers of different value is thus related to conditions of unequal development in the class struggle. Not in an abstract fashion, but taking into account the set of elements of the 'standard of living' – including vocational training – which capitalist development makes possible and within certain limits necessary at a definite moment, and the set of conditions that enables a particular fraction of wage-earners to make these into elements of its traditional lifestyle, in other words of the 'value of labour-power'.

Conclusion

The determination of the double relevance of the category of value, both quantitative (Chapter 2) and socio-political (Chapter 3), grasped in the unity of the concept of expenditure/consumption of 'labour-power', naturally led us to an examination of this latter notion. Eminently liable to convey economism in its commodity determination, it is, in reality, the site of a conceptual development that prevents this.

The propositions that Marx arrives at in his final drafts of *Capital* develop, in conformity with the demands of the theoretical space that he deploys, a specific relationship between value and price of labour-power. Its value is analysed according to a dual system of reference that I have called 'the . . . M . . . N . . . axis', and this escapes any possibility of economistic reading. Point N here in fact defines a *norm* that is not the norm of a reproduction imperative of the system, but includes also elements of 'free' consumption that are unrelated to the functioning of the producer. This norm is simply the historical result of the antagonistic confrontation over the division of the product, in given conditions of productivity. It is an effect inscribed in rights acquired (always precariously), in the light of which any infraction is characterised as 'robbery', and in a tradition that is always (relatively) recognised and, in this way, a principle of resistance; and it denotes the articulation of the relation of rights to the relation of forces. As for point M, the *minimum* value of labour-power, this denotes the conditions below which the latter is not reproduced as a power able to hold its place in production. But, here too, there is no functional necessity: this point can perfectly well be crossed, for the reproduction of the 'economic system' does not imply the reproduction of its agents 'at their value', nor even their reproduction in general. The system is open: it does not retain its agents.

Paradoxically, it is the category of 'price', which one might expect to simply denote 'market mechanisms', the mechanical effect of variations in supply and demand, that confirms here the value/price couple as an element in a theory of class struggle. In effect, the category of price denotes here something quite other than just the fluctuation, described in *Capital*, Volume Three, around the value of a commodity (or more precisely around its production price), leading to the *redistribution* of surplus-value among capitalists: it involves the *distribution* (between wage-earners and capitalists) of the value produced and thus belongs to the field of Volume One. The market here is one of a special type, in which the 'commodity' is also an actor, and labour-power likewise never just a commodity in too great or too little supply, but also an element in a more or less constituted group, its involvement in competition being limited by its capacity to organise itself into a relatively unified force, i.e. to constitute itself as a class. This is how the market relationship becomes a class relationship.

This analysis opens the way to that of the distinct movements in the value and price of labour-power. At the level of 'formal devalorisation', the law of motion of the value of labour-power denotes the tautological moment of its definition, its variation as a function of social productivity. What is involved here is a limit, and, in this sense, a virtuality. It encounters an obstacle that gives rise to a price movement opposed to the falling movement of value: the monetary nature of wages. For the capitalists, if they are to take advantage of relative surplus-value, must obtain a 'modification' of the wage 'contract'. The competitive relationship among capitalists, which determines the (virtual) movement of the value of labour-power, is thus supplemented by the antagonistic relationship between capitalists and wage-earners that determines the movement in the price of labour-power. The wage-earners draw support from the acquired wage norm, as a 'position' in the military sense of the term;

and, in this way, they tend, to the extent that their resistance has a lasting effect, to modify their 'standard of living'. The movement in the price of labour-power then translates into an effect on the movement of its value.

At the level of real devalorisation, the situation is the reverse of this. The 'simplification of the workers required' is here an obstacle that threatens the wage-earners. But the theoretical matrix is analogous. The 'economic law' determines a movement of value that is not mechanical in character, since it establishes a field polarised into obstacle/support, determining the labour market as a field of class struggle. And the price movement denotes the effect of the ability or inability of the wage-earners to overcome the atomisation of the market and constitute themselves into a relatively unified force. The value and price of labour-power, far from being inscribed in the sequential relationship of essence and phenomenon, form a couple of such kind that the category of price modifies in an original sense that of value: value is established in a class struggle defined by the question of the price of labour-power.

This articulation of value and price serves as a guide for exploring the confines of the system. A 'fall in the price of labour-power below its value', which expresses an infraction of the norm, is something different from a fall in value. Beyond the minimum (point M), 'pauperism' as a specific relationship of capitalism denotes those fractions of its agents, in particular those subject to the shocks of the industrial cycle, that are not fully reproduced in the form of wages. This expresses the 'openness' of the system, the reproduction of which does not imply that of its agents.

Of all these questions, that on which Marx displays most uncertainty, even inconsistency, is certainly that of the wage hierarchy. His explicit discourse, which highlights the costs inherent to training, often collapses into economism. The difficulty, in fact, consists in relating the general axiom (according to which training increases the 'cost of production of labour-power', thus contributing to its value) to its significance for the individuals affected. Current interpretations, either retrospective using the machine analogy, or prospective in terms of proletarian 'lineages', are analytically inadequate. What is actually needed is to distinguish, on the one hand, a general-abstract level, at which capitalist development demands that some workers are more skilled and gives rise to a confrontation around the distribution and costs of this training; and, on the other hand, an individual level, at which the fact that some individuals shoulder these costs is not the cause but the effect of a certain magnitude of the value of labour-power, a certain 'standard of living'. There is no relevant distinction between costs of this kind (which the wage-earner bears on behalf of her offspring) and other subsistence costs. In this sense, the wage hierarchy has no other 'foundation' than the class struggle and the variety of its 'circumstances'.

In these conditions, the definition of labour-power as a 'commodity', far from lowering the discourse into economism, belongs, on the contrary, to the 'essential connection' of the theory and characterises this as a discourse of historical materialism. It is certainly a metaphor, and the wage relationship cannot be reduced to the commodity relationship. But a metaphor in which the analytical components (use-value/value, value/price, market, etc.) re-appear charged with new determinations, which precisely define the specificity of the capitalist relationship in opposition to the commodity relationship: thus a conceptual metaphor.

Chapter Five
Relations of Production and Class Relations

We have seen the double face of the categories
of value and labour-power, a quantitative and a
qualitative one. We shall now proceed further in the
progress from abstract to concrete, which is that of
Marx's exposition: an analogous problematic asserts
itself at the level of the relations of production specific
to capitalism. This time, however, the articulation is
more complex: it involves the unity of a structure
that is economic and social, and the relationship of
this structure to its historical dynamic.[1]

This is a key moment in defining the object of
Capital, i.e. the scope and limits of what such a theory
can teach us. And it is starting from this central place
that the two prevailing tendencies of interpretation
are determined, divergent in form but mutually
supporting each other: the economistic tendency and
the politico-mythic tendency.

The debate on these questions goes back a long
way, but it has taken a new upturn in recent years
and given rise to a copious literature. See, in particular,
M. Freyssenet (1971), A. Berthoud (1974), and more
recently J.-C. Delaunay (1983 and 1984). If certain
results have been finally established, the fruit of a
better acquaintance with Marx's work, the question

---

[1] My *Théorie générale* proposes a complete redevelopment of 'class theory'. (Bidet
1999, Sections 511 to 524.)

is far from being completely resolved, and various one-sided views continue to coexist and obscure it. Some of these privilege the productive forces ('material' production), others the relations of production (the production of surplus-value, the specific relationship of exploitation). What they have in common, I believe, is a lack of articulation between the two things that is also the *articulation of the structure to its dynamic*, a matrix common to the economic and the sociopolitical, by way of which it is also possible to understand their unity.

I shall start by examining the notion of 'productive labour', within the strict limits of Marx's own texts. Then I shall go on to study the articulation of this with the category of 'social class' in the class-ifying or teleological conceptions that the workers' movement has frequently drawn from it. I shall propose some conclusions concerning the object of the theory and the limits of pertinence of the categories that constitute it.

1. Productive and unproductive labour

Marx takes up here a theme that was very important with the classical economists and located in a recognised debate. But he entirely refashions this by shifting it onto the ground of historical materialism. This intervention, in my belief, has been very poorly understood, and this is unavoidable unless a certain number of interlinked questions are clarified. First of all there is that of the interference between the level of the *universal* category, that of production in general, and the *specific* level of the theory of the capitalist mode of production. Connected to this is the question of the relationship between *theory* and *critique*, and the double aspect of its exposition, as the difference between them precisely bears on the heterogeneity of the relationship that these introduce between the universal and the specific. Finally, there is the relationship, nowhere made explicit and yet essential to the exposition, between 'productive labour' and 'unproductive function': these categories, which in *Capital* seem curiously ignorant of one another, form in reality two sides of the same coin, and are mutually illuminated by their respective development.

1.i   *The Marxian notion of productive labour in its 'essential determination'*

The use that Marx makes of the category of 'productive labour' can only be conceived as at the articulation of two determinations, which he respectively names 'essential' and 'secondary'.

The *'essential determination'* is as follows: the concept of productive labour specific to the capitalist mode of production does not include any reference to the content of production. This thesis of Marx calls for three remarks.

1.i.a   *Marx bases himself on Adam Smith against vulgar economics, yet at the same time criticises Smith's ambiguities*

The concept of productive labour, as Marx develops it in his critical texts bearing on the history of economic thought, constitutes first of all a rejection of the standpoint of vulgar economics, which, by assimilating productive labour to useful labour, includes in it the entirety of 'social functions'.

More precisely, Marx distinguishes two levels.

There is first that of labour taken in its general sense (*Capital*, Volume One, Chapter 7, Section 1), which analyses the 'movement of useful labour' or 'production of use-values'. This is labour in general as a process between man and nature. The question of *'productive labour'* is, then, that of this movement viewed 'from the point of view of its result, the product'. 'The process is extinguished in the product. The product of the process is a use-value, a piece of natural material adapted to human needs by means of a change in its form.'[2]

There is then the level of labour in capitalist society. Marx refers here to Smith, who distinguished two kinds of wage-labour, that which is 'exchanged against capital' and that which is 'exchanged against revenue'. In explaining that only the first of these is productive, Smith had the great merit of bringing to light, by extracting the physiocrats' notion of net value from its empiricist shell, the motive force of capitalist society as constituted by the valorisation of capital by wage-labour, as well as the principal social relationship of capital/labour as the essential characteristic of this society and principle of its entire social organisation.

---

[2] Marx 1976a, p. 287.

Marx thus opposes two concepts of production or 'productive labour': production in general, i.e. production of *use-value*, and specifically capitalist production or production of *surplus-value*. And he credits Smith with having defined this second notion, capitalist production, meaning 'productive labour' under capitalism.

Yet if, in his critique of vulgar economics, Marx bases himself on Smith, the fact remains that his analysis of productive labour is also directed against him, against the amalgam Smith effects between two definitions. The first of these is the one I indicated: productive labour is labour exchanged against capital. Marx views this as extremely important and as providing the genuine scientific definition of capitalist relations. But mixed in with it is a second definition, that no longer relates it simply to the nature of the social relationship, but to the *material* content of production ('a vendible commodity which endures').[3]

This second definition, which appears in Smith like an over-printing on the first, assimilates: 1) labour that is exchanged for *revenue* with the production of *services*, useful but evanescent (unproductive labour), and 2) labour exchanged for *capital* with the production of *material* objects, in which labour is fixed (productive labour).

Marx's critique of this second definition, a critique that by itself takes up a major part of the first volume of *Theories of Surplus-Value*, is as follows: this *immediate* supplement of a second characteristic of productive labour that Smith proposes (production of *material* objects) obscures his first contention. A. Berthoud (1977) has rightly shown that it is possible to understand *'materiality'* in Smith's text as denoting *'durability'*, and this, in turn, as denoting *'vendibility'*, thus bringing Smith's 'second' definition in line with his 'first'. But it is still enlightening to follow the procedure by which Marx rejects this reference to the 'material content'. This is less for his critique of Smith than in relation to the precisions we are thus given for Marx's own theory.

1.i.b *Marx puts forward a problematic that radically dissociates productive labour from the material character of the product*
This point is already implicit in Chapter 7 of Volume One of *Capital*. Against the *general* notion of productive labour defined in the first section of this

---

[3] Smith 1974, p. 430.

chapter as the production of use-value, Marx introduces in the second section the notion of the productive labour characteristic of the *capitalist* mode of production: the production of surplus-value, or of an increase in abstract wealth. Abstract, in the sense of abstraction made of the nature of this production, in particular whether its character is material or not.

In *Theories of Surplus-Value*, he sets out to demonstrate how, contrary to the 'second' definition offered by Smith,[4] a 'more superficial' definition,[5] the content of labour (useful/harmful, material/immaterial) does not affect the determination of its productive character, this term only being an abbreviated expression denoting 'the whole relationship and the form and manner in which labour-power figures in the capitalist production process'.[6] This proposition certainly forms the leitmotiv of the first volume of the *Theories*.[7]

Marx's major critical intervention consists in dissociating (capitalist) productive labour from material labour, and setting aside here the distinction between goods and services. On this point, he criticises both Smith[8] and Sismondi.[9] On the one hand, there can be unproductive material production.[10] Marx takes the example of the tailor who works from home, whose labour is realised in the trousers that his client buys from him, but which is unproductive from the fact that his commodity does not take the form of commodity capital. Likewise, the example of the cook.[11] Correlatively, immaterial production can be the act of productive labour. Theatre performances, etc., despite not providing any 'durable object', still give rise to a recuperation of the capitals committed, and at a profit. The 'so-called [*sogennante*] unproductive labour' is thus undeniably 'productive' in the capitalist sense of the term. 'The same is true,' Marx continues, 'of the labour of clerks employed by a lawyer in his office.'[12]

---

[4] Marx 1964, p. 154.
[5] Marx 1974, p. 286.
[6] Marx 1974, p. 383.
[7] Cf. already Marx 1973c, pp. 308 & 328–9.
[8] Marx 1973c, p. 328.
[9] Marx 1973c, p. 308.
[10] Marx 1964, p. 390.
[11] Marx 1964, p. 161.
[12] Marx 1964, p. 162.

In sum, there is no ambiguity in Marx's thesis: *'services' can be productive of surplus-value, just as labour that does not produce surplus-value can be realised in material objects.*[13]

In order for a service to form part of 'productive labour', it is necessary and sufficient for it to be a 'capitalist commodity', inscribed in a capitalist market structure that determines the time socially necessary for its production, in other words, its value. A labour-power thus situated can produce, for the benefit of capital, 'more value than it possesses itself'.

These texts have been frequently commented. Most often, the object is to discredit them theoretically, either by insisting on the transitional or marginal character of the 'cases' to which they allude, or by maintaining that these spheres of activity, because their 'production' is non-material, cannot participate in the production of *surplus-value*, even if they are a site of accumulation of *profit*. It is necessary therefore to examine whether the notion of surplus-value as a social relation, or of 'productive labour', is really applicable here, or whether, on the contrary, profits have to be analysed in this case in terms of transfers, as is the case with commercial 'services'. This question can only be answered by examining if the notion of commodity, as a unity of use-value and exchange-value, is applicable to services in this way, or whether it is reserved for material products.

1.i.c   *Marx theorises services, non-material commodities, as 'productive labour'*
There are three passages in *Capital* and in the *Theories* that offer elements for an analysis of productive labour in capitalist service enterprises. These all concern the transport of passengers, but the concepts that they deploy have a broader scope, as witness the application that Marx makes to the sphere of communication in general. I shall limit myself to the most explicit passage.[14] It clearly emerges here that capitalist services – contrary to the empiricist views of vulgar materialism – do not constitute a mere unproductive expenditure of capital, or (alternatively) an exchange of labour-power, but, rather, a specific modality of functioning of the social relationship of surplus-value.

> What the transport industry sells is the actual change of place itself. The
> useful effect [*Nutzeffekt*] produced is inseparably connected with the transport

---

[13] Marx 1964, p. 163; cf. also pp. 148–295 *passim* & 377–400.
[14] Marx 1978, pp. 132–4, but see also p. 234 and Marx 1964, pp. 399–400.

process, i.e. the production process specific to the transport industry. . . . The formula for the transport industry is thus $M - C \langle^{L}_{mp} \ldots P \ldots M'-$ for it is the production process itself, and not a product separable from it, that is paid for and consumed.[15]

The general formula for capitalist production, as we know, is as follows:

$$M - C - \{^{L}_{mp} \ldots P \ldots C' - M'$$

The possessor of money-capital M purchases commodities C (or in this particular case, labour-power L and means of production *mp*), and organises the production process P to produce the commodity C', which he sells and obtains M'. Marx sets against this here the particular schema of non-material production, characterised by the absence of C', or, more precisely, by the concomitant presence of this moment along with the production process P.

Marx defines the product of the production process here in a more abstract manner than he does in his usual exposition, in which the commodity figures in its more ordinary concrete aspect, as a *material* good. The example of transport – and transport is an appropriate example, corresponding to the most 'important'[16] case from the economic standpoint – presents an occasion for deployment of the more general concepts. Marx envisages the 'product of the production process' under the abstract form of a *'result'*, which can be either a 'material thing different from the elements of the productive capital',[17] or else a 'useful effect' indissolubly tied to the process itself. The theory of capitalist production calls for a concept that incorporates these two forms of expression, to denote the product in its full generality. This concept is that of the *commodity in general*. Thus Marx counts the 'useful effect' of a service among other commodities: 'this useful effect behaves just like other commodities'.[18] It is, indeed, a commodity, as shown by its being sold. '[W]hat the transport industry sells is the actual change of place itself': not the train, nor the carriage, nor the driver's labour-time. The theory of capitalist production thus transcends on principle the mere context of the production of material

---

[15] Marx 1978, p. 135.
[16] Ibid.
[17] Marx 1978, p. 134.
[18] Marx 1978, p. 135.

objects. And it does so above all because the theory of labour-value is indifferent to the form of the commodity, material or otherwise. Even if the product of labour, particularly if non-material, is not always marketable, the theory of the commodity is general.

Marx continues his analysis of the status of this type of labour with respect to the *reproduction* of capital, the cycle of this capital. The formula

$$M - C - \{ \begin{smallmatrix} L \\ - mp \end{smallmatrix} \ldots P \ldots C' - M'$$

puts into relief the fact that the 'services' sold by the capitalists all contribute to the accumulation of capital. This remains true whether the service is consumed 'productively' or 'unproductively' (as intermediate or final consumption, as we say today). For, in the latter case, if the value 'disappears' into consumption, it has still been acquired by the capitalist in the form of the equivalent M'. The production of services as use-values is simultaneously their disappearance as use-values, since it is inseparable from their consumption. In so far as they are commodities, i.e. a unity of use-value and exchange-value, services disappear into consumption at the same time as they are produced. But the 'exchange-value' does not disappear, since it reappears in M'. Services thus enter the process of capital accumulation every bit as much as material goods. In this text, therefore, Marx produces the concepts of a general theory of personal services destined for individual consumption, and locates these in the context of capitalist accumulation.

This amounts to a more rigorous perspective. For indifference to the materiality of the product does not simply involve a generalisation of the theory. It is the very condition for understanding it properly. Materiality is, in effect, closely associated with the idea of utility, or a certain form of utility, which is then seen as the *immediate* goal of capitalist production as such. What is specific to Marx's theory is that it locates use-value in a subaltern position in relation to what is the real immediate goal of capitalist production: surplus-value.

This is also the sense of his critique of Adam Smith, sometimes deemed excessive: Smith does not rigorously distinguish between use-value and value, since he does not conceive value independently of its inscription in the determinate forms of material wealth. This problematic prevents him from conceiving the development of the capitalist mode of production simply in terms of the accumulation of *abstract* wealth, and can lead to presenting it as inspired by a different logic, that of the accumulation of certain forms of use-value. This slippage from the first to the second definition of surplus-value impedes Smith from grasping the true nature of capitalist relations of production. Marx's claim to have been the first to draw the full conclusions from the distinction between use-value and value, and the importance he attached to this discovery, is thus understandable: it is only on the basis of this rigorously abstract notion of value, unconnected with any reference to a definite material content, that the specific logic of the capitalist system is apparent: the accumulation of abstract wealth or profit.

1.ii *Marx's notion of productive labour in its 'second determination'*

But Marx combines with this a second and seemingly contrary thesis: the concept of productive labour specific to the capitalist mode of production does include a reference to the material content of this production.

If the texts cited above have been appreciated differently, but, in my view, without the central question they raise being confronted, the reason for this is that Marx, after having applied himself at length to defining in its full purity the concept of productive labour as indifferent to the content of its result (goods or services), seems, at the end of the day, to admit that Smith's second definition remains by and large correct, in so far as capitalist production tends to be identical with material production.

In point of fact, to the 'specific difference' of productive labour, which is to produce surplus-value, Marx finally adds a 'second determination [*Nebenbestimmung*]', which is to produce *material* wealth.[19] This is indicated in an often-cited text from the *Theories*, which bears this significant title: 'supplementary definition of productive labour as labour which is realised in material wealth'.[20]

---

[19] Marx 1964, p. 156.
[20] Marx 1964, ibid., p. 397. Here is the full passage. 'In considering the essential relations of capitalist production it can therefore be **assumed** that the entire world of commodities, all spheres of material production – the production of material wealth – are (formally or really) subordinated to the capitalist mode of production (for this is what is happening more and more completely; [since it] **is the principal goal, and only if it is realised will the productive powers of labour be developed to their highest point**). On this **premise** – which expresses the limit [of this process] and *which is therefore constantly coming closer to an exact presentation of reality* – all labourers

Does Marx finally return to a procedure analogous to that which he criticises in Smith, which consists in defining the concept of productive by the combination of two 'criteria': as producing both surplus-value and material objects. Are the several chapters of the *Theories* devoted to excluding consideration of this latter 'criterion' then simply a speculative exercise with no genuine interest for the analysis of capitalist society? This is what seems to be the view of those contemporary commentators whom I shall return to below, and who tend to a cumulative-syncretic interpretation of the notion of productive labour. But, before turning to criticise them, it is necessary to make clear that the relevance of this concept lies in a quite different direction. Marx, in fact, qualifies the first definition of 'determining characteristic'[21] or 'specific difference'[22] and presents the second as expressing the movement of the capitalist mode of production towards a 'limit', as its 'tendency'. The relationship between the first and second definitions should therefore be interpreted as that of structure and tendency. In other words, the object of the Marxist theory of 'productive labour' is to explain the particular nature of the relationship between productive forces and capitalist relations of production:

> On the one hand, 'essentially': productive labour in the capitalist mode of production is the production of surplus-value, in the sense that this is the goal, the logic of this mode of production;
> On the other hand, 'tendentially': this logic leads to the development of material production, though within limits inherent to the contradictory character of these relations.

If this is the case, then, when Marx discusses 'productive labour' he introduces under this term a concept specific to the theory of the capitalist mode of production, one that denotes the specific manner in which the material foundations of social existence are constituted in it: the development of the

---

engaged in the production of commodities are wage-labourers, and the means of production in all these spheres confront them as capital. It can then be said to be a characteristic of *productive labourers*, that is, labourers producing capital, that their labour realises itself in *commodities*, as material wealth. And so *productive labour*, along with its determining characteristic – which takes no account whatsoever of the *content of labour* and is entirely independent of that content – would be given a second, different and subsidiary definition.' (Italics for Marx's emphases, bold for my own: J.B.)

[21] Ibid.
[22] Marx 1964, p. 156.

productive forces here has as its logic and limit the production of abstract wealth. We can then understand how the couple of productive and unproductive labour (in the specifically capitalist sense of the term) requires in *Capital* a second couple, that of 'productive/unproductive function', which denotes the contradictory moment of these relations, the tendency for productivity (of use-value) to be *limited* under capitalism. Study of this second couple, entirely distinct from the first though linked to it, will display the conditions in which the category of 'unproductive labour', in the general sense and no longer that specific to the capitalist mode of production, makes a return and finds a necessary place in the exposition of *Capital*.

1.iii   *The Marxian notion of the 'unproductive functions' specific to capitalism*

We shall see here the introduction of a different use of the notion 'productive' and a different discourse on production, which it is necessary to define in relation to the previous one.

1.iii.a   *What is an 'unproductive function'?*
In the second and third volumes of *Capital*, Marx makes his elaboration of the 'essential definition' more precise, distinguishing among the workers who exchange with capital a category who do not produce surplus-value, that of agents of circulation.

If we were to approach the question in a classifying spirit, this would give the following schema, in which 'productive' means 'producing surplus-value':

Wage-earners paid from *revenue*	....	} = unproductive
Wage-earners paid from *capital* {	Circulation sphere	
	Production sphere	= productive

And this is effectively the grid that Marx uses in Chapter 17 of Volume Three, where he examines the status of commercial workers: these workers do not produce surplus-value, but they assist their employer in appropriating it, i.e. in making profit.[23] In short, they are productive 'for capital' *in this sense*. But

---

[23] Marx 1981, pp. 404 ff. & 414.

they are not productive in the proper sense: they produce 'neither value nor surplus-value'.[24] Everything so far is clear.

In Chapter 6 of Volume Two, however, Marx tackles the question in an entirely different register: commercial workers are unproductive because they create 'neither value nor products'.[25] This is significantly different from the formulation that they produce 'neither value nor surplus-value'. More precisely, in the long section of this chapter devoted to 'pure circulation costs', where this labour is defined as unproductive, the category of surplus-value does not appear at all. It is not explicitly mentioned. If we recall that it is the category of surplus-value that defines productive labour,[26] we cannot fail to be surprised – unless we understand that Marx is actually dealing here with a completely different question. This is what he writes about the commercial worker:

> He performs a necessary function, because the reproduction process itself includes unproductive functions. He works as well as the next man, but the content of his labour creates neither value nor products. He is himself part of the *faux frais* of production. His usefulness does not lie in his transforming an unproductive function into a productive one, or unproductive labour into productive. . . . He is useful rather because a smaller part of society's labour-power and labour time is now tied up in these unproductive functions.[27]

The question Marx introduces here is completely different, it concerns an 'unproductive function', a function which, in the author's words, 'creates neither value nor products'.

The notion 'unproductive' is thus applied by Marx to the labour of circulation in two completely different senses: with respect to *surplus-value* (Volume Three, Chapter 17), and to the *product* (Volume Two, Chapter 6). In the first sense, this labour involves a pure 'expenditure of capital', a deduction from surplus-value. In the second sense, these workers perform an 'unproductive function', though an indispensable one.

The two senses are connected, in so far as without a product there can be no value, and hence no surplus-value. But it would be a misconstrual to

---

[24] Marx 1981, p. 406.
[25] Marx 1964, p. 209.
[26] Marx 1964, p. 387 etc.
[27] Marx 1978, pp. 209–10.

imagine that this simple relationship resolves the problem, and that these 'unproductive functions' are always connected with 'unproductive (of surplus-value) labour'. We must thus examine the question of 'unproductive functions' as a whole.

1.iii.b   *Unproductive functions in the circulation sphere*
The continuation of Chapter 6 of Volume Two offers a sketch of this question, which Marx presents as that of the *'faux frais'* of capitalism.

The production of *money* is called unproductive, as this does not enter into either 'individual' or 'productive' consumption.[28] It is precisely because it is rejected as use-value that it functions as money. We find here the category of production in general, or *production of use-values* (productive labour in general) as developed in Volume One, Chapter 7, Section 1, used in opposition to the *production of surplus-value* (productive labour in the capitalist mode of production) presented in Section 2.

Marx, moreover, later goes on to deal with the question of the production of money in terms that apply to the production of any other commodity: money possesses a definite value determined by the labour-time needed for its production. To the extent that the time needed to produce the workers' means of subsistence is less than this (and it is so in principle), there is *surplus labour, surplus-value,* and thus *productive labour.*[29] The conclusion must be drawn that productive labour is devoted here to an unproductive function, so that the identity of the term should not conceal the difference in concepts.

In this sense, the category of 'function' refers to the division of social labour between productive and unproductive spheres, not with respect to capitalist accumulation in the strict sense, the accumulation of surplus-value, but rather to the production of social wealth, i.e. goods destined for either intermediate or final consumption.[30] And the example of money thus expresses the difference of object between the category of *productive labour,* specific to the capitalist mode of production, and that of *productive function* (characteristic of productive labour in general), which is applicable to other modes of production.

The production of money, however, is not for Marx an absolutely unique case. He applies the same consideration to certain costs of *storage* and *book-keeping.*

---

[28] Marx 1964, p. 213.
[29] Marx 1978, pp. 400–1.
[30] Cf. Marx 1978, pp. 420–1.

Some aspects of this analysis remain vague. But the interesting point here is the emergence of a general problematic of 'overhead costs of capitalist circulation', 'unproductive functions' that are not identical with 'unproductive labour'. These overhead costs include both living and dead labour, labour 'unproductive of surplus-value' (commercial and banking labour, book-keeping) and labour 'productive of surplus-value' (production of the money commodity, warehouse labour and storage in general).

This category of 'overhead costs' bears on the overall productivity of labour as regards use-values entering into consumption. In the capitalist mode of production, these 'overheads' weigh on the *global* relationship between capital and the use-values produced, in the same way as any other factor of unproductivity may affect a *particular* capital.[31]

But this problematic, developed particularly for circulation, actually transcends this sphere. It is applicable, in principle, to the total process of social production. Circulation costs, besides, are defined by Marx as 'overhead costs of production'. If the question of overheads is one of a 'reduction of the productive power of labour', then it is possible to think that it may find application also in the sphere of production itself. And this is what we now have to examine.

1.iii.c *Unproductive functions in the production sphere*
This question of overheads, or the unproductive (in terms of use-value) expenditure of social labour, is equally raised by Marx in similar terms with respect to the tasks of *supervision*, which he presents as *partly unproductive, though fully productive of value and surplus-value.*

When he explains in Volume One the process by which the capitalist progressively dispenses with the tasks of supervision and delegates them – in a military metaphor – to 'officers (managers) and N.C.O.s (foremen, overseers)',[32] he criticises the 'political economist' who conceives the tasks of supervision as overheads only in the case of slavery, and does not see analogous contradictions in the capitalist mode of production, where tasks of superintendence and (technical) direction seem to him to possess a natural unity. For Marx, on the contrary, the labour of supervision specific to the

---

[31] Cf. Marx 1978, p. 216.
[32] Marx 1976a, p. 450.

capitalist mode of production is characterised by the fact that the organisation of production, being also an extraction of surplus-value, necessarily assumes a 'despotic' character. This illustrates how these tasks fall at least partly into the category of *'faux frais de production'* (Marx also uses the French term in the German edition). For the share of this managerial labour that is made necessary only by virtue of the antagonisms existing between the classes expresses a limitation on the productive power of social labour.[33]

In a section of *Theories* devoted to Smith, Marx summarises a passage from Smith's book that, as he sees it, defines productive labour correctly as labour which also reproduces a certain profit. 'Included among these productive workers, of course, are all those who contribute in one way or another to the production of the commodity, from the actual operative to the manager or engineer (as distinct from the capitalist).'[34] Marx comments: 'Productive labour is here defined from the standpoint of capitalist production, and Adam Smith here got to the very heart of the matter, hit the nail on the head.'[35]

In short, if, from the standpoint of the production of social wealth or use-values, the capitalist labour of management is to be classed under overheads (but only partially, since if it does indeed have the aspect of domination over the workers, it achieves this only by making the necessary 'connection of labour'), it is none the less immediately involved in the production of surplus-value and, in this sense, productive, by virtue of its function in a process which is *at one and the same time* a process of production and a process of valorisation,

The notion of overheads thus denotes here only the negative effect of capitalist relations of production on the productive power of labour. Or again the contradiction specific to the capitalist mode of production between productive forces and relations of production.

1.iv *Proposed general interpretation*

Marx's whole procedure is based on the distinction between two senses of the expression *'productive labour'*: productive in general and productive under capitalism. Labour is *productive in general* in so far as it produces use-values.

---

[33] Cf. again Marx 1981, pp. 507–12; Marx 1972, p. 507; 'Results', Marx 1976a, p. 1037.
[34] Marx 1964, p. 152.
[35] Marx 1964, p. 153. Cf. also Marx 1964, pp. 398–9; Marx 1972, p. 497.

But capitalist production is characterised by a different goal: the production of surplus-value. Labour is productive in this sense only if it is *productive of surplus-value.*

The '*essential determination*' of capitalism, according to Marx, is the production of surplus-value. This proposition includes two intentions that are both connected and distinct. The one is critical: aiming to dispatch the idea that capitalism is production as such, the 'socially natural' production of use-values. The other is theoretical: Marx rejects the idea that productive labour here is characterised by production of a material kind. He thus confers theoretical priority on the *structural* element: there is 'production' for capital to the extent that the process yields a value greater than its ingredients, and that this value, through the realisation of the product (whether of material or non-material character is irrelevant) takes the form of money. This is the theoretical priority of the relations of production over the productive forces, which is how a mode of production possesses a 'specific logic'.[36]

This essential determination is supplemented by a '*secondary definition*': a structure of this kind is precisely of such a nature (because each capitalist competing for surplus-value is led to seek an increase in productivity by using machinery) as to develop material production, to the point of being tendentially identified with this. The relation between 'essential' and 'second' definition thus denotes the articulation of structure and tendency, that of absolute to relative surplus-value. The 'surplus-value structure' which governs the capitalist mode of production proves in this sense to be very genuinely productive (in the general sense).

But this same structure is equally marked by contradictions, in the shape of principles of social unproductiveness, understood here in the sense of use-values (though sometimes also of surplus-value), principles that find increasing expression with the development of these tendencies, especially in the form

---

[36] Reichelt 1983 shows very pertinently the reversal that occurs in the course of development of Marx's theory. In *The German Ideology*, the relations of production correspond to historical stages in the development of the productive forces; in *Capital*, on the contrary, they determine the forces by giving them a content corresponding to their form. He also emphasises the problematic character of the theme of a contradiction between forces and relations of production, first proposed in relation to capitalism and subsequently transformed into a general axiom of historical materialism, in connection with a philosophy of history (pp. 50–5). A remarkable analysis of this 'contradiction' in *Capital* is also provided by Kocyba 1979.

of 'unproductive functions' linked either with the commodity character of the system or with its specifically capitalist character. Marx locates these both in the sphere of circulation and in that of production. He fails to provide on this subject a coherent set of categories giving a unified representation of the set of requirements, functions and practices that form this relative unproductiveness of the system and lead it to crises that can put its reproduction in question. His presentation proceeds by way of varying biases and terminologies that are not free of contradiction, so that the terms 'productive' and 'unproductive' denote, either in turn or even simultaneously, the various aspects I have distinguished. This subject, as we find it in Marx, also lacks the connection that is needed to the notion of *crisis*. But it goes without saying that the contradictions analysed here also form the preconditions for this.

The complexity of Marx's discourse here arises from the fact that he plays both polemically and theoretically on the two senses of the term. This gives rise to a triple proposition. 1) Under capitalism, production equals production of surplus-value, for this is necessarily the objective of the individual capitalist in competition. 2) A structure of this kind, however, is *genuinely productive*: its nature is to develop social wealth (even though this is never its purpose, only a means). 3) But this productivity is threatened by the contradiction in the structure, which increasingly develops its *unproductive functions*.

The difference between these two 'definitions' is thus identical with the articulation between Parts Three and Four of Volume One of *Capital*. The 'essential' definition denotes the actual structure of capitalist relations of production, presented in Part Three. The 'second' determination, though it really has nothing secondary about it, denotes the tendential law, presented from Part Four onward, according to which these relations of production take hold of spheres of material production and develop them, within limits and according to contradictions that are determined by the nature of these relations. The entire line of argument of Part Four, according to which the capitalist mode of production engenders the development of productivity, especially by mechanisation, and thus tends to become identical with the sphere of material production, rests therefore on the presentation of Part Three, which is a pure analysis of capitalist relations of production – not that the 'productive forces' are absent from this, since constant and variable capital are defined here, but because this moment of the theory is the one that expresses the logic of capitalist relations of production independently of the concrete nature of the productive forces and the movement that these relations give them. Surplus-value is as yet envisaged here only as absolute, and the subordination of labour to capital only as formal.

Marx thus expresses the theoretical priority of the relations of production. His propositions concerning the 'decisive characteristic' of productive labour express this as being defined outside of any reference to a particular content or a particular commodity, thus also any definite level of development of the productive forces; in short, they present it in terms of the relations of production. This does not mean that a definite level of development of the productive forces may not be required to establish capitalist relations of production, and therefore 'capitalist productive labour'. Simply that only the strict definition of capitalist relations of production as having profit as their purpose, and of productive labour as productive of surplus-value, abstract wealth indifferent as to its content, makes it possible to analyse the dialectical relationship between relations of production and productive forces. When Marx writes of essential and secondary here, he indicates not a primacy but a theoretical priority, an order that is necessarily followed in the exposition of the theory, which must start by establishing the nature of capitalist relations of production in order for the dialectical relationship between these relations and the productive forces to make its appearance, excluding any metaphysical precedence of one over the other. This involves, at the same time, the necessary distinction between what defines the structure of the capitalist mode of production, and what is expressed progressively in history as a function of the characteristic tendencies of this structure. The 'second characterisation' precisely refers to this development, i.e. to the dialectical relationship between productive forces and relations of production. And, for this reason, if it is 'second', it is no less important for all that.

As Marx's rigorous and conceptually comprehensive analysis of the 'transport of passengers' shows (cf. above), the concept of productive labour specific to the capitalist mode of production does not exclude on principle those commodities designated as non-material. These are either *'services'* whose particular use-value is defined by a modification in the physical person, or commodities in which the result of social labour takes the form of a vendible *'material inscription'* (patent, software program, etc.). And this tendency co-exists perfectly well with another tendency that consists in the fact that the majority of these labours are performed on the contrary as public services, in such a way that their results do not take the form of commodities. This question links up with another one, far wider and more complex, of knowing why and in what conditions certain fractions of social labour in capitalist societies (education, administration, health, research, etc.) take a non-commodity form, and are performed outside the immediate production process of surplus-value.[37]

1.v Critique of some empiricist interpretations

It is necessary, in my view, to revisit here the debate on these subjects that developed in the 1970s. This was marked by various confusions, which despite the contributions of the authors cited above, have not been entirely removed.

A confusion over the *general* concept of productive labour, often assimilated with that of the production of material goods in opposition to services. A confusion in particular as to the nature of the relationship to be established between this *general* concept and the *specific* concept that Marx defines as that of 'productive labour in the capitalist mode of production', where 'productive' refers to the relationship between the two definitions ('essential' and 'second') of capitalist production that it denotes.

Poulantzas, for example, proposed a rectification of Marx's definition in the following terms: 'productive labour, in the capitalist mode of production, is labour which produces surplus-value *while directly reproducing the material elements that serve as the substratum of the relation of exploitation'.*[38] He based himself here on the idea that the two definitions given by Marx with Chapter 7

---

[37] I leave aside here this problem of the status of non-commodity labour in capitalism and its relationship to commodity labour. There is no doubt that this was a blind point in Marx's theorisation. He contrasts in fact 'labour exchanged for capital' which produces use-value and value, with 'labour exchanged for revenue' which produces only use-value. Now the notion of value, as defined in the theory of the commodity, can certainly not be applied to the latter. But the fact still remains that all labour, being at the same time concrete labour and expenditure (abstract labour), requires a theorisation that grasps it in its relationship between these two aspects. This would be a different theorisation from that found in the first Part of *Capital*, since it involves a different kind of definition/orientation/stimulation from that which characterises commodity relationships (see below, Chapter 10).

[38] Poulantzas 1975, p. 216; his emphasis.

of *Capital* are not mutually exclusive but rather 'co-substantial', the second actually implying the first.[39]

This thesis does not seem to have originated with Poulantzas, being already present in an earlier work of Bettelheim: productive labour is labour paid by capital and reproducing 'the material elements that serve as supports for the relations of exploitation'.[40] This last clause excludes from the sphere of productive labour, for example, 'scientific work', or the 'production of information', by virtue of the fact that the products of this (patents, programs), even if they take 'the form of a commodity', are purely non-material.

The procedure followed here consists in constituting the category of productive labourers in the capitalist mode of production by the *combination* of two features: production of use-value (or material) and production of surplus-value. The same analysis can be found in the voluminous work of Nagels, fairly representative of orthodox Marxism. He interprets the two definitions as a 'play of criteria'.[41] The productive character of labour in capitalist society is measured by the manner in which it fulfils two conditions: to produce surplus-value and produce use-value.

The question raised was an important one, as it bears both on the quantitative *economic* representation of surplus-value (who produces surplus-value?) and thus the accumulation process, and on the *political* representation of social classes, particularly the working class (who experiences the 'surplus-value' relationship of exploitation?). But the procedure adopted led to an illegitimate use of these categories. It implied a standpoint of the Smithian type, according to which productive labour is labour that both 'yields' and produces material use-values.[42] By transforming into combined *criteria* the two 'definitions of productive labour under capitalism', of which, in reality, one (the 'essential determination') is of the order of the structure, the other (the 'second determination') a question of tendencies, this moment of the theory is conferred a premature *classificatory* significance, exorbitant in relation to the place of these categories in the architecture of the system.

---

[39] Poulantzas 1975, p. 220.

[40] Bettelheim 1972, p. 71.

[41] Nagels 1974, p. 204.

[42] An echo of this is again found in a work, otherwise highly enlightening, by J.-C. Delaunay (1984): 'since quantity of labour is an evanescent quantity, it can only endure if the result whose value it becomes is itself durable' (p. 81). Marx's analysis of the 'transport of passengers' studied above seems in my view to be directed precisely against this view.

That this debate has now rather faded into the past does not mean that these problems have been overcome or received a solution. I propose, on the contrary, to show how they are linked with general difficulties in the theory, and more precisely with its plan of articulating economics and politics, and within what limits this plan is successful.

2. Production and social classes

I shall now analyse the category of *'working class'*, in the sense that the French Marxist tradition gives to the political aspect of the relationship that defines the category of productive labour at the economic level, and show how the reference to the relationship of structure and tendency is at the basis of both its relative pertinence and its tendency to swing between theoretical and mythic status.

We pass here from the set of *labours* and the quantities of value that they determine, to the mass of *workers* and the social groups that they constitute: from economic problems of accumulation to socio-political problems of the constitution of classes. Or, rather, we shall first examine the theoretical conditions for this transition.

Let us leave aside for a moment the texts of *Capital* and consider that great category of social analysis as a whole, omnipresent in Marx and the entire revolutionary tradition, that of the 'working class'. What relation does this have with the so-called 'economic' categories that we have studied? To what extent do these authorise such a sociopolitical concept as that of 'working class'?

2.i *The notion of 'working class' and the categories of* Capital

We immediately come up against an irritating epistemological problem. The introduction of 'scientific' categories should in principle result in emptying of content the 'divisions in reality' inherent in the pre-scientific categories for which they substitute. Now, as far as the working class is concerned, Marxism simply seems to take over and repeat the customary representation of a familiar 'social category': does not the notion of 'working class' in Marxism denote by and large, just as in ordinary language, the sum of wage-earners employed in material production?

In reality, if we examine *Capital*, this apparent correspondence is immediately presented as quite problematic. For there is no category that could be interpreted in sociological terms as defining the outlines of an ensemble that might be identified with this supposedly familiar 'social group', the working class. Marx's analysis, in fact, makes two successive distinctions. First of all (following Smith), between two types of wage-earners: those paid from private or public *revenue* and those paid from *capital*. Then, within this latter category, between two sub-groups: wage-earners in *circulation*, not productive of surplus-value, and wage-earners in *production*, or 'productive workers' in the specific sense, i.e. producers of surplus-value.

Now, this latter concept embraces, as we have shown, the whole of capitalist production, including that of 'service commodities' (by which I mean not services tied to the purchase and sale of commodities, but commodities having the form of services), or again the whole of 'immediately productive' functions, including that of management and administration. It is thus wider than that of the working class, understood in the common sense of the 'class of wage-earners employed in material production'. It is quite clear, then, that the 'worker' of Volume One, the 'productive worker', does not exactly coincide with this 'social group' to which the current expression 'working class' refers in the Marxist tradition.

When Marxist literature equates 'productive workers' and 'working class' (and this is for example the interpretation of Mandel's *Traité marxiste d'économie politique*), which defines the working class as 'the totality of wage-earners who, by their action on the material means of production, create surplus-value and capital for the capitalists',[43] it violates the relationship between economics and politics by failing to recognise the articulation presented above between the so-called 'essential' definition, that of the relations of production or surplus-value, and the 'second' definition, that of the productive forces or material production, i.e. the articulation of structure and tendency.

From the standpoint of historical materialism, what defines the working class as a class, a historical social force, is not something like the 'brute fact' (an inadmissible notion, to be sure) of producing surplus-value. The mechanism of surplus-value certainly expresses the *interests* of the productive worker as contrary to that of the capitalists. But this is not enough to draw the conclusion that the exploited can be defined as the group of those who, having interests opposed to the exploiters, supposedly constitute by that fact alone a social

---

[43] Mandel 1972, vol. 1, p. 213.

force called not only to struggle against capital but actually to supplant it. All that the *structure* of exploitation expresses is the conflict of interests. But what provides the wage-earners with the *means* to defend their interests (and not just the *reason* to do so), the means to progressively form themselves into that historical force capable of overthrowing the power of the bourgeoisie, is a whole set of 'concrete conditions' which are precisely bound up with the 'second definition' of productive labour, this *tendency* for material production to develop under the specific forms of this mode of production. It is this whole set of conditions that Marx deals with in Parts Four and Seven of Volume One: the concentration of production and workers, over-exploitation bound up with fragmentation and mechanisation, relative homogenisation (despite the tendency for disparities to develop), the rising level of skill (along with the de-skilling of certain fractions), unification through the labour process itself, in sum, everything that constitutes the base of the process that leads to the trade-union, political and ideological organisation of the working class, and makes it capable of effectively challenging the permanence of the system based on private property of the means of production.

In other words, the concept of 'working class' can only be sought in the theory of 'productive labour' (productive of surplus-value). But it does not culminate in the classification directly authorised by considering the social relationship of surplus-value as defined in Part Three, a classification that would 'arrange' the various components of capitalist society in different columns: wage-earners in production, those in circulation, those working for the state, etc., and so obtain a distribution of the whole.[44] The concept of the capitalist relation of production experiences a 'development' in Part Four, the object of which is the set of *tendencies* that characterise this relationship: the tendency to increase material production according to a specific mode of collective labour that defines the working class not just by the opposition of its *interests* to those of the capitalist class (something that is already shown by the structure of the social relationship of surplus-value considered in the abstract moment of the formal subsumption of labour to capital), but also by the ensemble of *means* that it gradually comes to dispose of (number, cohesion, organisation, culture) and which define it as an *element of class struggle*. It is in this way that historical materialism is the theory of class struggle. Its

---

[44] See the remarkable analysis of Balibar 1974, pp. 138–54.

concepts thus escape any sociological interpretation in terms of social groups: they are concepts of the historical movement.

Such an approach leads more generally to investigating the 'tendencies' that mark the development of wage-earners in the spheres of 'circulation' and 'public spending'. This means raising the problem of class confrontation on a broader scale than that defined by Volume One, but following the same articulation of structure and tendency that underlies this.

But the question still clearly remains as to what kind of necessity such an articulation possesses: can we justifiably attribute such tendencies to this structure?

2.ii *Teleological category and strategic category*

Let us resume the analysis of the formation of social classes under capitalism starting from a different principle, that of the *unity of the processes of production and valorisation*. This prescribes two opposing perspectives.

The first of these offers a context for an expansion of the capitalist class. If the place of the capitalist in the class relationship is defined by the unity between *ownership* of the means of production with the function of organisation and control that derives from this,[45] the agents whom she enrols for these tasks as they become more complex find themselves integrated into the capitalist class, at least to the extent that they benefit from the process of exploitation.

The second perspective offers the context for an extension of the working class. Surplus-value, because it derives from the overall difference between the value of commodities produced by the capitalist unit (the individual capital) and the capital advanced, derives indivisibly from the collective labour process that takes place, in the light of which all the agents, including those of management, are 'productive' in the sense specific to capitalism, i.e. producers of surplus-value (except, of course, if they receive more than they put in).

In sociopolitical terms, the opposition is attributable, in the prevailing interpretation, to the fact that the organisation of the process of 'production/valorisation' tends to demand ever more co-ordinating work from an ever

---

[45] Cf. Marx 1976a, p. 291.

larger number of employees, who are thus caught in different degrees between two class assignations. It is not resolvable a priori in either direction, even if assimilation to the 'working class' seems more natural for those agents who are close to its conditions of life, and less so for the others. The fact that there is class struggle actually means a confrontation of strategies of the polar forces, each of which aims to group the intermediate elements around it in solidarity.

This is, at least, the 'revolutionary' interpretation of *Capital*. But here we reach the balancing point between the theoretical and the mythical status of the 'working class' and similar categories.

As a category of 'tendency', one that draws its sociopolitical content from the general characteristics of the tendencies of the capitalist mode of production, it seems built on a solid foundation: capital in its development produces its 'gravediggers', as the saying goes. Now, if the productive forces are certainly subject to a unilinear development (concentration, increase in productivity, introduction of science), likewise the correlative employment of labour-power (fragmentation/technicisation), the same does not apply to those sociopolitical aspects that are deemed to go together with this and produce the working class as political force: these aspects experience counter-tendencies, in the shape of the various factors that diversify and divide the working class, and that are both consciously and unconsciously promoted by the dominant forces.

The teleological interpretation maintains the natural supremacy of the 'positive' elements, those running in the sense of a consolidation of the working class, whereas, given the structure of the mode of production, the possibilities exist for the system to remain in equilibrium for at least very long periods – above all because a large part of the managerial staff can be integrated by the dominant class. It also rules out the end of capitalism meaning anything but the victory of the wage-earners as a whole, whereas it is conceivable in reality that other forms – complex and diffuse – of monopolisation of the production apparatus and the advantages to be had from its control can exist beyond capitalism.

The teleological interpretation was certainly Marx's own. Chapter 32 of Volume One, titled 'The Historical Tendency of Capitalist Accumulation' and oriented to a perspective of 'the negation of the negation',[46] clearly bears witness to this.

---

[46] Marx 1976a, p. 929.

Now, it seems to me that Marx had no basis for drawing such 'teleologically revolutionary' conclusions from his theory. In the contradictory play of factors, the site of unexpected turns that is the terrain of class struggle, nothing indicates *a priori* that the 'positive' factors (of reinforcement and unification of the working class) are naturally destined to triumph: the theory does not permit such *a priori* designation of one tendency as dominant. In this sense, it does not have a predictive value.

What it does present is a strategic significance: it teaches the dominated what factors unite and strengthen them, what measures must therefore be taken if this is the goal they aspire to. Marx takes up here Machiavelli's project.

In sum, if the articulation of structure and tendency is the first point to take into account for a theorisation of the sociopolitical moment of class categories, the second is the status of this category of tendency in a system of 'contradictory' tendencies: this status makes the category of the working class a strictly 'strategic' category in the sense I have indicated. And a category that turns to myth whenever teleology gets the upper hand.

We must thus reject the alternative proposed many times over, from Horkheimer to Habermas:[47] either *Capital* presents a 'critical theory' written 'from the standpoint of the proletariat', or else it constitutes a 'traditional theory', scientistic and positivist. Marx's exposition certainly displays the 'contradictions' of capitalist society, and on the basis of these the antagonism of standpoints and strategies, but the fundamental categories it is based on, those of Part One, in no way derive from a 'socialist standpoint' on society. The Marxian *theory* of capitalism certainly gave the socialist *project* a new turn. But theory and project are not defined by a mirror relationship that would subject the first to the 'standpoint' of the second, thus making it into a 'critical theory' in the sense in which its theoretical legitimacy would be a function of its critical legitimacy. On the contrary, if Marx gave new life to criticism, it was because he gave new life to theory.

---

[47] For Habermas's interpretation of *Capital*, see my article 'Habermas' in Bidet and Kouvelakis (eds.) (2007).

Conclusion

The Marxian propositions on 'productive labour' have been poorly understood. They provide a *theoretical-critical* expression of the concept of surplus-value based on the double sense of 'productive' (of use-value and of surplus-value): 'under capitalism only that which yields surplus-value is productive'. This is a subtle business, as the statement has a double meaning: 1) the immediate tension towards surplus-value (particular to the structure) is genuinely *productive*: it contains a historical tendency to the development of production; 2) but this is only within certain limits, which characterise its specific *unproductiveness* as manifested by contradictions, crises, etc. and flow from the fact that for capital, to produce is first and foremost to produce surplus-value.

A *theoretical* proposition, which puts forward the principle of an explanation of the historical course of these societies. A *critical* proposition, in so far as it marks the contradictions of this particular mode of production.

The Marxian exposition of 'productive labour' is thus nothing other than the exposition of surplus-value, but in a polemical form. Hence the particular and disturbing articulation of the contention, which progresses in two stages. 1) The *'essential definition'*, the assertion that under capitalism productive labour is labour that produces surplus-value, irrespective of the materiality or utility of the product. This thesis expresses both the generality of the theory (which also applies to non-material commodities), and above all its radicality (the purpose of production is not utility, use-value, but the increase in abstract value). 2) The *'second definition'*: this mode of production governed by surplus-value tends to develop material production. This second thesis must naturally be taken together with what Marx maintains concerning the *unproductive aspects* of the system: 'unproductive functions' bound up with commodity constraints and class antagonisms, the management of labour-power, crises.

These texts have broadly inspired two contrary interpretations. An *economistic* and empiricist interpretation which combines the two definitions as joint criteria, and a *structuralist* interpretation that disconnects them and recognises only the first. At the root of both positions is a certain misunderstanding of the key articulation of the theory, one of structure and tendency, that this duality of definitions expresses.

The issue in this discussion also bears on the relationship between the economic and the sociopolitical significance of the theory of surplus-value.

The economistic-empiricist interpretation proposes to identify the workers in capitalist material production (the working class) with the wage-earners of Volume One of *Capital*; the other insists on the non-worker character of a section of wage-earners, and thus tends to relativise the category of 'working class'. This is a battle in the dark.

The matter is only made clear if we consider that a category such as 'working class' – a social force opposed to another force, the class of owners of the means of production and organisers of the labour process – is not the sociopolitical underside of the structural moment of the theory. The social structure presented in Part Three of Volume One, a structure of exploitation, certainly displays an opposition of interests, but only the historical tendencies of this structure (towards the creation of a modern and concentrated proletariat, etc.) confer on the class the means to constitute itself as a social force, as well as the reasons for doing so. This, however, is a movement that goes well beyond what is traditionally called the working class.

Is this a truism? No, and first of all because it indicates that the object of the notion of class is not to classify but to offer a concept of the historical movement. This indeed is certainly how the user of the theory, the workers' movement, has understood things. But it is also not a truism because the workers' movement has itself tended to misconstrue the open character of the theory and turn its concepts into myths.

The 'working class' in effect becomes a myth if one extrapolates by arguing from the tendencies that affect the productive forces under capitalism (with its impact on wage-labour: increase in numbers, rise in abilities, concentration) to a globally positive effect on the development of a 'working class'. No more than the 'falling rate of profit', in which the favouring factors have no theoretical priority over those countering it, does the reinforcement of the working class have this kind of principled priority. If the capitalist class is characterised by the function of ownership and organisation of the means of production, it displays a capacity for expansion and ramification that, whilst certainly beset with contradictions (since the organisation is necessarily entrusted to employees who are increasingly subject to the common exploitation, the farther removed they are from the centre), structurally possesses a mass base. And it is faced with a class that many factors in the system may equally divide and weaken, above all the hierarchical organisation of labour that is characteristic of capitalism as such.

The teleological interpretation, that sees a steady strengthening of the working class leading to its ineluctable victory, has no logical basis in Marx's system. If *Capital* shows very well how capitalism does not have to fear economic collapse, and possesses the means (socially costly as they may be) for reducing its crises, its author suggests that its political end is inscribed in its tendency: the final assault is inevitable. In reality, however, other evolutions of capitalist society are perfectly possible, anchored in the traits of its structure, which facilitates various kinds of regroupment leading to different modes of restructuring.

The legitimate use of the theory is thus, in this sense, far more restricted. It simply permits the exploited to better determine what unites and what divides them, what runs in the direction of their constitution into a predominant and historically revolutionary force. All it provides is strategic concepts.

Chapter Six
The Start of the Exposition and Its Development

In the course of the conceptual development that has led us from value to labour-power and surplus-value, from the structure to its tendency, the question of the economic-political articulation that I have brought out displays at each stage the relationship between the status of the *categories* and the status of the *exposition* that orders the system of categories and in this way prescribes their pertinence.

The literature concerned with the plan and exposition of *Capital* deals above all with the relationship of this to the Hegelian model. It was, indeed, by drawing support from the Hegelian method that Marx managed to produce his theory, reworking the categorical field that he borrowed (or believed he borrowed) from Ricardo. This is the heart of the problem. It is necessary though, in my view, before dealing in the next chapter with the Hegel-Marx relationship as a whole, to proceed to a deeper study of two key questions: that of the *initial moment* of the exposition, corresponding to Part One of Volume One, and that of the transition from this initial moment to the second moment that forms the subject of Part Two – the *'transition to capital'*.

In each case, I shall follow the origin of Marx's texts in two stages. The first of these comprises the *Grundrisse* and the *'Urtext "Zur Kritik"'*,[1] the second

---

[1] [This 'Original Version' of *A Contribution to the Critique of Political Economy*, written

the *Contribution to the Critique of Political Economy* and *Capital*. I shall show how, in the two first versions, a particular definition of the initial moment as one of 'simple circulation' goes together with a specific conception of the transition to the second, that of a dialectical transition; and that the rejection of this in the later versions was bound up with a redefinition (which amounted to a rectification) of the object of each of these moments. In sum, therefore, the development of the system will appear as the correlate of a distancing movement from a certain recourse to the model of Hegel's *Logic*.

This demonstration seems necessary for a number of reasons. Firstly, because the work of the Althusserian school, which gave decisive indications in this direction, focused above all on the break between the young Marx and the Marx of maturity. Now, the first genuinely 'mature' exposition of the capitalist mode of production, that of the *Grundrisse* – 'mature' in the sense that it correctly articulates the question of surplus-value to its basis, value, and moreover to the transformed form of this, the price of production – remains largely enveloped in the forms of Hegelian philosophy, and is seen for this very reason, by several interpreters, as the 'richest' moment of Marx's thought.[2] This hindsight has also been fuelled by a number of works, especially since the 1960s, that have analysed and emphasised the Hegelian matrix in the *Grundrisse* and the signs of its persistence in *Capital*.[3] Finally and more recently,[4] a current has emerged that in seeking to release *Capital* from the Ricardian positivism that allegedly threatens it, proposes a return to the *Grundrisse*, in the conviction that the dialectic of this text offers the best chance for an authentic science of history.

1. The question of the initial moment of *Capital*

One of the most difficult problems that Marx had to face was precisely that of defining his point of departure. I propose to analyse here how Marx gradually overcame certain flagrant ambiguities that the earlier versions display (though even in *Capital* itself they leave some significant survivals),

---

in August–November 1858, is appended to the German edition of the *Grundrisse* (Marx 1974b, pp. 871–947), and cited from there.]

[2] Negri 1979.

[3] Cf. Reichelt 1970 and the works cited by D'Hondt and Texier, among others.

[4] Denis 1980.

aspects that are aberrant in relation to the general theory at work there. These incoherences follow from the interference between certain a priori conceptions of the theoretical order, borrowed from Hegel's *Logic*, and the particular constraints of the 'specific logic of the specific object'.

This interference, in my view, led to two major anomalies and contradictions, which I shall discuss in turn. On the one hand, the tendency to define the point of departure as that of the 'surface', and hence see the development of the exposition as a procedure *'from the surface down'*. On the other hand and more seriously, to relegate from Part One determinations that essentially belong there, that of the 'law of value' and that of 'competition', and then define this exposition as a route *'up to the surface'*. There are two conceptions involved here that form 'epistemological obstacles', at least in part obscuring the object of *Capital* and the status of its categories.

1.i *Preliminary remark: reaching the starting point*

The *1844 Manuscripts* not only fail to address the question of the starting point, but do not contain any significant fragment corresponding to Part One, i.e. no moment more 'abstract' than that of capital. The sequence from 'commodity relations' to 'capitalist relations' does not yet exist. The 'Comments on James Mill', written the same year, develop the same discourse (of the 'alienation' type), this time on the commodity relationship itself, without the articulation of this to the capitalist relationship being brought out. In these two texts, moreover, the category of 'private property' denotes both things indifferently. We are faced here with a nebulous beginning in which the polarity of money and capital is as yet indicated only faintly.

The same can still be said of a subsequent stage of development. In 1847, Marx proclaimed in *The Poverty of Philosophy* his adhesion to the 'Ricardian theory of value' in terms of labour-time.[5] In 'Wage Labour and Capital' (1849), however, his first systematic presentation of the capitalist production process, the category of value does not yet occupy the initial position one would then expect: it is presented only in the second section.[6] The first section, on the contrary, deals with what Marx calls the 'first question': *'What are wages? How*

---

[5] Marx 1976b, pp. 121 ff.
[6] Marx 1977a, p. 205.

are they determined?'[7] A great distance separates this presentation from that of a later popular booklet, *Wages, Price and Profit* of 1865, which finally displays a mastery of the system. Here, we read, on the contrary, that 'the first question we have to put is: What is the *value* of a commodity? How is it determined?'[8] In the meantime, Marx had written the *Grundrisse*, the main contribution of which is precisely the explicit articulation of value and surplus-value essential to the constitution of his theory.

And yet, in the investigations that make up the *Grundrisse*, this essential discovery is not immediately presented: it is only at the end of the discussion that the beginning is set in place. The first chapter, in fact, is presented as the 'chapter on money'. After a brief initial reference to the definition of commodity-value by labour-time, Marx sticks exclusively to a systematic analysis of the essence of money and its three functions: measurement, means of exchange, and material representative of the commodity. It is only gradually that he perceives the necessity of preceding this with a chapter devoted to value: while still at work on the *Grundrisse*, he assigns this chapter on money second place, writing at the head of it: 'II Kapital vom Geld'. Finally, on the last page of the draft, he introduces and embarks on a new first chapter headed '(1) Value':

> This whole section to be brought forward. The first category in which bourgeois wealth presents itself is that of the *commodity*. The commodity itself appears as unity of two aspects. It is *use value* ... [and] [v]ehicle of exchange value.[9]

This is, in substance, the same formulation found in the opening lines of both the *Critique* and *Capital*. This final page of the *Grundrisse* thus attests to the completion of the construction of the theory: Marx has at last conceived its beginning.

We can remark how the successive plans sketched in 1857 and 1858 illustrate this development. Thus, money, not mentioned in the first plan of September 1857,[10] initially occupies first place in this version. But a second plan of November 1857 already links it to exchange-value as object of the first

---

[7] Marx 1977a, p. 198; Marx's emphasis.
[8] Marx 1973d, p. 48.
[9] Marx 1973c, p. 881; Marx's emphases.
[10] Marx 1973c, p. 109.

section.[11] Then, in the letter to Lassalle of 11 March 1858, there appears the sequence: '1. Value, 2. Money, 3. Capital', which is found again in the index of June 1858.[12] Finally, in a letter to Engels of 20 November 1858, Marx proposes the headings: '1. Commodity. 2. Money or circulation. 3. Capital.'

The realisation of the necessity of 'starting with the commodity', however, did not remove all ambiguity. Indeed, two inadequate procedures were subsequently developed.

1.ii *The procedure 'from the surface down'*

The first ambiguity consisted in the tendency to consider that the right procedure was 'from the surface to the inner connection'.

This interpretation is very widespread, and found in some very different authors.[13] It is also found in those economists, like Kôzô Uno, who present Part One of *Capital* as a theory of circulation.[14]

It can clearly be characterised as 'ambiguous' only with regard to a certain idea of the 'legitimate' beginning, or the 'legitimate' status of the initial Part. And I see such a legitimate problematic as gradually asserting itself and being clearly proclaimed in *Capital*. It makes the object of Part One the definition of the commodity relationship in general, as a unity of *production* and *circulation*. It treats this relationship as an 'abstract sphere' of capitalist relations, corresponding to a more general level than that specific to bourgeois society, which is introduced in Part Two. This is what is still lacking in the earlier versions.

1.ii.a *Ambiguities of the* Grundrisse *and the 'Original Version' of the* Critique
As against the precept affirmed in the Preface to the *Critique*, which maintains that the scientific method proceeds from the abstract to the concrete, the *Grundrisse*, even though inspired by this precept, at the same time treats the most abstract moment as an element of the 'surface'. This tendency marks the exposition at several levels.

---

[11] Marx 1973c, p. 227.
[12] Marx 1973a, p. 855.
[13] Colletti 1976, p. 130; Theunissen 1975, p. 107; Steinvorth 1977, pp. 12–17; Meiners 1980, p. 243, etc.
[14] Uno 1980, pp. 1–18.

The text of the *Grundrisse* ('Notebook 1') actually begins very curiously. Not with a presentation of the initial categories, but with a long critique of utopian socialism in the course of which these categories emerge and are gradually asserted. This debate would seem to be well suited to organising the presentation around the question of the market (and the category of *commodity*) as a structure of both circulation and *production*. And yet, this is not the case: the object analysed is *money*. Commodity production only appears in the background, as the basis for the existence of money: it is not studied for itself.

Subsequently, however, in the section that deals with the transformation of money into capital, Marx explicitly develops money as the articulation of circulation (the 'chapter on money') and production (the 'chapter on capital').[15] The same idea is expressed in the fragments on the plan that are presented further on.[16]

In short, the theme of commodity production as such, which is an underlying presence that breaks through here and there (for example when Marx describes the 'division of labour'),[17] is obscured by the major organisational scheme according to which the first part of the exposition is devoted simply to circulation, and does not as yet deal with capital.

The first justification that Marx gives for this choice is a *historical* one: the first things exchanged were the surpluses produced in pre-commodity conditions, and it was only later on that the laws of exchange became the actual laws of production.[18] This historicist argument was abandoned in *Capital*, and not without reason. For things produced in a non-commodity fashion do not adequately correspond to the 'concept' of commodity (the object of the exposition), even if there is exchange. Marx seeks here to justify a theoretical process conceived in this way (1: circulation, 2: capital) in terms of the idea that the historical development of exchange 'leads to capital',[19] which then figures as the form of production adequate to commodity circulation. This construction is no more than a retrospective projection on history, and quite suspect as an order of theoretical development.

---

[15] Marx 1973c, pp. 225 ff.
[16] Marx 1973c, p. 320.
[17] Marx 1973c, pp. 171–2; cf. 'Original Version' of the *Critique*, Marx 1974b, p. 904.
[18] Marx 1973c, p. 226; 'Original Version', Marx 1974b, pp. 921–2.
[19] 'Original Version', Marx 1974b, p. 922.

This is indicated in the second justification, which this time is methodological:

> This still presents itself even on the surface of developed society as the directly available world of commodities. But by itself, it points beyond itself towards the economic relations which are posited as relations of production. The internal structure of production therefore forms the second section . . .[20]

This argument makes the 'surface' of *bourgeois* society the point of departure of the exposition. Marx has in mind here a 'Hegelian' plan ordered not historically but from abstract to concrete, and interprets this as a procedure moving from a *surface* sphere [*Oberfläche*], that of circulation, to a an *inner* sphere, that of production.[21] But nothing is less evident. For what particular reason requires that the most 'abstract' moment should also be the most 'superficial'?

1.ii.b *The rectification in* Capital
Capital finally brought a very clear response to this question, which put an end to the ambiguities of the 1857 draft.

It is sufficient to consider the organisation of Part One to assess the extent of the clarification effected. The title of this is 'Commodities and Money'. Not only does it discuss the commodity before speaking of money, but it deals with commodity *production* (Chapter 1, Sections 1 and 2) before analysing the value form as *exchange-value* (Section 3, 'The Value-Form, or Exchange-Value'). Exchange and circulation appear later, in Chapters 2 and 3. In short, Part One appears from the start as dealing with commodity production in general, or rather with the 'commodity relationship' as unity of a structure of production and circulation.

If we examine the terms in which Marx retrospectively defines the object of Part One (at the start of Part Two), we can also note how circulation is linked here to production.[22] Very significantly, too, what the 'Original Version' of the *Critique* calls the law of 'simple circulation'[23] is renamed in *Capital* the law of 'commodity production'.[24]

---

[20] Marx 1973c, p. 227.
[21] '[D]ie innere Gliederung der Produktion': Marx 1974b, p. 139.
[22] Marx 1976a, p. 247.
[23] Marx 1974b, p. 903.
[24] Marx 1973c, p. 733.

Both the *Critique* and *Capital* begin, it is true, with an almost identical sentence (the repetition of which emphasises its importance), one that can lend itself to confusion: 'The wealth of societies in which the capitalist mode of production prevails *appears* [*erscheint*] as an immense collection of commodities.'[25] Does not this statement establish us immediately at the level of *appearance* [*Erscheinung*], the surface? But the answer is no, as Marx's procedure here leads immediately from 'exchange-value' that 'appears first of all as the quantitative relation'[26] between commodities, to that which is its foundation but is not apparent: labour-time, abstract labour, socially necessary labour. In short, to the determinations specific to commodity *production* in general. Marx thus moves from 'exchange-value'[27] to value.[28] He certainly takes the first of these categories from ordinary consciousness, and, in this sense, the 'surface', but this is only to immediately criticise it and extract from this critique the category of value. Indeed, Marx precisely goes on to explain in Section 4 ('The Fetishism of the Commodity and Its Secret') how this value relationship rises 'to the surface'. This means, however, that there is nothing 'superficial' about this relationship. Besides, the fact – analysed at length in subsequent chapters of *Capital* – that ideology reads the capitalist relations of production as exchange relations, or that this is the appearance that the latter take 'on the surface', does not make the commodity relations presented in Part One into 'surface phenomena'.

In this sense, *Capital* thus removes all ambiguities; the abstract from which it departs is in no way the 'surface' of society.

1.iii   *The procedure 'up to the surface'*

If *Capital* clearly defines the beginning as the moment of commodity production, and no longer as 'simple circulation' or 'surface', clarity is still far from being attained as to the nature of this initial moment, the most abstract one, and the determinations specific to it.

We touch here on a decisive point, which indicates Marx's uncertainties concerning the object of the category of value. In actual fact, we come up

---

[25] Marx 1976a, p. 125; my emphasis: J.B.
[26] Marx 1976a, p. 126.
[27] Ibid.
[28] Marx 1976a, p. 128.

against an enormous paradox, so much so that it is amazing how this has not previously attracted the attention of Marxists, but has been glimpsed only very tangentially: Part One of Volume One does not include an exposition of the law of value, it is silent on some of the most essential determinations of it, and in particular those pertaining to the level of generality or abstraction specific to this Part, devoted to the commodity, i.e. the 'laws of the market'. Marx in effect postpones the exposition of competition to Volume Three, insisting that until then it is 'not time to speak of it'.

I shall show that there is here, with respect to the theory that Marx actually produces, a profound anomaly, damaging to its development, which follows from the reprise of a movement of Hegelian logic inadequate to the 'special logic of the special object'.

1.iii.a *The content of the category of 'value' employed in* Capital
If we take the category of value as this is presented in Part One – abstracting, on the one hand, from its possible employment outside of commodity relations (for example, under socialism) and, on the other hand, from the determination it receives under capitalism from the fact of its 'transformation into price of production' –, this implies a *precise categorial ensemble* that Marx was already quite familiar with and which is quite commonly found in his writings from 1857 to 1867. This is often asserted apropos capital, but what is involved here is the particular realisation of a more 'abstract' structure, that of the market in general.

On the one hand, there is the couple of 'individual values' and 'value' proper, implicit in Ricardo and explicitly addressed by Marx, in which the former[29] denote the quantities of labour employed by each individual exchanging producer (or particular capital), while the latter, still here called 'natural value', 'market value [*Marktwert*]'[30] or 'social value',[31] denotes the *quantity of labour necessary on average*. In this sense, the law of the determination of value by labour-time, and 'the immanent laws of capitalist production' in general, 'assert themselves as the coercive laws of competition'.[32]

---

[29] Marx 1969, pp. 211–13, etc.
[30] Ibid.; Marx 1981, p. 273.
[31] Marx 1976a, p. 434.
[32] Marx 1976a, p. 433.

On the other hand, there is the couple of 'value' and 'market price', inherited under this name from the Smithian tradition, in which the latter denotes the results of fluctuations in supply and demand. This concerns *competition between branches of industry*, or more precisely the general confrontation between all producers in commodity-producing society.

The *concept* of value, its definition by socially necessary labour-time, thus owes its pertinence here to the *law* of value understood as the law of the market. This asserts itself in the connection between these two aspects of competition among private producer-exchangers free in their choices of production and exchange, through which, in the market structure, *socialisation of labour* is effected, i.e. the appropriate distribution of activities and compulsion to labour. This is the particular mode of articulation that ties value and use-value, constituting the *market* system of stimulation and regulation of production. In short, the *concept* of value is inscribed in the *'law' of value*, a *market structure* that implies competition in two forms, within each branch and between branches.

1.iii.b   *The 'law of value' presented in Volume Three*
Now, one of the most surprising paradoxes of the plan of *Capital* is that this famous 'law of value' is officially presented only in Volume Three, more precisely in Part Two, Chapter 10, at the point where Marx undertakes to provide an explanation of the transformation of value into price of production, an explanation in terms of causes that are nothing else than the properties that capital possesses from the fact that it is based on a market structure, in other words on the law of value and the law of *competition* that is inherent to it.

It is only at this late moment of the exposition, on the occasion of a development specific to the theory of capital, that the law of value is presented in the entirety of its constitutive elements, according to the two couples that I indicated above.

Why does Marx refer to the 'law of value' precisely at this point in his exposition, and why does he need such an explicit analysis? The reason is that he intends here, in this Chapter 10, to provide the *explanation* of what in the previous chapter he had given only in tabular form, in other words the transformation of value into price of production. And this explanation is based on the 'law of value' as law of the competitive structure in general. It appears, in my view, as the assertion of the manifestation of this general law of value at a more 'concrete' level of the exposition: *in the same way* that producers spontaneously move into branches where supply is inferior to demand, and price accordingly higher than value, and conversely, and that from this fact value tends to assert itself as the axis of orientation of market prices, in such a way that the labour of the exchanger tends to be 'remunerated' by the product of a labour of the same magnitude, *so too* does the pressure exerted by the flow of capitals directed towards branches in which profit is higher than average determine the equality of rates of profit between branches, the equal 'remuneration' of all capitals engaged in exchange. In sum, therefore, it is the 'law of value' that decrees the competitive structure, as matrix of equalisation of rates of profit. We can thus understand why this law finds its necessary place at this point, at the moment when what has to be explained is the law of competition under capitalism. But it seems, at the same time, that this appears here only by way of a reminder, in order to present the particular form that it displays at this level of analysis. It remains therefore to determine the logical place of the question of competition in the general order of the exposition.

1.iii.c   *The 'law of value' presented in Part Four of Volume One*
If we go back through *Capital* with a view to seeking a previous place where the question of competition emerges, we come to the important Chapter 12 of Volume One, which provides the theoretical argument for the whole of Part Four devoted to relative surplus-value, in which Marx presents the principles of the capitalist's practice in the competition within his branch: to increase productivity by the improvement of mechanisation and the organisation of labour, in such a way as to obtain an 'extra' or 'differential' surplus-value in relation to his competitors.

Now, there are two reasons for surprise here. On the one hand, this couple 'extra surplus-value/relative surplus-value' that occupies an absolutely central place in the theory was only recognised by Marx at a very late stage. It does not yet appear either in the *Grundrisse*,[33] nor in the *1861–3 Manuscripts*, which present the first systematic draft of the future Part Four[34] without referring

---

[33] Marx 1973c, pp. 341–64.
[34] Marx and Engels 1988a, pp. 233–52.

to 'extra' surplus-value, nor again in *Theories of Surplus-Value*, even though this tackles the question of relative surplus-value at many points. It does not figure either in *Wages, Price and Profit*. On the other hand, this question is strangely overlooked by the subsequent Marxist tradition, as expressed by the fact that even today, many presentations either ignore it or travesty it in various ways, whereas it is a key point in the interpretation of the theory, a point at which the articulation between the 'individual' moment and the global moment of the class relationship is defined.

'Extra surplus-value is a variety of relative surplus-value,' says the *Dictionnaire économique et social*.[35] In the same sense, B. Marx defines it as 'another way of producing surplus-value, which can be equated with that of relative surplus-value in that it is bound up with the increase in productivity, but at the level of the individual firm rather than that of society as a whole'.[36] This is an empiricist approach that adds together heterogeneous categories which the theory defines by a systematic relationship. Lipietz offers a more satisfactory presentation of this relationship, but by modifying its place and function in the system.[37] He introduces the category after the study of accumulation, though Marx places it logically at the start of Part Four of Volume One, as a prerequisite of the accumulation mechanism. Lipietz characterises the presentation made in this Part as premature: 'Marx cannot resist the pleasure'[38] of presenting competition. Dallemagne neglects this articulation. He does not see that Marx deals with this question, which he believes is 'left hanging', and can thus write that 'the transition from formal subsumption to real subsumption is not organic'.[39] In actual fact, the object of Chapter 12 is nothing else than the principled exposition of this organic development, an exposition that precedes examination of the historical circumstances in which it is effected. Valier also takes up the idea that Volume One deals with 'capital in general', without the intervention of 'several capitals'.[40] The article on '*survaleur*' in the *Dictionnaire critique du marxisme* also deals with relative surplus-value without mentioning extra surplus-value.[41] Finally, according to

---

[35] Bouvier-Adam et al. 1975, p. 501.
[36] B. Marx 1979, p. 57.
[37] Lipietz 1979, pp. 270–4.
[38] Lipietz 1979, p. 270.
[39] Dallemagne 1978, pp. 89 & 90.
[40] Valier 1982, p. 25.
[41] Labica 1982.

the *Marx-Engels Begriffslexikon*, the capitalist who realises extra surplus-value 'does at the individual level what capital does at the global level with the production of relative surplus-value':[42] here again, no mention of the organic relationship between the two things.

We can understand now why Chapter 12 needs a closer examination. I shall dwell on the central section of the text,[43] which constitutes the hinge between the exposition of relative surplus-value[44] and that of extra surplus-value,[45] i.e. between a global problematic and a competitive individual problematic, and accordingly occupies a key theoretical position:

> The general and necessary tendencies of capital must be distinguished from their forms of appearance [*Erscheinungsformen*].
>
> While it is not our intention here to consider the way in which the immanent laws [*Tendenzen*] of capitalist production manifest themselves in the external movement [*Äussern*] of the individual capitalists, assert themselves as the coercive laws of competition, and therefore enter into the consciousness of the individual capitalist as the motives which drive him forward, this much is clear: a scientific analysis of competition is possible only if we can grasp the inner nature of capital, just as the apparent motions of the heavenly bodies are intelligible only to someone who is acquainted with their real motions, which are not perceptible to the senses. Nevertheless, for the understanding [*zum Verständnis*] of the production of relative surplus-value, and merely on the basis of the results already achieved, we may add the following remark.[46]

The exposition of extra surplus-value follows.

This text is surprising in a number of ways, and should be read in the double relationship that it maintains, on the one hand, with the *subsequent* moment that it denotes as being necessarily that of competition, and on the other hand, the *antecedent* moment from where this concept of competition actually derives.

---

[42] Lotter 1984, p. 231.
[43] Marx 1976a, p. 433.
[44] Marx 1976a, pp. 429–32.
[45] Marx 1976a, pp. 434–8.
[46] Marx 1976a, p. 433; cf. Marx 1973a, p. 335.

As far as the *subsequent* relationship is concerned (Volume Three), we should note first of all that Marx's awkwardness is clear: he tries to resist the necessity forced upon him of dealing here with competition, but despite his denials and references to a later moment, he ends up well and truly engaged in a full exposition of the principles of competition within the branch.

He maintains, moreover, that 'scientific analysis of competition presupposes' that of the 'intimate nature of capital'. Now the exposition that immediately follows shows, on the contrary, that the 'intimate nature' of capital (in the event, the historical tendency to relative surplus-value) can only be understood *on the basis of* competition (here in the form of the struggle for extra surplus-value), and this is also why the French edition which in this passage speaks not just of 'understanding' but of 'better understanding [*mieux comprendre*]', is faulty, since what is actually involved is simply to 'understand' relative surplus-value, in other words, to analyse the mechanism by which it is constituted, a mechanism situated in the competitive relationship of extra surplus-value.

Finally, Marx writes that the 'apparent movement' is intelligible only if the 'real movement' is known. What he is actually getting ready to explain is a tendency designated as 'real', i.e. relative surplus-value, which is perhaps not all that 'unapparent' (Marx, as we have noted, emphasises that Ricardo, who did not understand absolute surplus-value, did indeed see relative surplus-value), from the standpoint of a movement called apparent, i.e. extra surplus-value, which is equally real. It is simply that these two movements do not have the same kind of appearance, since they do not have the same kind of reality.

The thesis of this chapter, which is that of the whole of Part Four, can be summed up in one phrase: there is in capitalism a *historical tendency* to relative surplus-value, in other words to a relative decline in the value of labour-power resulting from an increase in productivity in the branches producing wage goods, because there is a *constant tension* among capitalists in *all* branches, arising from the fact that none of them has any future unless they succeed in raising their productivity as rapidly as their competitors. To put it another way, the competitive relationship between capitalists, far from being a subsequent category whose natural place would be Volume Three, is involved right from the start in explaining the global movement of capital, the production of surplus-value.

If we now look backward in a logical sense, we see that this theory of extra surplus-value is based, as the text here says, 'on the results already reached in the course of our investigations'. Marx remains imprecise as to what these 'results' might be; but they are necessarily of two kinds. On the one hand, there is the general theory of surplus-value, since the comparative fate of various competitors is analysed in the study of this. On the other hand, however, there is a whole register of concepts that Marx has not had to use in the theory of surplus-value, and that arise directly from Part One, i.e. from the theory of value: 'individual versus social value', 'simple labour versus complex'.

For individual and social value,[47] this involves, in an explicit terminology, a couple expressly implied in the basic exposition of value, which denotes this as determined by the 'labour time which is necessary on an average, or in other words is socially necessary'[48] in average conditions of skill, intensity and productivity. In Chapter 12, Marx thus gives a name – 'competition' – to something that has already been explained in Chapter 1. It seems remarkable to me, however, that this name has taken so long to disclose, and moreover that Volume Three tackles the same question with a different terminology. We might think that the difficulty of naming the thing, shown by the delay and the variation in appellation, is not unconnected with the difficulty that Marx has in defining the status of competition within his theory.

As for simple and complex labour,[49] these are also concepts that arise *directly* from the theory of value.[50] Directly, that is, without experiencing the intermediate re-elaboration specific to the theory of capital. For this couple (which, as we have seen, does not refer here to level of skill), denotes, in the competitive relationship of the 'law of value', the *inequality of productivity* that becomes decisive in capitalism and defines the field of extra surplus-value.

If this is the case, the category of extra surplus-value must be defined as the application to the theory of surplus-value of certain constitutive elements of the theory of value, more precisely those that define the competitive situation within a branch, as implied by this abstract market structure to which the 'law of value' in the specific sense refers. This reference to *competition*, far

---

[47] Marx 1976a, p. 434.
[48] Marx 1976a, p. 129.
[49] Marx 1976a, p. 435.
[50] Marx 1976a, p. 135.

from being a 'paedagogic' anticipation in relation to the moment where it needs to be introduced into the theory, as Marx suggests in the text I have analysed, is actually in its necessary place here, and, what is more, is simply a re-actualisation, at the level of the specifically capitalist relationship, of constitutive categories of the social relationship of value.[51]

1.iii.d   *The censorship of the categories of competition and the market in Chapter 1 of Volume One*

We cannot but be surprised by the fact that Marx, elsewhere so careful about the proper order of categories, does not develop systematically in Part One, and right in its first chapter that deals with the commodity, the structure of the market as a structure of competition.

As regards the first attempts at an exposition of this, I have shown Marx's difficulty in defining his point of departure. This also bears on the present aspect.

In the *Critique*, where Marx systematically develops the determinations of his initial concept, the commodity, there is no reference to the market structure except indirectly through the mention of 'necessary labour'.[52] But even this is badly articulated. For the category of 'general' labour, an epistemological obstacle, applies here, and very indistinctly at that, to both necessary labour and abstract labour. In effect, the schema for the transformation of individual labour into 'general' labour is drawn on to denote two different relationships: 1) the fact that individual labours are counted only as regards average (socially necessary) labour-time; 2) the fact that particular labours are compared between each other with respect to the abstract labour that they contain. The confusion is particularly marked in the fact that categories such as that of 'average', 'simple' or 'more complicated' labour are linked here to that of abstract labour and not that of socially necessary labour.[53]

Capital is far more clear on the categories of abstract and necessary labour, and also includes two developments bearing on the competitive structure.

---

[51] The analysis presented here is an alternative to recent readings (for example, Eldred et al. 1984, pp. 61–74), which, by making value less a category of production than one of exchange, reject the theory of the 'labour-form' and oppose to it that of the 'value-form'.

[52] Or even outside the systematic exposition; Marx 1971, p. 66.

[53] Marx 1971, p. 31.

Marx presents here, in the very first section, the problem of competition within the branch, by defining socially necessary labour as that performed 'with the average degree of skill and intensity', in the 'conditions of production normal for a society'.[54] And he immediately gives the example of competition between hand and machine weaving. Moreover, in the exposition of money as means of circulation, he introduces the question of the market,[55] but only from the standpoint of the establishment of a market price distinct from value, without indicating that this tends to modify the allocation of labour between different branches –, in short, from the standpoint of exchange rather than production. These are the only two passages in Part One that deal with the market structure as a competitive structure. It seems remarkable to me that at no point does he explicitly tackle this question, and even when it is touched on incidentally, this is expressly in the absence of not only the terms 'competition' and 'market' that are required by the context, but also the pairs of categories needed for the exposition: 'value/individual value', 'value/market price', which denote respectively competition within a branch and competition between branches. In other words the categorial ensemble with which value is defined at the general level of commodity production, which is that of Part One. It is impossible not to see here an anomaly, which we need to explain.

1.iii.e *Note: a criticism of Duménil's interpretation*

Duménil (1978) starts exactly from the problem I have mentioned here: Part One of Volume One does not mention the 'law of value'. He notes, however, that the *Critique* speaks of the 'concept' of value. And, on this basis, he develops the idea that the law is precisely nothing more than this concept. To present the concept is to present the law. To maintain that 'value is determined by socially necessary labour-time' is by that very token to maintain 'the internal and necessary connection [*inneren und notwendigen Zusammenhang*]' between the elements indicated. Against which, Duménil opposes an 'external relationship' between value and productive force, a relationship external to value and political economy. He means by this that the question of productive force would relate to a different order, that of use-value, of concrete labour,

---

[54] Marx 1971, p. 129.
[55] Marx 1971, p. 213.

which would be external to 'political economy' and belong to the realm of contingency, to the non-theorisable.

This analysis, which provides the guiding thread of an enormous and often stimulating study, strikes me as absolutely erroneous. Use-value is certainly 'external' to value, since it is a different basic concept, but it is not external to the 'law of value', and thus no more so to 'political economy', since this law concerns the commodity as unity of use-value and value. It is by virtue of the ensemble 'commodity/use-value/value' that a dynamic theoretical space exists, an explanatory model.

There is really nothing to be gained from a 'law of value' lacking any mention of use-value. For, if this 'law' possesses a definite content, it is that it defines the relations between competing producers capable of producing different quantities of a given product or use-value in the same time. 'Socially necessary labour-time' implies differential productivity giving rise to an average. This is not 'external to the law': it is something without which there is no object at all, since, if it is to govern anything, this law is from the start a law of *production* and not just of exchange. It is not possible to distinguish, as Duménil does, between law of exchange, law of value, and law of commodity production. In *Capital*, this is one and the same thing: a dynamic principle of production, a particular type of organisation of production (commodity production), i.e. of stimulation, regulation, co-ordination and orientation of production. It has no content except the dynamic relationship between value and use-value as defined by a market situation. And for this reason, too, the question of use-value and productivity cannot be relegated to the 'contingent' and 'non-theorisable', outside of political economy. Duménil's reading transforms the theory of *Capital* into pure formalism on the side of the theory of value, interpreted in strictly tautological terms, and into pure empiricism on the side of use-value, presented as mere contingency. A theory of this kind no longer has any object.

1.iii.f *Proposed interpretation*

The following question is then raised. If the law of value rightly occupies, as law of the market and effect of the competitive structure, the initial place in the exposition of the theory of the capitalist mode of production, why does Marx relegate it to Volume Three? Why, when he invokes it in Part Four of

Volume One, does he excuse himself as if it was not in its proper place there? Why does he censor so strictly its explicit appearance in Part One?

A first explanation could be that, in the theory of capital as a whole, he is concerned to extract an initial moment at which 'competition' does not intervene. This orientation is affirmed in the original project of dealing with 'capital in general' before tackling the 'competitive' relationship between capitals, in the sense in which this relationship gives rise to the transformation of values into production prices. It goes together with the rediscovery in 1857 of the Hegelian method of procedure from abstract to concrete, which was what enabled Marx to escape from Ricardianism. Ricardo, for his part, found himself almost immediately, in Section 4 of the first chapter of his *Principles*, in this 'space of competition between capitals', that of values modified as a function of organic composition. In this way, he lacked what alone could ensure a certain abstraction from competition: analysis of capitalist production at the most abstract level of value, the theoretical space of Volume One of *Capital*, with its specific categorical development, which makes it possible to present the central articulation of the system, the initial division of value produced into wages and surplus-value, along with the major tendencies of this structure of production. In short, it is the abstraction from competition, in this precise sense, which makes it possible to elaborate the global relationship between capital and labour.

This justification, however, comes up against a double limit.

On the one hand, the legitimate reasons that led Marx to abstract from capitalist competition in Parts Two and Three of *Capital*, resulting in the creation of this non-Ricardian space, that of the capital/labour relationship in general, apparently led him to neglect his method of exposition from abstract to concrete, according to which the set of categories pertaining to commodity production in general, and especially *competition in general* (and between branches), should have been presented as a determination of the market. In this light, a surprising misconstrual of the nature of the starting point can be read in the proposition that opens the exposition of exchange in the first edition of *Capital*:

> The commodity is an immediate [*unmittelbar*] unity of use-value and exchange value.... This contradiction must develop as soon as the commodity is no longer considered analytically, as it has been up till now, sometimes from

the standpoint of use-value, sometimes from that of exchange value, but effectively [*wirklich*] related to other commodities as a 'whole'.[56]

In fact, Marx forgets here that commodity *production* cannot be presented in terms of such successive changes in standpoint, but only from the start as an 'effective' unity of the two. The dialectical false windows [*unmittelbar/wirklich*], which, here again, are epistemological obstacles, hide the structure or prevent it from being adequately developed as a market structure with the totality of its 'immediate' determinations and their relationships, including that of competition.

On the other hand, the project of abstracting entirely from capitalist competition throughout Volume One comes up against a limit, since this notion is implicit in the exposition of relative surplus-value as articulated to that of extra surplus-value, and in the particular form of competition within the branch. I can now add that what really breaks down in the process of elaboration of *Capital*, beyond the articulation of 'capital in general' and 'multiple capitals', is the very idea of 'many', which disappears because it divides into two kinds of multiplicity corresponding to two aspects of competition, within the branch and between branches. It turns out that the couple of general and multiple, borrowed from the philosophical tradition, which Marx has resorted to a priori for heuristic purposes, does not yield what might be expected of it, since the 'multiple', i.e. the relationship between individual capitals, is immediately of two kinds in this theoretical object, with each of these having its own proper moment of introduction: one in Volume One, Part Four, the other in Volume Three, Part Two. In short, the specific logic of the specific object that is capital does not call for the relegation of competition to Volume Three, but rather a more complex distribution of this 'determination'.

The main inconvenience of this 'omission' from Marxist literature on the subject of extra surplus-value is that it goes in the direction of a mythical interpretation of the theory, precisely for lack of articulation between the individual moment and the global class relationship. 'Competition' as invoked here, far from leading us towards the 'surface of things', is located at the very

---

[56] Marx 1980, p. 44.

heart of the concept: the capitalist system constitutes a particular structure of integration of individual interests (here of capitalist individuals). There is no 'explanation' outside of this.

In actual fact, it is not relative surplus-value (the 'inner connection') that explains extra surplus-value (the 'surface'); it is not the tendency to accumulation (increase in productivity, machinery, etc.) that competition translates into reality; but rather the reverse.

For the system only has a *tendency* (to relative surplus-value, to increased productivity, to accumulation) from the fact of its *structure*. This involves *simultaneously* the relationship between classes, between the opposed elements of classes (industrialist and wage-earners), and between elements within each class, in this case the relationship of competition between capitalists. Only the structure can explain its tendencies, not vice versa. This is what the theme of 'essence' and 'surface' partially hides, tending to decompose elements of the tendency into the essence and elements of the structure into the surface.

The references to the tendencies of the system and the interests of the ruling class would be purely metaphysical if they were not linked to the question of the interests of the 'individuals' who compose the system, and the compulsions that weigh on them as individuals – individual capitals 'personified', as Marx says, by their holders. Capitalism possesses no general tendency unless this is connected with what moves individuals, with the structure of interests and compulsions that the competitive relationship defines. This is the object of the theory of extra surplus-value, which defines what constitutes the main dynamic of the capitalist structure, that through which it has a tendency, i.e. relative surplus-value. This determination is just as 'inner', 'essential' and 'primary' as the general class articulation that makes the bourgeoisie bearer of a project and common interest, thus of a general 'tendency'.

It is against this structural foundation of competition that modifications intervene (monopolies, economic role of the state), their development deriving from the tendencies of this structure. Marx basically explains how and why under capitalism *individuals* produce and organise production, exploit and accumulate, within what limits and contradictions. He explains this by inscribing the individual moment at the heart of his explanation, and not on some kind of 'surface'.

The reference to competition that forms the basis of Marx's theorisation (for, if there is censorship, what is censored is the presupposition of this discourse) is what gives it its dated character. And it goes without saying that capitalism has reached a stage at which quite different principles of regulation are now at work. But the same methodological attitude that links these tendencies to structures is still appropriate here, with these structures depicting the articulation of social forms to the individual positions that they imply, along with the interests, purposes, compulsions and contradictions that characterise them.

2. The 'transition to capital'

The articulation of Part One to the rest of the work is more important than any other since it traces the dividing line between what is and what is not specific to the capitalist mode of production (even if this is the only one to be completely commodified).

Marx provides four successive versions of this transition:

- that of the *Grundrisse*;[57]
- that of the 'Original Version' of the *Critique*;[58]
- that of the *1861–3 Manuscripts*;[59]
- finally, that of *Capital*, with changes between the first edition and the second and French editions.[60]

Just as with the nature of the 'initial moment', the break here was effected after the 'Original Version'. I shall accordingly formulate a rigorous critique of this text (and of the *Grundrisse*) on the basis of *Capital*. If I am right in doing so, it is not just because Marx happened to prefer this final text, but because it is possible to show how *Capital* proposes a construction in which the elements are logically arranged into a coherent theory, in the light of which the earlier expositions appear relatively artificial, revealing themselves according to the 'obligatory figures' of Hegelian logic, deployed a priori in an almost experimental manner. This exercise, however fruitful in many ways, also shows its limit, its inadequacy to the 'special logic of the special object'. And these preparatory texts have, in return, something precious to offer, in

---

[57] Marx 1973c, pp. 203–75.
[58] In Marx 1974b, pp. 871–947.
[59] Marx and Engels 1988a, pp. 9–171.
[60] See pp. 247–69 in the English edition.

that they clearly display, as if enlarged under the microscope, certain distortions that persist in *Capital*.

The analysis presented here thus goes diametrically against the interpretation proposed by Denis, who sees in the *Grundrisse* and above all in the 'Original Version' of the *Critique* the most fertile moment in Marx's analysis, where he is 'within an ace of revealing the authentic foundations of a genuine science of the commodity economy'.[61]

2.i *Critique of the* Grundrisse's *dialectic*

In the *Grundrisse*,[62] and again in the 'Original Version', Marx seeks a dialectical transition from money to capital. He attempts to base this on a movement located within the development of money itself and its functions. In its first function, as 'measure of value', it possesses only an ideal existence. In the second, that of 'means of circulation', depicted as C–M–M–C, it can only exist in the form of monetary sign. But, in its third function, that of 'money as money', figured M–C–C–M, it possesses a material existence adequate to the necessities of hoarding, payment, and international exchange, and it now presents two analogies with capital: it becomes an 'end in itself', it acquires 'an independent existence outside of circulation'.[63] We 'move on' in this way to capital.

This problematic is based on an erroneous representation of the 'chapter on money' as dealing with 'circulation', as opposed to the 'chapter on capital' which would deal with 'production'. I shall not dwell on this point here, leaving a critical treatment of it until later. But, remaining in the framework that Marx gives himself here, I simply formulate two fundamental objections concerning this figure M–C–C–M, which Marx sought to make into a principle of dialectical mediation: 1) it does not belong in this 'chapter'; 2) it does not provide any transition to capital.

1.iii.a *M–C–C–M does not belong in the 'chapter on money'*

Marx conceives the transition from the first chapter (circulation) to the second (capital) in terms of a dialectical movement in which the configuration

---

[61] Denis 1980, p. 201.
[62] Marx 1973c, pp. 201–3.
[63] Marx 1973c, p. 203.

M–C–C–M provides the mediation, constituting at the same time the 'final form of money' and the 'first concept of capital', the 'first form in which it appears'.[64] The configuration actually remains a form of simple circulation to the extent that it is formally possible as a sequence of two exchanges, thus *without a change in quantity*. And it is already a form of capital by its 'positive determinations', which make this movement something qualitatively distinct from C–M–M–C, as indicated by the different disposition of terms: money becomes the *end* of the process and *exists* from circulation. 'This movement . . . makes up the formal determination of commerce',[65] the capitalist activity.

This development, however, is completely illegitimate.

First of all, M–C–C–M cannot represent the third function of money. It is impossible to accept the thesis of the *Grundrisse*, explicit in several passages, that depicts the second function, that of means of circulation, as C–M–M–C, and the third function, that requiring its material presence and exercised in hoarding or accumulating,[66] payment,[67] and 'world money'[68] as M–C–C–M. The grand design, to develop the 'syllogism'[69] from money to capital, is readily discernible. It is with this aim in view that the articulation of the second and third functions is twice rehearsed as that of C–M–M–C to M–C–C–M.[70] The problem is that this last formula is quite inadequate to its object. Hoarding aims at money, but is restricted in itself to C–M, if not just appropriation by any means, just . . . M. The other two functions – payment and world money – imply money as mediation, thus C–M–M–C.

In actual fact, M–C–C–M corresponds to one object only, that of exchange, which is, moreover, regularly mentioned as soon as this formula appears.[71] But exchange does not belong in this chapter, even if this is, as the *Grundrisse* presents it, the study of simple 'circulation', since this activity is only given its meaning by the quantitative difference between M and M', i.e. as a specifically capitalist activity. It is impossible to 'isolate' it, as Marx would like, 'in its purely qualitative form', alongside the 'quantitative aspect visible

---

[64] Marx 1973c, p. 253.
[65] Ibid.
[66] Marx 1973c, p. 198.
[67] Marx 1973c, p. 235.
[68] Marx 1973c, p. 213.
[69] Marx 1973c, p. 202.
[70] Marx 1973c, pp. 203, 214–15.
[71] Marx 1973c, pp. 201, 202, 203, 215, 217, 253, etc.

in exchange'.[72] Its qualitative form, in isolation a meaningless behaviour, exists only by way of the quantitative difference itself.

The 'Original Version' takes up afresh this project of displaying in money *qua* money 'the adequate existence of exchange value, the general equivalent existing for itself and persisting in itself'. But it immediately goes on to add that 'the actual movement of the form M–C–M does not exist in simple circulation'.[73] The M–C–M figure of simple circulation is lacking in content [*inhaltlos*]. And the exposition revolves on itself, since Marx does not succeed in reaching his goal, which is that of establishing this form as one also lacking in sense [*Bedeutung*].[74] The only example he offers is that in which exchange only yields in return the money laid out. This can scarcely pass as the quintessence of exchange: the absence of quantitative difference in M–C–M is the suppression of its quality, of its meaning as social relationship.

In short, M–C–C–M (or M–C–M) is not the final form of money, does not correspond to its third function, and has no sense as a figure of 'simple circulation'.

2.iii.b   *M–C–C–M does not offer a 'dialectical' transition to capital*
Marx's attempt includes two distinct and complementary aspects. On the one hand, he anticipates by imposing on simple circulation a capitalist form (M–C–C–M). On the other, he analyses this specifically capitalist process on the basis of categories drawn from simple circulation. This might appear as a moment of mediation between circulation and capital. But it is not a legitimate procedure.

1) Marx artificially makes M–C–C–M stand for both hoarding (thus simple circulation) and exchange (thus capitalism).

Starting from the figure of *accumulating*, in which money is the goal, he maintains that 'this aspect already latently contains its quality as *capital*'.[75] He shows at the same time the *perspectives* opened by this form by virtue of its abstraction: indifference to the particular character of labour,[76] to the

---

[72] Marx 1973c, p. 202.
[73] Marx 1974b, p. 929.
[74] Marx 1974b, p. 930.
[75] Marx 1973c, p. 216; Marx's emphasis.
[76] Marx 1973c, p. 223.

individuality of its possessor, principle of unlimited craving for wealth in general;[77] and the *contradictions* this involves, that of presenting the universal form of wealth in a particular substance,[78] which provides only an imaginary pleasure, that of Midas.[79] The question of the transition to capital is then that of the overcoming of these contradictions (and their realisation at a higher level), in particular the contradiction between use-value and exchange-value, in such a form that its becoming use-value does not abolish its exchange-value and vice versa, and as a result, value is maintained in the continuity of a circuit. This is what Marx sees as being realised by the form M–C–C–M, as found in exchange. In historical terms, it is in exchange that capital finds its 'first form of appearance'.[80] But this is only the 'confirmation' of an order that is essentially conceived in the *Grundrisse* as theoretical.

In actual fact, as we have seen, M–C–C–M introduces something radically new: the concept of capital, of a value that is maintained in a cyclical process. Accumulating is in no way M–C–C–M because it is in no way capital; exchange, as figured by M–C–C–M, is capital. There is no possible mediation: M–C–C–M, being the very form of capital, cannot figure the transition from money to capital.

2) Marx fails in his attempt to make capitalist production dialectically appear simply on the basis of the categories of circulation.

The 'Original Version'[81] presents the most far-reaching analysis: in capital, exchange-value is opposed to use-value in such a way that instead of being simply separated from it in the 'petrified' form of an object without use, as is the case with hoarding, it 'asserts itself' in use-value itself by the 'real negation [*reale Negation*]' of the latter, i.e. its consumption, which is also the act that leads it to its 'active existence', the manifestation of its utility.

Marx apparently reached here the end of the genetic development from money to capital by simple dialectical analysis of the pair of opposites, use-value and exchange-value, that define the commodity. The opposition, first present in the 'price' form, develops then in the 'money' form, and culminates in the higher moment of the negation of use-value, its promotion to 'actual

---

[77] Ibid.
[78] Marx 1973c, p. 218.
[79] Marx 1973c, p. 233.
[80] Marx 1973c, pp. 256–9.
[81] In Marx 1974b, pp. 943–4; cf. also Marx 1973c, pp. 266–73.

existence [*das wirkliche Dasein*]'. A long-awaited moment at which 'use-value as use-value, the consumption of the commodity', 'posits exchange-value', displaying it as value 'in process'.

This brilliant dialectical development is, unfortunately, inconsistent.

First of all, the 'dialectic' rests on a faulty disposition (which *Capital* will correct): 1) simple *circulation*; 2) capitalist *production*. It is this that makes it possible to pass from the 'formal' to the 'actual [*wirklich*]'. It suffices that an initial moment has been posited at which production as yet intervenes only in a 'formal' fashion,[82] i.e. where a law of production linking use-value with exchange-value has not yet asserted itself. But this procedure is untenable, because it is possible to conceive circulation in general (simple circulation) without at the same time conceiving commodity production in general.

It is also necessary to note the misunderstanding about 'consumption', which is already sufficient to destroy the line of argument. What 'consumption' is involved here? Quite clearly, *productive* consumption, as the continuation of the text shows. But this is a restrictive shift in relation to a development remaining at the level of the opposition between exchange-value and use-value. For *non-productive* consumption, consumption in the ordinary sense of the term, is just as much an abolition of use-value that confirms its utility. Marx thus makes an unjustified slippage into productive consumption, in other words, production.

Finally, there is no real dialectical development. What does this 'positing' of exchange-value actually involve? Is it a transfer of the consumed use-value? This might be expected, since the exchange value must find its 'source' in use-value, 'aus ihm herstellen'.[83] In reality, however, there is nothing of the kind, since as Marx makes clear, the negation/confirmation of use-value that posits exchange-value 'is possible only in so far as the commodity is consumed by labour, its consumption appearing as objectification of labour and hence as creation of value'.[84] This last proposition destroys the whole dialectical scaffolding. It maintains, in effect, that it is not the use-value consumed, which has been the object in question up till now, that forms the principle of the positing of value and the promotion of capital as such: it is the introduction of labour as appropriated by capital, labour that valorises capital not to the

---

[82] Marx 1973c, p. 255.
[83] 'Original Version', Marx 1974b, p. 942.
[84] Marx 1974b, p. 943.

extent that it productively consumes use-values that are presented to it in the labour process, but rather that it is itself consumed (more precisely, as a function of the difference between its value and that which its own consumption produces).

This is not a dialectical development of the contradiction, simply an expansion of the framework. Marx adds at this point a new consideration, that of wage-labour, which capsizes the initial schema and produces a new theoretical field, that of capitalist relations proper. What proves to be impossible here is that the transition from one to the other should be at the same time its own development, a dialectical transition. In *Capital*, as we shall see, Marx finds the solution to this.

Colletti, exhuming the critique published by Trendelenburg in 1840, maintains that the secret of the movement of the Hegelian dialectic rests on the interpolation [*Einschiebung*] of a third term drawn from outside, that of experience.[85] It is clear, in any event, that this is indeed the case when Marx's presentation here suddenly introduces the wage-earner. But Colletti's error, which, to my mind, governs his entire interpretation of Marx's work, is to believe that Marx stuck to this dialectical problematic.

2.iii The non-dialectic of Capital

The Marxian conception of the transformation of money into capital undergoes a decisive break in the *Critique*, with *Capital* in this respect only continuing the new orientation. This break is characterised by the withdrawal from Part One of the M–C–M 'form', which now ceases to constitute the mediating figure common to both money (Part One) and capital (Part Two), to become a mere introductory 'formula' to the latter, thus removing from the transition from money to capital any dialectical character.

2.iii.a The disappearance of M–C–M from Part One

The *Critique*, to be sure, still apparently puts forward the thesis of the *Grundrisse* concerning the second function of money, that of 'means of circulation': 'the circulation process comprises two distinct types of circuit', C–M–C and M–C–M. But Marx goes on to add straightaway: 'In this section we are solely concerned

---

[85] Colletti 1984, p. 99.

with the first circuit, that is the one which directly expresses commodity circulation.'[86] And this indicates clearly that the former dialectical problematic has been abandoned: M–C–M is no longer recognised as belonging to this initial moment of the exposition, the most abstract, defined as that of 'the commodity', object of Chapter 1 of the *Critique*. Thus the principle of dialectical mediation disappears, the continuity of the same thing in the transition to something else.

Curiously, the *Critique* still opens its exposition of the 'third function of money' (money as money) with a development devoted to M–C–M.[87] But, here again, the argument stops short, and appears rather as an accidental residue of the procedure of the earlier versions. For, when he comes to the various aspects of this third form, Marx no longer makes any reference to M–C–M, but, on the contrary, characterises hoarding as C–M.[88]

The *1861–3 Manuscripts* recognise that M–C–M has 'nothing in common with hoarding, except that both of these are concerned with exchange-value'.[89] And *Capital* then correctly removes any mention of M–C–M in the exposition of money's third function.[90]

2.iii.b   *M–C–M, a 'form' in the* Grundrisse, *becomes a 'formula' in Part Two of* Capital

The problem in Part Two of *Capital* has a different shape. Here, the form M–C–M is in its proper place. Our comparative examination thus needs to focus on the way this is introduced in the successive versions and the role it plays there, which is no longer that of a 'form' but rather a mere 'formula'.

In this respect, the *1861–3 Manuscripts* are already very close to *Capital*. M–C–M no longer functions as the means of transition to capital, but belongs to it from the very start: 'The money which passes through this movement is *capital*.'[91] There is no longer a genuine continuity from C–M–C to M–C–M, no transition from one to the other.

In *Capital*, C–M–C fills the entire space of simple circulation. This is evident for the third function of money: 'hoarding' is only a temporary interruption

---

[86] Marx 1971, p. 87.
[87] Marx 1971, p. 122.
[88] Marx 1971, p. 127.
[89] Marx and Engels 1988a, p. 18.
[90] Marx 1976a, p. 227.
[91] Marx and Engels 1988a, p. 11; Marx's emphasis.

of the circuit, which money as 'means of payment' and money as 'world money' also describe in their fashion. M–C–M is thus introduced in Chapter 2 without preliminary mention in Chapter 1. The question now arises: where does M–C–M come from?

It should be stressed, once again, that M–C–M is not 'deduced' from Chapter 1, there is no 'genesis' or development from C–M–C to M–C–M. The latter appears as something new, though not entirely so, as its elements M and C have been defined in Chapter 1, just as have its two component relationships M–C and C–M. But this chapter does not offer anything that would make the circuit M–C–M conceivable; indeed, this initially appears as 'without purpose . . . and therefore absurd'.[92] Chapter 1 does not provide any reason for introducing it into the theory.

The object denoted by M–C–M' is introduced here not as a product of the exposition, but as an object already familiar to ordinary consciousness. 'Every day the same story is played out before our eyes':[93] money is accumulated by a process of purchase and sale. M–C–M' thus refers us here to a fact of experience, analogous to that other fact to which Marx appeals at the start of Part One: commodities are exchanged in definite quantitative relationships. And, in the same way that the analysis of Part One leads from the recognition of this quantitative relationship – exchange-value – to its foundation in determination by socially necessary labour-time, i.e. the *concept* of value, so it proceeds here from recognition of the specific sequence that capitalist circulation presents 'before our eyes' to the *concept* that (overcoming the contradiction in the 'formula' offered by experience) provides its explanation, that of surplus-value. The nature of the 'transformation' of money into capital is thus no longer the dialectical one that the 'Original Version' was still searching for. The exposition advances only by way of a new appeal to 'experience' which enables the introduction of new determinations, those of the wage relationship that are brought in to explain this experience.

The argument of Part Two is actually as follows:

> Chapter 4: the 'general formula for capital' is M–C–M', the transition from a given quantity of money to a greater quantity, by way of purchase and sale.

---

[92] Marx and Engels 1988a, p. 10.
[93] Marx 1976a, p. 247.

Chapter 5: this formula is 'contradictory', since the increase is achieved
by a series in which equivalents are exchanged.
Chapter 6: the only possible solution is that a particular commodity
produces more value than it possesses, and only labour-power fulfils
this condition.

We can thus understand the quite particular sense in which *Capital* proceeds
here (as at the start of Part One) from the 'appearance' or surface to the
essence. This is not a *general* movement of the exposition, as is the movement
from abstract to concrete, but an *isolated* intervention located on this major
axis, by which Marx relaunches the forward progress by an appeal to experience
(what we are familiar with through the categories of 'ordinary consciousness',
the notion of 'surface' denoting the correlate of this on the object side), but
then criticises this in the light of the previous categorical results. The progress,
quite justified, is by the addition of new qualities, compatible with the initial
ones but not deduced or developed from them dialectically, qualities moreover
that account for experience.

The status of the 'contradiction' in this development is not hard to grasp.
It is in no way a dialectical one. The contradictory formula M–C–M' does not
form part of the categorical development of the concept. It is indicated as an
ideological form of consciousness. It does not call for 'subsumption [*Aufhebung*]',
but, first of all, correction. A correction located at a certain remove from the
concept, which indicates, at the same time, its function in the social system
and its real contradictions.

All this is emphasised by a remarkable shift in terminology, which seems
to me to have remained unnoticed. In *Capital*, M–C–M' is referred to as a
'formula [*Formel*]' and no longer a 'form [*Form*]', as was still the case in the
1861–3 Manuscripts.[94] The shift is highly significant, especially as it affects the
titles of chapters.[95] Marx could not have put it more clearly that the starting
point here should not be taken in the sense of a form that was already defined
by the theory, but was rather a representation or formulation that had to be
criticised. And it is indeed this formulation that the analysis focuses on to
display its contradictions [*Widersprüche*], as indicated in the title of Chapter 5
('Contradictions in the General Formula'). This title is far more adequate to

---

[94] Marx and Engels 1988a, p. 9.
[95] Marx 1973a, pp. 161, 170.

the new course of the exposition than that which still figures in the *1861–3 Manuscripts*: 'Difficulties Arising from the Nature of Value'. In point of fact, the analysis that leads us to surplus-value, solution to these 'contradictions', is not that of the difficulties or contradictions of an *actual* form or social relationship (such as 'value', for example), but rather the solution to contradictions inherent to the *formulation* M–C–M', a series of exchanges that by definition are equal and yet yield an increased result. There is no question here of a dialectical contradiction inherent to a form, which would then call for a transition to the higher form. The contradiction is a logical one specific to an ordinary form of representation (analogous to that in the formula 'value of labour').[96]

The object of Part Two of *Capital* can only be, in the end, the quest for the conditions of possibility for a formula of this kind 'discovered' in ordinary experience. A quest conducted in the light of what Part One has taught us about M, C and their relationships. This condition – the existence in the system of labour-power as a 'commodity' and the particular relationships this implies – is introduced as the necessary result of the expression of the partial truth of this 'general' formula (capital does indeed increase from M to M' by passing through C) and of the contradiction it presents when taken as a simple formula of exchange.

There is then no place in *Capital* for a dialectical 'transition' from money, or simple circulation, to capital, neither as a 'dialectical transformation' of C–M–C nor in any other fashion.[97]

---

[96] D'Hondt (1981) reproaches the translator of the Éditions Sociales edition of the *Version primitive* for having translated *Form* as *formule*. His reason, however, is remarkable: the change from *Form* to *formule* sacrifices the Hegelian tenor of the exposition. But that is precisely what Marx was soon to do in *Capital*.

[97] In revising this text in 1999, I find nothing to change to this analysis of the 'transition to capital': Marx failed with his earlier dialectical attempts, and replaced these with a non-dialectical form. But I no longer see this conclusion as sufficient. In fact, in the interpretation I have meanwhile proposed in *Théorie de la modernité* (1990), and especially in *Théorie générale* (1999), the articulation of the market and capital is inscribed in a broader theoretical context, in which the opposition between market and organisation forms the first 'abstract' moment that develops ('returns') into capital. I already explained this in a preface to the Korean edition of *Que faire du 'Capital'?* (1994): 'the major insufficiency of Marx's theory is not that there is too much dialectics in *Capital*, but that there is not enough, at least in the sense that only a more general theory can enable the consistent deployment of the forms of the dialectic'. For further precision, see the Preface to the present edition.

2.iii.c *Note. From 'labour as subject' to 'labour-power': the retreat of*
philosophical terminology

In parallel with the application of a new form of transition to capital that
differs from the dialectical path, we see Marx gradually distance himself from
certain categorial developments taken from German philosophy, the Hegelian
in particular.[98]

I shall limit myself here to investigating the theme of 'labour capacity' or
Arbeitsvermögen as it is called in the 1861 text before developing into 'labour-
power [*Arbeitskraft*]' in 1867.[99]

This concerns a moment of the exposition that is evidently of great
importance: the introduction of the category of 'labour-power' as solution to
the problems raised by M–C–M'. The same moment occurs very precisely in
the different successive versions: the *Grundrisse*,[100] the 'Original Version' of
the *Critique*,[101] the *1861–3 Manuscripts*,[102] the standard German edition of
Capital,[103] then the French edition.[104] It does indeed seem that, each time, the
new formulation is proposed as a correction to its predecessor, even if Marx
does not make his re-working explicit. We see, in fact, in the first three of
these texts, a particular evolution of terminology and concepts, of which the
subsequent modifications, through to the French edition, are only a logical
extension.

The *Grundrisse* starts by denoting the opposite of 'objectified labour' as
'labour as subjectivity',[105] 'living subject', as well as 'capacity [*Fähigkeit*]', or
'possibility [*Möglichkeit*]'; the term 'labour capacity [*Arbeitsvermögen*]' only
arises later.[106]

---

[98] On the philosophical constellation surrounding the notion of *process* and its
development, see my article 'Traduire en allemand *Le Capital*' (Bidet 1985).

[99] Vadée, who devotes a number of pages of his *Marx, penseur du possible* (Vadée
1992) to my interpretation of this terminological shift, curiously ascribes to me the
idea that 'the concept of labour-power must be understood in the sense of energy or
mechanical force' (p. 284). My entire investigation has been precisely directed against
this kind of positivism. In a general sense, it is hard to argue against Vadée, his basic
postulate being that if Marx had changed his analysis he would have informed us.
This, of course, makes the investigation of texts quite useless.

[100] Marx 1973c, p. 272.

[101] Marx 1974b, p. 942.

[102] Marx and Engels 1988a, p. 35.

[103] Marx 1973a, p. 181.

[104] [Page 270 in the English edition (Marx 1976a).]

[105] Marx 1973c, p. 272.

[106] Marx 1973c, p. 293.

The 'Original Version' starts with analogous formulations: 'subjective [*subjektive*]', 'non-objective [*ungegenständliche*]' or 'living' labour.[107] But 'possibility' and 'faculty' are soon expressed as 'labour capacity', which becomes the standard term.

In the *1861–3 Manuscripts*,[108] Marx approaches the question in analogous terms. But the *subject* here is curiously effaced, only to be found in the indirect form of a non-object: 'non-objectified labour, *living labour*' (Marx's emphasis). If, however, we anticipate here and compare this text with that of *Capital*,[109] it is notable that the subject/object couple still plays an important role, in particular that the equivalent here for the 'objectification of labour' is 'objectification of labour capacity',[110] a formulation with a markedly anthropological character, just like 'realisation of his labour capacity' or the reference to labour existing outside of the 'subjectivity' of the labourer.[111] These various formulations, however, may be considered as simply residual, in so far as Marx no longer bases himself on them for theorising the transition to capital.

In the various texts of 1863, it is *Arbeitsvermögen* that figures most regularly. For instance, the section devoted to the 'converted form of the value of labour capacity [*Arbeitsvermögen*] in the value or price of labour'.[112] *Capital* sees a systematic shift in the corresponding text to 'labour-power [*Arbeitskraft*]'.

In *Capital*, labour-power is introduced brusquely at the start of Chapter 6,[113] without the subject/object theme. Marx visibly skips a passage of his draft (the 1861 manuscript), substituting for this a new definition of labour-power (physical and mental faculties, body and living personality) that has no reference to the subject. Labour 'capacity', which, in the 1861 manuscript, had a philosophical support ('potency, δυναμισ')[114] and was subsequently used as the standard term, is now no more than a memory: Marx speaks from now on only of '*labour-power*'.

Between the German and French editions, there is just one important change: the disappearance of the last remaining reference to the subject/object couple:

---

107 Marx 1974b, p. 942.
108 Marx and Engels 1988a, p. 35.
109 Marx 1976a; Marx 1973a, p. 181.
110 Marx and Engels 1988a, p. 36.
111 Marx and Engels 1988a, p. 37.
112 Marx 1994, p. 70.
113 Marx 1976a, p. 270.
114 Marx and Engels 1988a, p. 37.

the 'objectification of labour [*Vergegenständlichung von Arbeit*]' – a suppression that appears therefore as an extension of the previous changes.

Conclusion

We have tackled here two major problems concerning the structure of the exposition of *Capital* that are intimately linked: that of the beginning and that of the relationship of Part One of Volume One to the rest of the work. The issue at stake is considerable: the mode of introduction and articulation of the categories determines their theoretical status, and all the great problems raised about the theory of the capitalist mode of production refer back to this question.

Marx only succeeded very gradually and very partially in his formulation of the beginning. The *Grundrisse* and the 'Original Version' of the *Critique* were still dominated by a false conception. The most abstract moment, the one that in this exposition proceeding 'from abstract to concrete' constitutes the point of departure, is characterised at the same time as the 'surface' of society; and it is defined as that of 'simple *circulation*' in the sense of commodity circulation in general. From this point, the progress is inwards, towards the inner core of society and thus the theory of this, 'capitalist *production*'. But the historicising argument which presupposes a commodity circulation prior to commodity production is not justified, any more than the methodological line of argument according to which it is necessary to go from what is 'immediately present', the world of commodities, to the 'relations of production' that this implies. For the intelligible beginning that goes together with commodity circulation in general is commodity production in general. *Capital* finally draws the logical conclusion, since Part One of Volume One is devoted not to circulation, but to the abstract system of commodity production and circulation.

This schema of the 'surface' is opposed by a different and opposite one, though one equally inadequate to the requirements of the theory. As distinct from the former, this still heavily marks *Capital*. It is that of a progress from the essence to the surface. And it is competition, denoted as a category accessible to ordinary consciousness and constitutive of immediate practice under capitalism, that figures as this surface element, supposedly also the most 'concrete', towards which the exposition gradually develops. Marx claims to introduce competition only in Volume Three. In reality, however, the categories of competition within the branch are absolutely necessary to the presentation of extra surplus-value, a central mechanism of Volume One. And the first Part of *Capital* itself, in so far as it has the abstract system of commodity production and circulation as its legitimate object, implies the full system of market categories, i.e. the imbrication of two orders of competition: within a branch and between branches.

Marx's confusion here is palpable, along with its irksome epistemological consequences. It is confusing to maintain that Volume One deals only with capital in general, abstracting from 'multiple capitals'. This is only partially true. Volume One does indeed define, against Ricardo, a theoretical space prior to that of prices of production, which are the overall result of capitalist competition as such. But this space of Volume One itself includes certain determinations of competition. In censoring these, Marx was led to obscure the 'inter-individual' moment of class relations, and he thus opens the way to the teleological myth. His theory only presents a genuine explanation of the historical process to the extent that its tendencies can be referred to a specific structure, that of the capitalist mode of production. And this is only defined as a social structure in so far as purposes are defined in it that are from the start the wellspring of individual action. These purposes are inscribed in the structure, not in its tendencies. And, by overlooking in this way the individual moment, Marx opens the way to a tradition of sociopolitical analysis that has too often speculated as to the purposes (generally unavowed) of capital, promoted to the rank of a subject.

The other uncertainty, correlative to the first, bears on the articulation between the abstract moment of the commodity and that of capital. This is the whole problem of the 'double articulation' often mentioned in the previous chapters, and which, in Marx's exposition, takes the form of the problem of the 'transition to capital'.

In the *Grundrisse* and the 'Original Version', Marx defines the first moment as that of 'simple circulation', seeks a dialectical access to capital on this basis, and believes he has found it in the figure M–C–C–M. In reality, however, this is incapable of supplying the mediating element between the section on money or 'simple circulation' and the section on capital. There is no basis for its denoting the former, and the attempt to make it figure 'money as money' is unacceptable. If it does indeed represent exchange, this is already a specifically capitalist activity. The 'dialectical transition' rests, in fact, on a double strategy. On the one hand, Marx anticipates by imposing on simple circulation the figure M–C–C–M that does not belong to it. On the other, he tries retrospectively to make specifically capitalist production appear the result of a dialectical play of forms of circulation: exchange-value would assert itself in capitalist 'productive consumption' as the 'negation/affirmation' of use-value. But this does not hold water. For one thing, the same can be said of consumption in the ordinary sense. For another, Marx obscures the fact that in reality he is simply adding in here the determination of the wage relationship, rather than reaching it by a dialectical process.

In *Capital*, at the same time as he breaks with the previous succession of the moments of his exposition (1: simple circulation, 2: capitalist production) and introduces a new one (1: commodity production/circulation, 2: capitalist production/circulation), Marx establishes a radically different approach. He distributes the figures differently, assigning C–M–C to commodity relations and M–C–M' to capital. And this latter, M–C–M', is now denoted not as a 'form' but as a 'formula'. In this way, the procedure followed is no longer a dialectic of forms, nor a logical deduction, but a specific mode of progression that, by recourse to the 'ordinary experience' contained in the 'formula' M–C–M', and the critique of this based on the categorial results of Part One, is able to provide the means of presenting the new determinations, those of the capitalist relation of production.

The consequences of these uncertainties, which still mark the 'definitive' text of *Capital*, will be shown in the following chapters with respect to the theory of ideology (Chapter 8), the notion of the 'value-form' (Chapter 9) and the articulation between the levels of generality of the discourse on value (Chapter 10). First of all, however, we must examine the questions of the exposition more globally.

Chapter Seven

The Method of Exposition and the Hegelian Heritage

It might seem that everything has already been said on the relationship of Marx to Hegel. The essential point, however, still remains largely to be elucidated, despite all the studies devoted to it: the function of the figures of Hegel's *Logic* in the articulation of the theory of the capitalist mode of production. It is familiar enough how this question has given rise to a conflict of interpretations that divide the Marxist tradition. I want to show here that it must be approached on the basis of the problematic of the epistemological support/obstacle.

These problems can evidently not be tackled in their particularity without the broader ground on which they are located being appropriately cleared up first of all. I shall therefore discuss, in broad lines, the questions at issue concerning Marx's method of exposition: the reasons for rejecting a 'logico-historical reading', the foundations and difficulties of a 'categorial' reading, and the recent discussion on 'capital in general'.

Once this discourse of Marx and its 'manner' has been recognised, it will be possible to return to the supposed model: the discourse of Hegel. Not to its content, in so far as this bears on society and the 'dialectic of history', but, rather, the form of exposition and the particular figures that Marx found in Hegel's

Logic and used in constituting his own discourse: syllogism, being and essence, negation, transformation, transition, essence and manifestation, etc. And also to the anthropological theme that Marx likewise drew from German philosophy.

What happened to these figures and categories in the constitution and maturation of the Marxian system? What logical necessities led him to call on them or reject them? Was Marx a Hegelian? Did the special object that he constituted, the capitalist mode of production, require an exposition characterised by a 'special logic'? Or did the new theory rather develop by radically distancing itself from this?

1. On the method of exposition of *Capital*

When Marx embarked on drafting his 'political economy' in 1857, he attached great importance to the question of the mode of exposition, devoting to it an Introduction that has remained celebrated. His argument there, and the various fragments that have remained of his exchanges with Engels on this question, have unavoidably been loaded with ambiguities, since the Marxist tradition contains two interpretations of the method, one logico-historical and the other strictly categorial. The issue in this quarrel is far from being merely technical: it is a site of symbolic exclusion on which idealism and materialism are deemed to confront one another. In any case, it is here that the question of the object and the signification of *Capital* are determined.

1.i *Misunderstandings of the logico-historical interpretation*

The logico-historical interpretation is schematically expressed in a statement of Engels that is often cited by commentators: 'The logical method of treatment . . . , as a matter of fact, is nothing else but the historical method, only divested of its historical form and disturbing fortuities.'[1] This position is defined, in opposition to a strictly categorial interpretation, as being the *materialist* position: it claims to overcome the dialectical mode of Hegelian idealism thanks to a homology between theoretical development and the historical development that this expresses, adopting the figures of Hegelian

---

[1] Marx and Engels 1980, p. 475.

logic as forms of the real, and of history in particular. Beyond the 'zig-zags'[2] and other acrobatics at the level of events, there is thus an 'underlying unity',[3] such that 'the logically necessary transition from one moment to another is always in the final analysis the reflection of an actual historical transition'.[4] By this criterion, the other procedure, which does not seek in the theoretical progression a historically founding equivalent, is seen as idealistic.

The inclination to this logico-historical interpretation was very widespread in the East, for instance in Soviet and East-German manuals and in the *MEGA*. It prevailed for a long while in the literature of the Communist movement, and was developed in various ways by several authors such as Vygodsky, Holzkamp and Zeleny. It goes together with a conception that integrates historical materialism into a dialectical framework forming the common matrix of an analysis of social forms and a philosophical anthropology. And it is against this that Marxists influenced by the Frankfurt school developed a 'dialectical' reading (also favoured by certain Soviet writers). In contrast to both interpretations, the Althusserian current opposed a reading that was neither historicising nor dialectical.[5]

The debate on this point goes back to Marx and Engels themselves, and though certain methodological texts of Marx pre-date this, it can properly be traced back to 1859, the date of Engels's intervention cited above. Backhaus has shown particularly well how the often alleged opposition between Marx as particularly concerned with the categorial development and Engels as promoter and defender of the logico-historical line has to be seriously qualified.[6] Engels's review of the 1859 *Critique*, for example, simultaneously shows both kinds of approach. As for Marx, we are familiar with his concern to 'correct the idealist manner of the presentation'.[7] His declarations and remarks on the subject have since been systematically gathered.[8] We shall tackle certain

---

[2] Ibid.
[3] Sève 1974, p. 28.
[4] Sève 1974, p. 26.
[5] Cf. Establet 1965, pp. 333–9, and Althusser 1978.
[6] Backhaus 1974, 1975, 1978.
[7] Marx 1973c, p. 151.
[8] The *Marx-Lexikon* (1977) of Samezo Kuruma includes an entire volume of texts by Marx and Engels on method. The elements here are organised in terms of a systematic grid that covers the entire raft of questions that the Marxist tradition and recent debate has raised as to Marx's method.

problems of a categorial order later on.[9] Let us first examine what relationship this has with a historical order.

The 1857 Introduction maintains, as is well known, the methodological principle of a progress from 'abstract' to 'concrete', the latter being understood not as the real, but as the 'concrete of thought [*Gedankenconcretum*]' or culmination of theoretical elaboration. As to the question of knowing to what extent this order corresponds to that of the historical appearance of categories, Marx responds with a problematic 'That depends',[10] which I intend to examine here in the light of what his theory actually produces. This problem of the logico-historical relationship, too often posed at a general level, refers, in fact, to a range of very specific questions.

1. Certain sequences are expressly of a 'logical' order, and can scarcely bear any historical interpretation. These are, in turn, of two kinds. There are those organised by a logical presupposition: thus accumulation (Volume One, Part Seven) can only be dealt with after valorisation (Parts Three and Four), and there is a similar progression from simple reproduction to expanded reproduction (Chapters 23–4 of Volume One, Chapters 20–1 of Volume Two). Then there are those that form an investigation, organised in a far less constraining fashion, of different or complementary parts or aspects of the same structural ensemble: e.g. the different figures of the circuit in Volume Two, the division of surplus-value into profit, interest and rent in Volume Three.

2. A characteristic sequence of the theory is the sequence of structure and tendency, which again, by definition, cannot have a historical correlate: the tendency is the tendency of the structure, which remains immanent in the tendency. This is the articulation of Chapter 12 of Volume One to the chapters that follow.

3. As against this, the determination of tendency clearly introduces a type of discourse marked by a concordance between the order of categories, in this case that of successive stages in a tendential development, and the historical order that it is precisely the object of this discourse to define. For example,

---

[9] The diversity of appellations can already be noted here: 'logical' (Engels), 'dialectical' (F. Ilienkov), 'categorial (Schwarz), 'conceptual' (Bader 1975, pp. 77–86), 'constructive' (Schmidt 1972, p. 139); or again 'structural-historical' (Eberle and Hennig 1974), as opposed to 'event-historical'. This is indeed symptomatic of the diversity of interpretation among those who reject the logico-historical problematic.

[10] Marx 1973c, p. 100.

the advance from manufacture (Volume One, Chapter 14) to large-scale industry (Chapter 15).

4. 'Primitive accumulation' presents a totally different kind of historical articulation, since it does not involve the dynamic of a structure, but rather the history of its constitution, the 'genealogy' of its elements, as Balibar has well shown.[11] Marx emphasises this in the *Grundrisse*.[12] This exposition of earlier facts is possible only at the end, after the exposition of the structure and the definition of its elements have made it possible.

5. The articulation of commodity and capital represents a particular case. It is the major categorial articulation of the theory, prescribing a necessary order of exposition, and as well as this, it clearly has a particular historical pertinence: commodity relations existed prior to capitalism. But, as I have shown, the categorial development cannot draw support here from the historical sequence, and, besides, Marx failed in his quest for a 'dialectical' categorial development, sometimes conceived as logico-historical.

The pertinence of the developments of *Capital* is clearly conditional on this diversity of relationships between categorial and historical sequences being taken into account. The relationship between the theoretical exposition and its historical object thus in no way implies a supposed homology of orders, the function of which is only too visible: to give the outcome of capitalism the appearance of ineluctable simplicity that the discourse on capital can more readily display. (This, indeed, still occurs in *Capital*, in the famous Chapter 32 on 'The Historical Tendency of Capitalist Accumulation', often cited, but which, sadly, makes no further contribution to the analysis of bourgeois societies.)

1.ii   *General problems of the categorial exposition*

The precept of categorial development from abstract to concrete, which lies at the heart of the 1857 Introduction, is constantly reasserted in   rx's work, and visibly constitutes its directive principle. It raises a series of general questions which we should indicate before going on to examine how Marx applies himself to the exposition of his particular theory.

---

[11] Althusser and Balibar 1970, pp. 273–308.
[12] Marx 1973c, p. 459.

The first question involves the theory of science that this procedure implies.

The 'concrete', as we have said, is not the existing 'reality'. The abstract/concrete relationship is to be understood as something within the totality of thought that the theory provides: it is an ordering relationship within the theoretical. And it is as a totality thus constructed that the theory is an instrument for knowledge of the real. In this sense, it does 'reproduce' the latter, but it does so only by being constituted in its own specific order, abstract to concrete, which is different from the order of genesis of the real.

The term 'abstract' here is to be taken in two different senses. It is, first of all, the separate element of the concrete whole, the unilateral, the moment. In this sense, theory seeks to supersede it, and give it its rightful place in the totality. What is needed for this is to reconstruct the global articulation of the totality, starting from an abstract moment which, although holding first place, does not imply the other moments but is, rather, implied by them. In this way, the whole is produced according to a logical development, the culmination of which is the concrete not as real, but as the conceptually reproduced totality, which can thus serve as means for appropriation of the real.

The 'concrete' of *Capital* thus itself remains very abstract, since it culminates in the general determinations of the 'capitalist mode of production', something that exists only in particular 'social formations' or actual societies, with diverse social, political and cultural histories.[13]

The second problem concerns the ideological-critical focus of this development.

Before the theory is produced, there is already a 'concrete of thought', in the form of the spontaneous consciousness of the agents occupying a particular place in this mode of production. 'Science' establishes – at least this is its intention – an overall connection based on principles that this spontaneous consciousness does not provide. At the same time, it accounts for this, not simply by offering a criticism but by producing a theory of it, in other words showing what are the functional foundations, inherent to the structure theoretically produced, for the existence of these representations.

A 'consciousness' of this kind evidently does not possess the status of an empirical fact, which the finger of theory could simply point to in reality.

---

[13] These questions have been particularly developed in Althusser and Balibar 1970, and Colletti 1973, pp. 113–38.

It belongs itself to the tissue of the 'concrete of thought' that the theory produces: this 'consciousness' is simply what is implied by the social relations that the theory defines. The whole problem, then, which forms the object of the following chapter, is that of the compatibility between this structural approach to ideology and an exposition of the always fragmented structure in the gap between its abstract and its concrete aspects.

This discourse of the critique and theory of ideology forms a specific dimension of the categorial development from abstract to concrete, and raises specific problems. If it is necessarily linked to the major discourse, that which develops the actual social relations, it is still always posited in rupture with this, introducing a series of distinct discrepancies which await their own globalisation in a particular discourse possessing its own specific organisation.

The constitution of this discrepancy between two orders of categories, that of real relationships and that of ideology, is, moreover, an index of the gradual maturing of the theory. It is still only weakly marked in the preparatory texts, the *Grundrisse* for example, in which many categories refer to both registers. Only the separation of these orders makes possible a strict categorial exposition, but it also prescribes new tasks of articulation between the two.

The third problem concerns the relationship between the order of exposition and that of research.

Marx stresses that the difference between these two orders is purely formal.[14] The research process, however, by the very fact that it always tends to link phenomena to the principles on which they are based, and thus to posit earlier moments, regressively constitutes the chain from concrete to abstract. Marx, as we have seen, climbs towards his starting point from one version to the next. It must be added, however, that the order of research also proceeds from abstract to concrete. This is the case when Marx investigates the subsequent links that a particular moment of his exposition introduces, or seeks to define the nature of the relationship between two moments, for example the transition from money to capital, or from Volume One to Volume Two. He actually asks himself three kinds of question at the same time: What is the abstract presupposition of this concrete proposition? What conclusions follow from establishing this abstract principle? How is the mediation between the outlined theoretical moments effected? This is one and the same procedure,

---

[14] Marx 1976a, p. 102.

and can, in this case, be defined as that of a methodological circle: 'concrete-abstract-concrete'.

The final problem bears on the nature of this order of exposition.

Althusser opposes this 'production' to the 'auto-production' of the (Hegelian) dialectic, as well as to axiomatic 'deduction'. It is a discontinuous process introducing new determinations: '. . . far from proceeding by auto-production of concepts, Marx's thought proceeds rather by positing a concept, inaugurating the exploration (analysis) of the theoretical space opened and closed by this positing, then positing a new concept, expanding the theoretical field and so on.'[15]

I have analysed in the previous chapter, in connection with the 'transition from money to capital', the nature of the progression or development of the exposition. I have shown how, within a defined structural level, categories are introduced whose legitimacy does not derive from the fact of their 'deduction' on the basis of earlier categories, but, rather, from their connection in an intelligible overall structure which they form in their ensemble; and how the transition to a different level is constituted by the introduction of a new category (in this case, the labour-power commodity) that 'opens up' a new categorial ensemble.

But this still leaves unresolved the question of the legitimacy of this 'productive' intervention. As I see it, this must be sought in a double direction. The research method consists in fact – and nothing can be said about it outside of the comparative examination of the various successive drafts of the exposition, in which we can see it in operation – of a work performed simultaneously on the various moments of the theory, whether they are more abstract or more concrete, tending to adjust them and bring them into harmony with one another. But this takes place in two different movements. The more concrete moments *imply* the more abstract (the theory of surplus-value implies that of value, the notion of profit that of surplus-value), i.e. they can only be presented after the latter and on the basis these provide; and this in turn assumes a regressive procedure that elucidates the nature of the more abstract categories presupposed by the more concrete. On the other hand, however, the reflection also bears on what the more abstract categories *require*, to be genuinely explanatory of the real. The law of value is only a general principle of the

---

[15] Althusser 1978, pp. 17–18.

functioning of a mode of production if other subsequent determinations are also posited. Surplus-value can only constitute the general relationship of capital and labour if values are 'transformed' into prices of production. The more concrete implies the more abstract for its own elaboration; the more abstract implies the more concrete to constitute itself into an effective social rule. In this way an order of exposition of these diverse categories is imposed, so that their relationships define the set of conditions of existence of a capitalist structure.

This approach calls first of all for some general remarks. 1) Structural analysis is simultaneously that of the elements of functionality and elements of contradiction in the structure. 2) At the same level of abstraction, the structure may be defined from different perspectives: for instance, the different chapters on surplus-value in Volume One (Chapters 7 to 10), or on the circuit of capital in Volume Two (Chapters 1 to 3). The relationship of structure and tendency is inscribed in this framework, but, at the same time, constitutes a limit to it. The tendency can be presented only on the basis of the structure, yet it does not constitute a more 'concrete' moment in the sense indicated here. It simultaneously displays, moreover, both the functionality and the contradictions of the structure. It is a prelude to the exposition of the stages of the system, to anticipations of its future.

An exhaustive analysis of Marx's method remains, in my view, a task for the future. It would presuppose a full evaluation of the signification of the theory, based on the nature of the various conceptual linkages this includes, and the connection of each of its parts with the whole. Certain recent works, in particular the book by Schwarz,[16] which deals with the whole of *Capital* and the gradual establishment of its articulations by trial and error, enable this to be seen more clearly. The fact remains, however, that the representation made of its method is indissociable from that made of its content, in other words the response to the basic problems that I note throughout the present book.

With the publication of the last essential manuscripts, it is possible now to judge the great theoretical importance that Marx attributed to this order and the care he took to constantly reshape it through to the final draft, considering each articulation, each transition from one moment to the next as a theoretical

---

[16] Schwartz 1978.

question. An exhaustive examination of the plan would go beyond the limits of this work. But a useful glance at this problem and its implications can certainly be provided by examining the main question that Marx faced and that led him to modify his plan, i.e. the question of 'capital in general' (*das Kapital im allgemeinen*), which has generated a broad debate in recent years.

1.iii   *The question of the plan*

It is in the work of elaboration and re-elaboration of the plan of *Capital* that the 'logical' preoccupations Marx invested in the categorial development of the exposition are displayed most clearly. And this is why the debate concerning the changes in this plan that has been under way since the 1970s,[17] bears not just on Marx's conception of the exposition, but on his theory of science as a whole.

I propose to start by examining the main results of these investigations before going on to show their inadequacy; in my view, this is that they stop short on the threshold of the essential question, that of the legitimacy, in the light of the logic of the theory, of those aspects of the earlier plans that remain in the final version.

1.iii.a   *The debate on 'capital in general'*
We know that, in 1857, Marx proposed a work consisting of six books: I. capital; II. landed property; III. wage-labour; IV. the state; V. international trade; VI. the world market and crises. And that the 'book on capital' was itself divided into: A. capital in general (i. production; ii. circulation: iii. profit); B. competition; C. credit; D. joint-stock capital. We also know that the final version, *Capital*, corresponds approximately to 'capital in general', though Marx more or less integrated into it the contents of the section on 'competition' and the books on 'landed property' and 'wage-labour'. The essential thing in this shift was that he moved from a two-part division, most frequently expressed in terms of the couple 'capital in general/actual movement of capitals [*Kapital im allgemeinen/reele Bewegung der Kapitale*]' to the three-part division of the three existing volumes.

---

[17] Cf. in particular Wygodski 1967, 1976, 1980, Kogan 1967, Rosdolsky 1968, Tuchscheerer 1968, Schwarz 1978 and Muller 1978.

The initial two-part division went together with the founding procedure of the *Grundrisse*: it furnished the solution to the 'Ricardian' problems that Marx had already come up against, bound up with the discrepancy between value based on labour and observable prices. This solution was the use of a mode of exposition from abstract to concrete borrowed from Hegel's *Logic*. In the event, this method of development particularly permitted the essential cleavage between two theoretical moments: 1) the abstract sphere of value and surplus-value, that of 'capital in general'; 2) the concrete sphere of 'natural' prices resulting from competition between 'multiple capitals'. The relationship between the two spheres was ensured by a system of transfer of surplus-value between capitalists, giving each the average rate of profit. This initial plan in two main phases thus appeared completely suited to the requirements of the exposition. Hence the question: what is the meaning and the import of the subsequent change in Marx's plan?

The reasons and circumstances of this change are now known. It occurred during 1862 (not in 1864–5, as Rosdolsky still thought),[18] the year of *Theories of Surplus-Value* and the year in which the system took shape. As Vygodsky has noted,[19] it was at this time that Marx arrived at the solution to his problem, that of the mediation between value and price of production, since this was when he succeeded in conceiving and producing the numerical table of transfers, and he was thus able to put forward, in an operatory fashion, the law of capitalist competition as determining this modification by the double action it exerts, both between branches, ensuring each an average rate of profit, and within each branch, leading to unequal profits.[20] Starting from this strong point, he could now go to develop the category of profit into profit of enterprise, commercial profit, interest and rent – in a succession from abstract to concrete as rigorous and of the same nature as that which had led him to that point.[21] But, in doing so, he raised the question of 'multiple capitals' and competition. He dealt with this in the context of a broader exposition than that of the initial 'capital in general', which constitutes 'capital in its concept'. Rent, which was going to be treated separately in the 'book on landed property', now appeared, in the categorial succession, as a 'transformed

---

18 Rosdolsky 1980, p. 11.
19 Wygodski 1967, p. 116.
20 Marx 1969, p. 212.
21 Schwarz 1978, pp. 273–4.

form' of surplus-value, an ultimate transformation that followed from taking into consideration the general determination of capital that production is carried out on a definite piece of land which is private property. In short, once the principle of articulation between the two moments of the initial plan was formulated clearly, the second of these moments appeared in the categorial succession as forming along with the first the 'general concept of capital', whereas previously it had been the first moment that monopolised this 'general' status.

The question that interpreters now face, after noting that the term 'capital in general' disappears in the final version, is to know whether Marx finally did dispense with this concept, or whether it still remains, and if so, where. The argument of Rosdolsky, which emphasises the discontinuity, needs to be qualified. According to him, Marx ended up abandoning the separation previously established between the analysis of capital in general and the analysis of competition. This couple had only had a provisional heuristic function; at the end of the day, 'the original strict separation of the categories was simply a means of methodological abstraction, and could therefore be discarded as soon as the main task – the analysis of "capital in general" – had been carried out.'[22] In actual fact, the initial articulation remained. This is as presented in Part Two of Volume Three: value/price of production, or before and after the equalising of rates of profit by competition. It is essential to the theory, and thus to the order of exposition. But it is quite different in nature from the three-part division, which is drawn from generic concepts (production/circulation/their unity) and not from the specific concepts of the capitalist mode of production. In short, the two articulations are combined: the two-part one, based on what is specific to capital, and the three-part one, based on a more general economic matrix.

1.iii.b *Disappearance of the Hegelian scaffolding*
Beyond the important clarifications brought by this recent research, an essential question still remains, in my view: that of the legitimacy, in the light of certain logical constraints inherent to the theory, of this category of 'capital in general', and, more broadly, the dialectical context that it implies. The first plans

---

[22] Rosdolsky 1980, p. 41.

inscribed the whole of the exposition in the syllogistic Hegelian framework of universal/particular/singular,[23] and the couple 'capital in general/ multiple capitals' is a residue of this. We can show, however, that, in the final work, categories of this kind lose their organising function for the theory.[24]

Let us first examine the status of the *universal* in this discourse. Does it mean what is common [*gemeinsam*] to all capitals, as maintained by Müller?[25] Certainly not. For the surplus-value relation, as a relation of production, only applies immediately and in the strict sense to productive capitals. It should really be defined as the global and dominant relationship. It applies on the one hand to the total capital, and on the other hand to productive capital, which is thereby constituted as the dominant relationship in the system, that which 'frames' the system in its overall character. There is nothing illogical in this relationship denoting both the whole and the part. This is simply due to the other capitals being constituted by deduction of surplus-value from productive capital. In other words, M–C . . . P . . . C′–M′ depicts both the global process (containing the process M–C–M′ and M–M′), and the process specific to productive capital. Volume One is thus neither a theory of the firm (K. Luxembourg) nor a theory of individual capitals (Schwarz, who sees the treatment of the total capital as starting in Volume Two, Part Three).[26] It defines both the total capital and productive capital, and the latter both in its totality and in terms of the individual capitals that compose it, therefore in the relationship between totality and individuals (cf. relative surplus-value/extra surplus-value). This, accordingly, involves a specific structural configuration, in relation to which the qualification 'general' or 'universal' is not applicable.

As to the *particular*, this is found all over the place. In Volume Three, of course, which distinguishes the parts into which surplus-value is divided (profit of enterprise, commercial profit, interest and rent), and the corresponding

---

[23] Marx 1973c, pp. 264, 275.
[24] This conception of the three-part division: universal (Volume One)/particular (Volume Two)/singular (Volume Three) is far from having gone out of fashion. It can be found for example in the interpretation of Dallemagne 1978, p. 127: 'in Volume Two, he re-articulates particular capitals . . . in Volume Three, he re-articulates individual capitals. . . .' The manual published by the USSR Academy of Sciences in 1971, on the other hand, attributed the singular to Volume One, the particular to Volume Two (Part Three) and the general to Volume Three! (Cf. *Geschichte der Marxistischen Dialektik*, p. 321).
[25] Müller 1978, p. 138.
[26] Schwartz 1978, p. 240.

fractions of capital (industrial capital, commercial capital, financial capital, landed property). Likewise in Volume One, with the couple 'fixed capital/circulating capital', first presented in Chapter 15, Section 2 ('the value transferred by the machinery to the product'). This is, moreover, something Marx had understood with his first sketches of the syllogistic plan in the *Grundrisse*,[27] which proposed a general and hierarchical articulation of universal/particular/singular, in which the 'particular' turns up at different stages in the construction. But the experimental character of these attempts is manifest, as is their negative outcome: this external framework imposed on the specific categories of capital, far from taking account of their proper articulation, leads only to formal regroupings and inadequate linkages.

We might expect the *singular* to hold a better-established place in the context of exposition. For the procedure of the *Grundrisse*, which, as we have seen, goes together with Marx's solution to the 'Ricardian' problems he encountered, consisted in an ordering from abstract to concrete, from the universal moment of surplus-value to the singular moment of competition: 'capital in general' is regularly opposed to the 'actual movement of capitals in competition'. The second moment would then be that at which the individual (the individual capital) is reached. I have shown how competition has a necessary place right from Volume One, Part Four. In reality, it is the very category of 'singularity' that falls away here. It appears, in fact, that there are two singular relations, of which one, competition within a branch, arises in Volume One, and the other only in Volume Three. The category of singularity breaks up and collapses, in the sense that it is not able to unify the theoretical moment (a very real one, which constitutes the pivot of the exposition) opposed to 'capital in general'. The general rate of profit is indeed opposed to surplus-value, and price of production opposed to value. But singularity, the multiplicity of individual competing capitals, is found on both sides of this divide. Analogous conclusions, concerning competition between workers, can be drawn from the analysis I have provided of the concept of the value of labour-power.

Contrary, therefore, to what Marx foresaw in his initial plans, these categories of universal/particular/singular ceased to organise the exposition and prescribe

---

[27] Marx 1973c, pp. 264 & 275.

a hierarchical order between its various moments. There is no genuine universal relation, but a dominant and global one. Particularity is omnipresent, but it is diverse, cannot be unified as particularity, and is thus not theoretically pertinent. Singularity dissolves into a range of different relations. In short, even if such categories had served as a 'heuristic principle', the project that they initially designated proved a failure. Far from constituting the dialectical scaffolding of a dialectical theory, they offer only a quite ordinary meaning within articulations and categories specific to this special object that is the theory of the capitalist mode of production.

But this withdrawal of the reference to Hegel's *Logic* is set in the context of a more general change that we now have to examine.

2. Hegel, an epistemological support/obstacle

Hegel provided Marx with the most elaborated form of a thought that conceived society as a totality and this totality as developing on the basis of its contradictions. A general analysis of the Hegel/Marx relationship would go well beyond the confines of the present book.[28] I shall deal with this only in terms of the conception of Marx's exposition, and do so not by basing myself on Marx's own declarations,[29] but, rather, on what his discourse actually effects by way of its successive re-elaborations. I shall show how the Hegelian

---

[28] I refer here to the works that have stressed Marx's break, his introduction of a new kind of totality and a new conception of contradiction (Althusser and Balibar 1970; Balibar 1977, pp. 46–61).

[29] The most notable of these is in the Postface to the second German edition of *Capital*, in which Marx defines his method as 'dialectical' and inherited from Hegel. In actual fact, the explanation he offers (Marx 1976a, pp. 102–3) refers to the dialectical movement of society, not that of his exposition. More generally, Marx gives the Hegelian precept of development from abstract to concrete an interpretation that is no longer dialectical but rather 'genetic'. Thus he acknowledges classical political economy for having been able to pursue an 'analytical' procedure, bringing the multiplicity of wealth to a conceptual unity. He simply reproaches it for having left it at that and being 'not interested in elaborating how the various forms come into being' (Marx 1972, p. 500) – in the sense of developing the theoretical space that makes it possible to define first the determinations of value, then those of capital, or on a different level, first those of value, then those of price of production (cf. again Marx 1964, p. 76). This 'coming into being' contains the entire theoretical programme of the exposition, that of proceeding from abstract to concrete. (In *Théorie générale*, I deal with this question as a whole, and propose a 'dialectical' form of exposition in three books, in which the 'genetic' development is dialectically integrated. I argue that Marx lacked the resources for his dialectic, which presupposes in fact a quite different concept of 'metastructure'. See in particular Sections 141–2, 231–3, 412 & 423.)

inheritance of a dialectical form of exposition, the figures that this involves and certain anthropological themes that intervene, present an obstacle to the development of the analysis, at least at certain stages in the elaboration, to the point of obscuring certain aspects or rendering them enigmatic – even to the general meaning of the theory.

2.i Being/Essence [Sein/Wesen]

Following Engels's letter to Conrad Schmidt of 1 November 1891, various authors, including Theunissen,[30] equate *Sein* with *Warenzirkulation*, *Wesen* with *Produktion*, and *Begriff* with *Reproduction*. In English: Being = commodity circulation, Essence = production, Concept = reproduction. A reading of this kind can appeal to the *Grundrisse*, in particular the form taken by the 'transition to capital'. In reality, however, as we shall go on to see, this resort to the Hegelian dialectic brings theoretical effects in its wake that are extremely awkward.

In Essence, relation-to-self is relation to the other as something posited and mediatised, and in this way we reach the Ground [*Grund*] (cf. *Encyclopaedia*, Part One, Sections 111, 112, 121). This moment in Hegel's logic comprises the categories that make it possible to conceive the totality as a system. They are suited, on the one hand, to expressing the notion of mode of production, which is reached in passing from money to capital, in the sense of mode of production and social structure including the conditions of its reproduction. They are also suited to the notion of circuit taken from the tradition of political economy, that of a totality reproducing itself by virtue of the results of production forming the conditions for a repetition of the production process. The 'chapter on capital', in the spirit of the *Grundrisse*, is the exposition of a circuit in the context of a mode of production.

The first difficulty that Marx encountered was that of defining an 'immediate' first aspect as the point of departure, one whose immediate existence could be defined prior to the totality in which it found its mediation. A difficulty of adequately conceiving one part before this was reconstructed as *'pars totalis'*, i.e. with the characteristics that make it into part of this totality.

In the *Grundrisse*, as we have seen, 'simple circulation' plays this role of initial moment. It does not in itself contain the principle of its renewal. Only with production (that is, in the context of this text, with capital) do we pass from the 'presupposition' to the 'positing' of its moments, and thus to the 'ground'.[31] In the meantime, 'circulation . . . appears as that which is immediately present [*als unmittelbar vorhandene*] on the surface of bourgeois society'.[32] Production does not intervene in its exposition, except by providing its 'presupposition'. Marx does indeed indicate that value is determined by labour-time.[33] But, at this point, this is only a matter of introducing the determinations of the commodity in so far as it is exchanged (use-value, exchange value, money), not of developing the determinations of commodity production for themselves. Commodities here 'express aspects of social production' but 'are *not posited* in this character'.[34] In short, in the 'chapter on money', the commodity is developed as a category of circulation and not of production.

We have seen how this 'dialectical' transition from being to essence, from the presupposed to the posited, and more particularly from (simple) circulation to (capitalist) production, is effected in the *Grundrisse*. Whereas, in exchange, the commodity is alternately commodity and money, and each time is only either use-value or exchange-value,[35] in such a way that each category is only itself immediately, in productive consumption, whilst, on the contrary, exchange-value is 'preserved as exchange-value in use-value as use-value',[36] in the negation-affirmation of the latter that constitutes its consumption and 'posits exchange value' and nothing more. Here, we find realised the 'unity of identity and difference' between use-value and exchange-value, which in 'circulation . . . *in itself*, not posited as such',[37] appear only as each identical to itself and different from the other.

In this development, the Hegelian schema of transition from the immediate to the posited and mediatised is applied at the same time to circulation and exchange-value. More precisely, the 'positing' of circulation in the sense of overcoming its immediate being, its access to mediatisation, is simply the 'positing' of the elements of the commodity, their access to a higher unity in productive consumption. When Marx identifies this here with productive

---

[30] Theunissen 1974, p. 326.
[31] Marx 1973c, pp. 255 & 227.
[32] Marx 1973c, p. 255.
[33] Marx 1973c, p. 135.
[34] Marx 1973c, p. 227; Marx's emphasis.
[35] Cf. Marx 1973c, pp. 263–71; 'Original Version', Marx 1974b, pp. 935, 941.
[36] Marx 1974b, p. 942.
[37] Marx 1973c, p. 261; Marx's emphasis.

consumption *by wage-labour*[38] – a slippage whose unacceptable character I demonstrated in the previous chapter –, he believes he has thus effected the transition from simple circulation to commodity production, from money to capital, the circuit or permanent 'process'[39] in which circulation and production mediatise one another.

The result of the dialectical operation is quite triumphantly proclaimed. 'Thus, here was a circulation which presupposed a production in which only the overflow was created as exchange value; but it turned into a production which took place only in connection with circulation, a production which posited exchange values as its exclusive content.'[40] A return at a higher level, since circulation and production are now united in the circuit. It is not surprising to find here the Hegelian 'ground', since it is precisely this that constitutes 'the unity of identity and difference . . . , essence put explicitly as a totality' (*Encyclopaedia*, Section 121).

But the dynamic principle that makes a 'dialectical' development of this kind possible is located in the initial disequilibrium, where Marx starts by envisaging only circulation in general, independently of commodity production in general, even though the two belong together conceptually in the intelligible first step of the theory. The disappearance of the concept of commodity production in general (with the unfortunate theoretical consequences that I noted in the previous chapter) thus constitutes the price to be paid for circulation appearing as *being*, as 'immediate' and non-posited given, seeking its positing and mediatisation in capitalist production as its *essence*.

2.ii *Transformation* [Verwandlung]

One term, though not particularly Hegelian, well displays in *Capital* the mirage of a continuous development with a dialectical character; that of 'transformation [*Verwandlung*]', a universal tool that possesses the double property of rendering homogeneous the various relationships to which it is applied, and suggesting in the transition from one to the other that the process at work is a continuity.

---

[38] Cf. 'Original Version', Marx 1974b, p. 943.
[39] Marx 1973c, p. 258.
[40] Marx 1973c, p. 257.

We can distinguish three main usages of the term, which I shall designate as *X*, *Y* and *Z*.

X: In the description of a circuit (M–C–M, C–M–C, M–C . . . P . . . C'–M', etc.) it denotes the *metamorphosis* of value, its passage from one form to another. Thus, in Volume Two, Chapter 1,[41] or at various points in Volume One, although 'metamorphosis' (p. 200) cohabits here with more specific terms such as 'change of form [*Formwechsel*]' (p. 119) or 'conversion' (p. 709). The same applies to accumulation: 'transformation of surplus-value into capital' (p. 725).

Y: In the development of categories of the exposition, *Verwandlung* denotes the *passage* to the next category. It figures in this sense in several titles of Parts and Chapters. Volume One, Part Two: 'The Transformation of Money into Capital'; Volume Three, Part One: 'The Transformation of Surplus-Value into Profit . . .'; Part Two: 'The Transformation of Profit into Average Profit'; Part Four, 'The Transformation of Commodity Capital and Money Capital into Commercial Capital . . .'; Part Six, 'The Transformation of Surplus Profit into Ground-Rent'. In this second sense, *Verwandlung* may be replaced by (or associated with) *Übergang*, transition. This is the case in the Appendix to the first edition of *Capital*; here, where Marx writes that he took care over the 'dialectical' form, all the *Übergänge* are precisely noted,[42] yet they are sometimes also designated as *Verwandlungen*.[43] From the second edition onwards, it is this term that remains, translated as 'transition'.[44]

Z: A final usage concerns the *discrepancy* between ideological relations and real relations. For example, 'The Transformation of the Value (and Respectively the Price) of Labour-Power into Wages', the title of Chapter 19 of Volume One, referring to the representation of wages as the 'price of labour'. That this usage is not always well distinguished from the preceding one can be noted in a proposition like that which opens Chapter 21: 'The piece-wage is nothing but a converted [*verwandelt*] form of the time-wage, just as the time-wage is a converted form of the value or price of labour-power.'[45]

---

[41] Marx 1978, pp. 109–12, etc.
[42] Marx 1980, pp. 776–77, 781.
[43] Marx 1980, p. 783.
[44] Marx 1976a, p. 162.
[45] Marx 1976a, p. 692.

This terminological polyvalence is clearly a handicap for the development of the exposition. It expresses a certain initial confusion that Marx gradually overcame. In the *Grundrisse*, the two first kinds of 'transformation' (X = metamorphosis and Y = passage) are superimposed in the notion of 'becoming': 'the product becomes a commodity; the commodity becomes exchange value'[46] – a 'dialectical' form that Marx then set out to 'correct'. In sum, the relative unity of the initial scheme of the *Grundrisse* (becoming, transformation into) seems to me to reflect the reference to the model of Hegelian logic, in which all the 'passages' enjoy, in a sense, a homogeneous status. Marx's originality here is expressed in the fact that he steadily manages to diversify them: to distinguish the passage from one aspect to a complementary one within the same level of abstraction (elements of a structure, moments of a circuit) from the passage to a more 'concrete' level of real relationships, and from the gap between the latter and forms of representation. But this false generality of '*Verwandlung*' remains an awkward problem.

2.iii *Essence/manifestation* [Wesen/Erscheinung]

This couple, as we know, plays a key role in the theoretical elaboration. It enables Marx to distinguish (and re-connect) different levels, and in this way to break with both 'Ricardian' and 'vulgar' discourse while still accounting for these. But it also presents an obstacle to the extent that it designates in a univocal fashion several kinds of relationship that the theory should distinguish. There are at least four distinct usages of *Erscheinung*:

W: As a form of *historical* appearance. For example, commercial capital is the first 'form of appearance [*Erscheinungsform*]' of capital.[47]

X: As an *ideological* phenomenal form. For example, the representation of the value or price of labour-power as the price of labour.[48]

Y: As a *derivative* form on the abstract-concrete axis. This is, then, the opposition between the 'inner connection [*inneren Zusammenhang*]', i.e. the surplus-value relation, and the 'forms of manifestation' that are interest and rent.[49]

---

[46] Marx 1973c, pp. 146–7.
[47] Marx 1976a, p. 247; Marx 1973a, p. 161.
[48] Marx 1973a, p. 562. [The English edition has 'imaginary expression' (Marx 1976a, p. 677).]
[49] For example Marx 1976a, p. 490; Marx 1972, p. 489.

Z: As a form of *expression*, 'use-value becomes the form of appearance of its opposite, value.'[50]

This terminological indecisiveness contributes to a certain identity of the identical and the different, responsible in part for *Capital*'s 'dialectical' charm. We shall analyse certain effects of this in the following chapters. The superposition of *W* and *Y* amounts to a contamination between the historical and categorial orders. That of *X* and *Y* generates confusion between the development of *real* forms from abstract to concrete and the problem of ideological *representation*, a problem that weighs on the entire Marxian theorising of ideology. Finally, superposition of *X* and *Z* raises very difficult problems for the interpretation of the first chapter of *Capital*.[51]

The category of *Erscheinung* comes into play at different levels and in opposing senses. Presentation of competition as a 'form of appearance' makes Volume One, and especially its Part One, appear obscure, depriving them of a determination the 'essential' character of which I have already shown. The same goes for the metaphor of the 'surface', applied in the *Grundrisse* to the section on 'simple circulation': this only becomes an 'appearance' or 'surface' because Marx neglects the correlative category of 'commodity production in general' which in his finished theory belongs together with it. We should note that the *Grundrisse* creates in two distinct ways the initial imbalance that gives the impulse to the dialectical movement: both with the schema 'being/essence', which leads from 'simple' circulation as immediate given to its positing-integration into the capitalist totality, and likewise with the couple 'appearance/essence', which makes this 'simple' circulation into the surface, the application of dialectics assumes in both cases the (relative) effacement of 'commodity production in general'. This is corrected in *Capital*, at least up to a point.

---

[50] Marx 1976a, p. 148; Marx 1973a, p. 70.
[51] Characteristic of the Hegelianising reading is the tendency to use this notion as a universal tool to connect the most varied conceptual levels. For example, Badaloni (1976, p. 169) denotes both value ($c + v + s$) and price of production (cost + average profit) as 'phenomenal forms of a more general law' and a specifically universal one, according to which value is equal to labour contained.

2.iv   *Negation and 'negation of the negation'*

This figure organises the famous and prophetic Chapter 32 of Volume One: primitive expropriation of the 'immediate producer',[52] then the long march of capitalism, at the end of which 'the expropriators are expropriated'.[53] The defect of this kind of representation, and also undoubtedly its motivation, is the polarity and mirror relationship it establishes between the beginning and the end, obscuring their underlying incompatibility. In actual fact, the beginning is not 'expropriation': where this does take place, it is only one element among many in the origin and establishment of the capitalist structure. And the 'final' expropriation is itself a double one: that of the small capitalists which takes place throughout the development (concentration), and the 'revolutionary' one that expropriates the dominant class. The short cut of the 'negation of the negation' wipes out the distinction between the various aspects of this movement and the historical temporality that the theory of the mode of production presupposes: genetic, dynamic, and revolutionary crisis of the system. It gives the final result the false simplicity of the supposed beginning. It brushes aside the indispensable reflection on the diversity of possible outcomes, examination of the complex play of tendencies and counter-tendencies – though, undoubtedly, this is the most useful reflection that it can inspire on the future of contemporary capitalism.

2.v   *Alienation*

The category of alienation expresses in critical fashion the contradictory structure of capitalist relations as based on the disjunction of two relationships. *Production*: the worker produces goods, in the form of means of subsistence and of production. *Property*: the capitalist possesses the means of production, thus the goods produced. The notion of alienation presupposes the *rightful unity* of these two relationships under the schema of 'objectification'. A subject objectivises him- or herself into an object in so far as he or she produces and possesses this (controls it, consumes it, etc.). The capitalist contradiction is thus grasped as a disjunction of 'objectification': the 'objective conditions' of labour are separated from the 'subjective existence' of the non-owning labourer,

---

[52] Marx 1976a, p. 927.
[53] Marx 1976a, p. 929.

this subject is objectivised in an object that is a non-object, the 'objective existence' of the other, the capitalist.

Such, at least, is the form taken by this theme in the *Grundrisse*, especially in the long passage devoted to it,[54] in a style still close to that of the *1844 Manuscripts*. The subject/object couple here forms the central theoretical mechanism. Each member of the couple is defined in a very over-determined way. On the subject side, there is 'living labour', 'living labour-capacity', 'creative activity'. On the object side, there is 'objectivised labour', 'value', 'property, i.e. . . . the objective conditions of labour'. This object takes the form of 'the autonomous being-for-itself of value'. Not only does it escape the subject, it dominates him, 'personified' as a 'juridical person' with 'its own will and interest' and exercising 'domination' over the subject.[55] The subject 'is posited' therefore in this object, finding in it his own 'objectification', but in the form of an 'abstract, objectless, purely subjective poverty'.[56] He is posited as 'without substance', as a 'non-being'. Various other texts develop this theme.[57]

It is not hard to discern a basic weakness in this critical discourse: founded on categories of metaphysics, it is so indeterminate that it can be applied to any mode of production in which the labour of a dominated class produces the means of production appropriated by a ruling class. In no way is it specifically suited to the theory of the capitalist mode of production.

On the other hand, its insertion point is problematic even within this context.

In his initial orientation, in fact, Marx attaches it to the definition of the actual *structure* of the capitalist wage relationship. In the *Grundrisse*, and again in the *1861–3 Manuscripts*, alienation is presented as absolute, in the same sense as is poverty. This does *not* denote 'absolute pauperisation', the historical tendency to a decline in living standard or wages, but takes, rather, a structural sense, in which it is 'abstract, objectless, purely subjective poverty'.[58] More precisely, poverty and alienation figure here at the level of the future Part Two of Volume One. Marx uses them in an attempt to grasp capital otherwise than from its 'material side'; 'from its formal side' (as 'economic form', in his

---

[54] Marx 1973c, pp. 452–4.
[55] Marx 1973c, p. 452.
[56] Marx 1973c, p. 453.
[57] Cf. Marx 1973c, pp. 462 & 831–3; Marx 1972, p. 259; Marx 1976a, p. 990.
[58] Marx 1973c, p. 453.

terminology of this period), 'these objective conditions must confront labour as *alienated*, as *independent* powers'.[59] They denote the very structure of capitalist relations of production: dispossession/appropriation/domination.

In a second orientation, alienation comes to characterise, on the contrary, the *tendency* of this structure, an embryonic tendency from the time of the simplest co-operation (which, under capitalism, is 'a power alien to [the workers]')[60] that undergoes successive development[61] in stages via manufacture through to large-scale industry, when the worker, initially in control of the activities and practices of his trade, gradually becomes the appendix of the machine-tool, 'in the workshop as a whole, which . . . confronts the workers as an external power, dominating and enveloping them, in fact the power of capital itself and a form of its existence'.[62]

Marx's discourse here, by suffering from this lack of distinction between categories of structure and tendency, remains prior to historical materialism, a philosophy of history. This is then naturally continued by his assertion about communism, in which 'the objective moments of production are stripped of this form of alienation'.[63] The imperative of practical philosophy, which brings to light the disjunction between production and property as 'separation [*Trennung*]', in the strong sense of separation between subject and object, postulates their unity and projects this as the goal of the historical process.

This is a different kind of category from those that function operationally in *Capital*. As a globalising category (being alienated or not alienated), it presents an obstacle to the analysis of the relationships of a mode of production, which are always particular: the imperfect 'disposition [*Verfügung*]', the undecided distribution of the product (v, s) and of time (paid, unpaid), the distinction of different strata with varying relations to the product and to production. The category of alienation is not suited to the complex designation of the contradictions that develop in the complex architecture and dynamics of the system.

We can also note that, in *Capital*, this category disappears from the *structural* definition of surplus-value, i.e. from Parts Two and Three. And, in the moment of definition of the *tendency*, Part Four, it loses its philosophical reference (that

---

[59] Marx and Engels 1988a, p. 114; (Marx's emphasis; cf. also p. 35).
[60] Marx and Engels 1988a, p. 261.
[61] Marx 1972, p. 278.
[62] Marx and Engels 1988a, p. 278.
[63] Marx 1973c, p. 832.

of 'non-objective' objectification of the subject in the object) in favour of a sociopolitical characterisation: what the labourer finds facing him in the manufacturing workshop is the capitalist, personification of capital, who 'converts the worker into a crippled monstrosity' and appropriates his 'productive forces', in this way dominating him.[64] The same goes for large-scale industry. The theme of alienation undergoes here a transformation which, on the one hand, cuts it off from its philosophical origins (subject/object is replaced by worker/conditions of work), and, on the other hand, denotes in restrained fashion 'the technical subordination of the worker to the uniform motion of the instruments of labour'.[65] In this respect, the theme is somewhat banalised: it blends in with the general critique of the capitalist organisation of the labour process, having only the particular merit of founding this theoretically as the effect of a historically given mode of production. The French and English editions, which prune out the Hegelian themes,[66] show still greater distance from this category.

Conclusion

My project here is not to offer a complete study of Marx's method of exposition and its relation to that of Hegel, but, rather, to analyse these questions in the light of the interpretative contentions I have presented in the previous chapters, concerning the categories of *Capital* and the central structures of the system.

The 'logico-historical' interpretation has an apologetic function that is all too visible: it ascribes the historical future a necessity that derives from the deployment of a categorial logic. In reality, the analytical instruments that Marx introduced or perfected are usable only on condition that in place of presupposing a general homology of order between the presentation and its empirical object, consideration is paid to the specificity of the various articulations of the historical that the exposition implies (structure/tendency, origin/dynamic, etc.), a specificity that circumscribes the legitimate usage of the concepts in question.

---

[64] Marx 1976a, p. 481, etc.
[65] Marx 1976a, p. 549.
[66] Ibid.

The strictly categorial conception of an exposition proceeding from 'abstract' to 'concrete' refers to a definite theory of science, in which these form two poles of a systematic totality of thought, this being a means of theoretical appropriation of the real. It offers an ideological-critical focus inasmuch as this categorial ordering leads supposedly to forms of ordinary consciousness (a problem we shall take up in the next chapter), founded on principles that account for them and give the measure of their 'truth'. It implies a representation of theoretical investigation as linked to this ordered elaboration, an order that cannot be its own, as investigation, and yet polarises it.

On the basis of this analysis, which was, in part, a recapitulation of fairly common views, I took up again the question of 'capital in general', which, particularly since Rosdolsky's book, has been at the centre of discussions about the plan of *Capital*. Beyond the suspension of this category, which without disappearing, was integrated into the broader ensemble of 'capital according to its concept' from the time that Marx mastered his theoretical project in 1862, I wanted above all to show how an entire Hegelian categorial field initially invoked for this purpose, particularly in the *Grundrisse*, now disappeared: that around the 'general' or 'universal [*allgemein*]', and the triad of universal/particular/singular.

I demonstrated how it was necessary to analyse in analogous fashion certain particular dialectical figures that at various phases of Marx's drafts articulated different levels of the exposition and were dismissed, entirely or in part, as this matured. This applies to the couple 'being/essence [*Sein/Wesen*]', which opposes the immediacy of the given presupposition to its positing: this figure leads to a weakening of the initial moment of the theory, its intelligible first principle. It effectively prohibits thinking this as the unity of production and commodity circulation in general. The category of *Verwandlung*, transformation, provides an ambiguous operator, used in particular for three kinds of purpose: *metamorphosis* in the course of a circuit, *transition* along the axis from abstract to concrete in the sense of *Übergang*, and *discrepancy* between the actual relationship and the ideological relationship that this implies. This polysemy is the residue of original ambiguities not entirely overcome, the famous 'coquetting' with Hegel, which, in the event, expresses indistinctly various different ordering relationships of the exposition which are pertinent only in their particularity. The same goes for the category of appearance or manifestation [*Erscheinung*], which also acquires different uses: form of *historical* appearance, phenomenal-*ideological* form, *derivative* or secondary form on the abstract-concrete axis, form of *expression*. This terminological ambiguity often conceals an interference between categories of the real and categories of the ideological, between the historical and the categorial, the ideological and the expressive.

This progression could be continued to cover such 'dialectical' figures as the 'negation of the negation', which Marx uses with more or less explicit reference to Hegelian logic: likewise 'process', 'the infinite', 'circle', 'contradiction', 'reversal', and the 'quality/quantity' couple (which the *Grundrisse* applies to functions of money, in a dialectical development that disappears in *Capital*). We would be led with these to similar conclusions. The intensive experimental-instrumental usage made in the early versions led to a number of theoretical cul-de-sacs. A part of this apparatus persists in the later versions, but not without perpetuating a number of confusions. A certain simplification is the predominant tendency.

The same is finally true of the anthropological theme that plays such a large part in the *Grundrisse*, and fades away only very slowly. The central category of *alienation*, which rightly depicts the axis of philosophical critique, cannot for this reason be integrated into the categories of the capitalist mode of production. As a globalising category, with an immediately given globalism, it gives any other category it comes into contact with a dangerously teleological turn. Theory, however, is valid only to the extent to which the limits of the knowledge it provides are clearly defined, to the extent that the 'strategic' use that I have indicated can be distinguished from its teleological and mythic use.

The special object possesses special categories. It does not possess a special logic.

Chapter Eight
The Theorisation of the Ideological in *Capital*

Marx uses the term 'ideology' in a fairly broad sense, often relating it to idealism and denoting a view of the world specific to certain classes. In the period of *Capital*, he practically stopped using it;[1] this work offers a strictly sectoral analysis that deals only with the 'economic base' of capitalism. If I am discussing the term here despite this, it is because, in my view, there is the same project at work in *Capital* that was announced for the first time in *The German Ideology* at the very moment when the concept of mode of production was coined, along with the conceptual couples that are constitutive of it: productive forces and relations of production, dominant and dominated class – a project, however, that Marx could only embark on systematically once he had developed, from 1857 on, the theory of a definite mode of production, the capitalist mode. By constructing the system of socio-economic relations that defined this, he was finally in a position to study the ideological forms that characterised it, and thus to articulate science and ideology. Despite the varying terminology ('everyday consciousness', 'form of appearance', 'fetishism' etc.), Marx remains, in my

---

[1] Cf. Balibar 1983.

view, within the unity of this problematic, and, from this point on, possesses the means of developing it in a more rigorous manner, if, at the same time, a more restricted one.

These questions have given rise to a copious literature in the last fifty years, and a very uneven one. Many of its inadequacies derive from the fact that too little attention has been paid to the logical constraints bound up with the architecture of the development and the specific character of the concepts whose nature I have explained in the previous chapters. The interpretation I propose here is based on these clarifications. It evidently goes together with a definite conception of the maturation of Marx's theory: it is the distance he takes from certain aspects of Hegelian logic that makes possible the constitution of an approach that is not simply one of a *critique* of ideology, but, rather, what I shall call a *theory* of ideology, meaning a discourse that sets out to establish, in Marx's terms, 'the rationale of these forms of appearance', the necessary link between social structures and forms of representation.

1. The place of everyday consciousness: Volume 3

1.i *Why* Capital *has to be read backwards*

Capital must be read in the order presented. Yet, it is only at the end, and by way of conclusion, that it offers a specific theory of ideology. Volume 3 brings us to the 'concrete' level at which, according to the author, ideology belongs. In Volumes 1 and 2, the question is posed in an external fashion and as something incidental, most often in the form of a *critique* of ideology or even a mere indication of the *difference* between the reality of the structures that have been displayed and the spontaneous representation that their agents have of these. In Volume 3, on the contrary, ideology seems to have its proper place, in the sense of the place of its proper theorisation: not simply its description or its critique, but a theory that accounts for its forms. We are thus offered a problematic from which it is then possible to retrace the course of the work to Volume One and its opening chapter.

This is already announced in the first paragraph of Volume 3, where Marx recalls his overall project and expressly positions the question that I refer to as that of ideology:

> The configurations of capital, as developed in this volume, thus approach
> step by step the form in which they appear on the surface of society, in the
> action of different capitals on one another, i.e. in competition, and in the
> everyday consciousness of the agents of production themselves.[2]

This programmatic text contains two assertions.

The first is that we are here at a more 'concrete' level. Marx did, in fact,
distinguish already from 1857 between the 'inner connection', the level of
value and surplus-value (Volumes 1 and 2), and the 'derived' forms, the level
of profit and prices of production; this distinction forms the principle of the
plan of *Capital* and the very wellspring of the critique of political economy.

The second is that we reach here the realm of 'everyday consciousness', of
ideology. The relation between science and ideology is thus designated in the
articulation of the exposition of the theory. The most 'concrete' stage, in the
sense of the final stage of the successive determinations that form the exposition,
is seen as defining the field of consciousness. The contents of everyday
consciousness arise in the order of the exposition as the product of the
theoretical elaboration itself. They are in effect derived or developed [*entwickelt*]
on the basis of the forms of the 'inner connection'. And this is the very project
of a *theory* of ideology: to show what forms of consciousness are implied in
the practice of agents, in relation to the function they occupy in the system
that has progressively been defined.

This dual status of the determinations of Volume 3 is condensed in the
category *Erscheinungsform* ('form of appearance'), which can denote both a
form that is 'concrete' in the sense of derived, and the form of representation
specific to 'everyday consciousness'.

But what is the basis of this coincidence of the 'concrete' and the 'conscious'?
The answer would appear to be simple: the point of development that the
exposition of the actual forms reaches here is that at which capital is no longer
envisaged in general, but from the standpoint at which its movement can be
understood only on the basis of competition between individual capitals, thus
of the specific action of individual capitalists; and by virtue of this also from
the *standpoint* of the latter, in their own categories.

---

[2] Marx 1981, p. 117.

This answer however involves various difficulties that call for a re-examination of Volume 3 as a whole.

1.ii   *The functional 'everyday consciousness' of the competitive situation (Volume 1)*

The object of Part 1 of Volume 3 is to show that the capitalist, far from having any need for the 'scientific' concepts developed in the previous Volumes, necessarily resorts to quite different categories in order to exercise his specific function.

The capitalist does not have to understand the basis of value, i.e. labour-time. He only needs to produce a commodity whose price is greater than its costs of production, and the practices that are required for this purpose do not imply any differentiation between c and v. 'It makes no difference to the capitalist whether we see him as advancing the constant capital to make a profit out of his variable capital, or as advancing the variable capital in order to valorize his constant.'[3] He will necessarily relate his profit not to v, but to $c + v$. In his eyes, the origin of profit lies in the capital as a whole, and its magnitude will depend on his ability to economise his resources and obtain the most productive use of them. Such is the general theme of this Part, which relates the various aspects of the capitalist's activity, and his strategies in dealing with the problems he encounters, to this initial principle.

It is clear that this exposition, far from being a purely negative critique of the categories of the capitalist entrepreneur, is first of all more of a justification. For what is given a foundation here is the legitimacy of the capitalist's discourse as a *strategic* discourse, through a definition of the elements of its specific field. The capitalist, so Marx in substance explains, is committed to an economic calculation with a view to the best possible productive combination, that which brings the maximum production for the minimum outlay. More generally, his practice implies an 'economic science' in the sense of a theory of decision-making that will take into account each of the factors of production in the light of its technical characteristics.

Marx has certainly marked out the limits of this discourse in advance, since he inscribes it in *Capital* and more broadly in the context of a theory of history for which any *science* of society must be based on an analysis of the

---

[3] Marx 1981, pp. 132–3.

contradictions specific to each mode of production, and develop on the basis of these its explanation of social processes and varying social practices. In this sense, the 'micro-economic' representation inherent to capitalist practice accounts neither for the contradictory development of capitalist society as a whole, nor for the capitalist's practice in its generality (as a practice of extracting surplus-value). And, yet, precisely in this context, it acquires its own legitimacy: the theory of the capitalist mode of production explains the necessity for the capitalist of a discourse enabling him to assume his function in a coherent fashion, thus a discourse endowed with a definite strategic pertinence.

Marx applies here the programme that he set himself in drafting *The German Ideology*, which already maintained that the production of ideas is 'directly interwoven with the material activity and the material intercourse of men',[4] and 'the ruling ideas are nothing more than the ideal expression of the dominant material relationships'.[5] But he seeks to realise this here at the most abstract level of the relations of production, i.e. prior to the terrain he had initially occupied, that of political and philosophical ideologies. Also outside of any instrumental interpretation of the dominant ideology: representation, here, is functionally linked to the activity of the ruling class. Ideology certainly appears under a double face, both illusory and functional, but in an articulation in which the latter holds primacy. It is as function rather than illusion that ideology is strictly deduced: as a categorial ensemble implied in a function defined by the structure, that of the capitalist acting in the competitive relationship. Marx does not start from the necessity of a mask, as a primordial requirement that hides the fact of exploitation. In this sense, ideology is not 'censorship' in the Freudian sense, the transformation of an object that must remain concealed. For, if these categories do not express exploitation, it is simply because they offer a different representation of the increase in capital, adequate to the functions that are those of the organiser of this increase, the capitalist.

It thus appears that, at the moment when theoretical analysis reaches the level of individual behaviour, it can only grasp this in terms of *human* behaviour, as meaningful, by accounting for the consciousness that individuals have of their own activity.

---

[4] Marx 1976f, p. 37.
[5] Marx 1976f, p. 60.

We see here how Marx's procedure now differs from that of Volumes 1 and 2, in which he had systematically presented the real social relations, and, as regards ideology, was most often content to say that, if social relations were as he had defined them, then the prevailing representations were inadequate. In Volume 3, he shows the adequacy of these representations to the social functions that his theoretical construction has brought to light, or at least to one of these, that of the capitalist.

The limitations of this theorisation of ideology can be traced. By tying this to definite functions, it does not offer any explanation of the representations of agents occupying a different place in the social structure. It is articulated to a very definite level of capitalist practice, that corresponding to the individual capital as such; it has nothing to say, for example, as to what might be the capitalist ideology of those economic functions centralised at the level of the state apparatus, where this bears on strategies aiming at the overall success of the capitalist economy.

This first Part, moreover, still only sets out the terms of the problem. Marx still faces the hardest task, that of showing in what conditions these determinations specific to individual activity, determinations to which he ascribes the ideological representations, can be theoretically related to the concepts of Volume 1, in other words how the world of prices, that of the 'surface', is attached to that of values, that of the inner connection. This is why the investigation of the theory of ideology necessarily refers us to the problems dealt with in the following Part, which deals with the famous question of the transformation of values into prices.

1.iii   *The value/price transformation as the foundation of ideology (Volume Three, Part Two)*

The 'transformation of values into prices of production' is a transformation of real relationships, a (decisive) moment on the abstract-concrete axis. It carries a specific ideological effect.

This question, which is the object of a major controversy today, is only intelligible, in my view, if it is related to those principles that, beyond specifically capitalist relations of production, are those of commodity production in general.

Marx's concern here is to account for the well-known fact of political economy that, at first sight, seems contrary to what the theory presented in

Volume One might lead one to expect: a particular capital is normally rewarded as a function of its overall magnitude $(c + v)$, and not simply that of the variable capital v that it includes. Marx's intention is to show that this must be analysed as a particular application of the law of value.

This law, taken in general terms, must be understood not simply as a law of exchange but primarily as the law of production specific to the market situation, in which – the various producers competing in the production of various goods, and no individual or group having a monopoly on the manufacture of a particular commodity – each of them is forced to sell their product (and therefore have it manufactured) according to its 'socially necessary labour-time', on penalty of seeing other producers enter this branch until the price is equated with this. This competitive situation between branches constitutes the context of competition within the branch, in which the various producers can only obtain from their commodity a price corresponding to the 'average' time needed for its production, and not the actual time taken.

Marx also presents competition as the explanatory principle for the transformation of values into prices. In the same way that, in the abstract matrix of production in general, individual producers, supposedly mobile, only remain in their respective branch if their efforts are rewarded at least according to the time socially necessary for the manufacture of their products, i.e. if these are exchanged against products manufactured in the same time, so capitalists only remain in a branch if capitals are rewarded in accordance with their magnitude. This determines a constant tension towards an equilibrium corresponding to a price at which each kind of capital receives the average profit. 'Concretely', therefore, exchanges take place not at value $(c + v + s)$ but at what Marx calls 'price of production' $(c + v + average\ profit)$.

The law of value, as 'law of supply and demand', is such that, when it operates in conditions of capitalism, value is no longer the *immediate norm* of exchange. But, by the mediation of this transformation, it remains the regulative principle of exchange and production.

The presentation of the transformation gives a *theoretical* assignment of the categories specific to the capitalist, after the previous Part has displayed their *functional* legitimacy within the strict limits that we have seen: it shows in effect how they are related to the concepts of Volume One.

The existence of this transformation, as an element of the capitalist structure, determines the non-transparent character of the concept of value. For, even supposing that the more 'abstract' relations of production, those presenting themselves in terms of value and surplus-value, were transparent (in other words, that the ideological effect denoted by 'fetishism' could be ignored), this more 'concrete' moment, at which exchange is effected not at value but at price of production, introduces a criterion which is no longer that of labour-time but rather of a 'normal' profit added on to costs. The practical categories of the capitalist are now stripped of any possible reference to the couple of constant/variable capital, to surplus-value and value. 'With the transformation of values into prices of production, the very basis for determining value is now removed from view.'[6] In this sense, the transformation 'founds' the ideological representation.

1.iv *Metamorphoses of surplus-value and metamorphoses of ideology (Volume Three, Parts Four to Seven)*

It remains to be shown how the ideological representation, at the precise level which is that of Volume Three as a whole, comes to be redefined and 'transformed', as a function of those 'transformations' that produce the 'derivative forms' of surplus-value; these define real relationships, and must not be confused with the ideological categories to which they give rise.

1.iv.a *'Derivative' real relationships and corresponding ideological categories*
Profit divides into 'profit of enterprise', 'interest' and 'ground rent'. Marx deals first of all (Chapters 21 to 23 of Volume 3) with the couple 'interest/profit of enterprise' (industrial or commercial).

The existence of interest rests on the fact that capital (particularly money) can function immediately as a commodity (by being lent), and, in this form, fulfil functions useful to the system. The conditions that determine the rate of interest differ from those that preside over the formation of rates of profit. Thus, the commodity 'interest-bearing capital' presents a *uniform* rate at a given moment, whereas profit rates are unequal between individual capitals, as a function of the mechanism of extra surplus-value, and only tendentially equal between branches. This uniform rate possesses its specific laws of variation over time.

---

[6] Marx 1981, p. 268.

From this point of departure, Marx's analysis naturally moves from the level of real relationships to that of the representations inherent to the situations and practices that they determine: in themselves, interest and profit of enterprise are simply the parts into which surplus-value or profit in general divides, but, for the individual capitalist, and from the perspective of his position in the economic structure, these are two entities with no mutual connection. This couple therefore possesses a functional foundation and in this sense a legitimacy: 'interest is the fruit of capital in itself . . . , while profit of enterprise is the fruit of capital actually in process'.[7] Far from being a 'subjective conception', this division 'is based on an objective fact', as indicated above.

In the same manner, the social relations constitutive of ground-rent, which form the object of Part Six of Volume Three, give rise to a particular ideological construction. The real basis of this is the fact of the capitalisation of ground-rent: in the capitalist mode of production, the landowner necessarily behaves as a financial capitalist, as possessor of a capital from which he can draw an interest by entrusting it to another capitalist who puts it into operation by using it for the production of commodities. Land is, in fact, analogous to a capital the magnitude of which is determined by the relationship between ground-rent and interest. If the rent of a piece of land is £200 per hectare, and the interest rate is 5 per cent, then the 'value' of this land will be £4,000.[8] The categorisation is irrational; land is not the product of labour, hence it cannot have a value and does not constitute a capital. But it is nonetheless operational, since the capitalist's relationship to rent is the same as his relation to interest: a given capital will yield the same interest, whether it is lent to a capitalist entrepreneur or used to purchase land.

The various transformed forms of surplus-value give rise in this way to ideological categories which should not be confused with them.

1.iv.b *The 'external' connection of the ideological*
Through Parts Four, Five and Six of Volume Three, therefore, Marx traces a progressive distancing that leads from surplus-value to financial capital, each transformed form obscuring still more the original relationship between labour

---

[7] Marx 1981, p. 497.
[8] Cf. Marx 1976a, p. 760.

and the production of an increase in value.[9] He traces the schema of an external connection: from the progressive construction of the 'concrete' relationships there corresponds a movement of progressive obscuring. We are thus led in stages from M–C . . . P . . . C'–M' to M–M', the blinding moment at which 'the social relationship is consummated in the relationship of a thing, money, to itself'.[10]

Marx describes here a movement of 'externalisation [*Veräusserlichung*]' not in the sense as involving the 'essence of man', as was the case with the *Entäusserlichung* of the *1844 Manuscripts*, in which the subject becomes 'foreign' to itself, but, rather, to denote the nature of the relationship that exists between the derived form M–M' and the formula M–C . . . P . . . C'–M' which is its 'concept', and actually *explains* capitalist accumulation by reference to the process of production. This reference is absent from M–M': *Begrisffslosigkeit*, 'absence of the concept'.[11] Here, alienation is not an anthropological category, but a category in the theory of ideology. What it characterises is not the *reality* of the derived social relationship M–M', but the fact that the decisive moment of production is no longer recognisable here. It concerns the mode of *representation* bound up with this relationship.

It remains to be explained why the most concrete forms are also those in which the real relationships are least manifest. We might imagine that the presentation of *Capital* could go from abstract to concrete by particularisation of general relationships without the latter becoming hidden in this process. Why is it necessary to speak of surplus-value on the basis of the transformed forms being *invisible*, as we are invited to do by all the expressions that assign a necessary and ineluctable character to the ideological representations specific to the agents?[12]

This invisibility does not immediately refer to the impossibility for the empirically existing capitalist to grasp in one way or another the reality of his relationship to the wage-earner, but, rather, to the fact that the capitalist here is defined by his function and the representations that this implies. If the ideological structures are as strictly constructed as the 'real' structures, it is because they are a particular aspect of these. They belong to the same

---

[9] Cf. also Marx 1972, pp. 481–97.
[10] Marx 1981, p. 516.
[11] Rancière 1965, pp. 181 & 205.
[12] Marx 1981, pp. 498, 503, 504, 505.

'concrete of thought'. And the impossibility for the capitalist, thus defined, to 'see' surplus-value, corresponds, in my view, to the impossibility of a return in the theoretical order 'from concrete to abstract', i.e. of following in reverse the order of presentation of *Capital*: the impossibility of 'transforming' the derivative categories back into their original concepts, precisely because they are defined only by this antecedent determination, the initial intelligibility of the initial moment. To move from price of production to value would be to assume the theory of surplus-value, which is possible only on the basis of the principles that this implies, i.e. starting with labour-value. In other words, it is because there is no return path leading from the 'derivative' real forms to the 'inner connection' (since the order of presentation runs from the abstract to concrete), that the representations corresponding to these are not suited to giving access to this connection. Such is the external connection of the ideological, which imitates that of the moments of development of the real structures.

1.iv.c *The 'internal' connection of the ideological*

As early as Part One of Volume Three, Marx explains that, if value appears to the individual capitalist as cost of production, the increase can only appear to him correlatively as issuing from the sale of the commodity.[13]

This idea is taken up again in relation to the subsequent forms. The degree zero of their interrelationship, we might say, is constituted by the very fact that the elements (wages, profit, rent) appear all the more independent from one another, in that they seem to be formed according to 'incomprehensible laws'.[14] Separated in this way from the internal principle of their unity, surplus-value (and the law of the division between wages and surplus-value), they are freed for a new ideological reorganisation. And Marx precisely puts forward the idea of a mutual co-determination of these ideological representations.

The fact that the rate of interest is fixed from outside, and uniform, makes it appear as if profit of enterprise depends on the success of the individual capitalist in the competitive struggle, which, conversely, displays interest as deriving from capital itself.[15] The relative invisibility of the capitalist extortion

---

[13] Marx 1981, p. 128.
[14] Marx 1981, p. 1005.
[15] Marx 1981, p. 506.

of value that constitutes interest, on the other hand, makes profit of enterprise appear as a distinct phenomenon, not tied to capital as such, but to the enterprise as site of the capitalist's *activity*. At the same time, the origin of profit being located in the activity of the industrialist, the extortion that interest displays becomes a matter between capitalists. 'The social form of capital devolves on interest, but expressed in a neutral and indifferent form.'[16]

The cleavage between interest and profit of enterprise thus suggests a separation between the process of exploitation and the process of production, in terms of which the opposition between capital and labour is 'forgotten',[17] 'obliterated'[18] in the face of the opposition between the financier and the industrialist, the latter now figuring as simply 'a functionary independent of capital, as a simple bearer of the labour process in general; as a worker, and a wage-worker at that'.[19] This is the reason for 'the capitalist's way of conceiving things . . . grounds for the existence and (subjective) justification of profit as such',[20] and for the capitalist's 'right'[21] to this profit.

In sum, therefore, we have a reciprocal ideologising of the derivative social relations, which in their relationship produces a global effect: reduction of the capitalist process – which is a unity of the process of production and exploitation – to the process of production (or labour process) in general. In this way, the category of surplus-value is obliterated and, along with it, the category of value itself, so that a complete naturalisation of social relations is effected.

1.iv.d   *The ideological as system: 'vulgar economics'*
Such is the main object of final Part of Volume Three, 'The Revenues and Their Sources', the themes of which are already present in the section of *Theories* with virtually the same title.[22] 'Vulgar' economics consists in the systematic integration of the spontaneous categories and their transformation into explanatory schemata for the whole of economic life. In saying this, Marx is still at the stage of critique. He only produces a *theory* of 'vulgar economics'

---

[16] Ibid.
[17] Marx 1981, p. 504.
[18] Marx 1981, p. 503.
[19] Marx 1981, p. 505.
[20] Marx 1981, p. 507.
[21] Marx 1981, p. 504.
[22] Marx 1972, pp. 453–542.

as ideology when he succeeds in basing in the structure of the object itself the principle of this slippage that it effects, by way of which these categories of individual action are constituted as concepts of the economic totality.

Such, indeed, is the principle that Marx brings to light: it is a matter of formal homology between individual capital and total capital, expressed in the fact that the formula M–C . . . P . . . C'–M' can equally symbolise both things. This homology bears on their process or self-reproducing character, in which the result forms, at the same time, the precondition. Thus, for the individual capital, the new value created necessarily breaks down into three parts, one going to capital, a second to labour, and a third to land; the individual capital only continues in its process if the industrialist is in a position to ensure this division – to himself, to the workers and to the landowner – of their respective and 'proper' shares. These distributive categories of individual action apply equally to the overall process: they define the particularities of the reproduction of the capitalist structure, and thus also the conditions of capitalist production. The shares into which value is divided then appear as so many preconditions: interest, for example, becomes a cost of production, being for the individual capitalist a cost just as much as are wages.[23] In short, the practical reproduction schemata for individual capital, which offer an understanding of reproduction in terms of redivision, are applied to the overall process. The result is clearly a vision of the social system grasped in the moment of division of the product outside of the moment of production, and thus also outside of the determinate historical mode of social contradiction.

At the point we have now reached, a coherent schema of the ideological representation now presents itself. This is based on the discrepancy that exists between the level of the 'inner connection', that of Volumes One and Two, and the level of competition which is that of Volume Three. It displays its functional character in the fact that it responds to the requirements of the individual practice of the competing capitalists, constituting the principle of their strategic operational schemas. It corresponds to the moment at which the general laws are realised in individual action, and objective necessities consequently become subjective purposes. These practical categories vary according to the diversity of the functions of capital (industrial, commercial, financial), and in the connection of these functions they find their supporting

---

[23] Cf. Marx 1972, p. 513; Marx 1981, p. 1010.

principle in the ideological complex. The homology that exists between the process of reproduction of individual capital and that of total capital predisposes them to provide a representation of the latter in terms of the former, and build this into the system that Marx denotes as 'vulgar economics'.

This harmonious construction, however, involves some major obstacles that we must now go on to tackle.

2. The uncertainties in Marx's exposition

Two difficulties particularly arise. The first pertains to the mistake that I analysed at length in Chapter 6: the moment of *competition* does not properly belong to Volume Three, but is required for the presentation of extra and relative surplus-value already in Part Four of Volume One. As a result, the problematic that associates 'everyday consciousness' with the level of Volume Three, deemed to be that of competition, appears unfounded. The second follows from the inadequacy of the schema (despite its appearing to be complementary and corrective) of *inversion* that is used to express the presence of the ideological as early as the 'internal' determinations, those of Volume One, but does so in a philosophical mode loaded with ambiguities. Let us examine the nature of these difficulties, and the way in which Marx gradually escapes from them.

2.i *Competition and ideology at the various levels of the theory*

If competition, the moment of 'inter-individual' relations within the capitalist class, rightly belongs to Volume One, then the ideological, the system of representations involved in this individual action, does so as well. We have seen, moreover, how, despite his denials (since he officially relegates competition to Volume Three), Marx actually introduces, in Part Four of Volume One, both competition and along with it the 'consciousness' of the capitalist: it is in the form of competition that the laws of capital appear, and 'enter into the consciousness of the individual capitalist as the motives which drive him forward'.[24] The moment of individual practice is necessarily also that of the representations that underlie it.

---

[24] Marx 1976a, p. 433.

Two connected problems arise at this point.

1) These representations inherent to the individual practice as defined in Part Four of Volume One are far from being any kind of illusion, and partly coincide on the contrary with the 'scientific' categories that the theory proposes. The preoccupation with 'socially necessary time', or at least that of producing in the shortest possible time, imbues all capitalist conduct in the competitive situation. The determination of value constitutes, in this sense, a reference to spontaneous consciousness.

2) This interference between 'everyday' and 'theoretical' consciousness is conveyed from Volume One to Volume Three by the fact that the latter contains, after the transformation of value into price of production, a new presentation of the question of competition within the branch, this time in terms of price, and thus a presentation of 'extra profit' that requires the same categorial ensemble at the levels of both reality and consciousness.

The connection between these two problems is precisely displayed in a long passage from Volume Three dealing with the 'consciousness' of the capitalist taken at the level of 'extra profit' and its relationship to the determination of value.[25]

This text has a double interest, or, rather, its interest bears on the double character of its argument. On the one hand, the capitalist taken in his relationship to others in general is only 'interested' in the determination of value because 'right from the start . . . it is not values but rather prices of production differing from them that form the governing average prices in each sphere of production'.[26] Confrontation within a branch is conducted in terms of price of production and not value, and the latter, being invisible, cannot be the pole of 'interest'. On the other hand, however, they are so, and 'the value determination . . . interests and affects the individual capitalist' in so far as it brings 'extra profits' arising from the difference in productivity within the branch.[27]

In short, these forms of consciousness that are attributed to the capitalist motivated by profit, at the level of Volume Three, are simply a realisation of those belonging to the level of Volume One, and they display a relative

---

[25] Cf. Marx 1981, pp. 1009–10.
[26] Cf. Marx 1981, p. 1013.
[27] Ibid.

convergence with the categories of value. In other words, in an idea that Marx frequently reaffirms,[28] they show that the invisibility of value and surplus-value is only relative.

2.ii The theme of inversion [Verkehrung]

The schema of inversion occurs in Volume Three in two distinct modes. The first, which is found in Chapter 12, is inscribed in the general problematic that we have analysed. The second, in Chapter 2, is of a different nature, since it locates the principle of the ideological in the 'inner connection'. But it does this in terms of the philosophical critique of the young Marx, which here shows its insufficiency.

In Chapter 12, Marx draws a kind of balance-sheet of the ideological representations bound up with competition:

> In competition, therefore, everything appears upside down [verkehrt]. The finished configuration of economic relations, as these are visible on the surface, in their actual existence, and therefore also in the notions with which the bearers and agents of these relations seek to gain an understanding of them, is very different from the configuration of their inner core [Kerngestalt], which is essential but concealed, and the concept corresponding to it. It is in fact the very reverse [Verkehrung] and antithesis of this.[29]

The terms of this presentation are organised according to the following table, where $\rightarrow$ denotes an inversion, and $\leftrightarrow$ a relation of correspondence:

	Volume 1	Volume 3	
Essential hidden inner core	$\longrightarrow$	Finished form surface real existence	$\uparrow$
	inversion, difference opposition		
hidden concept		agents' representation	$\downarrow$

---

[28] Marx 1981, pp. 137–9, etc.
[29] Marx 1981, p. 311; Marx 1974a, p. 219 (Marx's emphasis); also Marx 1981, pp. 331, 428–9, 503–4, etc.

Inversion, here, does not characterise the relationship between the representation [*Vorstellung*] made by the agents and reality. On the contrary, this is (functionally) adequate at the 'concrete' level of the real relations of production, the 'finished' form. And it is the 'finished form' and 'representation' that together represent an inversion of the inner essence.

We should note that the term 'inversion' is not adequate here, since the relationships defined in Volume Three are not themselves the actual 'inversion' of those defined in Volume One, but simply located at a different level of the overall theoretical architecture. The 'inversion', or something deserving that name, appears only when the categories that characterise this level are applied in an 'essential' sense, i.e. concerning the production of surplus-value. What is then called 'inversion' is the fact that the non-worker appears as worker, capital as a thing, etc.[30]

In short, the relation characterises the relationship between the representations inherent to the level of reality of Volume Three, and the level of reality of Volume One. It is thus an ideological phenomenon, an inversion in the representation, a discrepancy between this and the reality (of Volume One), but which is supported in the reality (of Volume Three) to which it is in a certain sense adequate. This use of the theme of inversion is completely coherent with the entire theory of ideology that Marx offers in Volume Three and which I have presented in the first section of this chapter. At the same time, he extends this further. For there is a moment indicated here at which appearance [*Erscheinung*] becomes illusion [*Schein*]. The categories of competition constitute an *Erscheinung*, in the sense that an essential structure is effectively realised in a more concrete structure: the law of value is expressed in exchange at prices of production. This involves a *Schein*, in the sense that this order of expression is mistaken for the inner structure and thus gives a fallacious representation of it. This is why Marx speaks frequently in terms of error, confusion, etc. The illusion is analogous to Kant's transcendental illusion: an illegitimate use of categories that have their proper pertinence elsewhere. Here this is based on the functionality that I discussed in the first section. That, however, is where the analogy with Kant ends. For, on the one hand, the categories of appearance here are not those of science, but, on the contrary, are opposed to it. And, on the other hand, the existence of 'science',

---

[30] Cf. again Marx 1981, pp. 428–9, 513; Marx 1969, p. 69 ('umgekehrt').

which establishes the real order beyond the phenomenon by asserting its specific categories, proves the resistible character of the appearance, which, in effect, no longer relates to a universal structure of mind but, rather, to the representation inherent to a particular function in a determinate historical mode of production.

In Chapter 2, however, the notion of inversion is used in a quite different context, and not without certain ambiguities:

> [T]he way that surplus-value is transformed into the form of profit, by way of the rate of profit, is only a further extension of that inversion of subject and object which already occurs in the course of the production process itself. We saw in that case how all the subjective productive forces of labour present themselves as productive forces of capital.[31] On the one hand, value, i.e. the past labour that dominates living labour, is personified into the capitalist; on the other hand, the worker conversely appears as mere objectified labour-power, as a commodity. This inverted relationship necessarily gives rise, even in the simple relation of production itself, to a correspondingly inverted [*verkehrt*] conception of the situation, a transposed consciousness, which is further developed by the transformation and modifications of the circulation process proper.[32]

This time we have a very different table:

Volume One		Volume Three
Subject, living labour, worker, subjective force		Surplus-value
⟵⟶		↓
Object, past labour, capitalist objective force	Corresponding inverted representation	Profit

The inversion here, far from being tied to the moment of 'competition', is indicated as belonging to the real inner relationships themselves. It exists 'in the simple relation of production', the moment of surplus-value. It constitutes an original characteristic of the capitalist relation of production, which develops by way of the whole architecture reflected in the presentation. It is specified in its initial moment by the philosophical couple of subject/object and its

---

[31] Cf. Marx 1976a, p. 451.
[32] Marx 1981, p. 136; Marx 1974a, p. 55.

derivations. It requires, already in Volume One, a representation that is itself 'inverted'. Not in relation to the second member of the inversion of real relations (object, past labour, etc.), with which it indeed corresponds – and, in this sense, it is not 'wrong-headed'.[33] But rather in relation to the first member (subject, etc.). Here, the ideological inversion is only the reflection of the inversion in the structure itself. In Volume Three, this inversion is taken up and 'developed', which means that it is of the same type (subject/object) as that which has been defined in Volume One. But, at the same time, it forms the articulation between Volumes One and Three: between surplus-value and profit.

The difference between these two treatments of 'inversion' is apparent. In Chapter 2 of Volume Three, this characterises first of all the real relations, the reality of a world that is essentially inverted. But then it also characterises the representation that 'corresponds' to this. Hence we have the unsustainable paradox that ideology is a true figure of the world as it is. The same category of inversion defines the real relationship and the ideological one. There is thus no specific theorisation of the ideological, nor a theory of the real relations as distinct from that of their ideological inversion. In Chapter 12, on the contrary, inversion functions as the defining category of the ideological, and of the particular level of reality to which it corresponds, the distortion of the latter in relation to the inner connection; it denotes, in fact, not a real 'inversion' but, rather, the complex 'transformation' described in Parts One and Two. This text displays a greater maturity. The maturing of Marx's theory was a process in which the two conceptual orders, initially more or less associated in the critico-philosophical mist, came to be distinguished and related to another without ambiguity.

2.iii *Maturation of the theory of ideology*

This process of maturation appears to have affected other categories of the same order: 'turning into its opposite', 'appearance', 'personification/reification'. Let us consider here the two last of these.

'Appearance [*Erscheinung*]' figures in the first drafts of Volume One at the heart of an ambiguous assertion: 'the productive forces of labour . . . appear

---

[33] Ibid.

as *productive powers of capital*.[34] This is the theme of a long passage that reappears both in *Theories*,[35] and in 'Results' under the title 'mystification of capital'.[36] This heading seems to locate it in the theory of ideology. Yet the pivot of the assertion ('erscheinen als', 'sich stellen als . . . dar', 'treten als'; 'appear as', 'present themselves as') is ambiguous, each time raising the question whether this 'appearing' should be interpreted in terms of appearance or of actual emergence, and, if the latter, whether the emergence is historical or theoretical.

On the one hand, in fact, Marx seems to treat in terms of fetishism, of 'ideological' appearance, the attribution of a productive power to capital, something that actually flows from co-operative labour as such. On the other hand, he evidently makes a judgement about reality: capital must be said to be productive. On this point, he frequently strikes an opposing position to Ricardo, for whom '*only labour* is productive, not capital': this would mean understanding capital simply as a 'material substance', a means of production issuing from labour, and forgetting its '*specific character as form*, as a *relation of production* reflected into itself'.[37] Marx reproaches the economists with taking capital for a thing, and thus overlooking its specific efficacy as a form of property and organisation of labour, i.e. as a mode of production, the principle of the revolutionary historical role of capitalism.[38]

This ambiguity about 'appearing' should not be taken as mere confusion. But, to remove it, the two propositions that Marx's analysis implies must be articulated: 1) the productivity of labour *appears* to be that of capital, whereas it is simply that of the socialisation of human activity; 2) this productivity of labour *is* that of capital, because it is historically born and develops with capital (though not being naturally and eternally tied to it).

Marx cultivates here an ambiguous form of expression, and this ambiguity provides him with a critical-dialectical impulse. But this critique is, strictly speaking, a non-theory of ideology. Its actual force and explosive character derive from the tension created by the collision of two assertions combined in one: the productive force of labour *appears* as the productive force of capital, in other words it both is and is not. And this 'appearing' depicts a contradiction

---

[34] Marx 1964, p. 378; Marx's emphasis.
[35] Marx 1964, pp. 377–80.
[36] Marx 1976a, p. 1052.
[37] Marx 1973c, p. 309; Marx's emphases.
[38] Cf. Marx 1972, p. 273.

which calls for a great reversal. This category, however, from the very fact that it denotes both what is and what appears to be, cannot ensure a clear expression of the two, i.e. the articulation of the ideological to the real relationship.

In the subsequent text of *Capital*, Marx stops playing this game and the formulation becomes unambiguous. 'The socially productive power of labour ... appears as a power which capital possesses by its nature – a productive power inherent in capital.'[39] The expression now distinguishes on the one hand the 'content [*Inhalt*]', and, on the other, the 'mere form [*blosse Form*]'[40] or 'false appearance [*der falsche Schein*]'.[41] Appearance is, here, simply appearance.

2.iii.a   The 'person/thing' inversion

Certain texts present surplus-value as a personification of the thing and reification of the person.[42] Marx thus produces a critical statement that refers to the contradiction of this mode of production, its content of domination. But, very curiously, this critical assertion itself rests on the ideological statement that takes social relations for 'things': capital which is a thing becomes in the capitalist a person. The statement is paradoxical: Marx enters into the ideological discourse, bases himself on the ideological representation which takes the capital social relation for a thing, so as to constitute a 'critical' discourse. The ideological discourse is turned back into a discourse on the real, and this reversal generates a critique of reality. But the price of this is the fiction according to which it is things, products of labour, that dominate and 'reify' people.

This theme is also taken up in the presentation of the *1861–3 Manuscripts*, according to which the wage-earner is the 'mere personification of his own labour capacity'.[43] *Capital*, which generally follows the 1861 text here, selectively skips these passages.

The theme of personification is reserved from now on for the capitalist, not as 'personification of things' but rather 'personification of capital', of a 'social relation'. This personification cannot be conceived as the moment of any *inversion*. It denotes the fact that the capital relationship implies the capitalist

---

[39] Marx 1976a, p. 451; Marx 1973a, p. 353.
[40] Marx 1973a, p. 609.
[41] Marx 1973a, p. 555.
[42] Marx 1964, p. 380.
[43] Marx and Engels 1988a, pp. 38, 39–42.

function, and hence an agent whose principles of action are defined by the requirements of this function, 'his actions are a mere function of capital – endowed as capital is, in his person, with consciousness and a will'.[44]

In sum, therefore, once we recognise the inadequacy of the problematic that postpones a theorisation of the ideological to Volume Three, we have to maintain that the sketch of this at the level of Volume One, based on the critical schema of 'inversion', encounters a major obstacle. This follows from the fact that the *inverted world* (of 'alienation') and the *inverted image* (of 'fetishism') that corresponds to it are associated here, precisely where the task should be to distinguish the real relationships from their ideological representation. We certainly see this distinction gradually asserted, in the progressive treatments of the theme. But, so long as Marx adheres to this theme of 'inversion', he is unable to develop coherently the theorisation of the ideological which the moment of Volume One requires.

3. The 'raisons d'être' of the form of appearance (in Volume One)

In Volume One of *Capital*, Marx produces, for the first time, a systematic analysis of the representations implied at the level of the 'inner and essential connection'.[45] This is a brief (but famous) passage in Part Six. This Part breaks the course of the presentation. Whereas previous Parts served to establish theoretically the reality of the wage-labour relationship, Part 6 opens with a chapter bearing on the *representations* that these real relationships give of themselves. There is thus a 'transformation [*Verwandlung*]' at work here, and this as we have seen is a deceptive term. It habitually denotes a 'passage'

---

[44] Marx 1976a, p. 739.

[45] The immediately preceding version, that of 1863 (Marx 1994, pp. 61–86), does not offer a study of these *'raisons d'être'*. It only mentions this 'form [that] lacks conceptual rigour [*begriffslose Form*]' as a 'necessary *form of appearance* of the value of labour capacity' (p. 86; Marx's emphasis). The question is still tackled in a 'dialectical' fashion: insistence on the idea that there is an 'inverted form' that belongs to the 'real process of competition' (p. 77). We encounter here an old problem: if we recall that competition does not supposedly belong in Volume One, we can understand why Marx omitted this embarrassing consideration in the final draft of *Capital*. He insists that the concept of value 'is reversed into its direct opposite' (p. 83 & passim). This text of 1863, which deserves a particular study, is located in the process of maturation that I have indicated.

from one moment to another (more concrete) in the presentation of the categorial system of real relations, but it is used here for the articulation of the real relations to the ideological relation.

With this chapter we do not leave the 'inner connection' that is the object of Volume One, but we examine how: 'On the surface of bourgeois society the worker's wage appears as the price of labour.'[46] In short, the surface is not left for Volume Three. The abstract relations presented in Volume One also have 'their own' surface.

Marx does not just propose here a *critique* of these forms, which it is easy to show constitute 'an absurd tautology',[47] given that labour being the measure of value cannot have value itself. He intends to show how such 'irrational'[48] formulae as 'value of labour' or 'value of land' refer to actual social reality, and, in this way, produce a *theory* of the ideological representation, explaining by what 'necessity' social relations appear other than they are. In short, he intends to establish 'the *raison d'être* . . . of this form of appearance'.[49]

I shall analyse in turn and in order each of the eight '*raisons d'être*' that Marx puts forward here.[50]

3.i First reason

The exchange between labour and capital at first presents itself to our perceptions in exactly the same way as the sale and purchase of all other commodities. The buyer gives a certain sum of money, the seller an article which is something other than money. The legal mind recognises here, at most, a material difference, expressed in the legally equivalent formula: '*Do ut des, do ut facias, factio ut des, facio ut facias.*'[51]

Marx appeals here to 'perception [*Wahrnehmung*]', the spontaneous representation of the exchange between capital and labour. He indicates that such a representation integrates this type of exchange into the general framework of commodity exchange. 'The legal mind [*Rechtsbewusstsein*]' is not to be understood as a 'superstructural' element with its specific historicity –

---

[46] Marx 1973a, p. 557; Marx 1976a, p. 675.
[47] Ibid.
[48] Marx 1976a, p. 679.
[49] Marx 1976a, p. 681.
[50] Marx 1976a, pp. 681 ff.
[51] Cf. Marx 1973a, p. 563.

as the reference to the dated formulae of Roman law might suggest – but denotes the subjective categories implied by the act of exchange. To exchange is to exchange mine against yours, to assert my own ownership and that of another. These categories, far from being illusory, are implied in exchange as a meaningful behaviour, as this was analysed in Chapter 2 of Volume One.

These formulae, to which Marx frequently refers,[52] have the further advantage of recalling the equivalence of various forms of exchange, whether these involve past labour [*do*] or present [*facio*], i.e. a 'good' or a 'service'.

If there is illusion of any kind here, it is because the exchange relation in general presents a framework in which a transaction concerning a 'service' can be inscribed. This is attested by the identity of the legal form.

The argument is thus complete only by reference to the theory of fetishism: exchange in general does not bear 'on its forehead' its quantitative determination in terms of labour-time. The exchanging consciousness, however, is prepared to accept this relationship as exchange, since it includes the legal forms. And it cannot detect its particular character (by which it is something other than an exchange), since this bears on the quantitative element in value that escapes it.

In short, it is not at bottom the specific forms of wage-labour that mask the reality; the famously invisible boundary between the part of the working day that is paid and the part that is not paid is a function of the indiscernible magnitude of the value of labour-power, and thus an obscurity that bears on value at its basic level. The illegibility of surplus-value derives above all from the original illegibility of value. The counter-proof of this is that in serfdom the division between paid and unpaid labour is visible, because production does not have a commodity character.

3.ii *Second reason*

Further. Since exchange-value and use-value are in themselves incommensurable magnitudes, the expressions 'value of labour', 'price of labour', do not seem more irrational than the expressions 'value of cotton', 'price of cotton'.

In this case, value and use-value are commensurable because the use-value in question serves to produce a greater value. This consideration, which is

---

[52] Marx 1973c, p. 465; Marx 1964, p. 391; Marx 1976a, p. 1047.

that of the theory itself, breaks the category of 'value of labour' in two: value of labour-power and value of the product of labour. But, for all other commodities, and for the commodity relation in general, such dissociation has no place. People thus speak spontaneously of the 'value of labour', Marx seems to be saying, with the appearance of rationality.

Marx's procedure here is of a rather different order from the previous reason. It denotes the expression 'value of labour' as a kind of spontaneous (but erroneous) 'rationalisation' of the specific wage relationship, and is, to this extent, located at a less 'primary' level. But, from the fact that it concerns the possible subsumption of the wage relation into the commodity relation, it remains very close to the first remark.

3.iii   *Third reason*

> Moreover, the worker is paid after he has given his labour. In its function
> as a means of payment, money realizes, but only subsequently, the value
> or price of the article supplied – i.e. in this particular case, the value or price
> of the labour supplied.

After having 'given' or 'supplied [*geliefert*]' 'his labour'. Marx spins out the 'transformed form' like a metaphor. This time, he situates himself inside it to show the evidence for it. His approach, in fact, undergoes a total change. The first two remarks concerned the wage relation as a whole, and its ideological subsumption under the simple commodity structure. Ideology, one might say, was defined there as the function of a structure, a function of the structural inclusion of the wage relation in the commodity relation. Now Marx extracts the ideological element bound up with a particular practice that characterises the wage relation, that of subsequent payment. This practice clearly has other functions than that of producing this ideological effect. It constitutes a means of pressure on the worker and a saving for the capitalist. But it is, at the same time, also an ideological practice, in the sense of a particular arrangement of economic acts to sustain a certain ideological form. If wages were paid in advance, they would appear as the preparation of labour-power, and lose their immediate reference to labour itself. Subsequent payment makes wages seem a particular case of 'payment', in the sense of 'deferred payment', dissociation of exchange into a first phase of alienation (which obtains here through the entire period in which labour is 'supplied'), and a second phase of acquisition (which, here, comprises just the final instant of payment). The wage appears when the whole labour has been supplied. In short, this particular practice of *subsequent payment* – which the capitalist structure in principle requires because it is essential to the wage relation as a relation of force, so much so that, when it does not exist, it is because substitutes for it have been found – far from expressing the wage as a specific relationship, makes it possible to inscribe it in the general framework of commodity transactions: any exchange can involves a deferred payment. We should note, however, that the analysis here is no longer located at the level of the general *structure*, as was earlier the case, but that of a *particular practice* inherent to this structure.

3.iv   *Fourth reason*

I shall base myself here on the French version,[53] which is longer and attests to a certain reworking. The argument falls into two parts:

> Finally, the use-value *supplied* by the worker to the capitalist is not *in fact* his labour-power but its function, a specific form of useful labour. In all *appearance*, what the capitalist pays for is thus the value of the utility that the worker *gives* him, the value of labour – and not that of the labour-power, which it seems that the worker does not *alienate*.
>
> The twofold utility of labour does not emerge simply from experience of practical life – its property of satisfying a need, which it has in common with every commodity, and that of creating value, which distinguishes it from all commodities and excludes it, as formative element of value, from any possibility of having a value itself.[54]

This time, the argument is situated not at the quantitative level of a confusion between two magnitudes (value produced/value of labour-power), but, rather, a confusion between two concepts (labour/labour-power), more precisely

---

[53] [This is one of the relatively few passages where the English edition does not follow the French.]

[54] Marx 1983, fasc. 2, p. 211; my emphases: J.B. [Cf. Marx 1976a, p. 681.]

the non-perception of labour-power as a commodity in the ideological representation.

The first assertion opposes reality and appearance.

In appearance, the worker 'does not alienate' his labour-power, says Marx, recalling in this way that in reality he does alienate it.

As far as reality is concerned, Marx employs a different term: the worker 'supplies [*liefert*]' the use of his labour-power, its function, he does not supply his labour-power.

Marx proposes in this way to explain the appearance and determine its '*raison d'être*'. Paradoxically, however, his explanation supposes that a whole section of the appearance does conform to 'reality'. It is implicitly but clearly to be understood that the fact that the worker supplies 'the use of his labour-power' is a *manifest* reality, a reality that appears.

This gives us, for 'alienate' and 'supply', the following table of usages:

The worker		his labour-power	the use of his labour-power
In reality	alienates	+	
	supplies	–	+
In appearance	alienates	–	
	supplies	–	+

In the register of 'supply', reality and appearance coincide. In that of 'alienation', on the contrary, they are opposed: labour-power does not 'seem' to be 'alienated', and this is precisely why a *raison d'être* is needed. Marx, however, does not provide this, except by moving to a different level, that of supply, which is deemed to provide the explanation: the worker does not 'supply' his labour-power, and so he does not seem to alienate it. The *raison d'être* is thus located in the discrepancy between alienating and supplying, in the fact that the worker does not 'supply' the power that he alienates.

We clearly have here, and under the same theoretical constraints, a turn of expression analogous to that which was already used to define the wage relation in Part Two of Volume One: the wage-worker 'disposes' of his labour-power (here he does not 'supply' it), but has to put it at the 'disposal' of the capitalist (here he 'alienates' it). The 'sale' of labour-power, as we saw, remains a metaphor to the extent that the buyer does not dispose of it as a thing, but only in a 'political' relationship. The purchase of labour-power ensures the full 'disposition' of its future product, but not of the actual producer.

What is supplied is the possibility of a definite use of labour-power, determined in the confrontation between director and directed within the production process.

To make the discrepancy between *alienated* and *supplied* the principle of ideological representation is to connect the invisibility of the sale of labour-power with the fact that this is never a total alienation, a sale in the strict sense. Marx does not dwell on this point, it is not an established position. It is, however, a perilous one, precisely because it is particularly strategic. To clarify this point, in fact, means not just showing the metaphorical character of the category of the sale of labour-power (where the metaphor does not jeopardise Marx's 'scientific' system, but indicates the impossibility of a positivist interpretation of it), but also the moment of truth of ideology. There is something true in everyday consciousness, Marx acknowledges: labour-power is not 'supplied', not sold in the same sense as a thing is. An 'ideological' assertion of this kind has a purchase on reality to the extent that it questions the commodity status of labour-power, its status of a pure thing. It shows that there is in the structure of the capitalist mode of production a feature that prevents the category of *value of labour-power* from appearing, this feature being that the commodity character of this power cannot appear: the free wage-worker does not hand himself over as a thing. This subjective moment cannot be reduced to a mere appearance without denying what Marx calls the 'essential determination' of the capitalist relation. Nothing would weaken the theory more than to oppose the freedom of the circulation sphere to the servitude of the production sphere. For, if this servitude is not slavery, if this dominated class has more than any other the prospect of being a class in struggle, this is due to the effect in the order of production of a freedom that pertains to the order of circulation, the freedom to change masters. It is this moment of truth that is indicated in the above table, that of the coincidence between reality and appearance.

As for the 'ideological' in the ideological assertion, this follows from the fact that the latter denotes what is put at capital's disposal as 'labour', thus denying that labour is only supplied if it is already 'mastered' – in the class relation that is 'always already' there – by the master of the process who must exert his grip on labour-power to obtain its 'function'. Exchange, in fact, contains a contract, and thus posits the self as free. Hence the exchange of labour-power involves a denial that labour is supplied already mastered, a denial of the alienation of labour-power, of its commodity status. A denial of the moment of truth of this metaphor: the capitalist only buys in so far as he can compel this power to perform more social labour than it contains. A moment at which he is the merchant and labour-power the merchandise.

The second assertion is connected to the former in a curious way, as both a critique of it and a supplementary argument. It asserts, in fact, the condition of visibility of the reality of the surplus-value relation: to have pierced the secret of value, of labour as general, formative of value and hence itself a non-value. This is certainly, first of all, a critique of the ideological representation, conveyed in a sense by the previous assertion: theory as the recognised reality is opposed to it. But these theoretical conditions of visibility are nothing more than the practical conditions of invisibility that define what the invisibility of surplus-value is attached to: the specific invisibility of the value relation. Just as 'value . . . does not have its description branded on its forehead',[55] neither is labour branded as being the former of value. This is an argument that is additional to the previous, in the sense that it refers us to a further foundation of the ideological position, at the most abstract level of value. An argument that proceeds not from the critique of ideology but from its *theory*, from the explanation of its '*raisons d'être*'. But by being theory, it is also the most radical critique.

3.v   *Fifth reason*

> Let us put ourselves in the place of the worker who receives for 12 hours of labour the value-product of, say, 6 hours of labour, namely 3 shillings. For him, in fact, his 12 hours of labour is the means of buying the 3 shillings. . . . Every change in the amount of the equivalent that he receives therefore necessarily appears to him as a change in the value or price of his 12 hours of labour.[56]

Marx puts forward here the idea that labour plays for every worker the role of universal equivalent, i.e. an immutable principle for any comparison. He puts himself in the shoes of the worker in so far as the latter is involved in an exchange process.

---

[55] Marx 1976a, p. 167.
[56] Marx 1976a, p. 681; Marx 1973a, p. 563.

In this exchange, it is only the 'service' that visibly bears in it the 'time and trouble' that constitutes it. It thus becomes the first term in the comparison. 'What initially concerns producers in practice', one might say of the wage-earners, taking up the language Marx applies to the 'exchangers' of simple commodity production,[57] is 'how much of some other product they get', in this case for their labour. The ideological equivalence of wage-labour and service is fuelled by the non-transparent character of exchange in general. Once more again, the place of ideology is referred to a higher degree of abstraction, the level of value.

3.vi *Sixth reason*

> Let us consider, on the other hand, the capitalist.[58]

The same reference to his 'practical interests', the pursuit of which in this case simply consists in buying, as with any other article, 'for as little money as possible'; we are thus again referred to the exchange relation and its specific non-transparency, which affects the capitalist's entire exchanging practice.

3.vii *Seventh reason*

> Moreover, the actual movement of wages presents phenomena which seem to prove that it is not the value of labour-power which is paid, but the value of its function, of labour itself. . . . (1) Changes in wages owing to changes in the length of the working day. One might as well conclude that it is not the value of a machine which is paid, but that of its operation, because it costs more to hire a machine for a week than for a day.[59]

Here, Marx touches on the specific level. The 'form of expression' is not related to the capitalist relation in general, but to the particularity of wage practice in its fundamental form, time-wages, of which the others, such as piece-wages, are 'transformations' (in the sense of particular modes of performing this labour-time). No immanent law of this social relation fixes the length of the working day, which is, on the contrary, implied to be undefined, except for

---

[57] Marx 1976a, p. 167.
[58] Marx 1976a, p. 682.
[59] Ibid; Marx 1973a, p. 564.

its minimum, that of paid working-time. This particularity implies the adequate practical character of labour's 'hourly rate' and in general the 'price of labour',[60] which Marx deals with in the following chapter. The category is implied in the procedure which the two 'partners' follow in establishing the wage relation, just as are the categories of profit inherent to the practice of capitalism that are presented at the start of Volume Three (cf. Section 1 of the present chapter).

3.viii *Eighth reason*

> (2) Individual differences between the wages of different workers who perform the same function.[61]

If we want to relate this statement to its implications in the theory, we have to proceed once more in the direction of the abstract moment of the commodity, i.e. of Part One. For these differences in wages are related to the differences in 'diligence, skill, or strength' and thus make the individual wage 'appear to vary in keeping with the results of his own work and its individual quality', as Marx indicates in the 'Results'.[62] The categories used here, 'diligence', 'skill', etc. are those used in Chapter 1 of *Capital* apropos the quality of socially necessary labour. And the argument here consists, in effect, of showing that, if the wage relation is hidden by exchange and seems to be reabsorbed into this, it is because in production for exchange in general, 'individual' capacities are taken into account to the extent that they lead to different performance [*Leistung*], determining the greater or lesser quantity of commodities, and thus value, produced in a given working time. Marx seems here to situate himself on the terrain of the 'mistake': from the (supposed) *proportionality* between values produced and wages received, the observer concludes a relation of *equality*.

This brief and very concentrated text is not the only place where Marx tackles the question of the foundation of the ideological representation of the wage relation, but here he gathers together all strands of his argument. It is rather heterogeneous, in an unmastered way, as Marx only imperfectly

---

[60] Marx 1976a, p. 684.
[61] Marx 1976a, p. 682; Marx 1973a, p. 564.
[62] Marx 1976a, p. 1032.

distinguishes the different levels at which he situates himself. An effort of analysis is thus needed to relate each proposition to its particular presuppositions, its points of attachment in the architecture of the theory. That is also to say that this analysis flows into the general interpretation of the theory proposed here.

The main conclusion to extract is that Marx's analysis tends to shift the question of ideology from the 'wage relation' to the 'commodity relation' moment. More precisely, if the wage relation presents itself as an exchange relation, this is first of all by virtue of a non-transparency that pertains to the exchange relation in general. In short, the ideology of the wage relation is dominated by commodity fetishism.

This is why, in the first reason cited above, the wage relation has the (legal) form of exchange. There is not a quantitative equality. But this is never legible in exchange, for labour-value is not empirically given. The second reason refers us to the relation between use-value and exchange-value that is not generally visible. In the same way, the second part of the fourth reason recalls that the ability of labour to create value is not given simply from 'experience of practical life'. What is involved here is the requisite 'value' of surplus-value. The fifth reason shows how the equivalence that presents wage-labour as a service is fuelled by the non-transparency of exchange. The sixth reason, that of the capitalist, simply recalls that for him this is simply an exchange because, approaching exchange as a fetishist, he naturally includes wage-labour as part of it. The seventh reason also refers to problems inherent to the commodity: the supposed equivalence of the 'service' and the 'good' that is hired (the *ut des* and the *ut facias*).

If this were all, the theorisation of the ideology bound up with wage-labour would be entirely related to the ideological aspect of value, to 'fetishism'. But other determinations of the ideological have appeared in the process, relating to the specificity of wage relations.

On the one hand, the problem that emerges from the fourth reason, the invisibility of the sale and purchase of labour-power (the belief that it is simply labour that is sold), also arises because the worker does not 'supply' this in the same way that a physical good is supplied. We may recall that the capitalist both 'disposes' and does not dispose of labour-power. The 'commodity' here is a metaphor. And, precisely because this alienation is not total, it is not legible as a sale. The ideological moment here would then be identified with a fit of truth, the deciphering of the metaphor, if it did not fall back into an inferior representation that takes what is supplied as 'labour'. We have here, in this sense, a specific effect of the ideological structure. The different variants of wage practice still need to be investigated (time-wages, piece-wages, etc.) as well as related ideological effects.

Something quite different is presented as the third reason, which we have to call an 'ideological practice': subsequent payment. This is not an ideological effect of the structure, but, rather, a practical arrangement suited to the structure as a structure of exploitation, an arrangement that has particular ideological effects.

As for the seventh reason, Marx indicates how the wage relation itself, for its practical application, requires such categories as the 'price' of an hour's labour or a week's, thus a 'price of labour' in general. This is the pragmatic face of the ideological category.

In these three last cases, however, even if we are not faced with an ideological effect of the 'commodity' structural level, but, rather, an effect specific to the level of the wage relation, the latter is still supported by the original opacity of commodity exchange, since it is always with this relation that the wage relationship is identified.

In short, everything leads us to confront the initial moment of the ideological complex, commodity fetishism.

Conclusion

Volume Three of *Capital* is explicitly presented as the moment at which the exposition, developing from abstract to concrete, reaches the categories of 'everyday consciousness' and accounts for their functional necessity in capitalist society. Here, in fact, we reach, beyond the 'inner connection' of the system taken in its entirety, the 'surface' moment by which the general laws are implemented: that of competition, the action of the individual capitalist, which effectively supposes the application of a system of operational categories. Marx shows how this system has no need for the concepts of surplus-value or even of value, and yet it still has its specific pertinence: it rationally organises the practice of the individual capitalist, providing him with the foundations for his economic calculation. But this theory of ideology has its sole basis in the theory of the transformation of values into prices of production which analytically connects the world of competition with the inner connection, thus explaining both why the operational categories of the capitalist are out of line with value, and why it is impossible to advance from them to surplus-value and value, which they render illegible. In brief, why there is no path from ideology to science. Starting from here, Marx offers not simply a critique but a theory of 'vulgar economics' as ideology, i.e. an explanation for its emergence; and this by way of the homology that exists between the reproduction of the individual capital and that of the social capital. The basis of 'capitalist ideology' is thus shown in its double aspect of illusion and functionality, but in an articulation in which the latter has primacy. For it is in terms of its functionality that it is 'deduced', and not in the name of the need for a mask or illusion, these arising only as effects. Ideology, then, is not censorship in the Freudian sense.

The ideological, defined here as implicit in the capitalist function, clearly constitutes an essential determinant of class struggle: this discourse of the manipulation and handling of labour as one ingredient of production among others, with the relation of appropriation being given here as an exchange relation, constitutes a discourse of domination. For what is designated here as a 'function' only is so in a system based on antagonism. Domination, however, has no need to hide itself; it is hidden *in advance*. It does not have to play tricks: it is opacity. Always imperfect opacity, as we shall see, and the domination likewise.

This form of theorisation, which posits the ideological in Volume Three, encounters a major obstacle in the fact that the determinations of competition, and hence those of individual practice, do not properly belong to this volume at all, but are implied in the presentation of surplus-value and even value, as I have shown in Chapter 6. The question of everyday consciousness is thus not really connected to a more 'concrete' moment of the exposition: it must be articulated to its different levels of abstraction. We can note that a different schema, that of 'inversion', is mobilised precisely to denote the ideological in a more global fashion. But this is an ambiguous category, to be found in two different versions. The first, in Marx's early texts, is critico-philosophical: the *real* inversion of an alienated world. The other is more homogeneous with the theorisation of ideology defined above: inverted *representation* of the real. In actual fact, Volume Three establishes on this point something quite different from an 'inversion'; it shows how appearance [*Erscheinung*] becomes an amphibological principle of illusion [*Schein*], in the sense of an illegitimate use of categories which have their proper pertinence elsewhere. As for the critico-philosophical schema of 'inversion', it is used to denote simultaneously the real and the ideological, being and appearance. It is thus unsuited to providing the framework of a theory that has to conceive these in their distinction and mutual relationship. Marx progressively disengages himself from this as he discovers the necessity for a 'fragmented' theory of the ideological corresponding to that of the exposition's process without subject: this would consist in determining, at each moment of the exposition, the representations that it implies in the agent whose function and practice it defines. The ideological conceived in this way can clearly not be globalised in a historical transcendental subjectivity.

In *Capital*, which presents the definitive version of Volume One, the effort of theorisation of the ideological adopted at this level is focused in Part Six, more particularly in a series of very abrupt statements, the terms of which I have explained by relating each of them to the various moments of the theory to which they connect. These propositions are very heterogeneous. Some of them relate the representation of wages as the 'price of labour' to the wage structure itself (fourth and seventh reason) and to the functional categories this requires, or else to the form of particular practices involved in it (third reason). They run in the sense indicated by the programme of a theorisation of the ideological that is graduated from abstract to concrete. Others, however, diverse yet convergent, refer the problem upstream, towards the theory of value and 'fetishism': it would then be the commodity relationship itself, implied in the surplus-value relation, that provides the ultimate principle of the ideological representation.

The next step to be undertaken is thus prescribed for us here: to resume our study of the first chapter of *Capital* on the basis of the analysis of labour-value already conducted – the structure of the 'beginning', Marx's method and his general approach to the ideological. Our aim will be to introduce a new clarity into these highly controversial questions.

Chapter Nine

The Theory of the Value-Form

In my judgement, the immense literature to which Sections 3 and 4 of Chapter 1 of *Capital* have given rise has produced disappointing results. It must be said that the problem is in no way simple: this section, the most worked-over by Marx himself, is also perhaps the most unfinished. Evidence of this is given by the discordant statements that remain; these can orient interpretation in different directions. Two main opposing attitudes have been taken. On the one hand, there is that which ignores these texts. This is often the case with arguments by economists, but it is also the tendency of a certain orthodox tradition, which has always been embarrassed by the handling of categories of expression and representation. On the other hand, there is that which, by virtue of the philosophical elements that the text comprises, lays strong emphasis on these and seeks in them a general principle of interpretation not just for the question of ideo-logy, but for the theory as a whole. The weakness of this is that it often separates these sections from the two preceding ones, which present something without which the notion of the value-form would be deprived of content, i.e. the very concept of value in the sense of labour-value. This approach, besides, leads to neglecting the double settling of accounts that Marx accomplishes in these pages – with both

Ricardo and Hegel. It tends, rather, to a Hegelian restoration of the theory, just as the other attitude veers into Ricardianism. The elements of clarification that I have proposed on each of these points will therefore be mobilised in the interpretation presented here.

The chief object of reflection will be the nature of the relation between the two sections, in other words between the 'value-form' and 'fetishism'. I propose, in effect, to show how the theory of fetishism is not based, or at least should not be based, on the theory of the value-form, but is rather directly articulated to the social relations that the concept of value defines; and that the form or expression of value, far from pertaining to the categories of ideology, belongs, on the contrary, to the register of meaning and rationality inherent to the commodity structure in its functionality. The ideological, in fact, exists precisely in this gap between meaning and consciousness.[1]

1. Why the historical or logico-historical interpretation cannot be relevant

I shall confine myself to examining the questions raised as to the theory's coherence by the 'little phrases' that Marx inserted into Section 3 of Chapter 1 in the second edition of *Capital*, and the historical considerations developed in Chapter 2. These elements are sufficient to grasp the problem as a whole.

In the second edition, Marx says of the 'simple, isolated, or accidental form of value' that 'this form, it is plain, appears in practice only in the early stages, when the products of labour are converted into commodities by accidental occasional exchanges'.[2] He thus assimilates this form to a supposed historical stage, that of pre-monetary exchange. The same goes for the second form, the 'total or expanded form of value', which 'comes into actual existence for the first time when a particular product of labour, such as cattle, is no longer exceptionally, but habitually exchanged for various other commodities'.[3]

---

[1] Sections 1 to 5 of this chapter are summarised in my *Théorie de la modernité*, pp. 227–9, and Section 6 on pp. 230–2. The question of fetishism (Section 6), in its link with the theory of value, I have re-examined in *Théorie générale*, particularly at pp. 438–9.

[2] Marx 1976a, p. 158.

[3] Ibid.

It is clear that Marx confuses here two senses of development, the categorial and the historical. It is tempting to see him as embarking on the programme he had proposed in the *Grundrisse*: 'to correct the idealist manner of the presentation, which makes it seem as if it were merely a matter of conceptual determinations and of the dialectic of these concepts'.[4] In reality, these two 'little phrases' are foreign bodies in a context that is fundamentally 'categorial'.

This should be seen in connection with a closer reading of Chapter 2, in which some have wanted to see a return to historicism, written in the spirit of Engels's injunctions. Marx turns here to the question of the origin of money, but this time in a historical style.[5] He characterises the first form, which he now calls 'direct exchange', by the fact that 'their [commodities'] quantitative exchange-relation is at first determined purely by chance', but then gradually comes to be governed by production time. From here, Marx passes directly to the third form, explaining that 'the need for this form first develops with the increase in the number and variety of the commodities entering into the process of exchange'.[6] He examines the factors determining the choice of general equivalent. This is initially the quality of being an imported product, or a basic object of utility. Later, with the appearance of products that are by their concrete nature more suited to this function – the previous metals, divisible and homogeneous – the fourth form ('the money form')[7] is reached.

These precisions are sufficient to show, I believe, that the 'forms' invoked here are of a completely different nature to those of Chapter 1.

In Chapter 1, the first form is defined on the basis of exchange at value. There is nothing approximate about it. If 'chance' comes into it at all, it cannot be 'the quantitative proportion in which it is exchanged' ('ihr quantitatives Austauschverhältnis'),[8] which, on the contrary, forms the object of a development that defines it strictly: '(ii) the quantitative determinacy of the relative form of value'.[9] It does not have a history. That of Chapter 2 presents the supposed history of the appearance of a barter based on labour-value.

---

[4] Marx 1973c, p. 151.
[5] Marx 1976a, pp. 180–4.
[6] Marx 1976a, p. 182.
[7] Marx 1976a, p. 184.
[8] Marx 1973a, p. 102.
[9] Marx 1976a, p. 144.

The second form of Chapter 1 does not appear in the following chapter, for a very good reason. It cannot depict any historical 'stage'. It is defined in effect by the property of the relation of equivalence to be open to any commodity in the system. Moreover, and above all, given the reversibility of the relation of the expression of value, a second form existing historically would function at the same time as the third form for all who exchanged their various commodities against this single commodity.

The third form, in Chapter 2, thus directly follows on from the first. And the question raised here is that of its gradual emergence, the transition from 'direct exchange' to exchange mediated by a general equivalent.

There remains the problem of the fourth form, that introducing the precious metals, a problem whose theoretical interest often remains unnoticed. It is often interpreted either as an illustration of the fact that Marx combines in his approach the categorial and the historical. Or else, on the contrary, it is reduced to the third form, considered as the culminating point of the categorial development, beyond which there is a transition to the empirical-historical order; which amounts to saying that the theoretical place of gold is form C. Neither of these interpretations is adequate. We have to grasp that form D initially has a strictly theoretical significance, that of defining the concrete characteristics that the universal equivalent has to possess in order to be adequate to its function of representing abstract labour. In this sense, the qualities of durability/divisibility/homogeneity invoked here are not initially the qualities of the empirical product that is precious metal, but rather define a priori the conditions that are required for the universal equivalent. These are determinations that go together with the categorial ensemble of Chapter 1. This is why this form warrants a legitimate place within the theoretical exposition, even if the determinations that it introduces are of a particular order, concerning the money commodity as a monetary use-value and the concrete properties implied by its *function* of universal equivalent.[10]

The interpretation in terms of categorial order, by which the theory of the capitalist mode of production exists as a theory, totally excludes interpretation in terms of historical order: the transformation of the 'forms' into 'stages' empties the theory of its meaning. The sequence of forms A–B–C–D, which

---

[10] Cf. Marx 1973c, pp. 174 ff.

is not susceptible to historical transcription, is even less capable of 'reflecting' a historical order.

But this does mean there is not a close link, if not between two supposed 'orders', then between two questions that a certain logicising approach totally connects: between the study of the systematic conditions of possibility of a structure, and the conditions of its historical emergence.

Chapter 1 presents a set of conditions of possibility of a commodity structure, and thus, at the same time, the 'contradictions' that such a structure comprises (for example, separation between production and the realisation of the product), and the functional arrangements by which these are overcome (in the event, by the general equivalent). The 'difficulties' specific to the historical emergence of such a system clearly involve the 'contradictions' of this system and the establishment of elements of functionality. In this sense, as Marx correctly says in the *Grundrisse* apropos primitive accumulation or the emergence of the capitalist mode of production (and he illustrates this in Part 8 of *Capital*, Volume One), the structural definition of a system is the 'key to the interpretation' of its historical origin.[11] This remark, even if far too abstract, applies to the question of the emergence of commodity relations.

Marx did not explicitly address this last point, or see that the problem was raised in the same terms. Hence the slippages that we have noted. This close relationship between structure and origin, though not in terms of order, still constitutes the genuinely 'materialist' perspective on the question.

2. The notion of form or expression of value, as distinct from the notion of relative value

Before coming on to the principle of development of the four 'forms of value', we first have to be clear about the actual notion of form of expression of value.

I propose here to show how the legitimate object of this moment of the exposition is to establish that money forms the adequate expression of value. And that this problematic of expression can be established only under a condition that Marx only comes to appreciate very slowly, and is lacking from many interpretations, i.e. that we are able to distinguish it from the problematic of relative value.

---

[11] Marx 1973c, p. 459.

The issue here does not just concern the origin of Marx's theory, in other words the fact, in my view poorly recognised, that it is here that Marx consummates his break with Ricardo. It also bears on the present-day, post-Sraffa debate, where we see that by neutralising this moment of the exposition by its reinterpretation as 'relative value' (even by those who claim to follow Marx), the theory of *Capital* is returned to the order of political economy.

2.i *The terminology of Section 3*

The orthodox tradition has not addressed all the specific elements of Marx's terminology, which is varying and vague in this passage. The economistic tradition has 'Ricardianised' them, as we shall see, by understanding the 'relative form of value' as 'relative value'. The Hegelian tradition has neutralised the specifically Marxian categories by way of the Hegelian instruments that Marx employed. In sum, the various notions that articulate the discourse have not been investigated in a consistent fashion.

On the first page of this section, Marx puts forward a number of categories, the main ones being *Wertform* [value-form], *Tauschwert* [exchange-value], *Wertverhältnis* [value-relation] and *Wertausdruck* [expression of value].

The first two of these, *Wertform* and *Tauschwert*, associated and identified, form the title of this section, 'the value-form, or exchange-value', yet they do not play the role that this privileged position might lead us to expect. In fact, 'exchange-value', mentioned on p. 139, only reappears once, and not until p. 177. And the category of 'value-form', though without losing the unity of its signification, breaks down into the various categories in which it appears, on the one hand, the two poles of the 'relative form' and the 'equivalent form', on the other, the sequence of four forms: 'simple', 'developed', general' and 'monetary'.

The two latter categories, *Wertverhältnis* and *Wertausdruck*, have not been addressed by the Marxist tradition, and are not retained as elements of the theory's systematic ensemble. It is these, however, that articulate the question forming the object of the section, 'to trace the development of the expression of value contained in the value-relation of commodities'.[12]

---

[12] Marx 1976a, p. 139. An important articulation, which is repeated on pp. 140, 149 & 151; cf. Marx 1980, p. 771.

2.i.a   Wertverhältnis, *value-relation*

The *value-relation* in this couple represents the element supposedly known at this moment in the exposition, precisely the element on the basis of which Marx seeks to determine the 'expression of value'. This term did not figure in Sections 1 and 2; it involves a consideration that did not enter into their object. But it is deduced from this; it simply denotes that the exchange-value of commodities as such is regulated by value: once Marx has shown that the basis of exchange-value is value, he returns to this exchange-value and interprets it as a relationship between the values of commodities.

2.i.b   Wertausdruck, *expression of value*

The 'expression of value', omnipresent in the text here, is the term that comes to duplicate and most often replace that of value-form [*Wertform*]. Not only is it a synonym for this, but above all a definition: the commodity possesses a 'value-form' in so far as it possesses an *expression* of its value. In other words, this third section, far from constituting an inessential philosophical trimming, raises an essential question: that of the problem of the expression inherent to the commodity relation.

And it is because *Wertform* denotes the expression of value that it is better translated not by 'value-form' but by 'form of value'. The term 'value-form' is actually ambiguous. It could mean: 1) the fact that value is a *social form*, what I have denoted by the market structure or 'commodity production-circulation' taken in abstraction; 2) the *ideological* (or 'fetishised') *representation* of value, in the sense that Marx often speaks of the 'wage form' meaning ideological representation of the wage relation; 3) the fact that the social form 'value', the social relation, possesses an adequate *form of expression* which is the form of value. It is clearly the third sense that is meant here, and is better translated not as 'value-form' but rather 'form of value'.

2.i.c   Tauschwert, *exchange-value*

It is on the basis of these two first terms, the meanings of which are stable, that we can go on to make clear that of the third term, 'exchange-value [*Tauschwert*]', which, on the contrary, is defined at different levels of the exposition. In the first section, this 'appears first of all as the quantitative relation' between commodities.[13] It thus denotes what is to be explained, and

---

[13] Marx 1976a, p. 126.

is explained by the 'theory of value' that follows.[14] 'Value' (i.e. labour-value) here is the theoretical concept that accounts for the everyday, pre-theoretical category of 'exchange-value'; it presents the foundation of this merely quantitative relation between commodities that 'exchange-value' initially is. But this latter category functions at a different level when it is identified, in the third section, with the 'form of value'.[15] It no longer denotes just relative value, even in reference to value, which would be still the 'Ricardian' perspective of the relationship of the labour-value of one commodity to that of another, a perspective culminating in the consideration of changes in relative values. It denotes the problematic that we have still to analyse, that of the expression of value.[16]

2.ii   *The object of Section 3: the expression of value*

It is impossible to stress too strongly, I believe, that the specific object of this section is to develop a non-Ricardian space of value and a non-Ricardian theory of money, based on the fact that value not only asserts itself here as a quantitative relationship, but also finds here the expression of its quality as abstract labour.

The question here is to show that the money commodity constitutes the adequate expression of value, adequate to its concept [*Wertbegriff*],[17] that is to value defined as quantity of abstract labour. Marx replies to this question of knowing how value is manifested in exchange in a series of stages familiar to the reader of *Capital*. The most simple value relationship, that established between two commodities, provides the initial determinations, in particular the bipolarity (symmetrical, but in a particular sense, as we shall see) of what is expressed and what expresses it. The inadequacy of this first form consists in its restriction to just one kind of commodity. The second form certainly

---

[14] Marx 1976a, pp. 127–30.

[15] [Following the author's argument above, I have generally rendered *forme de la valeur* (*Wertform*) from here on as 'form of value', not 'value-form' as it appears in the English editions.]

[16] These precisions seem to me all the more necessary in that the most varying opinions agree on the relationship between exchange-value and value. Thus Grevet (1971, p. 30) distinguishes them as different magnitudes, and uses 'exchange-value' to denote market price. B. Marx (1979, p. 34) uses a similar terminology. Benetti (1974, p. 137) perceives a 'contradiction' between them, the 'point of departure for the Marxist analysis of money'. Zech sees 'value' as a universal category bound up with the division of labour, and 'exchange-value' as a category specific to capitalism (1983, pp. 80–1).

[17] Marx 1980, p. 779.

displays how the expression of value is indifferent to the nature of the commodity that expresses it, but it is only the third form that brings the expression of value *adequate* to the value relation: at the moment when all commodities express their value in 'one single kind of commodity set apart from the rest',[18] which is rejected as a use-value, they are expressed in this as value, i.e. as abstract labour.

It must still be added that this does not happen without a residue. And that is why, at the end of this analysis, I shall have to show how the problematic of the form of value includes a further dimension, which is proclaimed in the terms 'expression of value in a use-value'.

2.iii *Confusion of the Ricardianising interpretation: the debate on the equivalence relationship*

The problematic of the 'expression of value' is only established gradually, replacing the inadequate one of 'relative value'. In the first chapter of the 1867 edition, it is 'relative value' that defines the theoretical space of the future Section 3; and Marx successively studies its 'quantitative aspect' and 'forms'.[19] In the Appendix, the latter become 'forms of value', and Marx forges the couple 'relative form/equivalent form', where 'relative' acquires a new meaning. In the 1873 edition, he analyses this 'relative form' first in terms of its content, then its quantity,[20] the latter referring to the problem of 'relative value', a function of changes in the absolute values of commodities on the market. In short, 'relative value' now takes its place in the framework of the 'form or expression of value', of which it represents the sole quantitative determination.

This shift can be summed up in the following table:

1867: investigation of *relative value*
    quantity
    forms (A, B, C)

1873: investigation of the *form of value*, or expression of value
    relative form   ⎫
      content   ⎬ form A, etc.
      quantity (= relative value)
    equivalent form   ⎭

---

[18] Marx 1976a, p. 158.
[19] Marx 1980, pp. 13–15 and 15–34.
[20] Cf. Marx 1976a, p. 144.

At the present time, a resurgence of the perspective of relative value is to be found in the discussion as to whether the character of the expression of value is or is not 'symmetrical'.[21] This debate is located within a broader one bearing on the nature of the relationship 'x of commodity A is worth y of commodity B'; should this be considered an equivalence in the logical sense, a relationship that is *transitive, reflexive* and *symmetrical*? The response to these questions depends precisely on the object assigned to the moment of the theory constituted by this Section 3.

One ambiguity, which has given rise to a number of questions, arises from the fact that Marx puts forward simultaneously a double formulation:

x commodity A = y commodity B;

x commodity A is worth y commodity B.[22]

In actual fact, the first relationship, bearing the 'equals' sign and thus constituting a relationship of equivalence, can in itself only involve the 'value relationship'. It is already realised in Section 2 before the problem of expression arises, being introduced here only by way of reminder. Between commodities exchanged there exists an equality in terms of quantity of labour embodied, and thus a logical equivalence as value.

The second relationship, 'x commodity A is worth y commodity B', corresponds more strictly to what Marx characterises as the expression of the value of the commodity alienated in the use-value of the commodity acquired. It is of a different nature, and cannot, to my mind, be qualified as an equivalence in the logical sense. A detailed investigation of this question will enable us to better discern in what way the relationship of expression differs from the simple value relationship.

I leave aside the question of 'transitivity' which is not relevant here, and it is clear that the relationship is also not one of 'reflexivity'. For it asserts that the value can be expressed only by a *different* commodity, more precisely

---

[21] See in particular, besides Becker (1972), Krause (1973, pp. 19–46), who concludes the existence of a relation of equivalence ('the value relation is a relation of equivalence', p. 40). In reality, however, what is investigated under the name of the 'form of value' is something quite different, the relation of exchange. Klaus (1972, p. 300) reaches the same conclusion, though ignoring the role of use-value. Göhler (1980) on the other hand ignores the exchange-value of the second term (pp. 58–70). See below on Benetti and Cartelier.

[22] Marx 1976a, p. 139.

by the only thing in this latter that can be the bearer of this difference, its use-value.

Finally, it also cannot strictly speaking be called a 'symmetrical' relationship, as would be for example the relationship 'has the same value as', since the two poles of the value form are heterogeneous (relative/equivalent) as regards the relationship that this defines. Marx does indeed say that the formula '20 yards of linen = 1 coat . . . also includes its converse';[23] and he adds that 'in this case I must reverse the equation'. But this consideration is not sufficient. It is not just a question of a further statement, such as could only be obtained by reversing the relationship 'has the same value as'. There is also a different subject, who expresses the value of the coat in the linen. As distinct from the relationship 'has the same value as', or the equality relationship of value in which the subject is indeterminate and which in the same assertion functions in both directions, we have here a *couple* of indissociable 'symmetrical' relations, this duality arising from the fact that, as a relationship of expression, and hence of meaning, these have a specific direction for each of the two parties involved. A meaning of two distinct acts provided with meaning, expressing themselves in two expressions of value.

In conclusion, the two expressions 'x commodity A = y commodity B' and 'x commodity A is worth y commodity B' are each of a different nature. The first denotes the value relationship, the second the expression of value. If the second is reduced to the first, by attributing to it the properties of the relationship of equivalence or one of these, there is a strong risk of remaining at a pre-Marxian stage, within the Ricardian problematic of relative values.

2.iv   *Remark: the interpretation of Benetti and Cartelier*

The interpretation recently proposed by Benetti and Cartelier represents one of the most advanced analytical attempts in this direction.

What gives their argument an apparent foundation is the support it seems to find in what they call 'form III',[24] in which the relationship exists between all commodities, which they depict in the following manner:[25]

---

[23] Marx 1976a, p. 140.
[24] [Called 'form C' in the English editions.]
[25] Benetti and Cartelier 1980, pp. 153–4.

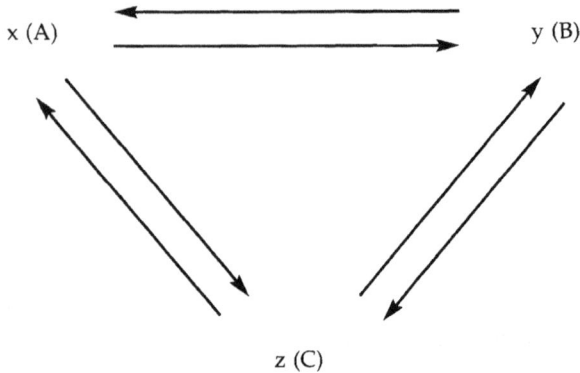

They conclude from this form that it is impossible to consider money as a commodity. Indeed:

> [S]ince every commodity can be equivalent to every other commodity, we have in total n (n-1) possible prices, which for Marx comes down to saying that it is no longer a question of commodities but of simple products. . . . Hence the conclusion: the general equivalent cannot be found in the set defined by the n processes. . . . This is what Marx demonstrates.
>
> The theory of forms demonstrates that the general equivalent cannot be a commodity.

The reader of *Capital*, however, will understand perfectly well that Marx developed his theory quite differently and arrived at the opposite conclusion, that the commodity implies money and that money is a commodity – at least in the case of metallic money. In point of fact, this is not a general theory of money under capitalism, but simply of one of its limiting forms.

The interpretation of Benetti and Cartelier is only possible on the basis of a complete misunderstanding. This so-called 'form C' does not exist in *Capital* as a moment in the origin of money. The figure that they invoke under this name is mentioned by Marx on various occasions, but in a quite different context.

On the one hand, at the end of the exposition in the *Critique*[26] and in the first edition of *Capital*; and it is this latter text that our authors cite. Here, however, it bears the name 'form D', which it is better to leave in place.

---

[26] Marx 1971, p. 52.

On the other hand, in the Appendix and the French edition of *Capital*,[27] as a 'generalisation' of form B. And the change of place that Marx effects here does constitute an evident correction. We must remark here that this figure is now invoked with respect to the limitations of form B. What Marx means by this is precisely that the *concept* of value does not find expression in this way, i.e. that such a 'form' is not involved in the origin of money. What form B offers is simply that it expresses the indifference of the expression of value to the concrete nature of the equivalent commodity, i.e. to its use-value. But its generalisation, in what the first edition calls 'form D', does not make any contribution. Marx invokes it only with a negative purpose, to show what the origin of the money-form cannot be.

This is the reason, as against what these authors believe, why the figure that they invoke cannot constitute a moment of the theory of the form of value. It only appears in Marx's exposition by way of an expression of the order of research, as an 'imaginary experiment' with a negative result. For, if the 'demonstration' had culminated in the 'form D' of the first edition, there would not actually have been a form of value, not an adequate expression of value, no relationship expressed between values, but simply a juxtaposition of products. Marx indeed himself concludes in the first edition that this 'form D' is an impasse: 'If each commodity opposes its own natural form to all other commodities as a general equivalent form, then all commodities exclude all others from the general equivalent form and consequently exclude themselves from the socially valid representation of their magnitude of value.'[28]

Marx indicates, then, that 1) every commodity can be the general equivalent, but 2) if they all are at once then there is no longer an expression of value, therefore 3) it is necessary to settle for form C, which assumes that effectively in a given system only one commodity at a time plays this role.

In sum, these two authors enclose Marx in a Ricardian problematic of 'relative value', one of 'measurement' that has no place for 'form'. They thus overlook the fact that Marx has already, in the theoretical space he inaugurates, that of labour-value, settled in Sections 1 and 2 the problem of the *measure* of value on the basis of its substance; the problem he now discusses is something quite different, that of the *expression* of this value.

---

[27] Marx 1980, p. 778; Marx 1976a, pp. 157 ff.
[28] Marx 1980, p. 34.

3. Epistemological history of Chapter 1, Section 3

To proceed further in this interpretation, we have now to read this section in the movement of its re-writing. Not in order to 'clarify' the French text by reference to the German, then to the first edition, and so on, until we finally reach the *Grundrisse*.[29] But rather to indicate what breaks were needed for Marx to establish the most developed form of his theoretical discourse.

What in the *Grundrisse* most resembles a beginning, a founding moment where the initial concepts are presented, is the passage on 'the origin and essence of money'.[30] Starting from the definition of the value of a commodity in terms of labour-time, and developing the relationship between commodity and money from one end to the other, this occupies in broad terms the theoretical space of the future Chapter 1 of *Capital*. Now, this passage terminates with the celebrated remark:

> It will be necessary later . . . to correct the idealist manner of the presentation, which makes it seem as if it were merely a matter of conceptual determinations and of the dialectic of these concepts. Above all in the case of the phrase: product (or activity) becomes commodity; commodity, exchange-value; exchange-value, money.[31]

Hence the questions: what precisely does this 'manner' of the *Grundrisse* consist in? What is 'idealist' or 'dialectical' about it? How was it subsequently corrected? And what, if anything, of this remains in the subsequent versions?

The first thing that should strike the reader familiar with *Capital* is the absence in this entire passage of the category of *use-value* – an incredible absence, which, however, does not seem to have been noted by commentators. There is no mention here of the use-value/exchange-value couple, even though Marx was sufficiently aware of its importance as to use it in the very title of the first section of *The Poverty of Philosophy*. Where 'use-value' would be expected, we find instead the idea that the commodity possesses its 'form of natural existence' in the 'product'.[32] The assignment of the category 'natural' (which, in *Capital*, becomes rare and marginal) to this element in the couple in its relationship to the other, called 'social' ('value is their social relation,

---

[29] The path commonly followed: cf. Fischer 1978, Fausto 1982.
[30] Marx 1973c, pp. 140–51.
[31] Marx 1976a, p. 151.
[32] Marx 1973c, pp. 141, 145, 147.

their economic quality')[33] seems to me to have no theoretical justification. Use-value and concrete labour refer to *social* needs, to the *social* division of labour. They no more refer to anything natural than does the famous 'physiological expenditure' that determines value. What is occurring here is a 'forced naturalisation', the function of which is to establish in this 'natural' moment an *initial* moment, legitimising it as such and providing at the same time the initial imbalance in the motivating disequilibrium that will kick off the 'dialectical' exposition.

For what is opposed to this 'natural identity with itself' of the commodity is that by virtue of which it is initially 'distinct from itself': its exchange-value.[34] The *dynamic discrepancy* consists in that, on the one hand, we have the natural properties of the commodity as it exists in 'its natural existence', and on the other 'its property as value'. Since the latter has no natural existence, it 'must obtain [*muss gewinnen*]' one corresponding to it, that is, corresponding to the characteristics of its 'property': divisibility, equality, universality, exchangeability, measure.[35] This is what money with its 'special qualities' provides.

The discrepancy is thus resolved into a 'duplication [*Verdopplung*]'. This mystical figure denotes a relationship of identification/distinction that will characterise not only the relationship of the *initial entity*, the commodity, to its two '*forms of existence*', product and value (it *is* these, and yet *differs* from them),[36] but also the relationship that obtains *between these two forms*. Each of them is the other, but in so far as it is itself: value is 'the product as value', and the product is 'value as the product'.[37] Finally, between the commodity and money: 'als Wert ist sie Geld', 'as *value*, it is commodity'.[38]

In this *mariage-à-trois* or even *quatre*, the couples intertwine and their perspectives become tangled. When Marx speaks of the commodity, he attributes it two forms of existence: the 'natural' product and the exchange-value as money.[39] But when he starts with value, he discovers that this 'exists in' both the commodity and money.[40] In other words, instead of the two

---

[33] Marx 1973c, p. 141.
[34] Marx 1973c, p. 142.
[35] Ibid.
[36] Marx 1973c, pp. 147 and 142.
[37] Marx 1973c, p. 143.
[38] Marx 1973c, p. 141: Marx's emphasis.
[39] Marx 1976a, p. 141.
[40] Marx 1976a, p. 150.

couples that *Capital* offers, the commodity couple (use-value/value) and the money couple (use-value/value), we have a kind of triple: two 'forms of existence' (product/money) and also something that exists in them and is denoted sometimes as commodity and sometimes as value. When it is the commodity that is attributed this 'double form of existence', it is certainly its articulation into use-value and value that is denoted, but Marx then overlooks the autonomy of the commodity, saying that this 'exists as value in money', whereas, in terms of his own theory, its value 'exists' in itself only in so far as it is the product of a certain time of labour. When, on the other hand, the 'double existence' is attributed to value, it is the autonomy of money that Marx overlooks, for in the money commodity what 'exists' is its *own* value, not that of the commodity.

This defect in the 'dialectical' analysis is particularly evident in the category of *money*, which is not explicitly analysed here as a commodity. Later on, though still rather marginally, we are indeed reminded that money is a commodity. Yet Marx does not explicitly address the question of what makes money a commodity in the strict sense, its articulation into use-value and value. On the contrary, money, though it is invoked as a form of existence, as an adequate embodiment of exchange-value, as 'material', only appears initially in the form of a 'symbol' or 'cipher',[41] whether represented or real: for example, 'a piece of paper or leather'.[42] In short, in this passage, if exchange-value 'engenders' money, it is above all as a 'separate existence, in isolation from the product',[43] as no matter what kind of materiality, and not a commodity proper.

We can readily see what Marx tried to do with this 'dialectical' formulation of the problem: to set in motion the categorial exposition. But such a motion can only be sustained by an identity that pervades its different moments. Thus some of these *'exist'* in others, they *'are'* others *'in so far as'*. By way of this oscillating hypostatisation, what can be said about one moment can be said about another, but Marx does not manage to escape from the initial collision between commodity and money, as he has not yet conducted the preliminary analysis of the former with its specific categorial field. (He would

---

[41] Marx 1976a, pp. 141–4 passim.
[42] Marx 1976a, p. 144.
[43] Marx 1976a, p. 145.

shortly go on to do this in the *Critique*.) Not having untangled the two terms, money and commodity, in the double and distinct relationship that characterises each of these, he is unable to navigate the space between them.

While waiting to discover his true point of departure, and thus also his true 'manner', for this lies entirely in the articulation of the departure, Marx sought his way forward, drawing on Hegel's *Logic*, in the identity/difference of commodity and money. But, just as bad money drives out good, so the bad got the better here too.

Let us now examine the first truly developed versions of the analysis of the form of value, those of the first edition of *Capital*, where one version is to be found in Chapter One and another in the Appendix.

If we start with the 1867 version of Chapter One and consider it in retrospect, it is easy to see how the support that Marx initially sought in certain philosophical categories tends to disappear.

Thus an entire passage here develops the origin of the commodity in terms of an explicit personification: it 'behaves', 'makes itself equal', 'relates to itself as a value', 'is distinguished [. . .] from itself as use-value', 'it provides its value being with a value form distinct from its immediate existence'.[44] The 1872 text, in reworking this theme, refashions it by placing the object at a distance; its movement is now simply the movement stamped on it: 'We may twist and turn a single commodity as we wish . . .'.[45] The notion of 'natural form' is certainly still found, but it no longer plays a motor role, being integrated rather into the problematic of use-value.

An ostentatiously Hegelian articulation, already found in the *Critique*,[46] linked together in the first edition the presentation of the commodity and that of exchange (Chapters 1 and 2 in the final version):

> The commodity is the immediate unity of use-value and exchange-value, and thus of two opposites. It is thus an immediate contradiction. The contradiction must develop, as soon as it is considered no longer, as has been the case up to now, in an analytic manner, sometimes from the standpoint of use-value and sometimes from that of exchange-value, but is actually

---

[44] Marx 1980, p. 16.
[45] Marx 1976a, p. 138.
[46] Marx 1971, p. 50.

> related to another commodity as a whole. The effective [*wirklich*] relationship
> between commodities is the process of exchange.[47]

This linkage is, to my mind, not simply artificial, but completely irrelevant. In fact, the presentation of commodity production (Sections 1 and 2), and equally that of the form of value (Section 3), make sense only by considering the unity of use-value and value. This disappears in the second edition.

If we now relate the 1867 version of Chapter 1 to the Appendix to this same edition, we see that the latter denotes the object of investigation no longer as being relative value, but, rather, the 'form of value', a notion that had previously been only weakly distinguished from the former. And this new approach is expressed in the fact that the analysis is from now on organised entirely around the couple that was only sketched briefly in Chapter 1, that of 'relative form/equivalent form', thanks to which the problematic of the *expression* of value is now established. This new procedure, which starts completely from the duality of this bipolar couple in which one logically implies the other, must, in my view, be related to the abandonment (incomplete but noticeable) of the discourse on 'the commodity that is first found in its immediate form, then takes a distinct form', in short the abandonment of certain wellsprings of the 'dialectical development' that were particularly active in the 1867 version of Chapter 1. Paradoxically, the Appendix, which ostentatiously bears the external signs of dialectics (with its *Übergänge* carefully noted) is less dialectical in its content than is Chapter 1.

As regards a comparison of the Appendix with the text of the second edition (which takes it over, enriched with elements from the previous Chapter 1), I shall confine myself to a single point: Marx leaves out an entire philosophical development concerning the 'second peculiarity' of the equivalent form ('concrete labour becomes the form of manifestation of its opposite, abstract human labour').[48] More precisely – and this illustrates perfectly Marx's development and the evident reticence he has to give up certain old philosophical tools even when they have become false friends – in the second edition he places this text in a note, and omits it entirely in the French edition, followed also in later editions.[49] Here is the essential passage:

---

[47] Marx 1980, p. 44.
[48] Marx 1976a, p. 150.
[49] [Including the English edition.]

What is palpable and concrete counts only as phenomenal form or determinate form of realisation of what is abstract and general. For example . . . it is not the *work of the tailor* contained in the *equivalent* suit that possesses the *general property* of being also human labour. On the contrary, being human labour counts as its essence, while being the work of the tailor counts only as the phenomenal form or particular form of realisation of this essence that it has.[50]

Marx criticises this inversion as equivalent to saying: that 'law . . . is realised in both Roman and Germanic law'. He denounces here a 'mystical *connection*',[51] already indicated in Chapter 1 of the 1867 edition: 'it is as if, alongside lions and tigers . . . there also existed the animal'.[52] This passage rehearses a Feuerbachian theme from *The Holy Family*, as Dognin points out in a note to his French translation. Its origin is the conception of the 'abstraction' of abstract labour as a property, *Eigenschaft*,[53] or as Marx clearly puts it in Chapter 1, a mere 'object of thought', *Gedankending*,[54] the result of an operation that abstracts the common properties of sensory objects, and promotes these to a separate existence.

The impossibility of such a proposition in the context of Marx's theory erupts when the idea is maintained that 'abstract labour' is something quite distinct from a general property, an object of thought. But this is what happens ever more clearly as abstract labour comes gradually to be defined as expenditure.[55] In this respect, certain contentions of the second edition are unequivocal rebuttals of those made in 1867 on the *Gedankending*:

[The] labour objectified in the values of commodities is not just presented negatively, as labour in which abstraction is made from all the concrete forms and useful properties of actual work. Its own positive nature is explicitly brought out, namely the fact that it is the reduction of all kinds

---

[50] Marx 1980, p. 771; my emphases: J.B.
[51] Ibid.
[52] Marx 1980, p. 73.
[53] Marx 1980, p. 771.
[54] Marx 1980, p. 17.
[55] Dognin 1977 (Vol. 2, p. 67) provides here an analysis that is very interesting, but insufficient both in an 'upstream' sense (he sees the texts from 1867 I have cited as a critique of Hegel; they certainly are, but first and foremost a critique of capitalism as an inverted world) and a 'downstream' (the category of 'expenditure' does not, to my mind, ultimately express a 'physiological truth' but rather a concept of the social).

of actual labour to their common character of being human labour in general, of being the expenditure of human labour-power.[56]

Such abstraction is not that of 'law in general' in relation to 'Roman law' or 'Germanic law'; it is not the 'generality'. For 'labour in general' is both abstract *and* concrete. The correlate of value is not labour in general, but abstract labour in the sense of expenditure.

Logically enough, Marx finally abandons such contentions. He gradually avoids the traps inherent in the philosophical conceptualisation, which has served as a heuristic instrument. It has given a name to that cleavage within the category of labour that Marx considered one of his main discoveries: the 'abstract/concrete labour' couple. But the connotations that this category brought with it from its philosophical history prove to be parasitical.

The French edition, while it does have certain inadequacies, is located, as I have shown elsewhere,[57] in a continuing development from one version to the next. The elimination of certain philosophical categories, such as the articulation 'singular/particular/universal', the subject/object problematic [*Vergegenständlichung*], and that of automatisation [*Selbstständigkeit*], far from being an oversight of the translator, attest on the contrary to the ongoing process of theoretical maturation.

4. What dialectic of the form of value?

This history of the text enables us to go on now to tackle, after the historicising and Ricardianising readings, the 'dialectical-teleological' interpretation that a whole tradition has proposed.[58] The very nature of the project that Marx conducted excludes this kind of discourse.[59]

I shall take as my main reference here the important work that G. Göhler has devoted to this section on the 'form of value', and which contains an

---

[56] Marx 1976a, pp. 159–60.

[57] Bidet 1985; cf. in the contrary sense D'Hondt 1981 and 1985.

[58] Found for example in the texts of Theunissen, Bader, Fausto, Fischer that I have mentioned; cf. also Fulda 1975, p. 208; Lange 1978, p. 14.

[59] I should make clear that there is in fact no possibility of dialectical development in a theoretical context that is one of the market alone, and in the concept of money that secures the closure of this figure. The dialectical motor only arises with the relationship between market and organisation, its co-implied opposite. I return to this point in *Théorie de la modernité* (pp. 226–33) and the whole of *Théorie générale*.

overall summary of the debate.[60] He shows very well Marx's progressive distancing from the dialectic, but, in my view, he does not at all demonstrate the basis of this.

Concerning the *Critique*, he attributes to this an 'emphatically' Hegelian dialectic, to which he opposes the 'reduced' dialectic of *Capital*. This does not seem to me a pertinent distinction. The *Critique* offers, in fact, an initial and very schematic presentation of the form of value,[61] lacking any 'dialectical' character. As for the exchange structure, though Marx does deal with this here on the basis of the 'contradiction' that derives from the fact that in exchange commodities must assert themselves as both similar and different, and enter into exchange as values, although they are value only by way of exchange, the universal equivalent finally intervenes here as the 'solution to the contradiction'.[62] But nothing in all this seems to me 'emphatically' dialectical. The presentation of exchange, moreover, is hardly any different in *Capital*, which refers to the same 'contradictory conditions' and their solution thanks to money in exchange and circulation.[63] The foundation of this procedure is, to my mind, sufficiently clear: in so far as the structure has not yet been described down to the last of its functional aspects, it displays 'contradictions' that these latter eventually resolve. In this sense, the procedure 'from contradiction to solution' necessarily marks the organisation of the presentation. But this 'manner' is stripped of those features characteristic of Hegel's *Logic*: identity/difference of moments, and their superseding in a higher unity. It is, rather, what Hegel terms a mere 'dialectic of the understanding'.

Regarding the 'form of value' as developed in *Capital*, the mistake of several writers (including Göhler) consists, in my view, in believing that the only movement is that from form A to form D. Marx, however, actually envisages the origin in a broader framework, which includes the ensemble 'commodity production/expression of value'. He proposes to 'deduce from the analysis of the commodity, and particularly of the value of the commodity, the form in which this becomes exchange-value'.[64] This 'deduction' assumes a point of origin, which, as I will show, is nothing other than the 'concept of value',

---

[60] Göhler 1980.
[61] Marx 1971, pp. 38 ff.
[62] Marx 1971, p. 48.
[63] Marx 1976a, p. 192.
[64] Marx 1976a, p.

Wertbegriff,[65] as presented in Sections 1 and 2 of Chapter 1, in the theory of commodity production. And the object of Section 3 under consideration here is to define how value as thus conceived finds an adequate expression, thus to determine a new condition of possibility, a new aspect of the commodity structure, after its production aspect has already been presented. The question Marx answers is, how is the property that commodities are 'values', i.e. their property of being entities whose measurement is determined by the quantity of abstract labour, expressed in exchange?

This relationship between commodity production and expression of value, which totally escapes Göhler, forms the principle of the non-teleological character of the presentation. Marx's discourse here, far from evolving towards the concept as happens in Hegel's *Logic*, has this as its initial reference.

That does not mean that there are not still in *Capital* traces of an Hegelian procedure in this sense (cf. form A that 'must undergo' a series of metamorphoses';[66] which contains the money-form D in 'germ'),[67] but such expressions function purely as metaphor, given that they arise under the sway of a quite different problematic. It is illegitimate for instance, as Göhler does,[68] to include as 'vestiges' of the Hegelian dialectic Marx's references to the 'inadequacies' of the value-form, which at each stage ensure its transition to the next form, as these 'inadequacies' are only so in relation to what we already know from the preceding presentation of the concept of value.

But this retrospective character, which it is important to stress as against the teleological interpretation, is also linked together with a prospective element.

Göhler, moreover, sticks to this latter: the new determination that each stage brings is not already contained in the preceding one, but arises by the introduction of 'additional conditions'.[69] Thus, in his view, we pass from form A to form B by introducing the condition of generalised exchange (which cannot follow from form A, which abstracts from the exchange process). But he does not tell us what the principle of these 'additions' is, and so they risk appearing arbitrary. It is not enough to say that Marx's analysis presents a

---

[65] Marx 1980, p. 779, cf. Marx 1973a, p. 74; Marx 1972, p. 112.
[66] Marx 1976a, p. 154.
[67] Marx 1976a, p. 163.
[68] Göhler 1980, p. 146 and 149–52.
[69] Göhler 1980, p. 156.

'differentiation of a fundamental model already given' in form A. What needs to be indicated is the basis for this movement.

Now it is true that, in Marx's text, this principle of development remains obscure. The successive advances seem to flow from a series of decisions on the part of the analyst, so there is a great need to explain their status. We pass to form B because 'the series of different simple expressions of that value' is 'indefinitely expandable',[70] and to form C 'if we reverse the series'.[71] But what justifies such decisions?

To my mind, there are two aspects in this Section 3 that must be distinguished.

On the one hand, the introduction of a new series of categories, which define the problematic of expression: bipolarity of the relative and equivalent forms, use-value of the equivalent as support for the expression of value. These categories denote a new aspect of the commodity structure of production and exchange: they are not 'deduced' from previous categories, any more than are the categories of exchange (Chapter 2) or circulation (Volume Two) from those of production (Volume One). In this respect, there is simply a logical *order* of introduction of categories, within one and the same structural level.

On the other hand, there is the trajectory from form A to form C, which progressively determines the set of conditions necessary for the expression of value. These conditions are defined on the basis of the problematic of the 'expression of value', and as a function of what we already know of the 'value relationship' (and thus of its principle, the 'concept of value', which is what is being expressed here). There is a decisive point that I shall express in the form of the following thesis. It is because the 'value relationship [*Wertverhältnis*]' is, in mathematical terminology, a 'total' relationship, that is, extending to the totality of elements in the set, that the 'expression of value [*Wertausdruck*]' may be legitimately generalised, and this is how we pass from form A, which defined the minimal condition for the expression of value (i.e. that there are at least two bipolar terms), to form B, which maintains that the expression of value involves the whole set of commodities in the system. And it is because the 'value relationship' is a 'symmetrical' relationship that 'the expression of value', form B, can pass on to form C.

---

[70] Marx 1976a, p. 154.
[71] Marx 1976a, p. 157.

In short, as Marx puts it, 'Our analysis has shown that the form of value, that is, the expression of the value of a commodity, arises from the nature of commodity-value',[72] where this 'nature' denotes what in the Appendix is called the 'concept' of value [*Wertbegriff*], a concept defined in the abstract theory of commodity *production*. We can thus see the extent to which the censorship of the question of commodity production burdens the entire analysis of the form of value.

We have still to examine the sense in which the presentation proceeds from abstract to concrete, and from the hidden to the apparent.

The origin of the form of value, Marx explains, leads us 'from its simplest, almost imperceptible outline to the dazzling money-form'.[73] But this is still not sufficient basis for a dialectical development. For what is most hidden here is initially what the theory calls the most 'simple' or 'abstract', on which other more complex moments can base themselves. This 'most abstract' is the most hidden because it is the start of the chain of scientific propositions that must be completed. (This, moreover, defines form A as a *theoretical* moment: for in what way would 'barter' as supposed historical fact be 'almost imperceptible'?) The most evident is what belongs to the empirical realm, to the experience of agents in the system, including our own, but can be explained only by linking it to the simple first principles of the theory. In this respect, *Capital* meets its objective of being social science, enabling what is observable and attested to by everyday consciousness to be related to the first principles of the object being studied. It is sometimes said that the procedure in this section is different in kind from that which prevails in the rest of *Capital*. In actual fact, this procedure has a shorter trajectory because it is located at a higher level of abstraction, where the chain of mediations is shorter. But just like that which connects Volume One with Volume Three, it goes from principles to 'dazzling' consciousness, though remaining a 'mystery'[74] as long as it is not linked to the first principles.

The theoretical space of Chapter 1, which as yet presents only the most general categories of a commodity structure, thus already leads in an orderly fashion to the surface, to the appearance. But the problem is that this appearance

---

[72] Marx 1976a, p. 152.
[73] Marx 1976a, p. 139.
[74] Ibid.

is doubly constituted, and it is this duality that will now concern us: on the one hand, the *expression of value* as a vehicle of meaning; on the other hand, the appearance of a mythified meaning in *fetishism*.

5. The expression of value 'in use-value'

Commentators have left in obscurity a tremendous paradox that is crucial for the interpretation of *Capital*. Knowing that there is no commensurability between value and use-value, what meaning can the idea have that Marx puts forward here of 'the expression of a value in use-value'? I intend, contrary to the usual approach, to propose the following answer, which goes together with an overall conception of the 'start of the theory': the category 'expression of value' concerns the *rationality* of the commodity relationship as a unity (at the level of exchange) of use-value and value.

This is a point that the 'orthodox' tradition scarcely illuminated, and on which some very varied opinions have been offered. Krahl[75] proposed a 'Frankfurt'-type interpretation: the expression of value in a use-value constitutes a process of 'reification', a 'reifying *quid pro quo*', a 'conceptual reflection of value'. Benetti and Cartelier also see here a fall into materiality, but, for them, this is a critique addressed to Marx.[76] Göhler proposes that, in the expression of value, the use-value of commodity A refers to the function of satisfaction and that of commodity B to the function of expression.[77] Ruben sees the expression of value (form A) as the 'language' level,[78] which he also understands as the level of the concrete. Finally, these authors quite generally link this 'expression of value in use-value' to the question of fetishism. For Lange, there is here a naturalisation of value that culminates in the fetishism of money.[79] For Fischer, Section 3 provides the 'structure of inversion [*Verkehrung*]' of Section 4.[80] This diversity of interpretations only indicates how necessary it is to take up the study of this problem.

---

[75] Krahl 1971, p. 40 etc.
[76] Benetti and Cartelier 1980, pp. 144–5.
[77] Göhler 1978, p. 80 etc.
[78] Ruben 1978, passim.
[79] Lange 1978, p. 17.
[80] Fischer 1978, p. 76.

5.i *First aspect*

The question can, in fact, only be clearly posed on the basis of an explanation of the categorial system that underlies Marx's arguments and represents labour (and subsequently exchange in its link to this) as *rational activity*, establishing a relationship between means and ends. The double determination of labour must be analysed in this sense, since expenditure here constitutes the means of all means, and *qua* rational activity aims at obtaining a use-value. In subsistence consumption, the unity is immediate: for each product there is a relationship between the *expenditure* it requires and the *result* that it brings. I propose, in a way that may initially seem paradoxical, but the justification for which will soon become clear, to call the relation between these two poles the 'relation of expression'. In commodity production, the same thing happens, with the difference that there exists the *mediation* of exchange. This establishes a relationship between the *expenditure* that the production of commodity A requires, and the *utility* that through exchange will be found in commodity B. This relationship is not that which marginalist theory establishes between utilities, nor that ascribed to Marx when his theory of value is presented as based on consideration of values alone, to the exclusion of use-values. It is a relation between a value that results from the expenditure of labour-power, and a use-value. This relation expresses the rationality of commodity production, or of the law of value. It characterises the commodity system as a system of meaningful behaviour. The practice of each partner is rational in that, via the expenditure he agrees to for the production of his product, he aims at the product being useful for the other.[81]

The commodity is indeed a unity of use-value and value, but this unity is not completed in the individual commodity, it articulates the relation between commodities, which is a relation between values and a relation between utilities, and only in this way unites value and utility. At the level of commodity production, the question of socially necessary time (productivity) and that of the equilibrium of the productive system denote this interaction between abstract and concrete labour which is already involved in the relationship of one expenditure to others, characterised by their specific results. At the level of exchange, what Marx terms the expression of value denotes this same

---

[81] Cf. the pertinent analysis of Delaunay and Gadrey 1979, pp. 262–7.

network of crosswise relations between use-value and value, and belongs to the paradigm of the exchanging producer, even when this is realised in dissociation, as is the case with the exchanging non-producer.

The expression of value is, in reality, something other than the measure of value or its definition. If expression were measurement, Marx would not be able to speak of the expression of a value 'in a use-value': use-value would then be incapable by definition of providing the shadow of a beginning of a measurement. The category of 'measure', of which the brief presentation in the *Critique* makes inflationary use,[82] significantly disappears from this section in *Capital*. This does not mean that consideration of the quantity of value disappears, but that the problem here is not to measure it (this is already achieved in Section 1) but, rather, to see how it is *expressed* in exchange.

One may well object that Marx characterises this 'expression of value in use-value' as a *quid pro pro*, that he places it at the centre of the 'contradictions of the equivalent form', since it is in fact this that is responsible for the 'peculiarities of the equivalent form':[83] 'use-value becomes the form of expression of its opposite, value', and 'concrete labour . . . of abstract human labour'.[84]

These statements and their context actually deserve a good deal of attention, starting with the surprising assertion:

> Since a commodity cannot be related to itself as equivalent, and therefore *cannot make its own physical shape into the expression of its own value*, it must be related to another commodity as equivalent, and therefore must make the physical shape of another commodity into its own value-form.[85]

It is surprising first of all because, instead of showing in what way there is a 'contradiction', Marx shows, on the contrary, the *necessity* of this form of expression (contradiction appears only in the sense of the fetishist illusion: 'the coat . . . seems to be endowed with its equivalent form . . . by nature').[86] But the greatest surprise is in the premise that the value of a commodity cannot be expressed in its own use-value[87] . . . whereas it is expressed in

---

[82] Marx 1971, p. 39.
[83] Marx 1976a, p. 148.
[84] Marx 1976a, p. 150.
[85] Marx 1976a, p. 148; my emphasis: J.B.
[86] Marx 1976a, p. 149.
[87] This second part of the premise cannot be interpreted, as Forest (1984, p. 68) suggests, as an 'anti-tautological rule': use-value is not 'the same thing' as value.

another commodity, i.e. in the use-value of the latter. In short, the relation of expression of value is defined as a relation that, if it could be realised in the commodity's own value, would not have to seek expression in the use-value of another, and as a relation that, in any case, involves the relationship between values and use-values. The *Critique*, besides, had opened the presentation of the value-form with general propositions that pose the problem as follows:

> The exchange value of one commodity thus manifests itself in the use-values
> of other commodities. In fact the exchange-value of one commodity expressed
> in the use-value of another commodity represents equivalence.[88]

In *Capital*, Marx himself indicates what the nature of the relationship between the 'value' and the 'use-value' of the same product might be – but, in this case, one would precisely not speak of 'value'. He transports us indeed, at the close of the first chapter, to the place where this relationship exists: Robinson Crusoe's island, where Defoe's protagonist has naturally to consider 'the labour-time that specific quantities of these products have on average cost him'.[89] And the same goes for a peasant family in a subsistence economy, which represents the different use-values for what they are: 'so many products of its collective labour'.[90] A situation is thus defined where there is as yet no need for expression in another product.

It is significant that Marx, in his progress from one form to the next in quest of an adequate expression of value, does not count the fact of finding expression 'in the use-value of another commodity' as a lack. The 'insufficiency'[91] of the simple form A is purely a function of its limitation to exchange with one kind of commodity. The same goes for form B: if Marx notes that 'it has no single, unified form of appearance',[92] it remains that expression in the endless series of use-values already provides abstract labour with 'its completed or total form of appearance . . . by the totality of its particular forms'.[93]

---

[88] Marx 1971, p. 38.
[89] Marx 1976a, pp. 169–70.
[90] Marx 1976a, p. 171.
[91] Marx 1976a, p. 154.
[92] Marx 1976a, p. 157.
[93] Ibid.

5.ii *Second aspect*

A turn is effected here. For, if it is true that, with forms C and D, commodities find their expression of value in the 'natural form' of the general equivalent,[94] what is thus expressed is something different, i.e. a quantity of abstract labour. Marx accordingly starts the discussion of form C with a break: 'By this form, commodities are, *for the first time*, really brought into relation with each other as values.'[95] This, moreover, is often what is retained from discussions of Section 3: thanks to money, commodities can be related to one another as values.

If we stopped here, however, there would be a total discontinuity between what Marx puts under the category of expression of value the first time 'in the use-value of . . .', and the second time 'as a value'. In actual fact, if there is a continuity in the problematic of expression of value, it is because this denotes, at the same time as a relation between values, the relation of the value of a commodity to the use-values to which it gives access. The general form of value is that which assures general exchangeability, in other words is open to all the use-values of a system: 'The commodity which has been set apart as the universal equivalent is . . . simultaneously . . . a use-value for everybody or a universal use-value.'[96] It thus realises the programme inherent in the category of expression of value as this functions already in form A: to assure the rationality of the procedure as a relation between expenditure of labour and the obtaining of a utility. And it realises this adequately, that is, it makes possible the commodity system of production and exchange as an integrated system of rational behaviours. It makes exchange possible not by way of a subterfuge, but because it makes possible the expression of value.

The unity of the two aspects of the problematic of the expression of value follows from the fact that, if there is 'abstract' labour, this is only ever the case with respect to the social complementarity of labour, in other words the circulation of utility within a society, or communication between the utilities produced. It is logical, therefore, that the moment at which the value of a commodity is adequately expressed, as abstract labour, should also be the

---

[94] Marx 1976a, p. 159.
[95] Marx 1976a, p. 158; my emphasis: J.B.
[96] Marx 1971, p. 48.

moment of its exchangeability with all use-values of the system, hence the communicability of this particular labour with all others. The value of a commodity is expressed in the money commodity because there appears here, from the fact that the use-value of money is excluded, the pure expenditure of labour that constitutes the substance of value, and also because access is given here to every use-value of the system. And this, to my mind, is what must clearly be disentangled before tackling the obscure converse side of this relationship that Marx called 'fetishism'.

6. Fetishism, a structural category of the ideology of commodity production

On the basis of this interpretation of the concept of value and the form of value, we can now introduce the category of 'fetishism', the paradigm of the ideological in *Capital*. We can now take up the questions left in suspense at the end of the last chapter, devoted to ideology, which refer back to this point of origin.

I shall argue that there are three interpretations, each suggested by certain texts of Marx but relatively heterogeneous in nature: an interpretation as *reification*, an interpretation by way of the *value-form*, and a *structural* interpretation. And that what is specific to the last of these, which Marx did not arrive at until his final version, is that it ensures the connection between the field of the ideological and that of economic relations.

I have returned to these questions in my *Explication et reconstruction du 'Capital'*,[97] starting from the analysis of the ontological status of the 'meta-structure', in a perspective that integrates the Hegelian element of Marx's presentation (the dialectic of being and appearance) into a Spinozist context.

6.i   *The interpretation in terms of reification-alienation*

It is impossible here to examine here the whole Marxist tradition that has organised its discourse around the themes of alienation-reification-fetishism. Firstly because this is an immense and diverse literature. We would have to go back to authors who, even before the appearance of the *Grundrisse* in 1939,

---

[97] Bidet 2004, pp. 63–85 and 208–18.

had from the early years of the century engaged in the Feuerbachian interpretation of *Capital*. Particularly notable here is Hammacher (1904), the precursor of such 'critical' themes. Lukács's *History and Class Consciousness* would have to be assessed along with its large posterity, or at least its influence not only on the Frankfurt school, but also the Hungarians, Italians and French. The works of Althusser and his followers showed the difference in kind between the categories of the young Marx and those of his maturity. I shall limit myself therefore to a few remarks concerning the *Grundrisse*, a text in which the concepts of Marx's youth and maturity are intermingled, and which offers the working model that this interpretation has reproduced (ad infinitum . . .) on *Capital* itself.

The *1844 Manuscripts* present the first significant references to fetishism and 'economic' alienation.[98] The *Grundrisse*, the novelty of which consists in particular in starting its presentation at the most abstract point, that of the value relation or commodity relation, transfers to this higher level the problematic initially developed apropos the wage relation, and with it the anthropological burden initially assigned to this. Marx thus combines the discourse of capitalist alienation, according to which my product or 'essence' becomes capital, the property of another, and is made the instrument of class domination, with the more general discourse of reification, according to which the relation between persons becomes and/or appears as a relation between things by virtue of the commodity structure itself.[99]

And/or: this is the whole problem that a reading of the *Grundrisse* faces, as this text develops (at the very point that in *Capital* will be that of 'fetishism'), at the end of its presentation of the commodity and money, a discourse freighted with remarkable ambiguity. A typical statement is this one: 'their mutual interconnection . . . here appears as something alien to them, autonomous, as a thing . . . personal capacity [is transformed] into objective wealth'.[100] Is what 'appears' a mere appearance? Or rather the expression of the essence of the commodity relationship? The ambiguity is insurmountable. Reification involves both the inverted being and the inverted representation of this being. More precisely, 'reification' denotes an 'appearing' that Marx

---

[98] Cf. Labica 1982, article 'Aliénation'.
[99] I have shown in Chapter 3 how the 'Comments on James Mill' (1844) already contained indications in this sense.
[100] Marx 1973c, p. 157; cf. pp. 160, 163–4.

grasps as 'being', i.e. as an essential determination; and 'fetishism' denotes the kind of representation implied in this essential determination. (And, since properly capitalist relations take this to its apogee, we find fetishism again at each moment of the presentation.)

I have shown what an epistemological obstacle to a theorisation of the ideological is presented by this figure of 'appearance' and 'inversion'. We must now add the obstacles of the couples 'man/thing' and 'subject/object', which cannot provide what the theory requires: particular categories corresponding to each structural level. The entire interest of the propositions of *Capital* on the subject of ideology, to my mind, arises from the fact that they disintegrate this globalised category of 'subject' and only assign types of representation to agents 'theoretically' constituted by their position in a space hierarchically arranged from abstract to concrete. In the 'process without subject' of the theoretical presentation there is also no place for an 'ideological' subject, as the ideological is determined here according to the radically discontinuous moments of the same process. Here, on the contrary, in the interpretation in terms of reification-alienation, the hierarchical grid collapses, since the same 'man/thing' thematic depicts both the relationship of the exchanging producer to the commodity system and that of the proletarian to the capitalist system.[101] But this is a question of categories applicable to any society (and we know how successfully they have been applied to post-capitalist societies!), in other words categories foreign to the theory of a definite mode of production.[102]

6.ii   *The value-form interpretation*

This second interpretation presents itself (at least at first sight) as the opposite of the previous one. It is based not on the theme of the inversion of use-values into exchange-values, the concrete into the abstract, but on the inversion by which value is represented in the form of use-value.

---

[101] Cf. Marx 1973c, pp. 196, 452.

[102] I return to this 'hierarchical' interpretation of the theory of ideology in the context of the *Théorie générale* for the analysis of modern society in general, in its collectivist as well as its capitalist form. And I have also recently discussed this question in 'L'aliénation selon *Le Capital*, ou que faire de Marx?', forthcoming in *La Pensée*, 2007, showing in what sense a certain concept of alienation is central to *Capital*, which makes a radical distinction between the alienation inherent in the market and the particular alienation inherent to capitalism.

It draws support from the analysis of the form of value, and particularly from Marx's assertion that in the expression '10 yards of cloth are worth 1 coat', the coat which is in the equivalent form seems to possess by nature this property of being exchangeable.

Several authors adopt this position,[103] which can certainly find support in certain passages in *Capital*.[104] The 1867 text presented a specific line of argument, located within the analysis of form A. Though mentioned only in passing in Chapter 1,[105] this figured in the Appendix as the 'fourth peculiarity of the equivalent form'.[106] And it is found again in the 1873 edition, this time apropos the 'first peculiarity'.[107]

The argument can be summed up as follows. In 'x of A is worth y of B', the first member is relative (it 'is related to'), whilst the second on the other hand 'is already something in itself'. The coat 'seems to be endowed with its equivalent form, its property of direct exchangeability, by nature, just as much as its property of being heavy or its ability to keep us warm'.[108] The first member in itself 'indicates that it conceals a social relation', while the second 'expresses value . . . and is therefore endowed with the form of value by nature itself'.[109]

The intrinsic fragility of these propositions is shown very well by this addition to the 1873 edition, which can be generalised as follows: every relative property is only the confirmation of a natural property. But this then should apply to the relative form as much as the equivalent form. These views are really incompatible with the theory. There is, in fact, a complete discrepancy between the analysis of the expression of value, which, as we have seen, is that of the conditions under which the value of commodities is expressed in exchange, i.e. their quality of being the product of abstract labour, and the analysis of fetishism, which shows, on the contrary, that what is present in the principle of exchange as an integrated rational practice escapes the

---

[103] For instance Berger 1974, p. 97, who refers to Backhaus; Projektgruppe Entwicklung des Marxchen Systems 1973, p. 147, Godelier 1977, pp. 11, 248, Fischer 1978, p. 48, Lange 1978, p. 17, Dallemagne 1978, p. 39, Bischoff 1981, p. 245 etc.
[104] Marx 1976a, pp. 147, 184–5.
[105] Marx 1980, pp. 22–3.
[106] Marx 1980, pp. 883–5.
[107] Marx 1976a, pp. 148–50.
[108] Marx 1980, p. 23.
[109] Marx 1976a, p. 149.

consciousness of the exchangers themselves. Section 3 analyses the way in which this behaviour is provided with meaning, a meaning adequate to the requirements of the system, in which commodities are exchanged as values and thus as abstract labour (that is, also as giving access to every kind of concrete wealth). Section 4 analyses the *consciousness* that the agents have of this. Ideology exists by way of this discrepancy between the logic of behaviour and the consciousness of agents. This section cannot be understood as an illustration or development of Section 3.

The discrepancy can be grasped more readily if we refer to the analysis provided above of the value-form as a non-'equivalent' relation. We can then understand that the 'propositions of fetishism' are representations of the 'value relationship', *Wertverhältnis*, but not duplicates of the expression of value, *Wertausdruck*. They concern the relation of commodities 'among themselves', the view that the agents have of the entire system of circulation and exchange. These propositions thus constitute relations of equivalence (reflexive, transitive, symmetrical). Analysis of the value-form, on the other hand, involves the intersection of two symmetrical propositions establishing an asymmetrical relationship. 'Form of value' and 'fetishism' thus do indeed form two categorial structures of basically different kinds.

This does not mean that the moment of money, that of the form of value, is not marked by fetishism. There is certainly a 'money fetish',[110] but money and the form of value do not constitute its point of origin.[111] And this is what we now have to establish.

6.iii The structural interpretation

The second edition of *Capital* contains a different explanation, and one compatible with the requirements of the system.[112] Here is the essential passage:

> Since the producers do not come into social contact until they exchange the products of their labour, the specific social characteristics of their private labours appear only within this exchange. In other words, the labour of the private individual manifests itself as an element of the total labour of society

---

[110] Marx 1976a, p. 187.

[111] In the contrary sense, cf. the approach of Forest (1984, p. 36): the money-form is the foundation of fetishism, as it constitutes an 'expression of the quantity' of value that 'hides its quality', i.e. its determination by labour-time.

[112] Marx 1976a, pp. 165–8.

only through the relations which the act of exchange establishes between the products, and, through their mediation, between the producers.[113]

Everything is said. We may note that the reference here is to exchanging producers, categories that the section on fetishism explicitly introduces. More precisely, dissociated categories of producers and exchangers. The whole argument turns around the idea that the producers enter into contact only as exchangers.

What does it mean to 'come into social contact' as producers? Marx provides here some real and imagined examples. Robinson Crusoe is in contact with himself as producer; he knows that his product costs him labour. The same applies to the 'associated' labour of the patriarchal household and that of future communism; the producers come into contact as producers by the fact that they consciously divide up the tasks. And the same would also be true of commodity production, *if* each person knew the time socially necessary to produce each product. For producer A would then know the conditions under which she confronted competitors within her branch, and the conditions in which producers in other branches produced the objects that they offered in exchange for those that cost A the time that she knew. There would then be no commodity fetishism. The law of value would be transparent. No science would be necessary.

Why, then, is this law unknown to the producers in the present case? Quite simply, because its global mechanism exceeds the field of experience of the private producer. For the overall production process of a commodity society, which is precisely what makes labours 'equal'[114] – a word that actually denotes here this complex confrontation between labours whose *inequality* within the branch is continuously renewed by modifications in the comparative conditions of productivity, and whose *equality* between branches is always caught between the inverse effects that market movements repeatedly exert –, is not the object of immediate experience, as would be the case with a system of a priori planning. If there is commodity fetishism, this is to the exact degree that the law of value as law of the market presiding over the exchanges between labours is not known as such by the producers, i.e. the degree to which the latter, in their activities and production choices, do not make consideration

---

[113] Marx 1976a, p. 165.
[114] Marx 1976a, p. 164.

of the comparative production times of the various objects exchanged on the market a conscious principle of their behaviour.

What does it mean that they 'do not come into social contact until they exchange'? The private producer adjusts her behaviour as a function of information that is provided to her in exchange by variation in market prices. Fetishism thus exists thanks to this indirect and a posteriori character of the relationship between individual and global production that characterises the commodity system. The movement of market prices indicates to the private producer the productive (or exchanging) behaviour to follow, but does not offer direct access to the principles of functioning of the system. Its operational categories are thus not of such kind as to give her access to the overall system as this is governed by the law of value. That can only be the fruit of a scientific elaboration, based on observations and (theoretical) practices of a different order. In the absence of theoretical knowledge, the exchange relation thus appears as a simple fact, and is imputed to the nature of the things themselves.

And yet the system and its foundation, the law of value, are not totally opaque to the producer. She too necessarily raises the question of the different use she could make of his time, and can represent to herself the comparative production times of a certain number of products. It is on this basis, moreover, that scientific research and presentation are possible. The structure of commodity production does not possess any essential opacity. And this is why, as the *Critique* puts it, 'everybody understands more or less clearly' that this is a relationship between people.[115]

We can grasp here the crucial importance of this theoretical moment for the conception of the ideological in the economic base as whole. Marx does not just provide here, for the first time in the order of the exposition, a discourse out of joint with the major discourse of *Capital*, which concerns the actual relations: he moves from these to their representations, and shows at the same time how the latter also belong to actuality and to the object of the theory. And this discrepancy is repeated throughout the exposition, each time that Marx presents the categories inherent to the practice of the agents that these levels define. But this moment of fetishism, since it is linked to the most basic relation of production, governs the entire subsequent ideological complex.

---

[115] Marx 1971, pp. 34–5.

Balibar has presented a number of objections to the principle of a structural interpretation. To my mind, however, these are removed by the considerations that Marx develops in the second edition of *Capital*. 'The theory of fetishism', writes Balibar, 'thus remains in *Capital* a (philosophical) genesis of the subject, comparable with others to be found in classical philosophy, but with this critical variation . . .: it is a genesis of the subject as alienated subject'. He sees the 'structuralist' approach in which fetishism is an 'effect of the structure', 'an effect on individuals of the place they occupy as subjects in the exchange structure, in relation to commodities', as 'the strict theoretical equivalent' of this humanist problematic:

> The question of the (structural) place is equivalent to the question of the (human) subject, if the sole fact of occupying a place in the system of social relations (exchange relations in particular) also establishes a perspective, a representation, and finally a consciousness of this system (even a 'false' consciousness), and is sufficient to explain it.[116]

It seems to me, on the contrary, that the necessary reference which Balibar makes to the 'ideological apparatuses'[117] and their historical development in no way excludes consideration of the relations of production in their ideological dimension.

In fact, as I have shown, the arguments proposed in the 1873 edition are not only located outside of the alienation-reification problematic of the *Grundrisse* (which can be appropriately characterised as Hegelian-Feuerbachian), but continue to link fetishism not to the simple structure of exchange but rather to the connection between exchange relations and relations of production in the commodity system. The purpose of historical materialism is thereby realised: to show that these representations are not based exclusively on autonomous relations and their history, but implied first of all by the relations of production themselves. There is certainly nothing here that might claim to substitute for an investigation of 'specifically ideological' social relations. The problem is simply that of their articulation to economic relations, including the ideological component of these.

It might be objected here that fetishism thus defined remains a 'structural effect', hence a case of '(structural) genesis of the subject'.

---

[116] Balibar 1974, pp. 223–4.
[117] Balibar 1974, p. 221.

A structural effect, certainly. But in the sense that structures define the context of practices, of which it is legitimate to ask what representations they require on the part of their agents. Marx's analysis consists in showing that the fact of being an agent in a structure does *not* provide an adequate representation. The structure is not transparent to its agents: they do not have the perspective on it that science provides. And Marx gives the structural reason for this: the exchanging producers only grasp the overall process in their capacity as exchangers. They do not need to be aware of how value is determined by the structure of production. The explanatory matrix is of the same kind as that which Marx proposes in the first part of Volume Three, apropos the categories inherent to the capitalist's practice. At the same time, this 'effect' has nothing to do with any structuralist fatalism, since the exchanging producer always has various ideas about production and the relationship between time and value.

But this does not involve the genesis of a subject. Marx's 'structuralism' is not of such a kind as to generate a subject. No more can the 'development of the concept of capital' be assimilated to that of a subject, since it concerns the development of an overall structure according to a categorial order with a logical hierarchy, in no way giving rise to the steady and cumulative advance of a total agent that would figure as the 'subject of the system' (nor indeed of various class-subjects). The categorial development of the structure actually consists in a radical principle of fragmentation and dissemination of the ideological representation. Each structural level presents its specific effects, its particular conditions of visibility and invisibility, giving rise to practices that possess their own pertinent references. An ensemble of this kind does not produce a subject.

Marx's procedure is initially negative. He simply proposes that the social agent has no spontaneous representation of the social reality such as science establishes. He is then led to inquire what representations actually are implied by the practices inherent to the functions of the system he has constructed. These are the narrow limits of the highly theoretical design that he pursues. And what is defined in this way is something that exceeds the representations, not only escaping them but, at the same time, being obscured by them in so far as they are representations of the social totality. This obscuring, moreover, is something quite other than a simple technical given of production. It involves for a start the 'law of value' to the extent that this forms a determinate structure of constraint on production, a semi-concept requiring the class relationship in which the 'political compulsion' that I analysed is exerted. Ideology forms the 'un-thought' of the socio-political relationship, and in this way its naturalisation and legitimisation.

Conditions certainly exist that tend to unify the ideological complex. These bear on the relationship that unites the different levels of actual relations. Among these, for example, is the illegibility of the law of value: this extends to that of specifically capitalist relations, which can only be deciphered as relations of exploitation on the basis of the theory of value. At the same time, the *general* (commodity) conditions for this illegibility of the law of value are overdetermined by the *particular* conditions that flow from the capitalist relation as such, in particular the transformation of value into price of production. But this unity of the ideological complex is not of such kind as to define the unity of an ideological subject. Any coherence it acquires is always fragmentary and fragile. The structural approach does not prescribe any fatalism for ideology. At every level, Marx shows how the law of value can be glimpsed somehow or another. And it is on this basis that theorisation is possible, as well as the critique of the system and the revolutionary struggle for its destruction.

Conclusion

The exploration of the problematic of the ideological back to its point of origin has led us to analyse the relationship established by *Capital* between the theory of the 'form of value' and that of 'fetishism', the nub of the conflict between different interpretations.

The object of Section 3 of Chapter 1 is properly the 'form of value' rather than the 'value-form', i.e. the adequate expression of the 'value relation' defined by the 'concept of value' presented in the first two sections. It is only at a late stage that Marx frees himself from the classical problematic of 'relative value', still present in 1867. But this is a key moment in his 'break', and one that is not well understood, as attested by the ongoing debate on the nature of the relationship 'x of A is worth y of B'. The relationship of equivalence contained in the 'value relation', which is reflexive, transitive and symmetrical, and in relative value, must be distinguished from the pair of symmetrical relationships and expressions contained in the 'form of value'.

In the *Grundrisse*, the exposition presents a dialectical form inspired by Hegelian logic and inadequate to the object. In the 1867 edition, the Appendix introduces the decisive couple of the relative and equivalent forms, which enabled the problematic of the relative form to be superseded. But the theme of essence and phenomenon still predominates here, obscuring the specific terrain of the theory.

In *Capital*, where the exposition takes a form more in conformity with the requirements of the theory, there is no longer any 'dialectic of the form of value'. The main weakness of commentaries on this has been that they do not correctly link the form of value to the 'concept of value', in other words to the abstract structure of commodity production which precedes it and of which it is supposed to provide the adequate expression. It is in this way, in fact, that the exposition displays not a teleological character but rather an analytical or retrospective one; it is in this way that the 'value relation' is a 'total' relationship in the mathematical sense, and the 'expression of value' can be generalised from form A to form C. This procedure is not merely 'deductive', as it is accompanied by the introduction of new categories (such as the 'relative/equivalent' couple) in such a way that the total configuration of the structure is progressively established.

Sections 3 and 4 of Chapter 1 tend respectively to determine the forms of meaning and of consciousness inherent to this social structure. The problem here bears on the fact that these forms are relatively disconnected: on the one hand, the 'form of value' implied in the rationality of commodity production, on the other, its ideological representation or 'fetishism'.

The 'form of value' actually denotes the rationality of the commodity relationship as a unity of use-value and value at the level of exchange. This is apparent as soon as we consider Marx's statement: 'since the value of a commodity cannot be expressed in its own use-value . . .'. A strange statement, unless it is related to its implicit alternative: pre-commodity production in which labour-time *is* directly 'expressed' in the use-value it creates and the consumption of which it permits. Such is the 'expression' that 'x of commodity A' finds, under commodity production, in 'y of commodity B'. An expression of value in use-value, which is neither inversion nor mystification, but denotes first and foremost the rationality of the commodity-form. If the money commodity is the form of the adequate expression of value, it is simultaneously because 1) being an excluded use-value, and thus pure value, it expresses the substance of this, abstract labour, the expenditure of labour-power; 2) conjointly (and this conjunction, this unity of two facets of the 'expression of value' constitutes the rationality of the structure) because, in this way, it offers access to any use-value in the system.

If this is the case, then the question of fetishism is of a quite different nature from that of the form of value: it (alone) designates the ideological. And, as Marx presents it in the second edition, it does so in a structural sense. The principle of the overall process of commodity production, the law of value, is not the object of immediate experience for the producer. And the latter has no need for it in his practice, which is governed by other indicators, i.e. market prices, which show him the path to follow. Because of this, commodity relations appear to him only through the categories of exchange. Such is the point of origin of the ideological complex that is developed throughout *Capital*. This invisibility of the law of value also involves that of exploitation, the concept of which depends on it. Step by step, all these categories of capitalism are subsumed under the relationship of exchange. This obscurity however can be resisted, since the law of value does not present any essentially invisible character. When theory produces this law, it displays the antagonistic nature of social relations. And the fetishism that is unaware of it is also the distorted consciousness of the sociopolitical character of capitalist relations and its foundation, the enforced expenditure of labour-power.

This analysis of the level of ideology has led us to the initial categories of the theory of the capitalist mode of production, those concerning value. What now remains is to cross this barrier and investigate the foundation of this starting point, the more general discourse that the theory of value and the theory of the capitalist mode of production imply.

Chapter Ten

The Economy in General and Historical Materialism

The discourse of *Capital* is articulated to a variety of more general notions and ideas that constitute its presuppositions. This point is one of the least elucidated in Marx's elaboration. What is involved here is something repressed, to the extent that he was driven by the awareness that his strength was a function of his ability to restrict himself to a very definite terrain, to make the system of categories specific to the capitalist mode of production function as a whole and exclusively. But it is apparent in many places that this specialised discourse is not self-sufficient, and here Marx has to appeal explicitly to a meta-language in order to properly grasp the particular thing that he wants to speak about.

This is the case at the very start of his project: he can only posit its initial categories by defining certain categories that are still more general. And if we consider his horizon, the object of his entire procedure, it is impossible to totally dissociate the analysis of a specific society (in terms of its particular categories) from general propositions for a future society.

This question is essential, since, whilst Marx's theory is trivialised and loses its whole pertinence as soon as it is absorbed into the generalities of philosophy and economics, his specific discourse can only be fully understood by an explanation of its relationship to these generalities.

The procedures of philosophising the discourse of *Capital* have already been analysed in the previous chapters (6 to 9). It is the economistic tendency, the more current today, that we have still to explore.

A prerequisite of this, however – and this will be the object of the first section here – will be to examine the status of *generality* in Marx's supposedly 'economic' work. It will appear diverse, in a diversity that has not adequately been considered: generality of historical materialism and generality of an economics; generality of the 'labour process in general' introduced in the course of the exposition, and generality that has to be presupposed at its beginning; generality of rational and balanced production/reproduction that surfaces in Volume Two at the heart of the specific discourse, and generality of the discourse on the future society, which finds a place only on the margin of this.

The result will be one of clarifications and uncertainties. It will make possible – the subject of the second section – a discussion of the recent problematic that has developed around the work of Sraffa, and compels us to rethink Marx's relationship to Ricardo. Is it necessary, as Marx did, to read Ricardo as theorising, unknown to himself, the particular historical object of capitalist society? Or should we rather base ourselves on Sraffa's achievement, understood as the development of a pure economics, and see in this the foundation of a strictly general discipline?

I propose to show how a re-examination of this kind leads to a radical re-reading of Marx's discourse, and can contribute in this way to the current debate concerning the foundations of his theory of capitalist production.[1]

1. The various generalities that *Capital* presupposes

1.i *Three kinds of generality*

In the 1857 Introduction, at the end of the famous passage on 'the method of political economy', Marx announces his intention to begin the study of

---

[1] I return to this question of general presuppositions on a new ('metastructural') basis in *Théorie générale*, particularly the first two chapters.

bourgeois society with a first part devoted to the 'general, abstract determinants which obtain in more or less all forms of society'.[2] But this idea is no sooner advanced than it seems to be abandoned, since the various plans that vie with each other in the *Grundrisse* no longer mention it, and begin, on the contrary, with money, which effectively forms the manuscript's point of departure. In reality, however, Marx does not entirely abandon the original project. And, in any case, he returns to it again in a significant text that does not seem to have attracted the attention of commentators. He reaffirms here his intention to write a section on 'production in general',[3] as a preliminary to the study of capital and of value. But he also states that what this must contain will only be clear after the study of capital has been completed.

The real cause of the difficulty is that this beginning includes, if we relate it to the various aspects of Marx's discussion, three distinct configurations:

1) the general categories of economics;
2) the categories of the labour process in general;
3) the categories of the mode of production in general.

Now, in the entire period that Marx was working on *Capital* (from 1857 to his death), he made only one overall attempt at a preliminary exposition of these general categories: this is the 1857 Introduction, Sections 1 and 2 of which are respectively titled 'Production' and 'The General Relation of Production to Distribution, Exchange and Consumption'.[4] The preliminary generalities here are thus those of 'economics', i.e. the first kind.

In the same context, discussing the 'common characteristics' of 'all epochs of production' (p. 85), Marx invokes the categories of 'production in general' (i.e. the second kind): subject/object in the sense of humanity/nature, past labour/present labour, instrument. These are categories that are to be found each time that Marx returns to the question of the 'labour process in general', especially in *Capital*.[5] They appear here as belonging by right to the initial and most abstract moment of the exposition.

At the same time, the 1857 Introduction displays the presence of the third kind of generality. Its fourth section,[6] in fact, invokes the set of concepts

---

[2] Marx 1973c, p. 108.
[3] Marx 1973c, p. 320, also p. 304.
[4] Marx 1973c, pp. 83 & 88.
[5] Marx 1976a, pp. 283–92.
[6] Marx 1973c, pp. 109–11.

defining the 'mode of production': 'means of production and relations of production', 'relations of production and relations of circulation', 'forms of the state and forms of consciousness' that correspond to the former, 'productive forces'/'relations of production'.

Nowhere else does Marx systematically attempt to elucidate the various presuppositions of his theory of the capitalist mode of production, and the relationship between the three kinds of generality that I have distinguished remains unclear. He sometimes tends to downplay the question, calling these generalities that are prior to the specification of particular historical 'forms' 'leathery commonplaces'.[7] It is only tangentially that he ever broaches it. This is the case with the labour process in general, which is introduced only in the interest of understanding, by way of antithesis, the process of capitalist production.[8] And the same goes for the general categories of economics, which are never again presented for their own sake. As for the categories of historical materialism, indicated in the 1859 Preface to the *Critique*, nowhere in *Capital* was there a suitable place to present them.

I shall confine myself here to three categories: *labour*, *value*, and *reproduction*. And I shall show that the ambiguity which surrounds them, affecting part of the discourse of *Capital* and locating it at the pivot between the scientific and the utopian, is displayed in the highest degree in Marx's approach to socialism.

1.ii   *The labour process in general (Volume One, Chapter 7)*

'Labour in general' is, naturally, the first generality in general economic discourse: it is indifferent to the various forms of society. But it does not figure at the start of *Capital*, which ostentatiously begins with the most abstract categories specific to the capitalist mode of production: commodity categories. To be sure, these are also valid to a certain extent in other types of society. But they are implicit in the very definition of capitalism, and it is in this sense that they are presented at the start of *Capital*: it is impossible to present this specific system of production without beginning with them. 'Labour in general', on the contrary, does not belong to this specificity. And so it cannot figure as the start of the 'development from abstract to concrete' that is constitutive of

---

[7] Marx 1973c, p. 853, cf. pp. 881, 85, 320.
[8] Marx 1976a, pp. 283–92.

the theory of the capitalist mode of production. If this were taken as the beginning, there would not be a proper development, but simply a discontinuous transition,[9] a leap to a different kind of discourse, now implying the consideration of historically defined relations of production. The way that *Capital* opens, however, does involve a disadvantage: there is no confrontation between the universal category of labour in general and the 'dual character of labour' posited at the start of *Capital*,[10] so that the jump from the general discourse to the specific could be analysed. This is the mark of an initial uncertainty that has an impact on the work as a whole.

Yet Marx does indeed provide this presentation of 'labour in general'. He even does so at the same place in each successive version of his text: just before the exposition of surplus-value, and in order to show the difference between capitalist production and production in general: in the *Grundrisse*,[11] the *1861–3 Manuscripts*,[12] and in *Capital*.[13] But it is precisely the contradictions that can be noted between these different versions that are highly significant of the uncertainty I have mentioned, and the efforts that Marx made to conceal this.

The text of the *Grundrisse* already introduces almost all the determinations to be found in the corresponding section of *Capital*: activity, raw material, instrument, object, result, precondition, objectified (past) labour, product. It leaves a rather disturbing impression, however, to discover in this exclusive club of universal characteristics an unexpected guest: 'value'. The product is, in fact, understood here as 'objectified labour', and this defined as 'substance of value'.[14] Moreover, Marx also locates here the 'expenditure of labour-power', which he combines with its 'consumption': 'labour also is consumed by being employed, set into motion, and a certain amount of the worker's muscular force etc. is thus expended, so that he exhausts himself'.[15] Even if this passage leads to the notion of 'use-value' as the result of the process, a notion that will subsequently give the presentation its title, yet the attribute of generality, the determinations of abstract labour, go together here with the notion of

---

[9] Cf. Marx 1973c, p. 259.
[10] Marx 1976a, p. 131.
[11] Marx 1973c, pp. 297 ff.
[12] Marx and Engels 1988a, pp. 54–64.
[13] Marx 1976a, pp. 283–92.
[14] Marx 1973c, p. 298.
[15] Marx 1973c, p. 300.

'expenditure', the 'objectification of labour',[16] which has regularly functioned to denote the basis of 'labour-value' in the earlier sections of the manuscript.[17] In short, from the *Grundrisse* onwards, Marx experiences a difficulty in formulating an exposition of 'labour in general' that does not involve the specific determinations of what *Capital* subsequently calls 'abstract labour'.

The exposition in the *1861–3 Manuscripts* is much longer and more explicit. It differs from the *Grundrisse* on one essential point: the reference to 'value' and the 'substance of value' disappears. Marx's preoccupation is evidently to produce an analysis of labour that is separate from the notion of value and thus from the reference to labour-time. This is heralded in the thesis that is developed at greatest length here: the means of production issuing from labour only appear under the rubric of their use-value, and the labour contained in them is described here as 'irrelevant [*gleichgültig*]', 'extinguished [*aufgehoben*]' or 'obliterated'.[18] In short, defining the labour process 'in its general form'[19] means defining it exclusively in terms of use-values. It matters little, says Marx, that these are the product of labour: 'if they fell ready-made from the sky they would perform the same service'.[20] A strange argument, for the means of labour precisely do not fall from the sky, and only possess use-value from the fact that they are the product of a certain labour. More strange still is the reference (repeated in *Capital*) to this previous labour being forgotten, and remembered only in the poor operation of the instrument: the 'saw that does not saw', fruit of a 'poor' labour :[21] this is to appeal to the evidence of fetishism, which, it is true, ignores the labour in use-value. Furthermore, the category of 'labour contained' in the means of labour should impress itself all the more on Marx, in so far as he claims here to be conducting an analysis in terms of 'process', a process in which the result becomes condition, the posited presupposition. The purging of the 'abstract labour' factor, moreover, is still incomplete in the 1861 text, since Marx does not manage to define 'the process of labour in general' without reference to the 'expenditure' and 'using up' of labour-power, its 'consumption'.[22] The very

---

[16] Marx 1973c, p. 299.
[17] Marx 1973c, pp. 134–43 *passim*.
[18] Marx and Engels 1988a, p. 61.
[19] Marx and Engels 1988a, p. 64.
[20] Marx and Engels 1988a, p. 61.
[21] Ibid. Cf. Marx 1976a, p. 289.
[22] Marx and Engels 1988a, p. 59.

effort of dialectisation that presents 'effective labour [*wirkliche Arbeit*]' as the synthesis of past and present *concrete* labour in the actuality of their mutual consumption ('the form-giving activity consumes the object and materialises itself')[23] gives the game away – extinguishing [*Aufhebung*] is achieved in consumption! Chased out of the door, the abstract 'aspect' returns through the window.

In the *1861–3 Manuscripts*, in short, Marx still presents the whole set of categories inherent to the notion of 'labour in general' in a double aspect: 'use-value/expenditure'.

This is what Marx systematically obscures in the definitive version, that of *Capital*.[24] If this text is taken for what it is, the result of the re-working of its predecessors, we can be sensitive to the changes it brings: the suppression of any reference to 'expenditure', and even to 'labour capacity' – in place of which we find 'man', 'the worker' –, the externalising of 'consumption' cited both before and after this text on 'labour in general',[25] but not actually in it. We find, moreover, but only beneath the surface, the elements of the problematic of 'effective labour'. In sum, this section of *Capital* is remarkably purged, in relation to earlier versions, of all categories that, like those of 'concrete/abstract labour', 'particular/general', 'expenditure', 'value', 'substance of value', 'objectivisation', do not fit into the strict framework of the production of use-values (and thus of 'concrete' labour) that Marx undertakes to present here, so he can go on to display the specific characteristics of the production of surplus-value.[26]

But can the category of 'labour in general' be legitimately constructed by excluding the determinations of expenditure and abstract labour? Marx, as we shall see, finally reserves these for Part One of *Capital*. I propose, however, to show that this procedure expresses an uncertainty that is heavy with consequences, and rebounds on the status of particular categories at other levels, in other words that of commodity production (with which *Capital* opens), that of economics in general, and that of the socialist economy.

---

[23] Ibid.; cf. p. 63.
[24] Marx 1976a, pp. 283–90.
[25] Marx 1976a, pp. 283 & 290.
[26] Marx 1976a, pp. 293–306.

1.iii   *The initial concepts of* Capital *(Volume One, Chapter 1)*

Let us first examine the most abstract categories with which *Capital* commences, those defining the two 'factors of the commodity' and the 'double character of labour'.[27] What is the nature of their 'generality'?

'Use-value' and 'value' figure in the title of the first section of Chapter 1 as the 'factors' of the commodity, i.e. the determinations that constitute it in their distinction and their relationship. This is, officially, the first abstract configuration. To my mind, however, it is not entirely legitimate.

The couple suffers from a certain inequality. 'Use-value', always named first, is presented as endowed with a status of higher generality. Paradoxically, it is as an absolutely general category that it figures here in its capacity as a 'factor' of a specific and historically determined category, that of the 'commodity', whereas the other 'factor', that of 'value', is supposed to share the same historical determination as the latter. Use-value is defined by recourse to other generalities: 'needs', nature, 'man' and his 'subsistence', and 'consumption'. 'Use-values . . . constitute the material content of wealth, whatever its social form may be.'[28] In the French edition, they provide the heading – 'la production de valeurs d'usage' – for the exposition of the 'labour process in general'.[29] And we find this same tendency to the 'naturalisation' of use-value (which dominated the problematic of the *Grundrisse*) in statements of the kind: 'the natural form of commodity B becomes the value-form of commodity A'.[30]

We might wonder why 'use-value' should be privileged in this way vis-à-vis 'value', which also possesses its own generality: see, for example, Marx's various statements that emphasise how 'economy of labour time'[31] is a universal 'law' (a notion that remains to be defined). If this does not appear in *Capital*, it is because 'expenditure' is introduced only at the end of an explanation opened by a highly 'specific' concept, that of 'exchange-value', which has a place only in commodity society. The theory of 'labour-value' is presented in

---

[27] Among the several studies bearing on the beginning of *Capital*, we should note those of Macherey 1975 (pp. 213–55), the Projektgruppe Entwicklung des Marxschen Systems 1973, Ricci 1974 (pp. 105–33), Bader et al. 1975 (pp. 87–100), Brinkmann 1975 (pp. 13–82) and Forest 1984.

[28] Marx 1976a, p. 126.

[29] Marx 1983, fasc. 1, p. 180.

[30] Marx 1976a, p. 144.

[31] Marx 1973c, p. 173.

fact as the answer to the question of the basis of the exchange relationship: socially necessary labour-time. This category implies the comparability of different labours, hence the consideration of what they have in common, that of being expenditure of labour-power. But this presentation should not conceal from us that, beyond the commodity structure, which is a particular mode of organisation of 'expenditure', this expenditure is a universal element.

In order to remove ambiguities, therefore, it is necessary to render to the concept of labour in general what belongs to it: 'all labour aims at a use-value' (a particular one, by virtue of which it is a labour of a particular kind); and 'all labour is expenditure of labour-power'. The couple 'use-value/expenditure of labour-power' gives us an absolutely general concept, which denotes labour as a rational behaviour in general: the effecting of an expenditure with the view to a utility. Each term here denotes the *naturalness* of the social nature of labour: use-value possesses a natural foundation, expenditure presents natural limits. But equally denoted is its *sociality* (in general): use-value and expenditure are socially determined.

These general determinations of labour, however, if they are implicit in the start of the exposition, do not themselves constitute this start, which, by virtue of being the start of the exposition of the theory of the capitalist mode of production, is produced by the operation that specifies these categories: their insertion into the commodity structure itself, as this is sketched out in Part One of *Capital*.

We now come to the categories of Section 2:[32] 'concrete labour' and 'abstract labour'. These are in themselves, and for the same reasons, absolutely 'general'. For in every social form, inasmuch as there exists a division of labour, labours are distinguished concretely, while they have in common the property of being an expenditure of labour-power, i.e. abstract labour.

We cannot follow Marx when he makes this 'abstraction' into a category specific to commodity production as such. The notion of abstraction understood in this way, moreover, tends to denote the negation of use-value. Now this, in the strict register of the theory of *Capital*, can only concern surplus-value as 'social logic': an orientation towards absolute wealth at the expense of specific use-values. This attribution does not have a place in the exposition of commodity relations as such.

---

[32] Marx 1976a, pp. 131 ff.

We can also not follow Marx in his correlative tendency to reject the abstract character of labour in its generality, and reserve this description for the relationship that contains money. For if money expresses abstraction, pure expenditure of labour, this is only, in my view, a specific expression of the commodity relationship. It certainly refers to abstract labour and belongs, as Marx says, to 'the essence of value', but in the specific sense in which the 'law of value' denotes the mode of regulation (of expenditure of labour) specific to the commodity relationship as such.

The start of the exposition of the theory of the capitalist mode of production, the exposition of its initial moment, that of the commodity relations of production and exchange, consists, then, in that a double pair of general concepts ('use-value/concrete labour', 'expenditure of labour-power/abstract labour') is specified by its inscription in the commodity structure, or the law of value.

1.iv   The generality of the concepts of reproduction

The categories of reproduction pose an analogous problem.

They seem, at first sight, to be no more than specific notions of the theory of the capitalist mode of production, appearing at a necessary moment in the exposition of this. In two aspects, however, this development goes beyond the categorial field specific to capital.

The first aspect is the easier to recognise. It follows from the introduction, at this moment of the exposition, of categories of a general character. There is, on the one hand, the distinction, within use-value, of two sectors, that of means of subsistence and that of means of production. And, on the other hand, the consideration of the relations between the major 'functions' listed already in the 1857 Introduction: production, consumption, exchange, distribution.

The second aspect, on the other hand, seems to me to have been overlooked. It concerns the status of the category of 'value' in the context defined by these reproduction schemas. Apparently, Marx was not aware of modifying this category, but only of introducing it into a new ensemble, in which commodities would be analysed as both use-value and value.[33] A difficulty arises, however, from the fact that this category of value, which in Volume One possessed the

---

[33] Cf. Marx 1978, p. 463.

status of a category of contradiction, appears here in a quite different fashion, a category of pure functionality (and thus a general category, as we shall go on to see).

Value is a *category of contradiction*, yet only virtually so in the initial moment that I have defined as that of the commodity structure of production and exchange, from the fact that a structure of this kind contains in virtual form contradictions that can exist as such only in capital. But, on the other hand, the contradictions that this develops are analysed in part precisely as an instantiation of these virtualities that pertain to value as it is defined by the commodity structure. The predominance of the logic of abstract wealth, denoted by the notion of surplus-value, signifies a contradiction between the classes that form such a society. And, by this fact, value forms a category of the contradiction.

But it is as a *non-contradictory category* that value intervenes in the reproduction schemas, which in effect denote a norm: that of the conditions of equilibrium of the structure, that of a non-contradictory functioning and development of production. Non-contradictory in the sense that its different elements harmonise into a coherent whole. The social contradiction is evidently not posited here as suppressed; it is only this moment of the exposition that abstracts from it. The consumption of a part of the product by the non-producer appears here only under the rubric of an element in the reproduction of the system.

A problem is therefore posed: how to explain that, within the same theory founded on value, this category presents two such distinct statuses?

The response is to be sought in the fact that two kinds of discourse interfere here. For there is no suspension of the specific discourse: Part Three of Volume Two constitutes a necessary moment because it is on this basis, at least in part, that it is possible to analyse the contradictions of capitalism in relation to these norms of harmony and maintenance of use-values – in other words, to analyse crises. But this moment of the exposition appeals to a different discourse in which 'value' functions in a non-specific sense. For the fact that these schemata are expressed *in values* is not a function of the specificity of the discourse as one bearing on capitalist or commodity-producing society, but, rather, of the legitimacy of a *general* category of value. They do not, in fact, contain any significant element of the motives and tendencies specific to a particular mode of production. And they can be equivalently interpreted as results of market mechanisms or as objectives in an a priori plan. Labour-time here is a purely technical given, and the question raised about it is that of its rational allocation. It appears as 'labour-value in general', outside the framework of the 'law of value' (in the sense of law of commodity structure), outside the particularity of a mode of production characterised by its definite order of social compulsion. It is labour as expenditure independent of the system in which this is obtained and regulated. This confirms the above assertions concerning the nature of the initial concepts of *Capital* and their relations with the universal concepts that they imply.

The problem is that Marx is not fully aware of the determinations that he produces here, and, as a result, this complex of categories is developed in his texts in an ambiguous manner, which marks his approach to socialism.

1.v *Marx's discourse on socialism*

At the time of the *Grundrisse*, Marx proposed to conclude the general work he envisaged with an analysis of the transition to socialism. The most detailed plan that figures in this text ends as follows: 'Dissolution of the mode of production and form of society based on exchange value. Real positing of individual labour as social and vice versa.'[34] Marx was not to realise this project. Nowhere did he develop the categories of *Capital* into categories of the transition to socialism. At most, he presented the specific 'circumstances' of capitalism that favoured either its collapse or on the contrary its continuation. In Marx's maturity, discourse on socialism would be a separate discourse, not directly articulated to his masterwork. This relative disjunction, which we might have expected Marx to theorise (i.e. that he would investigate what distinguished the theory of an existing society from the project of a future society), actually conceals several uncertainties, which favour illegitimate and distorting recombinations of his discourse. These ambiguities – on which the project of 'scientific socialism' rests, and more broadly, the totalising discourse that developed in the Marxist tradition – refer, once again, to the category of value.

The expression 'law of value', rare in *Capital* but common in *Theories of Surplus-Value*, initially possesses a particular sense. It is used in the context of the analysis of capitalism, and refers to its character as commodity

---

[34] Marx 1973c, p. 264.

production, by which value is determined in the market by labour-time; it is situated in the tradition of English political economy, which Marx stressed had been unable, with the exception of Ricardo, to maintain this principle in its analysis of capital. This is the 'law of value',[35] denoted indifferently in the German original as *Gesetz des Wertes*,[36] *Gesetz der Werte*,[37] or 'law of values of commodities'.[38] It is invoked each time that precapitalist commodity production comes into the picture,[39] as well as when capitalism is analysed in its market mechanisms. Thus, in Part Four of Volume One, the 'law of value' is indicated as the specific way in which the market regulates proportionality in the allocation of labour to different branches.[40] Marx contrasts this with the a priori planning within the firm that prefigures socialism. This category 'law of value' is implicitly and legitimately present in the presuppositions of Part One of Volume One.

Marx presents this 'law of value' as the historic form of a universal law, which he never invokes except in such incidental remarks.

In the *Grundrisse*, the universal law is indicated as that of economy and proportionate distribution of labour-time.[41] The letter to Kugelmann of 11 July 1868 affirms its 'self-evident'[42] character, the evidence being that the principle of production is labour and its proportionate distribution between branches. This is a 'natural law', expressed in a 'mode of appearance [*Erscheinungsweise*]' that is historically determined.[43] The 'law of value' is thus the realisation of this natural law in a society based on 'private property'.

The note on Adolph Wagner expresses a similar idea:

> [T]he 'value' of the commodity merely expresses in a historically developed form something which also exists in all other historical forms of society, albeit if *in a different form, namely the social character of labour*, insofar as this exists as *expenditure of 'social' labour-power*.[44]

---

[35] Marx 1972, p. 29.
[36] Marx 1969, p. 403; Marx 1972, pp. 8, 23.
[37] '[L]aw of values': Marx 1976d, pp. 160, 399, 401.
[38] 'Gesetz der Warenwerte': Marx 1976d, p. 159.
[39] Marx 1981, pp. 277–8, for example.
[40] Marx 1976a, p. 465.
[41] Marx 1973c, p. 173.
[42] [Marx uses the English term in a letter otherwise written in German.]
[43] Marx and Engels 1988b, p. 68.
[44] Marx and Engels 1989, p. 551.

Marx adds that the same goes for use-value, which is also a 'historically determined form of something that exists in all social forms'.[45] In sum, use-value and value are, in this respect, placed on the same footing, as particular forms of universal categories.

Marx ascribes this law to Robinson Crusoe as generic figure of labouring society,[46] and it is also that of the future communist society.[47] *Theories of Surplus-Value* makes this particularly clear: '*Time of labour,*[48] even if exchange-value is eliminated, always remains the creative substance of wealth and the measure of the *cost* of its production.'[49]

A 'law' of this kind is confined, as we shall see, to asserting the general relationship between the fact that labour is always 'expended', and the fact that as rational activity aiming at use-values it is important for it to be reduced to a minimum and divided in proportion to social needs. So this is in no way a 'law' in the sense that this term functions in 'law of value', that of a structure the existence of which is established by historical materialism for a determinate kind of society, and possesses, as a theoretical object, an explanatory value, because it denotes a particular system of compulsion to produce and interest in producing. It is, rather, a general matrix logically prior to the determinations specific to historical materialism as a theory of modes of production.

In his texts on communism, Marx defines this basically in terms of certain particular determinations of this general matrix: production would be effected according to a plan, appropriation of the production process and the product being collective at the same time as individual, and the state losing its *raison d'être* as an organ of domination. These determinations are of a different kind from those of the theories of modes of production: they are *normative*, indicating what kind of order has to be given to the expenditure and distribution of social labour.

These are certainly notions that go together with the *critique* of capitalist society. And in this sense, they are 'theoretico-critical' in the expression coined by Cotten.[50] But, precisely by being articulated in the socialist project, they acquire a new status that seems to have escaped Marx.

---

[45] Ibid.
[46] Marx 1976a, p. 169.
[47] Marx 1976a, p. 171.
[48] [Marx uses the English term here.]
[49] Marx 1972, p. 257: Marx's emphasis.
[50] Cotten 1984.

This is particularly noticeable, as I showed in Chapter 3, in the *Critique of the Gotha Programme*, where Marx develops the theme that communism will also be based on value, and apart from the impossibility of exploitation, 'the same principle . . . as that which regulates the exchange of commodities as far as this is an exchange of equal values'.[51] Hence the proposal of 'labour certificates'. The ambiguity of this, however, is that it ignores the distinction between two concepts of value that Marx's theory itself produced: site of contradiction versus norm of harmony. It is, of course, in this second register that his prescriptive discourse on socialism is located. He maintains, in fact, that, under socialism, exploitation will disappear (labour certificates assuring an equitable distribution), likewise the market (replaced by the plan) and fetishism (the plan rendering production 'transparent'). All that remains of the concept of value, in reality, is the idea of a rational general distribution of labour-time. But what disappear without being replaced are the explanatory determinations of socialisation, as Marx expounded these apropos capitalism. And, along with these, the theoretical use of the category of value, in the sense that there is a 'theory' of the capitalist mode of production.

Marx certainly went beyond his utopian forerunners, to the extent that he established more clearly what the overthrow of capitalism implies (abolition of both wage and commodity relations) and how this is possible only through the development of its contradictions. But he shared the utopians' premises inasmuch as he failed to perceive the radical difference of status between the explanatory categories specific to a particular mode of production, and general or normative categories. His discourse on socialism is, in reality, prescriptive: it affirms the unity of theoretical reason (rationality of production) and practical reason (equality of participation). To neglect the essential difference between this discourse and the theory of the capitalist mode of production is to locate the former in a strict continuity with the latter, and thus attribute it a status of 'science' that it cannot claim.

This does not mean that the Marxian discourse on socialism does not indicate social contradiction. On the contrary, this appears below the surface in certain inescapable modalities of language and its significant amphibologies: 'To serve as a measure labour must be determined by duration or intensity.'[52]

---

[51] Marx 1974c, p. 346.
[52] Ibid.

Or again, it has to be determined in how much time a certain quantum of product 'must' be produced.[53] Is this agreement on times a *necessity* for a rational plan, an *imperative* of the plan for the worker, or a requirement in various senses of the term? The ambiguity remains. The same goes for 'regulation [*Regelung*]'[54] and 'control'.[55] In all these invocations, we can note the indeterminacy of the agent:

> If wages are reduced to their general basis . . . if this share is freed from its capitalist limit and expanded . . . ; if surplus labour and surplus product are also reduced, to the degree needed under the given conditions of production . . . if both wages and surplus-value are stripped of their capitalist character . . .[56]

The missing subject here, absent in the impersonal form, is at one and the same time that of the theorist who embarks on this imaginary experiment, that of the revolutionary movement that 'strips' these determinations of their capitalist character, and that of the future 'society' that is supposed to ensure these equilibria by a plan.

We see here how Marx envisages these contradictions only in general terms, as contradictions between individuals and the collective, and in the manner of their ideal abolition under the impulse of an ideally unified collective. This shift to the general is a shift to a different kind of discourse from that of historical materialism. A difference that remains un-thought by Marx, and is obscured in the tradition by the theme of 'scientific socialism'.

Marx also failed to think through the different principles of his various discourses.

The analysis of 'production in general', presented in Chapter 7 of Volume One, is biased by an prejudice that led him to progressively set aside the category of 'abstract labour' as used in the configuration presented at the start of the exposition of *Capital*. This, in turn, proves to be relatively inadequate to its object, since it couples use-value, a category supposed to be absolutely general, with value, supposed (at least in this form) to be specific to commodity relations. I have shown how these both possess a universal significance,

---

[53] Marx 1973c, p. 157.
[54] Marx 1981, p. 991.
[55] Marx 1978, pp. 544–5.
[56] Marx 1981, pp. 1015–16.

likewise the categories of labour (concrete and abstract). And that these two couples here obtain a status of particularity from the commodity structure itself, defined by the determinations of private property and competition.

As against this, what appears at the moment of the exposition of reproduction is a general category of value. This, in fact, defines a level of generality that is functional and normative, neutralising the contradictions inherent to the commodity and capitalist category of value though without the special discourse on capital being interrupted. In this way, a *positive* discourse on value is produced, which can in principle be transposed to other modes of production.

Marx's assertions concerning socialism are again based on this *general* matrix of value. This category, stripped of its commodity determinations, is now introduced into the context of an ethical-normative discourse, the other side of the critical discourse on capitalism. Marx failed to see that he had thus changed terrain, and that his discourse on socialism, proceeding outside the framework of the problematic of historical materialism, was of a different kind from that of *Capital*. This ambiguity is repeated both by those who make *Capital* into a simple 'critique of political economy' and by those who speak of 'scientific socialism'.

2. Labour-value in pure economics and in historical materialism

The recent development of neo-Ricardianism, and the work of Sraffa in particular, have re-awakened these questions, which, in Marx's work, remain in the background, and concern the articulation of particular categories, specific to the mode of production, with general categories – in other words, the problem of the relationship between historical materialism and 'pure economics'. The problem is immense, and here I shall only tackle it from the standpoint of the interpretation of *Capital*.

2.i *From Marx to Sraffa*

The starting-point here is 1862 (this story is now well established, thanks to Dostaler's *Valeur et prix*),[57] when Marx explained, in a letter to Engels, the

---

[57] Dostaler 1978.

solution to the problem raised for the theory of labour-value by the existence of a uniform rate of profit, proportional not to the amount of labour employed, but to the total capital invested: this was a simple *redistribution* of surplus-value within the capitalist class. Such is the idea that Marx developed in his 'second economic manuscript',[58] and clarified in the draft of 1865, the text that Engels edited in 1894 to become Part 2 of Volume Three.

Sombart argued already in 1894 that Volume Three rendered Volume One useless: labour-value could not be accepted as a 'fact of experience', though it remained a 'fact of thought'. Böhm-Bawerk, in 1896, pushed this criticism to its logical conclusion. The main thrust of his approach lay, as I see it, in the conception of value as an exchange relationship. From this starting-point, he rejected the notion of total surplus-value, which made it possible to define a general rate of profit and hence a system of prices based on surplus-value. He went on to criticise, on the basis of the problematic of prices of production, the logic of Marx's system: wages, the variation of which modifies the rate of profit and hence the system of prices, are an element foreign to the law of value, and yet they are supposed to determine the amount of surplus-value. In sum, a contradiction between Volume One and Volume Three.

The 'revisionists', in the wake of Sombart, took a middle position. For them, Volume One offered a satisfactory sociology, but marginalism was the basis for a scientific economics. At the same time, a rehabilitation of the Ricardian problematic was developed. In 1905, Tugan-Baranowksi opened the way by showing Marx's 'mistake' in his transformation table, which measures output in prices of production and input in values, linking this question with that of the reproduction schemas. Shortly after, basing himself on the formalisation of Ricardian theory of production prices carried out by Dmitriev, Bortkiewicz 'rectified' Marx's schemas by describing a system of reproduction entirely in prices of production as follows:[59]

For a schema of simple reproduction in terms of values, let:

$c_1 + v_1 + s_1 = C$, means of production sector,

$c_2 + v_2 + s_2 = V$, wage sector,

$c_3 + v_3 + s_3 = S$, sector of capitalist consumption;

---

[58] Marx 1988 and 1994.
[59] Bortkiewicz 1907.

the condition for reproduction is then expressed as:

$$C = c_1 + c_2 + c_3$$
$$V = v_1 + v_2 + v_3$$
$$S = s_1 + s_2 + s_3$$

The transformation into prices of production gives the following result:

$$(c_1p_c + v_1p_v)(1 + r) = Cp_c$$
$$(c_2p_c + v_2p_v)(1 + r) = Vp_v$$
$$(c_3p_c + v_3p_v)(1 + r) = Sp_s$$

where c_1p_c denotes the input of constant capital involved in the production of C at the price of C; likewise for v_1p_v, etc. And r = the general rate of profit.

This gives three equations and four unknowns (r, p_c, p_v, p_s).

Bortkiewicz completed the system by positing that $p_s = 1$. In this way, both prices and the rate of profit are simultaneously determined, and a standard is defined by using the third sector.

This 'rectification of Marx's mistake' could initially pass for a contribution to Marxist theory (though the author's intention was, rather, a reconciliation between Marx and Walras). In actual fact, however, it introduced a completely different perspective, amounting to the abandonment of any reference to labour-value, since an equation in terms of commodities could now give a complete table of the economy in physical quantities at definite prices, without reference to the question of labour-time.

This is what Sraffa's system later presented, in a model along the following lines:[60]

$$(A_ap_a + B_ap_b + \ldots + K_ap_k)(1 + r) = Ap_a$$
$$(A_bp_a + B_bp_b + \ldots + K_pp_k)(1 + r) = Bp_b$$

$$\cdots\cdots\cdots\cdots\cdots\cdots\cdots\cdots\cdots\cdots\cdots\cdots$$

$$(A_kp_a + B_kp_b + \ldots + K_kp_k)(1 + r) = Kp_k$$

The set of equations represents an economic system, and each equation a particular commodity. A_a denotes the quantity of input A entering into the production of A; p_a its unit price; (1 + r) the rate of profit.

---

[60] Sraffa 1960, p. 11.

At the end of the day here, we have gone far beyond the transformation of values into prices of production: to a system where the concept of labour-value, the very foundation of Marx's edifice, is put in question. This is what we now need to examine more closely.

2.ii   *The criticisms addressed to Sraffa 'in the name of Marxism', and their rebuttal*

It is beyond the present remit to give a presentation of Sraffa's system. It would not do justice to this, moreover, to reduce it to a stage – even the final one – in the transformation problem. What is involved is actually an attempt to constitute an alternative to neoclassical theory. The latter, basing its theory of value on the concepts of marginal utility and scarcity, reduces the sphere of production, central to Ricardo, to an element subordinate to the sphere of exchange. Sraffa proposed a return to the classical perspective of prices of production, and developed a solution to the problems that this encountered. First of all, he achieved Ricardo's project of an 'invariable measure of value', a measure that made it possible to control the effects exerted on the system by the unequal organic composition of capitals and the variation in the ratio of wages to profit, and to determine in this way 'real' and not just relative variations. On this basis, he developed a theory that, owing to a certain proximity between its categories and those of Marx (and their common opposition to the 'vulgar' economics of the neoclassical school), as well as the filiation that it claimed in relation to the classics, seemed to many to locate itself in a broad continuity with Marxism, but that nonetheless displays, upon analysis, a radical difference from this.

A number of authors, who expressed themselves in the collection *Interventions en économie politique* and the journal *Cahiers d'économie*, conducted in the 1970s a critique of Sraffa in the name of Marxism.[61] We can summarise some of its essential arguments as follows.

1) It focused first of all on the nature of the category of labour in Sraffa's theory. The difficulty particularly appeared in Section 11, which introduced a model including direct labour alongside other inputs:

$$(A_a p_a + B_a p_b + \ldots + K_a p_k)(1 + r) + L_a w = A p_a$$

---

[61] This was a broad international debate. A significant aspect was the virulent form it took in the GDR around the writings of Ruben (cf. Ruben and Wagner 1980, Damerow et al. 1983).

where L_aw denotes the quantity of direct labour (L) needed for the production of commodity A, in terms of its price (w) or wage.

It is clear that this 'labour at a given price' is an entirely different category from that of the 'labour' that figures in Marx's schemata. In Volume One of *Capital*, at least, labour presents itself in fact 'in person' in so far as it produces value, independently of the wage that the worker receives. The quantity $v + s$ that represents the value produced is independent of the relationship established between v and s, and thus of the wage. In Sraffa, on the contrary, labour and wages always appear as associated, and this association is what gives them their pertinence in the model.[62] It is literally inexact to say that there is in Sraffa an 'assimilation of labour to wages' or that L_aw represents simply 'wage quantities',[63] since, in actual fact, the equations also depict the physical reality of the inputs, not just their prices. The essential point, however, as the authors show, is that labour here is always associated with its price, and from this fact functions as a commodity. As the very title of Sraffa's work proclaims, its subject is the 'production of commodities by means of commodities'. In other words, the commodity considered here is not labour-power but 'labour', just as in classical economics. A radical difference therefore in relation to Marx.

2) The best illustration of this is given by the approach Sraffa proposes of a homogenisation of labour:

> We suppose labour to be uniform in quality or, what amounts to the same thing, we assume any differences in quality to have been previously reduced to equivalent differences in quantity so that each unit of labour receives the same wage.[64]

What then is this principle of homogenisation? We might initially believe it was a matter of abstract labour, since the aim of the operation is to aggregate various kinds of labour. In reality, however, Sraffa's very choice of hypothesis gives his procedure a completely different sense. If equality of wages meant equality of the 'quality' of labours, we could just as well take into consideration the diversity of labours and their 'qualities' by ascribing them distinct wage rates. If labours exist in society in a hierarchy of quality (or, as Marx sometimes

---

[62] Cf. Benetti 1974, p. 139.
[63] Benetti, Brunhoff and Cartelier 1976, p. 35.
[64] Sraffa 1960, p. 10.

says, of 'complexity'), they function as commodities of distinct natures, with distinct prices. This is a simple corollary of the first principle, according to which labour is only ever present in the theory with an ascribed price.[65]

3) The transformation of the set of inputs in terms of 'dated labour' may seem to return us to Marx's problematic, since it takes inputs as a series of labours 'embodied' in the commodity, and the inputs that these imply. In reality, it reproduces the same procedure.

The equation for the production of a commodity is thus expressed as:

$$L_aw + L_{a1}w (1 + r) + \ldots L_{an}w (1 + r)^n + Ap_a$$

where a composite rate of interest is applied, corresponding to the labours of previous years (the most recent year being given by L_aw).

It is clear that the reduction of all inputs in this way does not change their nature. 'What is actually involved is a reduction to dated amounts of wages.'[66] More precisely, of dated 'labours with given prices'.

4) A further criticism follows from this: Sraffa tackles the wage relation essentially as a category of distribution. This criticism has been ascribed to the fact that, in Sraffa's formulations, wages appear as paid post factum, and thus as a deduction from the net product. However this may be, even a different procedure that counts units of labour as inputs advanced at the start of the period and assigned a rate of profit would still mean that Sraffa's models, by tying labour to its wage characteristic, do not grasp it as an element of production except in its relationship to the problem of distribution. Here, again, Marx and Sraffa diverge.

5) Finally, the criticism that we have seen directed against the category of labour evidently bears on the problematic as a whole. Sraffa's world, like that of Ricardo, is in a sense a world of relative values.[67] Certainly, the very object of the theory of the standard commodity is to tie the level of prices of production to that of 'values', i.e. to enable determination of the real variation in case of a variation in relative values, in the sense that this follows from a change in the conditions of production. On this point, Sraffa completes the Ricardian

---

[65] Cf. Arena and Maricic 1977.
[66] Benetti 1974, p. 139.
[67] Benetti, Brunhoff and Cartelier 1976, p. 39.

project, resolving the difficulty arising from the fact that a variation in the wage/profit relationship affects prices differently according to the organic composition of the capitals involved. In this sense, he breaks the circle of relative values. But he still does not reach the terrain of absolute value in Marx's sense, since the labour to which he refers is always considered in terms of price.

6) From this standpoint, the 'resemblances' with Marx's system appear very precarious. We certainly have a system of production regulated by a uniform rate of profit, in which the surplus is divided between wages and profits, in such a way that there is an opposition between these two categories of distribution. In reality, however, the analytical framework of the system does not allow an explanation of the 'origin' of profit,[68] the same criticism that Marx already made of Ricardo. Or, at least, the notion of 'explaining the origin' acquires a completely different sense. The system makes it possible to indicate the various changes in other elements that are capable of making the rate of profit vary. But its object is not to define the foundations of the actual tendencies of a social system.

We must add, however, that certain of these authors, in particular Benetti and Cartelier, develop a kind of see-saw that combines a Marxist critique of Sraffa with a critique of Marx based on a Sraffa-type re-reading of the classics, the whole process leading to a radical questioning of the edifice built on 'labour-value'.

A first level of analysis consists in showing the specificity of the classics in relation to Marx.

In the light of Sraffa's system, a new reading of the classical economists has developed based on the idea that by resolving the problems that they raised, Sraffa revealed what was essential in them. This reading is also a critique of the interpretation Marx proposed of the classics when he indicated them as his precursors, attributing to them a discourse founded on labour-value. A whole series of studies have thus set out to display the heterogeneity of the classical problematics in relation to that of Marx, and to the problematic that he endowed them with. Cartelier, who revealed,[69] underlying the whole 'classical' literature, a 'system of prices' based on consideration of the surplus

---

[68] Benetti, Berthomieu and Cartelier 1975, p. 22.
[69] Cartelier 1976.

product and the rules that preside over its distribution, taking into account the reproduction constraint of the economy in question. Re-read on the basis of Sraffa's indications, Ricardo ceases to be the theorist of labour-value and more generally the precursor of Marx.[70]

This assertion of the specificity of the discourse of the classical economists, however, makes that of Marx appear as discrepant with it, and more generally with the whole terrain and object of 'political economy'.

According to these authors, in fact, Marx was wrong when he located himself in the line of classical political economy and believed he needed to draw support from it. He was wrong to believe that it had already begun to penetrate the 'inner connection' of capital,[71] its internal structure as a mode of production. In reality, the gap between the two problematics was total. Not only is it impossible to 'demonstrate the validity of Marxism by basing oneself on the principles of political economy',[72] for if the attempt is made to transform values into prices, the result is enclosure within a system of prices that makes value useless. The very intention underlying this position of continuity has to be abandoned: there is not in Marx any takeover and superseding of the classical discourse, 'there is not a Marxian or Marxist "political economy" at all'.[73]

But the whole problem is to know what the basis of the theory of exploitation might then be. Marx constructed it on the basis of the initial category of the commodity as unity of use-value and value, the latter being understood as 'labour-value'. If this last is rejected, the edifice floats in a vacuum. And this is indeed the conclusion drawn by certain authors: after having criticised Sraffa's category of labour, it is now that of Marx that is put in question.[74]

This oscillating movement between Marx and Sraffa seems to me sufficiently representative of a certain trend in the debate, and shows the degree to which the question of the relationship between historical materialism and political economy deserves to be deepened. That is why I now see the need to return, at the end of this book, to the considerations with which it opened, and which were the particular object of Chapters 2 and 3: the significance of the theory

---

[70] Benetti 1975, p. 213; Gilibert 1976, p. 96; Deleplace 1977, p. 183.
[71] Cartelier 1976, p. 229.
[72] Benetti, Berthomieu and Cartelier 1975, p. 92.
[73] Benetti, Berthomieu and Cartelier 1975, p. 72.
[74] Cf. Benetti and Cartelier 1980.

of labour-value. I want to show how the 'Sraffa shock', far from disqualifying this, has, on the contrary, brought out (at the same time as certain difficult problems) its specific originality and rationality.

2.iii   *Propositions on the interpretation and articulation of the respective discourses of Marx and Sraffa*

The appearance of Sraffa's system brought reflection on the categories of *Capital* to a critical point. It appeared at the end of a series of attempts to 'correct Marx's mistake' and correctly expressed the transition from values to prices of production in a way that respected the rules of reproduction. But, by doing so, it finally set itself up as an independent system for which Volume One of *Capital* became useless, its categories apparently losing their relevance. A crisis of this kind can be overcome only if it is possible to show that there is a legitimate place for a variety of discourses each having their own object, and to determine the nature of their relationships.

It seems to me that we have to distinguish three orders: that of the 'mode of production', that of 'pure' economics, and that of a 'normative' theory of planning. The theoretical objects of these three orders are entangled in the same concrete object, their categories presenting the same proximity and difference as the theories as a whole.[75]

The first order is that of the 'theory of the mode of production', in our particular case the capitalist mode, which is an example of the theories that historical materialism enables us to construct, as an analysis of societies, on the basis of the relationship between productive forces and relations of production. This analysis gives first priority to consideration of the nature and mode of ownership of the means of production, and traces on this basis the economic articulation of classes, the exploitation of a dominated class by a dominant one, the manner of obtaining surplus labour (and thus also labour in general), the relationships within each of these classes and the historical tendencies specific to these structures and thus these societies.

---

[75] This triple problematic evidently possesses a long history. The original 'revisionism' was already moving in this element, and we find a similar distinction in the analysis of Croce 1981 (pp. 91–182). I clearly return to it here on a quite different basis, that of labour-value and its fate in the three distinct orders. As far as pure economics was concerned, 'revisionism' drew on the theory of marginal utility, not that of labour-value.

The second order may be described as 'pure economics'. This description, if applied to Sraffa's system, is not without certain difficulties, since this presupposes the existence of a uniform rate of profit, which can be seen as the specific effect of a capitalist structure (with the assumption of perfect competition). Leaving this point aside, however, we can consider the essential differences between the respective discourses of Sraffa and Marx.

The third order, that of the normative planning of labour, will not be examined here.

What is specific to a theory like Sraffa's is not its analysis of the contradictions *specific* to a society, its real tendencies or even its specific functioning, but rather the *general* functional relationships that it maintains. It takes as given the techniques of production along with corresponding quantities of inputs and outputs. The system of prices and distribution that is functionally bound up with these can only be fixed by an exogenous determination: a particular variation in the wage/profit relationship, for example, will lead to a determinate change in the system of prices (as a function of which a more productive technique is substituted for another). In sum, we are here in a relational world of interdependent elements, but one that always assumes an 'outside' providing information on what might modify it. We can thus understand how the same factors that constitute its limit also constitute its necessary articulation to another theoretical field: for example, that which indicates why there is a change in distribution. It is on the basis of such 'external' information that the system displays its capacity to produce new knowledge. And it is clear that the 'theory of the mode of production' is of such a kind as to claim this function of an 'external principle'.

The first question now raised is that of knowing if the respective status of these two theories is such that they can refer to each other. And this can only be answered by a comparative study of their heterogeneous constructions of the category of labour.

Paradoxically, what we have to return to here is the 'double articulation' of *Capital*, i.e. the division between Part One of Volume One and the rest of the work; it is here, in fact, that a category of labour is defined that has no place in Sraffa's system. The paradox lies in the fact that it is at an abstract formal level, at which the capitalist specificity has still to appear (the fact that one of the commodities is labour-power), that the category of labour is determined, able to serve as the basis for the theory of the capitalist mode of production in opposition to the discourse of pure economics. It is also a paradox that this category of labour is only produced by the construction of a model of the market in general, or a model of simple commodity production and circulation.

I propose to show that the particularity of this model (which is implied in the presentation of 'the commodity' in Part One of Volume One) is that it shows us *labour before wages*, what I will call here 'naked labour', something that a system of prices of production cannot produce.

In actual fact, if in Sraffa's system it is possible to write the equations 'in labour', this involves a preliminary model that is *superseded* once a rate of profit is introduced. For the counterpart of this is a rate of wages, and labour becomes a commodity ascribed a price. In Marx's system, on the contrary, Part One of Volume One defines a category of labour that remains *within* the system, and is not abolished as a relevant element by the introduction of wages. What is actually constructed in this initial abstract moment is the concept of 'naked labour', something that belongs to a quite different universe from that of pure economics: the field of historical materialism, which is not one of pure functional relationships, but of this particular relation, always both technical and political, that gives the particular meaning of the Marxist concept of the 'economic base'.

The object of Part One of Volume One might then be seen as the deconstruction of the concept of labour specific to classical economics, and the elaboration of an abstract theory of naked labour, labour independent of any wage ascription. Labour is then considered on the one hand in its *social effect*, which presents a double aspect according to whether the focus is on its place in the division of labour, in which it is a certain concrete labour, or its comparability with any other labour, which derives from what is common to all labour, the property of being a certain expenditure of labour-power. On the other hand, labour is considered in its *social performance*, i.e. according to the mechanism that makes it both a certain (concrete) labour and (abstract) labour pure and simple. A mechanism of this kind, which explains how labour produces its effect, why and how it is performed, is given by the market structure in general, through which labour is confirmed as a meaningful activity: the commodity system appears as a system of compulsion exerted on the 'individual' elements that compose it, but with these confirming at the same time the rationality of their behaviour. Thanks to the mediation of money, all labour, on condition that it produces the commodities in demand and is performed in the requisite conditions, is 'remunerated', but in a quite different manner than by a wage: by the product of the same quantity of labour. The important thing, in this abstract initial figure of the market, is that in relation to the classical schemas – as the post-Sraffa reading of them characterises these – labour is disconnected from wages. The question raised, to which as yet we have only a partial answer, is not that of the relative prices of the elements (including labour), but rather that of knowing why and how labour is performed and the labouring activities of a society are rationally integrated. It is the question of the compulsion, stimulation and regulation of labour. And this is prior to the consideration of labour as ascribed a wage.

This is important to spell out since, from a Sraffian point of view, this 'remuneration' by a product of equal value to that which labour realises may appear as the kind of wage that precedes the appearance of profit in the logical development of the presentation.

The mistake, to my mind, would be to read this initial 'model' retrospectively on the basis of 'profit-rate models', as for example Meek does,[76] projecting an initial moment at which profit does not exist and as a consequence the product contains only 'wages' (on top of the reproduction of the material means of production). The schema of Part One should not be read as a 'wages only' schema, but rather as a 'wage-less' schema, in which consideration of wages does not occur. It presents the *general* effect of the competitive structure: in commodity-producing society, products tend to be exchanged proportionately to the quantity of labour that they require. The worker appears in this first Part only under the heading of expenditure of labour and utility of labour, not that of his remuneration or reproduction.

This 'law' is not established simply to depict a world of individual workers who find in commodity B, which they acquire by alienating the commodity A that they produce, a 'wage' corresponding to their labour. It also governs the relation between capitalist firms. It is indeed this same law, in the event this same structure of integration of productive behaviour that is the market, which has the effect of weighting this principle according to the organic composition of capital. Competition brings each element a 'remuneration' proportionate to what it invests in production (at least in a theoretical universe

---

[76] Meek 1973, pp. xxxiv–xxxvi; cf. Meek 1967, pp. 164–7.

of perfect competition). There should thus be nothing surprising about an adequate exposition of the transformation of values into prices of production.[77]

In short, the individuals in Part One are not workers prior to profit, they are entities (individuals or firms) in their relationship as exchanging producers, analysed before wages are taken into consideration as pure 'sites' at which labour is performed, and via labour, products destined for exchange. Whether the exchanging unit of production is an individual or a firm, commodities are exchanged, after taking into account the weighting that follows from their organic composition, in proportion to the labour they involve.

Evidently, Part One only defines in a formal fashion the producing machine that is the competitive structure. Part Three shows how the compulsion to produce (and the regulation of production) is effected in a class relation, the capitalists exerting on their employees the market compulsion that is exerted on them. It is in this dynamic context that the question of wages arises, in such a way that this category cannot abolish that of naked labour in the way that the 'profit models' abolish, by substituting themselves in the operational analysis of the concrete society, the 'profit-less' models of Marxo-Ricardianism. The latter, in effect, depict isolated moments in the exposition, those needed for the successive presentation of categories (wages, profit) that will subsequently be made to function simultaneously, since the object of the theory is the study of their functional relationships. 'Naked labour', on the contrary, remains present as such in the system. Its theoretical function does not disappear, but gives rise to different questions from that of wages (for example, the confrontation over the length of the working day), or at least relatively different ones (for example, in the problematic of extra surplus-value, which is linked with the pressure on labour needed for production). As for the surplus-value structure in general, it does not initially define a division of the product, it does not define labour as 'a factor to which a share of the product goes'. It describes a structure in which a certain labour is performed against a certain remuneration (corresponding to a part of this labour). It thus defines the conditions of performance of this labour, a 'mode of production' as Marx calls it.

We can now understand in what sense Marx founded a different kind of discourse from that of Sraffa, one which yields different kinds of information.

---

[77] Cf. Duménil 1982 and Lipietz 1982, 1983.

Marx defined how labour is performed in a commodity structure, and how a competitive capitalist structure constitutes a system of interests and powers such that one class 'exploits' another, which stimulates production, yet within limits that derive from this contradiction of interests between the two classes. This treatment can clearly be extended to more complex structures than that of perfect 'competition', and the problematic is serviceable also for the study of non-capitalist societies as specific modes of production (on condition that appropriate theories of these are provided).

If this is the case, then it is necessary to re-examine the Marxian category of 'transformation'. It conceals, in certain usages at least, a type of gap between levels such that the notions involved cannot figure together in the same 'model', i.e. they cannot be adequately defined by the hierarchical relationship between them. The transition from Part One to Part Two of Volume One, from money to capital, is here also the transition from naked labour to wage-labour. It is this articulation that must be elucidated if we are to maintain that Marx proposed something other in his theory of surplus-value than what Bortkiewicz called a theory of 'deduction', in other words a particular theory of distribution. For this, it is necessary to understand how naked labour *remains* beneath wage-labour: in Parts Two and Three, the question of labour is not reduced to that of wages, nor to that of the introduction of labour as a commodity. There remains here, but 'transformed' by the fact of its appropriation by the capitalist, the question of labour-'power', its productive implementation. Hence the consideration of the power of capital that compels it (in a way that is not that of a mere instrument), and also that of the structural compulsion that is exerted on the capitalist and determined by the market, which rewards labours as a function of their productivity, i.e. their capacity to produce a commodity in the least time, and in this way establishes its principle of rationality, the law of value.

The subsequent moments cannot dispense with the category of value, for the reason that this is not a category of distribution but initially one of production, and so cannot be challenged by a 'transformation' that is a function of the organic composition and the norms of distribution. These are certainly also categories of production, but as such they only express in a particular fashion the norms that the law of value establishes in general, and that are ensured under capitalism by the competitive structure (which provides the background to any state regulation under capitalism).

The transition to prices of production effected in Part Two of Volume Three thus possesses a double significance. On the one hand, it does indeed form a moment of the theory of the capitalist mode of production, since it is with the category of the uniform rate of profit that the problems bearing on accumulation and its contradictions (Part Three) are raised, in a more 'concrete' manner than in Volume One, as well as that of the division of profit into profit of enterprise, commercial profit, interest and rent (Parts Four to Seven). On the other hand, it marks the articulation between the discourse of historical materialism and that of a 'pure' political economy. This latter, however, does not make the former useless. Quite the contrary, for if this 'transition' defines their mutual exteriority (and if from this standpoint it is for the theory of the capitalist mode of production a 'passage to the limit'), its existence also continues their tie, their point of contact, which accounts for the necessity for the system of pure economics to be provided with exogenous information (but on the basis of categories that are sufficiently homogenous to intervene in it) before producing the least information.

Between the two systems, therefore, it is necessary to conceive both their difference and their communication. And it seems as if the most difficult thing in this matter has been to conceive of their difference. The touchstone of this certainly lies in the distinct treatment of the category of labour, as those who set out to formulate the 'Marxist critique' of Sraffa have made clear. But beyond this critique, as I see it, it was necessary to define positively the specifically Marxian treatment of the category of labour, such as this is implied in the competitive and capitalist structure. A treatment that I have denoted by the concept of naked labour, and which seems to me to constitute the principle of a scientific discourse on value, that of historical materialism.

2.iv   Consequences for the interpretation of Capital

On the basis of these propositions, it is possible to undertake a further clarification of the exposition of *Capital*, taking into account the fact that the three orders of discourse that I have distinguished coexist in it, and that their articulation, the necessity of which did not escape the author, was neither completed nor even formulated in an explicit fashion.

In the 1857 Introduction, Marx presented in turn two kinds of generality, without defining the relationship between them. On the one hand, the *generalities of historical materialism*: productive forces/relations of production, ruling and dominated classes.[78] These generalities only interest us here to the extent that they provide the general context in which the initial categories of Volume One are defined as categories of historical materialism. On the other hand, the *functional generalities of economics*, categories to be found in all modes of production: production, consumption, distribution, circulation.[79] To my mind, this project of a preliminary exposition of the 'general, abstract determinants',[80] the 'abstract moments with which no real historical stage of production can be grasped',[81] must be interpreted as a project of constituting the field of a 'pure economics': a set of categories inadequate to informing us about concrete reality without the mediation of theories of particular modes of production, but necessary for the exposition of these and possessing its own specific consistency and rationality.

The problem then consists in determining which elements of *Capital* relate to this 'generality', and how the general and the specific (in the sense of what is specific to the particular mode of production) are articulated at each level. The problem is complex and difficult, and I shall only try to indicate here some of its aspects.

1) It is necessary first of all to determine what relates to the register of 'economics in general'. This is certainly the case for categories such as those of 'production/circulation/distribution', or those forming 'the labour process in general'. But the most interesting question is undoubtedly raised by the system of prices of production, which, as we have seen, is developed in a discourse independent from the founding categories of the capitalist mode of production. We know, moreover, that this system also includes the categories of reproduction.

2) We then need to examine how the 'specific' discourse, that of the theory of the mode of production, only develops by developing at the same time a general discourse. The category of 'reproduction' provides an example of this: it refers at the same time to the *reproduction of the economy*, and, in this sense, is expressed in the equilibrium character of the system of its production equations, and to the *reproduction of the mode of production*, in the sense in which this is the reproduction of the class relationship, the ownership of the

---

78 Marx 1973c, pp. 108–9.
79 Marx 1973c, pp. 88–100.
80 Marx 1973c, p. 108.
81 Marx 1973c, p. 88.

means of production by the ruling class. The first can be studied independently of the second, but not vice versa.

3) From this starting point, it is possible to indicate, in the light of the clarifications for which Sraffa's system provided the opportunity, the slippages in Marx's discourse, his tendencies to escape from the field of 'historical materialism' and move to considerations that relate to that of 'pure' economics.

An example of this is furnished by Marx's hesitations concerning 'skilled labour'. In fact, as I showed in Chapter 2, it is quite unjustified to argue, as the German edition does in particular, from the greater value of labour-power to a greater value of the product. The theory of labour-value expressly forbids deducing the magnitude of the value of the product from that of the labour-power that produces it. It leads, rather, to interpreting the level of skill and its effect on production in the analytical framework of the 'collective labourer', within the 'extra surplus-value' relationship, thus as a dimension of the difference between the productivity of individual firms. It discards at the same time the 'pure' notion of competing workers, substituting for it that of the labour market as a class relation, in which capital always encounters the wage-earners in a certain condition of mutual cohesion (according to a whole series of principles of diversification that the development of the system defines in particular historical circumstances). But the discourse of pure economics naturally tends to argue from the magnitude of the product's 'value' to the value of the 'labour', for just as capitals receive a remuneration proportional to their magnitude, so 'labours', supposed to exist in pure competition, will tend to receive a remuneration proportional to their social effectiveness. The theoretical constraints of the problematic of the 'mode of production' are such that this kind of autonomising of the question has no place in its theoretical field, though it is perfectly legitimate in the context of a normative theory of planning.

Conclusion

Investigation of the status of these 'generalities' in the background of the theory of the capitalist mode of production has led us to recognise several distinct orders, often invoked and constantly implied in Marx's work, but not acknowledged in their specificity and their reciprocal relationships.

There are first of all the generalities of *historical materialism*, familiar from other presentations, from *The German Ideology* to the Preface to the 1859 *Critique*: productive forces/relations of production, dominant/dominated classes, labour process and reproduction, ideology, the state, etc.

There are then those of *'the economy' in general*, common to complex social systems: production/circulation/distribution/reproduction, etc. We should note that these are also susceptible to a different use from that of historical materialism, since they also serve to define, outside the problematic of contradiction and social antagonisms, the general conditions of economic functionality, as is the case in Part Three of Volume Two of *Capital*.

Finally, the Marxian discourse on *socialism* itself appeared as a general discourse, based on a general-legislative use of the category of labour-value, thus participating in the mode of generality of the 'contradiction-free' discourse, but also participating by its critical side in that of the antagonism whose abolition it projects, which makes it a discourse out of phase with historical materialism yet located in relation to it.

Behind these three orders there is the most abstract moment, that of the *labour process in general*, which already includes the determinations of use-value/concrete labour, expenditure/abstract labour. This is ultimately a particular mode of treatment of these categories that rightly characterises each of the three orders of generality.

The first, historical materialism, approaches societies from the standpoint of their antagonistic articulation and thus the relationship of domination, grasping labour in its relationship to the class compulsions that determine it both in its concrete content and as expenditure. This involves the *general* foundation of the category of labour-value as a category of historical materialism, the notion of this present at the start of *Capital* constituting a particular figure, that which is specific to the capitalist mode of production and is formed by what I have called the 'double articulation', commodity/capitalist. A category of this kind, as a category of historical materialism, possesses a broader field of application than simply the capitalist mode of production. It is valid, in particular, for postcapitalist societies, on condition that a specific theory of these is produced. In capitalism itself, it calls for a specific theorisation wherever non-commodity labour is involved (of which particular forms are developed in this society).

The second order, that of 'pure economics', is characterised by abstraction from the problematic of social antagonism (even if it can contribute to an analysis of this). This is also why labour no longer appears here as 'naked' labour, i.e. from the simple standpoint of its performance and effects, but rather as assigned a remuneration, in a general economic system in which all inputs and outputs are considered with proportions and 'prices' adequate to reproduction. In this sense, all elements of the system, and labour itself, are 'commodities', both products and means of production.

The third order participates in both. It focuses on the construction of a rationally economic society, in a theoretical and a practical sense. But this 'legislative' mode of thought can only formulate its requirements in relation to norms that historical materialism evaluates at the same time as it discovers them; only by being the *theory* of 'modes of production', i.e. of politico-economic relations, does it make possible the *critique* of society as a condition of any normative proposition.

General Conclusions

I have shown at the root of the theory of the capitalist mode of production the link that it establishes between economics and politics. But the whole difficulty then consists of understanding this interaction. Hence the tendencies towards dissociation that are observable today, as they have been throughout the history of Marxism. Either economics is conceived in a positivist manner, developing the space for calculation opened up by labour-value in an autonomous way. Or else, analysis of structures and social relations is privileged, with value and surplus-value being retained only as necessary metaphors. To the present attempts to escape these dead ends, either by a 'dialecticisation' that seeks support in the *Grundrisse*, or a 'politicisation' that articulates the theory around the wage relation and thence around the state, I have proposed a different path that consists in pushing the question of the interaction between economics and politics back to the initial concept of 'labour-value', as the *political*-economic foundation of the capitalist mode of production within the element of historical materialism.

This thesis is intimately linked with another one, concerning the genesis of the theory (from 1857 on), which considers this as a heuristic process in the course of which, and to the extent that its specific concepts were set in place and their specific logical constraints established, we can see the steady disappearance of the role of the philosophical categories, often of Hegelian origin, that served as support but became epistemological obstacles. It is linked to the first thesis, in so far as the distance Marx took in relation to the philosophical and particularly dialectical element was correlative to his ability to constitute his theory on the basis of 'labour-value' and conceive the unity of the *political*-economic concept of the capitalist mode of production from this starting-point.

Before drawing the final lessons from this investigation, I want to show, by developing the main conclusions I have already reached, the necessary unity of this double approach, focusing simultaneously on the logic of the system and the process of its elaboration.

The category of 'naked labour' defined in the previous chapter only makes explicit the category of labour-value with which I began, and which I noted was the most inescapable and new, the genuine cornerstone of the theory, despite being often considered suspect. For, by the tiny distance that consists in considering labour first of all outside of the wage relation, Marx opened a non-Ricardian space. This novelty, of which he was not fully aware, actually imposed on him a difficult programme of reinterpretation of the place of the 'qualitative' determinations of labour (more or less 'productive', 'skilled', 'intense') in his theory. Most often, he either appeals to self-evidence, or postpones consideration until later. In reality, Marx betrays a certain degree of confusion, the recognised problem of *measurement* developing only by way of a chiaroscuro definition of the *substance* to be measured. Thus, the initial identifications of 'abstract' labour as 'simple' or 'average', from which he never completed freed himself, translate the nostalgia for a 'substantial standard' adequate to the mastery of this space. Theorisation of 'more productive' labour offered a coherent logical matrix corresponding to the requirements of historical materialism, with its organisation in terms of structure and tendency. But that of 'skill' presented a whole set of traps, which Marx, though possessing the necessary principles, never succeeded in escaping. As for 'intensity' of labour, he only managed to deal with this by way of two kinds of metaphor, one technical and the other geometric, both of which have a certain operational application, but as metaphors leave a residue that overspills this quantitative context. For what the metaphors obscure, or at least imply without showing it, is the very fact of labour as intensity or 'expenditure', beyond its more or less intensive character, by which it escapes any economistic reduction and demands a sociopolitical determination.

Intensity, in fact, denaturalises duration. For there is no expenditure that is not socially determined, and thus a compulsion. And this is what is denoted here as the 'consumption of labour-power' by the capitalist. There is thus effected, in this determination of labour-value as expenditure, a sociopolitical transformation of the initial economic category. 'Abstract labour' simultaneously opens up the space of economics and the space of class struggle, as a single 'political-economic' space. The classical economists had no conception of 'expenditure' because they had no conception of compulsion. Marx, on the contrary, constituted the wage relation (compulsion/acquiescence) as a moment of his theory and an operator in its space. The 'inherence of money in value', a breaking-point with Ricardo, belongs to the same order: money is only the form of value because it is adequate to the abstraction of this as mere expenditure. A compulsory expenditure, by which the presence of money in (labour-) value is the presence of the political. This is conceived only in the 'double articulation' of the *market* that prescribes expenditure at the same time as its content, and the *class relation* according to which this compulsion is exerted by some people upon others. Here, value and capital form semi-concepts, the former, anticipating the second that will follow it in the exposition, still bearing only a 'latent' contradiction. Now, this essential liaison between theory of value and theory of the class relation (a category of historical materialism) was forgotten by Marx when he set himself the task of conceiving socialism in the *Critique of the Gotha Programme*: he believed he was deploying 'the same principle' of value, though this now lacked any historical conception of socialisation, such as is necessarily required in an anticipation of this kind. Marx thus opened the way to a new and damaging separation between economics and politics. His category of labour-value, however, already denoted by itself the insuperable character of the politico-economic contradiction. Certainly, it does not in itself supply any concrete element of the theory of the state (even the bourgeois state), but it does mark the site of the articulation of politics to economics, prior to the wage relationship.

If the category of labour-power, which marks the transition from the first moment of the theory (commodity) to the second (capital), is inscribed in the field thus defined, it is paradoxically by way of the couple 'value/price of labour-power' which slowly emerges from its philosophical cocoon, and may be seen as the most economistic category. Not only is 'value' actually analysed here, on an axis which I have defined as the axis ... M ... N ..., where the norm (N) is not that of the reproduction of labour-power as such, but represents the articulation of the relation of rights (won) to the balance of forces, and where the minimum (M) likewise does not correspond to any functional requirement of the system, which is, by nature, 'open' so that its reproduction does not imply that of its immediate elements, the working agents. But the category of 'price', which belongs here to the space of Volume One, far from aligning this commodity together with all others, denotes that of the 'value' of labour-power as a category of class struggle: in fact, beyond the relations of supply and demand, a price of this kind is the fruit of the ability of the workers to form themselves into a relatively unified force, the 'market' existing here only as a class relation. Study of the distinct but connected movements of the value and price of labour-power in the moments of formal and real devalorisation permits the development of this concept of the norm as a 'position' in class struggle, though a position whose intrinsic fragility is displayed by the limits of 'pauperism', the 'reduction of the price of labour-power below its value', etc. The same goes for the examination of the category of the 'hierarchy of value' of labour-powers, a prime site of economism (even for Marx), which reveals on the one hand its *general* pertinence – for capitalist development requires 'skills', and a struggle is waged around their distribution and price – and on the other hand the impossibility of applying this category to *individuals*, since to benefit from it is always the effect and not the cause of the value of labour-power. It is thus metaphorical to call labour-power a *commodity*, but a *conceptual* metaphor, since all its determinations without exception necessarily reappear here, though transformed into political-economic categories.

Analysis of this relation of production, capitalist wage-labour, in its relationship to the productive forces, opens the way to two classical themes, that of 'productive labour' and that of the 'working class', traditionally perceived as two sides of the same coin in Marx's problematic, one economic and the other sociopolitical. In reality, the Marxian theme of 'productive labour' forms a theoretico-critical presentation of the theory of the capitalist mode of production, and, by this fact, articulates and contrasts the specific categories of capitalist production with 'universal' categories. This is a discourse that grasps the system in its relationship of structure to tendency, and thus also to its ultimate destiny. This is how it invokes the discourse on the 'working class', considered as the historical force born out of the system and able to lead it to its breaking point. But this politico-economic articulation, explicit in the tradition, hides many pitfalls and fuels several myths. This 'working class' cannot be defined structurally by the surplus-value relation: it exists only by way of tendency. And what pertains to the historical tendencies of the system also touches other social categories besides the 'working class'. Above all, these 'tendencies' have nothing unilateral about them: they are also tendencies towards the division of the wage-earners and the construction of a mass 'support' for capital. The legitimate use of the theory is thus only strategic: it is an instrument of analysis supplied for the struggle against the system, but offers no guarantee as to its future. In no way does it permit the 'prediction' of socialism at the end of capitalism. The epistemological equivalence of tendencies and counter-tendencies precludes any teleological interpretation of the theory.

This epistemological investigation of the founding categories of the system calls for an investigation of its *exposition*, as it is the precise place they occupy here that defines their legitimate use. It is important to grasp Marx's theory in the history of its production, even within the period of his 'maturity'. If we consider the major articulation of this exposition, that between commodity relations in general and specifically capitalist relations, a decisive break is perceptible between the 'first economic manuscript' (i.e. the *Grundrisse*, to which the 'Original Version' of the *Critique* should be joined), marked by the project of a 'dialectical' development, and the published *Critique*, which inaugurated a new mode of presentation. I have shown the ineffective character in all respects of the first attempt, which sought to proceed 'from the surface to the essence': not only was the 'dialectical' strategy deployed in the service of an inadequate order of development (simple circulation/capitalist production), but schemata of mediation were proposed (around the figure M–C–M) that were completely inconsistent. We must speak here of a real failure of the dialectical development of the exposition, but a failure that gave rise to a rectification that was steadily confirmed through to *Capital*: the initial theoretical moment here is not that of 'circulation' but that of *commodity production and circulation* in general, and from there we move on to the second moment – to capital – by way of a constructive progression that does not present any 'dialectical' claim. The fact remains that, if the procedure 'from surface to essence' disappears in *Capital*, a different and opposite one broadly persists, the procedure from the essence or 'internal connection' (Volume One) to the 'phenomenon' (Volume Three), from capital in general to multiple capitals in competition. I have shown the equally artificial character of this mode of exposition, since, in effect, the categories of competition, being those of the market in general, are required at the start of Volume One, and later in Part Four. The result is an obscuring of the inter-individual moment, giving the impulse to a mythical interpretation of capital as a collective subject and depriving the explanation of its foundation, which requires consideration of the interests and purposes of individuals as equally 'essential' as that of the class unity that they constitute.

Considered as a whole, the method of exposition of *Capital*, which is defined as the development of the theoretical object from abstract to concrete, is inspired by Hegel's *Logic*. Marx found in this the way to overcome the 'Ricardian' problems that he encountered, elaborating the level of value in all its implications before considering that of price of production. The Hegelian legacy is thus decisive. But it is also the basis for a wide field of 'epistemological obstacles'. The very idea of 'capital in general' is initially integrated into a matrix of 'universal/particular/singular' with a syllogistic purpose, which gradually proves to be an artificial architecture in which false windows hide the relevant articulations. The couple 'being/essence' prevents the initial moment of the exposition, that of commodity production and circulation in general, from being conceived in its theoretical autonomy, and misleadingly suggests that 'simple circulation' could form the point of departure. The notion of a 'dialectical transition' to the following moment, likewise that of 'reversal into its opposite' and 'negation of the negation', trigger destructive short-circuits: these deceptive figures, cobbled together in defiance of the logical possibilities of the system and the teachings of the theory, are gradually eliminated between one draft and the next.[1] Even in *Capital* a trace of this

---

[1] In my *Théorie générale* I give a central place to the concept of 'reversal into its opposite' (para 412b). I propose that Marx, in opening this question in *Capital*, lacked the means of its dialectic, which turns to an ambiguous historicism, as illustrated by the use he made of it in Chapter 32 of Volume 3 on the 'negation of the negation', which would be very plausible if the 'organisation' mediation did not have the same status of a 'class factor' as the 'market' mediation. On the historicising of the dialectic by Marx, see also my *Théorie de la modernité*, Conclusions, in particular p. 293.

ambiguity is still to be found, surrounding terms such as *Verwandlung*, which means in turn metamorphosis (of value), dialectical transition, ideological gap; and *Erscheingungform*, used alternately for historical form, form of appearance, of derivation or of expression. This approximate dialectical terminology suggests an uncertain interference between categories, which are invoked to denote both real relations and ideological ones, logical moments and historical. It neutralises the analytical moments in a teleological whirlpool.

A steady distancing from Hegelian themes was also for Marx the very way in which a theory of ideology became possible: not just a critique, but an explanation of its forms based on the properties of definite structures. If we leave aside the theme of 'inversion', particularly in the philosophical tone that it takes in the earlier versions, where it acts as a real epistemological obstacle, we find in *Capital* two major perspectives bearing on ideology. One of these is articulated in Volume Three, defined as the moment at which the 'most concrete forms' are approached, those of inter-individual (competitive) relations and the representations of 'everyday consciousness' that these imply. It gives rise to a very coherent development that justifies the categorical universe peculiar to the capitalist as adequate to the particular level of his practice, this being based on the structural reality of ratios in prices of production, of such kind that a reduction to values, i.e. of ideology to science, is impossible. Ideology is presented here under its double aspect of illusion and functionality, but with the latter having primacy: it is under the positive heading of this functionality, and not from the abstract argument of a necessary censorship, that ideology is 'deduced'. Yet this edifice has a defect: it is not legitimate to relegate to Volume Three the moment of competition, the individual and the appearance. Correlatively, however, it is also quite possible to establish the assertion of a different perspective, relating the ideological *Erscheinungsform* not to a particular moment of the exposition (located towards the 'concrete'), but rather to each of the moments defined on the abstract/ concrete axis. A richer perspective that posits the theory of the ideological outside of the theory of the subject, making it emerge throughout a process without a subject. Its culmination is the analysis of the wage relation in Part Six of Volume One, which relates this both to the properties of the surplus-value structure (and the practices attaching to it) and to those of the underlying commodity structure, as the ultimate principle of the ideological.

The two expositions of this question in the first chapter of *Capital*, that of the 'form of value' (Section 3) and that of 'fetishism' (Section 4), must, in my view, be interpreted in opposition: the first belongs to the register of meaning, the rationality of practices within the system, while the second belongs to the register of ideology. Fetishism does not depend on the form of value, it is not a function of this. The form of value is, in fact, the adequate expression of the value relation. It should not be confused with 'relative value', which constitutes a relationship of equivalence, itself being analysed as a pair of symmetrical relationships and expressions. This is the point Marx reaches at the end of his final drafts. The 'form of value', far from developing in a dialectical-teleological fashion, is retrospectively defined in its relationship to the 'value relation' (or 'concept of value') presented in the first two sections of the chapter; it is because this form is a total relationship, and one of equivalence, that it is possible to proceed from form A to forms B and C. The last of these gives the genuine expression of value because the universal equivalent, by its exclusion of use-value, is pure value, pure representative of abstract labour, of expenditure; but also and correlatively, because in Marx's paradoxical formula it realises 'the expression of value in use-value', giving access to every use-value in the system. Such is the category of the form or expression of value with its double aspect, as implied by the rationality and functionality of the system of commodity production in general.

'Commodity fetishism', on the contrary, denotes the gap between consciousness and this meaning, and so cannot be deduced from the 'form of value'. Its basis was only clearly shown in the second edition of *Capital*, which ascribes it to the fact that the law of value is not for the commodity producer an object of experience, his behaviour being directly governed by the indicators presented by market prices. Commodity relations thus appear to the agents defined by this structure only via exchange categories. This form of theorisation is homogeneous to that which Marx presents apropos the capitalist in Volume Three and the wage-earner in Part Six of Volume One. It implies only a relative 'invisibility' of the law of value (and by this relative character, science is made possible). But it makes the 'fetish' form attached to the commodity relation – and thus to the most abstract and most general relation – the centre of the entire ideological complex of the capitalist mode of production.

The status of the 'generalities' is one of the least elucidated questions as regards the object of *Capital*, and yet one of the most decisive. Thus 'labour in general' suddenly appears at the start of Part Three, a fragment of the meta-discourse without which the discourse of *Capital* could not be defined in its specificity. Marx reshaped this meta-discourse several times from one version to the next, but in this case not in a very convincing manner. For the most general moment can itself be conceived only as the articulation of two couples: use-value and the concrete labour that produces it, 'expenditure' (of labour) and the abstract labour that this constitutes. In other words, the production of exchange-value requires expenditure, and, in this sense, every labour is both concrete and abstract. And it is the mode of treatment of this generality that determines the different types of discourse involved, imperfectly distinguished as these are in *Capital*. *Historical materialism* grasps the process in its determinate sociopolitical context, in such a way that expenditure is articulated here to the social compulsion; the theory of the capitalist mode of production is an example of this discourse, the object of which is a form of society in which expenditure is compelled by the market, and the compulsion (in the 'political' sense I have given the term) exerted by the class possessing the means of production. The discourse of *pure economics*, as based with Sraffa on reference to labour, is distinguished by the fact that it grasps this in a contradiction-free sense (only indirectly, in terms of distribution). Labour here is a commodity endowed with a wage, and not 'naked labour'; this discourse can only produce information on the basis of external data supplied by the theoretical forms which take concrete historical societies as their object. From the time of the 1857 Introduction, Marx recognised and noted these two types of generality, but without articulating them theoretically, so that they surreptitiously interact with each other in *Capital*, in which general elements surface, particularly in the analysis of reproduction, that are valid for any complex system of production. This interaction is indeed necessary, but it is effected by obscuring the fact that the category of 'labour-value' possesses here in Volume Two a completely different status than it has in Volume One: a contradiction-free status. As for the third form of discourse, that bearing on *socialism*, which is connected to the second by the legislative use that it makes of the organising categories of labour, this escapes utopianism only if it is inscribed in the continuity of historical materialism, from which it must receive its critical principle. This bears on the relationship it establishes between the technical realities of the labour process and its sociopolitical framework, in which particular forms of compulsion and social domination are involved in the performance of labour. Here again, though Marx broke with utopianism by locating socialism at the end of a process of radical destruction of capitalism, he reverts to it when he posits the labour-value of the future as free from antagonism, thus opening the way to an apologetic reversal of his discourse.

To return finally to the overall questions raised at the start of this book, we can say that it has led to a double conclusion. The first point concerns the nature of certain fundamental ambiguities in *Capital* and their resonance in the crisis of contemporary Marxism.

Thus, to limit ourselves to a very few examples, *labour-value* turns out to be torn between its supposedly Ricardian provenance and its genuine novelty. The *labour-power commodity*, likewise, between its tautological economistic definition and its sociopolitical implications outside the commodity sphere. *Productive labour*, between its structuralist definition (in terms of social relations), its empiricist definition (in terms of the productive forces), and an eclectic definition that draws on both. The *starting-point of the exposition*, between its representation as surface and as the initial abstraction. The *transition to capital*, between dialectic and constructivism. *Ideology*, between its localisation at a derivative level and its dissemination across the whole set of moments. The universal *value-form*, between the idea that it is an adequate expression of value and the idea that it opens the way to fetishism. And so on.

It is clear that uncertainties of this kind make the use of such notions as 'value', 'production', etc. disputable, all the more so in that contemporary societies present more complex forms, which can only be related to the categories of *Capital* to the extent that these are released from their descriptive/ empiricist shell, the nineteenth-century guise which in places still sticks to them, and are reduced to their most abstract form. The establishment of new categorical systems, borrowed from social formations that precede or follow capitalism, naturally presents the same requirements. The traditional uses of the theory, whether as instrument for scientific analysis of past and present societies, or as reference for political practice, are certainly as fertile as ever. But the uncertainties I have mentioned tend to translate into the form of an empiricism (economistic or sociologistic) that greatly affects the credibility of

Marxist discourse. And as for the attempts at reconstruction founded either on 'dialecticisation' and return to Hegel,[2] or on confrontation with and consequent absorption by Ricardo and Sraffa, they do not strike me as responding to the internal logic of the theory and the particular nature of the conceptual field that it traces.

An alternative path suggests itself: precisely that indicated in the gradual constitution of the work, between 1857 and 1875, in the movement by which Marx steadily distanced himself from both Hegel and Ricardo. The emergence of specific forms, which in the course of this difficult origin were substituted for the Hegelian and Ricardian elements, went together with an uninterrupted movement of theoretical reconstruction that clearly needs to be taken still further. It thus appears that the theory of labour-value refers, beyond the question of measurement, to that of the 'substance' to be measured: and, outside of any substantialism, it implies the consideration of 'naked labour', something quite outside the Ricardian field, and defined prior to wages as a *political*-economic category that characterises a historically given space of expenditure/compulsion, opening simultaneously a space of quantity and a space of class struggle. Thus the *money-form*, interpreted not dialectically and teleologically, but in relation to what it is 'adequate' to, commodity production, already embodies the power of abstraction in the face of this nakedness, since it expresses value both *as* value and *in* use-value. However, if the initial moment of this double articulation that forms the capitalist structure is indeed that of commodity production in general, this intelligible beginning presents itself as pure functionality, logically prior to the opposition that appears only with the positing of the class relation. The notion of *labour-power as commodity*, which mediates this double articulation, must then be reinterpreted as a conceptual metaphor, since it only effects this mediation of the concept by way of the unique significance that the notions of appropriation, value and price, along with their movements, assume around norms forming a position in the class struggle. But it is the metaphor that is conceptual, and not the concept that is metaphorical. The capitalist structure, being constituted by the addition of this particular 'commodity' that produces a surplus, needs to be seen in terms of structure and tendency (a couple very often misconstrued),

---

[2] The 'dialectical' rerun of the Marxian project is, to my mind, conceivable only on the 'metastructural' basis that I propose in the first book of my *Théorie générale*.

which delimits the pertinence of the set of categories: surplus-value, productive labour, working class, etc. It is only to the extent that this tendency is understood as being ultimately located in the play of individual or collective strategies that it is possible to escape the mythical-teleological interpretation. Nothing authorises the integration of the concepts of philosophical anthropology here as specific analytical categories: 'My analytical method does not proceed from *man*, but from the economically given social period.'[3] The theorisation of the *ideological* breaks out from abstract to concrete throughout a process of exposition without a subject. *Other discourses* are thus possible around the theory of the capitalist mode of production, analogous and connected to it, but which, because they are general (pure economics, or normative), remain out of phase with it and stripped of the political characterisation that it has.

Marx's great work is thus not definable either as economics, sociology, or critique (of political economy). As an unfinished fragment of a general theory of the capitalist mode of production, it constitutes a *'political* economy', but in the singular sense that the programme of historical materialism defines, this sense being first of all that of conceiving the inseparable conjunction of these two terms. And it is only to the extent that this programme succeeds that it constitutes an original discourse and carries a critique.

---

[3] Marx 1989, p. 551.

References

Editions of Marx and Engels's works cited

Marx, Karl 1964, *Theories of Surplus-Value*, Part 1, London: Lawrence and Wishart.
Marx, Karl 1969, *Theories of Surplus-Value*, Part 2, London: Lawrence and Wishart.
Marx, Karl 1971, *A Contribution to the Critique of Political Economy*, London: Lawrence and Wishart.
Marx, Karl 1972, *Theories of Surplus-Value*, Part 3, London: Lawrence and Wishart.
Marx, Karl 1973a, *Das Kapital, Buch I*, Berlin (East): Dietz Verlag.
Marx, Karl 1973b, *Das Kapital, Buch II*, Berlin (East): Dietz Verlag.
Marx, Karl 1973c, *Grundrisse*, London: Allen Lane.
Marx, Karl 1974a, *Das Kapital, Buch III*, Berlin (East): Dietz Verlag.
Marx, Karl 1974b, *Grundrisse der Kritik der politischen Ökonomie*, Berlin (East): Dietz Verlag.
Marx, Karl 1974c, *The First International and After*, Harmondsworth: Penguin.
Marx, Karl 1976a, *Capital, Volume One*, Harmondsworth: Penguin.
Marx, Karl 1976b, *Theorien über den Mehrwert*, erster Teil, Berlin (East): Dietz Verlag.
Marx, Karl 1976c, *Theorien über den Mehrwert*, zweiter Teil, Berlin (East): Dietz Verlag.
Marx, Karl 1976d, *Theorien über den Mehrwert*, dritter Teil, Berlin (East): Dietz Verlag.
Marx, Karl 1977, *Un chapitre inédit du 'Capital'*, Paris: Coll. 10/18.
Marx, Karl 1978, *Capital, Volume Two*, Harmondsworth: Penguin.
Marx, Karl 1980, *Das Kapital, Buch I* [reprint of 1867 edition], Hildesheim: Gerstenberg Verlag.
Marx, Karl 1981, *Capital, Volume Three*, Harmondsworth: Penguin.
Marx, Karl 1981, *Le Capital* [in eight fascicules], Paris: Éditions Sociales.
Marx, Karl and Engels, Frederick 1975, *Collected Works*, Volume 3, London: Lawrence and Wishart.
Marx, Karl and Engels, Frederick 1976a, *Collected Works*, Volume 6, London: Lawrence and Wishart.
Marx, Karl and Engels, Frederick 1976b, *The German Ideology*, London: Lawrence and Wishart.
Marx, Karl and Engels, Frederick 1977, *Collected Works*, Volume 9, London: Lawrence and Wishart.
Marx, Karl and Engels, Frederick 1980, *Collected Works*, Volume 16, London: Lawrence and Wishart.
Marx, Karl and Engels, Frederick 1987, *Collected Works*, Volume 25, London: Lawrence and Wishart.
Marx, Karl and Engels, Frederick 1988a, *Collected Works*, Volume 30, London: Lawrence and Wishart.
Marx, Karl and Engels, Frederick 1988b, *Collected Works*, Volume 43, London: Lawrence and Wishart.
Marx, Karl and Engels, Frederick 1989, *Collected Works*, Volume 24, London: Lawrence and Wishart.
Marx, Karl and Engels, Frederick 1994, *Collected Works*, Volume 34, London: Lawrence and Wishart.

Other authors and works cited

Althusser, Louis 1978, 'Avant-Propos' to Gérard Duménil, *Le Concept de loi économique dans 'Le Capital'*, Paris: Maspero.
Althusser, Louis and Etienne Balibar 1970, *Reading 'Capital'*, London: NLB.
Backhaus, Hans-Georg 1974, 1975, 1978, 'Materialien zur Rekonstruktion der Marxschen Werttheorie', 1, 2, & 3, *Gesellschaft. Beiträge zur Marxschen Theorie*, 1, 3, & 11: 52–77, 122–159, & 16–117.
Backhaus, Hans-Georg 1997, *Dialektik der Wertform*, Freiburg: Ça ira-Verlag.
Badaloni, Nicola 1976, *Pour le communisme*, Paris: Mouton.
Bader, Veit M. (et al.) 1975, *Krise und Kapitalismus bei Marx*, Cologne: Europäische Verlagsanstalt.
Balibar, Étienne 1974, 'Plus-value et classes sociales', in *Cinq études du matérialisme historique*, Paris: Maspero.
Balibar, Étienne 1977, 'A nouveau sur la contradiction', in *Sur la dialectique*, Paris: Éditions Sociales.
Balibar, Étienne 1983, 'La vacillation de l'idéologie dans le marxisme', *Raison présente*, 66: 97–116.
Baudelot, Christian, Roger Establet and Jacques Malemort 1974, *La petite bourgeoisie en France*, Paris: Maspero.
Becker, Werner 1972, *Kritik der Marxschen Wertlehre. Die methodische Irrationalität der ökonomischen Basistheorien des 'Kapitals'*, Hamburg: Hoffmann und Campe.
Benetti, Carlo 1974, *Valeur et répartition*, Paris: Maspero.
Benetti, Carlo 1975, 'Travail commandé, surproduit et plus-value', *Cahiers d'Économie Politique*, 2.
Benetti, Carlo, Claude Berthomieu, and Jean Cartelier 1975, *Économie classique, économie vulgaire*, Paris: Maspero.
Benetti, Carlo, Suzanne De Brunhoff, and Jean Cartelier 1976, 'Eléments pour une critique marxiste de Sraffa', *Cahiers d'Économie Politique*, 3.
Benetti, Carlo and Jean Cartelier 1980, *Marchands, salariat et capitalistes*, Paris: Maspero.
Berger J. 1974, 'Der gesellschaftstheoretische Gehalt der Marxschen Werttheorie', in *Marx und Marxismus heute*, edited by G. Breitenburger and G. Schnitzler, Hamburg: Hoffmann und Campe.
Bernstein, Eduard 1899, 'Zur Theorie des Arbeitwerths', *Neue Zeit*.
Bettelheim, Charles 1972, 'Préface' to Manuel Janko and Daniel Furjot, *Informatique et capitalisme*, Paris: Maspero.
Bidet, Jacques 1986, 'Traduire en allemand *Le Capital*', in *Marx, cent ans après*, edited by G. Labica, Paris: Presses Universitaires de France.
Bidet, Jacques 1990, *Théorie de la modernité*, Paris: Presses Universitaires de France.
Bidet, Jacques 1998 (with Jean-Marc Lachaud), *Habermas: Une politique délibérative*, Paris: Presses Universitaires de France.
Bidet, Jacques 1999, *Théorie générale, Théorie du droit, de l'économie et de la politique*, Paris: Presses Universitaires de France.
Bidet, Jacques 2003a, 'Paradoxes marxiens de la marchandise', *Actuel Marx*, 34: 11–16.
Bidet, Jacques 2003b, 'La structure de classe de la société capitaliste', *Mouvements*, 26: 79–86.
Bidet, Jacques 2003c, 'Reconstruire le *Capital* pour reconstruire la théorie de la société moderne', *Revue Philosophique de Louvain*, 102, 2: 242–58.
Bidet, Jacques 2004a, 'Marx critico del mercato. Pro e contro dell'approccio francofortese al *Capitale*', *Critica Marxista*, 6.
Bidet, Jacques 2004b, *Explication et reconstruction du 'Capital'*, Paris: Presses Universitaires de France.
Bidet, Jacques 2005a, 'La ricostruzione metastrutturale del *Capital*', in *Sulle tracce di un fantasma*, edited by Marcello Musto, Rome: Manifestolibri.
Bidet, Jacques 2005b, 'The Rule of Imperialism and the Global-State in Gestation', *Traces*, 4
Bidet, Jacques 2005c, 'The Dialectician's Interpretation of *Capital*. On Christopher Arthur's, *The New Dialectic and Marx's "Capital"'*, *Historical Materialism*, 13, 2: 121–46.

Bidet, Jacques 2007a, 'Kôzô Uno and His School: A Pure Theory of Capitalism', in Bidet and Kouvelakis (eds.) 2007.

Bidet, Jacques 2007b, 'New Interpretations of Capital', in Bidet and Kouvelakis (eds.) 2007.

Bidet, Jacques 2007c, 'Explanation and Reconstruction of Marx's Capital', in Rethinking Marxism, forthcoming.

Bidet, Jacques 2007d, 'La "méthode de Marx" selon Michael Hardt et Toni Negri', Multitudes.

Bidet, Jacques and Stathis Kouvelakis (eds.) 2007, Critical Companion to Contemporary Marxism, HM Book Series, Leiden: Brill.

Bischoff, Joachim 1981, Grundbegriffe der marxistischen Theorie, Hamburg: VSA.

Böhm-Bawerk, Eugen von 1973 [1926], Karl Marx and the Close of His System, Clifton: Kelley.

Bortkiewicz, Ladislaus von 1906–7, 'Wertrechnung und Preisrechnung im Marxschen System', Archiv für Sozialwissenschaft und Sozialpolitik, 25: 10–51, 445–88.

Bouvier-Adam, M., J. Ibarrola and N. Pasquarelli, 1975, Dictionnaire économique et social, Paris: Éditions Sociales.

Brinkmann, Heinrich 1975, Die Ware. Zu Fragen der Logik und Methode im 'Kapital'. Eine Einführung, Giessen: Focus Verlag.

Cartelier, Jean 1976, Surproduit et reproduction, Paris: PUG/Maspero.

Cartelier, Lysiane. 1980, 'Contribution à l'étude des rapports entre État et travail salarié', Revue économique, 31, 1: 67–87.

Colletti, Lucio 1973, Marxism and Hegel, London: NLB.

Colletti, Lucio 1984, Le déclin du marxisme, Paris: Presses Universitaires de France.

Cotten, Jean-Pierre 1984, 'L'appropriation collective et/ou sociale', Raison Présente, 70: 93–102.

Croce, Benedetto 1981, Historical Materialism and the Economics of Karl Marx, London: Cass.

Dallemagne, Jean-Luc 1978, L'économie du 'Capital', Paris: Maspero.

Damerow Peter, Peter Furth, and Wolfgang Lefebvre 1983, Arbeit und Philosophie, Bochum: Germinal Verlag.

Delaunay, Jean-Claude (with Jean Gadrey) 1979, Nouveau cours d'économie politique, Paris: Cujas.

Delaunay, Jean-Claude 1984, Salariat et plus-value en France, Presses de la Fondation Nationale des Sciences Politiques.

Deleplace, Ghislain 1979, Théories du capitalisme: une introduction, Paris: PUG /Maspero.

Denis, Henri 1980, L'économie de Marx. Histoire d'un échec, Paris: Presses Universitaires de France.

D'Hondt, Jacques 1981, 'La disparition des choses dans le matérialisme de Marx', La Pensée, 219: 43–61.

D'Hondt, Jacques 1986, 'La traduction tendancieuse du Capital par Joseph Roy', in L'Oeuvre de Marx, un siècle après, edited by G. Labica), Paris: Presses Universitaires de France.

Dognin, Paul-Dominique 1977, Les 'sentiers escarpés' de Karl Marx, 2 vols, Paris: Cerf.

Dostaler, Gilles 1978, Marx, la valeur et l'économie politique, Paris: Anthropos.

Duménil, Gérard 1982, 'Une approche fonctionnelle du théorème marxien fondamental d'Okishi-Moroshima', Cahiers d'Économie Politique, 7: 129–39.

Eberle, Friedrich and Eike Hennig, 974, 'Anmerkungen zum Verhältnis von Theorie und Empirie', Gesellschaft, 2: 2.

Eldred, Michael, M. Hanlon, L. Kleiber, and M. Roth, 1984, La Forma-valore, Laicata Editore.

Establet, Roger 1965, 'Présentation du plan du Capital', in L. Althusser et al., Lire 'Le Capital', Paris: Maspero.

Fausto, Ruy 1982, 'Sur la forme de la valeur et le fétichisme', Critiques de l'Économie Politique, 18: 133–58.

Fischer, Anton M. 1978, Der reale Schein und die Theorie des Kapitals bei Karl Marx, Zurich: Europa Verlag.

Forest, H.M. 1984, 'Introduction', in *Marx, Le Capital (chapitre 1)*, Paris: Hachette.

Fulda, Hans Friedrich 1975, 'These zur Dialektik als Darstellungsmethode (im "Kapital" von Marx)', in *Hegel-Jahrbuch*, 1974, edited by W.R. Beyer, Cologne: Pahl-Rugenstein Verlag.

Galander, Ehrenfried and Ulrike 1979, 'Probleme der Marxschen politischen Ökonomie', *Deutsche Zeitschrift für Philosophie*, 10.

Geschichte der marxistischen Dialektik 1974, Berlin (East): Dietz Verlag.

Gilibert, G. 1976, 'Travail commandé, incorporé et marchandise étalon', *Cahiers d'Économie Politique*, 3: 89–101.

Godelier, Maurice 1977, *Horizon, trajets marxistes en anthropologie*, 2 vols, Paris: Maspero.

Göhler, Gerhard 1980, *Die Reduktion der Dialektik durch Marx*, Stuttgart: Klett-Cotta.

Grevet, P. 1971, 'La hiérarchie des salaries', *Économie et politique*, 202.

Ilienkov, F. 1974, 'Logisches und Historisches', in *Geschichte der materialistischen Dialektik*, Berlin (East): Dietz Verlag.

Klaus, Georg 1972, *Moderne Logik*, Berlin (East): Deutscher Verlag de Wissenschaften.

Kocyba, Hermann 1979, *Widerspruch und Theoriestruktur: zur Darstellungsmethode im Marxschen 'Kapital'*, Frankfurt: Materialis Verlag.

Kogan, A.M. 1976, 'Das Problem des Wertes im "Kapital" von Karl Marx. Ausgangspunkt für die weitere Forschung', *Arbeitsblätter zur Marx-Engels Forschung*, 1.

Krahl, Hans-Jürgen 1971, 'Zur Wesenslogik der Marxschen Warenanalyse', in *Konstitution und Klassenkampf*, Frankfurt: Verlag Neue Kritik.

Krause, Ulrich 1979, *Geld und abstrakte Arbeit. Über die analytischen Grundlagen der politischen Ökonomie*, Frankfurt: Campus Verlag.

Kuruma Samezo (ed.) 1977, *Marx-Lexikon zur politischen Ökonomie*, Second Edition, Vaduz: Topos Verlag.

Labica, Georges 1976, *Le Statut marxiste de la philosophie*, Paris: Éditions Dialectiques.

Labica, Georges (ed.) (with G. Bensussan) 1982, *Dictionnaire critique du marxisme*, Paris: Presses Universitaires de France.

Lange, Ernst-Michael 1978, 'Wertformanalyse. Geldkritik und die Konstruktion des Fetischismus bei Marx', *Neue Hefte für Philosophie*, 13: 1–46.

Lefebvre, Jean-Pierre 1979, 'Les deux sens de "forces productives" chez Marx', *La Pensée*, 207: 122–34.

Lefebvre, Jean-Pierre 1983, 'Introduction', in *K. Marx, Le Capital (Livre 1)*, Paris: Éditions Sociales.

Lipietz, Alain 1979, *Crise et inflation, pourquoi*, Paris: Maspero.

Lipietz, Alain 1982, 'Retour au problème de la "transformation des valeurs en prix de production"', *Cahiers d'Économie Politique*, 7: 141–65.

Lipietz, Alain 1983, *Le Monde enchanté*, Paris: La Découverte/Maspero.

Lippi, Marco 1976, *Marx, il valore come costo sociale reale*, Milan: Etas libri.

Lotter, Konrad, Reinhard Meiners, and Elmar Treptow 1984, *Marx-Engels Begriffslexikon*, Munich: Beck.

Markus, Gyorgy 1984, 'Portée et limite des concepts de l'idéologie chez Marx', *Les Temps Modernes*, 415: 1407–33.

Marx, Bernard 1979, *L'économie capitaliste: fonctionnement et évolution, contradictions et crises*, Paris: Éditions Sociales.

Meiners, Reinhard 1980, *Methodenprobleme bei Marx und ihr Bezug zur Hegelschen Philosophie*, Munich: Minerva.

Müller, Manfred 1978, *Auf dem Wege zum Kapital. Zur Entwicklung des Kapitalbegriffs von Marx in den Jahren 1857–1863*, Berlin: Verlag Das Europäische Buch.

Nagels, Jacques 1974, *Travail collectif et travail productif dans l'évolution de la pensée marxiste*, Brussels: Editions de l'Université libre de Bruxelles.

Negri, Antonio 1979, *Marx au-delà de Marx*, Paris: Bourgois.

Pareto, Vilfredo 1965 [1902–3], *Les systèmes socialistes*, Geneva: Droz.

Poulantzas, Nicos 1975, *Classes in Contemporary Capitalism*, London: NLB.

Projektgruppe Entwicklung des Marxschen Systems 1973, *Das Kapitel vom Geld*, Berlin: Verlag für das Studium der Arbeiterbewegung.

Rancière, Jacques 1965, 'Le concept de critique et la critique de l'économie politique des *Manuscrits de 1844* au *Capital*', in L. Althusser et al., *Lire 'Le Capital'*, Volume 1, Paris: Maspero.

Reichelt, Helmut 1970, *Zur logischen Struktur des Kapitalbegriffs bei Karl Marx*, Frankfurt: Europäische Verlagsanstalt.

Ricardo, David 1971, *The Principles of Political Economy and Taxation*, Harmondsworth: Penguin.

Ricardo, David 1951, 'Absolute Value and Exchangeable Value', in *The Works and Correspondence of David Ricardo*, edited by P. Sraffa, Cambridge: Cambridge University Press, Volume 4.

Ricci, F. 1974, 'Structure logique du paragraphe 1 du *Capital*', in *La Logique de Marx*, edited by Jacques d'Hondt, Paris: Presses Universitaires de France.

Rosdolsky, Roman 1968, 'La signification du *Capital* pour la recherche marxiste contemporaine', in *En partant du 'Capital'*, edited by Victor Fay, Paris: Editions Anthropos.

Rosdolsky, Roman 1980, *The Making of Marx's 'Capital'*, London: Pluto Press.

Roubine, Isaak 1978, *Essai sur la théorie de la valeur de Marx*, Paris: Maspero.

Ruben, Peter 1978, *Dialektik und Arbeit der Philosophie*, Cologne: Pahl-Rugenstein.

Ruben, Peter and Hans Wagner 1980, 'Sozialistische Wertform und dialektischer Widerspruch', *Deutsche Zeitschrift für Philosophie*, 10: 1218–30.

Schmidt, Alfred 1972, *Geschichte und Struktur. Fragen einer marxistischen Historik*, Munich: C. Hanser.

Schwarz, Winfried 1978, *Vom Rohentwurf zum Kapital. Die Strukturgeschichte des Marxchen Hauptwerkes*, Berlin (West): Verlag Das Europäische Buch.

Sève, Lucien 1978, 'Introduction', in Karl Marx and Friedrich Engels, *Textes sur la méthode de la science économique*, Paris: Éditions Sociales.

Smith, Adam 1970, *The Wealth of Nations*, Harmondsworth: Penguin.

Sraffa, Piero 1960, *Production of Commodities by Means of Commodities*, Cambridge: Cambridge University Press.

Steinvorth, Ulrich 1977, *Eine analytische Interpretation der Marxschen Dialektik*, Meisenheim am Glan: Hain.

Texier, Jacques 1977, 'Sur la détermination en dernière instance (Marx et/ou Althusser)', in *Sur la dialectique*, Paris: CERM.

Texier, Jacques 1982, 'Le privilège épistémologique du présent et la nécessité du moment génétique dans les *Grundrisse* de K. Marx', *La Pensée*, 225: 40–52.

Texier, Jacques 1984, 'L'automation et la fin du capital dans les *Grundrisse* de K. Marx', *Raison Présente*, 70: 67–92.

Theunissen, Michael 1974, 'Krise der Macht, Thesen zur Theorie des dialektischen Widerspruchs', *Hegel-Jahrbuch*, edited by W.R. Beyer, Cologne: Pahl-Rugenstein Verlag.

Theunissen, Michael 1975, 'Unkorrigierte Nachschrift der Heidelberger Vorlesung "Hegel und Marx", aus dem Wintersemester 1974/75'.

Tosel, André 1979, 'Les critiques de la politique chez Marx', in Étienne Balibar, Cesare Luporini, André Tosel, *Marx et sa critique de la politique*, Paris: Maspero.

Traité marxiste d'économie politique. Le capitalisme monopoliste d'Etat 1972, Paris: Éditions Sociales

Tuchscheerer, W. 1968, *Bevor das Kapital entstand: die Herausbildung und Entwicklung der ökonomischen Theorie von Karl Marx in der Zeit von 1843 bis 1858*, Berlin (East): Akademie Verlag.

Uno, Kôzô 1980, *Principles of Political Economy*, Brighton: Harvester Press.

Vadée, Michel 1974, 'La critique de l'abstraction par Marx', in *Logique de Marx*, edited by Jacques d'Hondt, Paris: Presses Universitaires de France.

Vadée, Michel 1992, *Marx, penseur du possible*, Paris: Méridiens-Klinksieck.

Valier, Jacques 1982, *Une critique de l'économie politique*, Paris: Maspero.

Wygodski, Witali Solomonowitsch 1967, *Die Geschichte einer grossen Entdeckung: über die Entstehung des Werkes 'Das Kapital' von Karl Marx*, Berlin (East): Dietz Verlag.

Wygodski, Witali Solomonowitsch 1976, *Wie 'Das Kapital' entstand*, Berlin (East): Dietz Verlag.

Wygodski, Witali Solomonowitsch 1980, *Das Werden der ökonomischen Theorie von K. Marx*, Berlin (East): Dietz Verlag.

Zech, R. 1983, 'Produktivkräfte und Produktionsverhältnisse in der Kritik der politischen ökonomie', in K. Marx, *Produktivkräfte und Produktionsverhältnisse: Entstehung, Funktion u. Wandel e. Theorems der materialistischen Geschichtsauffassung*, Berlin: Ullstein.

Index

www.ingramcontent.com/pod-product-compliance
Lightning Source LLC
Chambersburg PA
CBHW060024030426
42334CB00019B/2170